Sister Judith Ann Lewis

*EMERGING
PATTERNS OF
SUPERVISION*

McGRAW-HILL SERIES IN EDUCATION

ARNO A. BELLACK *Teachers College, Columbia University*
*Consulting Editor, Supervision, Curriculum, and
Methods in Education*

PHILIP M. CLARK *Ohio State University*
*Consulting Editor, Psychology and
Human Development in Education*

WALTER F. JOHNSON *Michigan State University*
*Consulting Editor, Guidance, Counseling, and
Student Personnel in Education*

The Late HAROLD A. BENJAMIN *was Consulting Editor of
the Foundations of Education Series from its
inception in 1935 until January 1969.*

SUPERVISION, CURRICULUM, AND METHODS IN EDUCATION

ARNO A. BELLACK *Consulting Editor*

BATCHELDER, McGLASSON, AND SCHORLING Student Teaching in Secondary Schools

BENT, KRONENBERG, AND BOARDMAN Principles of Secondary Education

BROWN, LEWIS, AND HARCLEROAD AV Instruction: Media and Methods

BUTLER, WREN, AND BANKS The Teaching of Secondary Mathematics

LEFEVRE Linguistics and the Teaching of Reading

LUCIO AND McNEIL Supervision: A Synthesis of Thought and Action

MACKENZIE Toward a New Curriculum in Physical Education

MARKS, PURDY, AND KINNEY Teaching Elementary School Mathematics for Understanding

MASSIALAS AND COX Inquiry in Social Studies

MICHAELIS, GROSSMAN, AND SCOTT New Designs for the Elementary School Curriculum

PHENIX Realms of Meaning

SERGIOVANNI AND STARRATT Emerging Patterns of Supervision: Human Perspectives

STOREN The Disadvantaged Early Adolescent: More Effective Teaching

STRANG, McCULLOUGH, AND TRAXLER The Improvement of Reading

WINGO AND SCHORLING Elementary School Student Teaching

Emerging Patterns of Supervision: Human Perspectives

Thomas J. Sergiovanni
University of Illinois

Robert J. Starratt
Fairfield University

McGraw-Hill Book Company
*New York, St. Louis, San Francisco, Düsseldorf,
London, Mexico, Panama, Sydney, Toronto*

Emerging Patterns of Supervision: Human Perspectives

Library of Congress Catalog Card Number 74-128792

56310

234567890MAMM7987654321

This book was set in Fairfield by ·The Maple Press Company,
and printed on permanent paper and bound by The Maple Press
Company. The designer was Marsha Cohen; the drawings were
done by Joseph Buchner. The editors were Nat LaMar and Paula
Henson. Les Kaplan supervised production.

Preface

The process of education, once described by Mark Hopkins as a teacher sitting on a log and talking to his student, has become in too many cases the teacher sitting on his student and talking to the log. Understandably enough, no one benefits from such an arrangement, not even the log. One reason why such a situation arises is that the log on which the teacher sits is quite uncomfortable. Another is that often about as much ingenuity and imagination is expected from teachers as one might expect from a log, and teachers therefore transfer this appraisal to their students. Older patterns of supervision, with their stress on authority, compliance, and control, and with their identification of wisdom with hierarchical position, put teachers in the position of passively accepting the directives of the principal, supervisor, or department chairman. In turn, teachers have tended to view their students in the same passive position in relation to them.

Supervision, however, is more usefully viewed as a process rather than as a unique function of role. Therefore, while this book is appropriate for those who hold supervisory titles, it is intended for all who have supervisory responsibility—and who behave in supervisory ways.

Emerging Patterns of Supervision: Human Perspectives has as its primary goal the humanizing of American education. It is composed of two parts; the first is concerned with supervising the human school, and the second is concerned with supervising the human curriculum. We believe that humanizing education, with its focus on self-actualization of youngsters, can be achieved only in a humanizing organization which focuses on self-actualization of teachers and other educational professionals. Our aim is not to help those who behave in supervisory ways to become instructional leaders as this role is usually defined, but to help them to facilitate the emergence of instructional leadership throughout the professional staff. In this effort we describe patterns of supervision and of curriculum development which do not presently dominate America's schools but which exist in enough schools so that they form an emerging pattern for supervision in the decades ahead.

Part I presents and builds upon a synthesizing theory of supervision composed of three classes of variables which interact dynamically in determining supervisory effectiveness. The theory proposes that certain manifestations of the school as an organization, of the school's prevailing authority system and certain styles of beliefs, assumptions, and behaviors exhibited by administrators and supervisors, affect the human organization of the school in a positive way; others, in a neutral way; and still others, in a negative way. The theory further proposes that school success—that is, maximum intellectual, social, and emotional development—is enhanced only as the school as an organization becomes a human organization. Certain essential skills of supervisors, such as planning, communicating, and changing and facilitating group supervision, are also included in Part I.

Part II deals with that primary concern of both teachers and other supervisory personnel—curriculum development. After describing the curriculum programs presently operative in schools and some aspects of the social system of the school which affect the adoption and implementation of these programs, it introduces the reader to the general process of curriculum development. A unique model of the student's learning environment is then offered which provides a framework both for planning curriculum-instructional programs and for evaluating deficiencies in current programs. The focus of Part II, however, is primarily on the human curriculum, and the reader is exposed to both the process of planning for and the content of one tentative human curriculum. The critical question of evaluation completes the treatment of the human curriculum.

Responsibility for both parts of the book is shared jointly by both authors. Part I, however, was developed by T. J. Sergiovanni, while Part II bears the stamp of R. J. Starratt. The book as a whole could not have been written without the many long hours of discussion, argument, and mutual encouragement which the authors were privileged to share.

Several people reacted to parts of this book, either in chapter form or in the form of related papers. Among them were Harry Broudy, Fred D. Carver, and Lloyd McCleary. This acknowledgment does not imply that the reactors agree with all the book's contents or that they should share in any of the book's shortcomings. Rensis Likert was particularly generous in permitting us to use material from his book, *The Human Organization: Its Management and Value*. This book is for the children of our households and for all the children of the world, with the hope that they may find peace.

Thomas J. Sergiovanni
Robert J. Starratt

Contents

Part One
SUPERVISING
THE HUMAN
SCHOOL

Introduction: The Nature of Supervision

Fundamental changes have taken place in American education in recent years. Many of these changes are simply priming the pump for those yet to come. Statements referring to change are not new to those who are members of the educational profession, but this does not lessen the importance of such statements. While attempting to plot the type, direction, and intensity of change may be risky, if not simply premature, certain obvious trends, issues, and developments are clear. Each of these trends has potential for increasing the significance of supervision in American schools *if* the assumptions, attitudes, and behaviors which constitute contemporary supervisory practices reflect these changes.

The trends, issues, and developments which are emerging as significant supervisory problems and patterns follow. They are not arranged in order of importance or in accordance with a systematic framework simply because the priorities and frameworks are themselves causes of considerable controversy.

1. *Knowledge explosion.* The frontiers of knowledge are expanding rapidly. Curriculum expansion in schools and increased reliance on content specialists reflect this trend.
2. *Militancy.* There is an increased and seemingly never-ending expression by teachers, students, and other school inhabitants for control over themselves, their work environment, and their destiny.
3. *Personal specialization.* This is a reflection of the sophisticated and expanded specialization of teachers in terms of professional and academic training, interests, and performance. This phenomenon is not to be confused with task specialization but is more akin to the appearance of the medical specialist.
4. *Pluralism.* The diversification of power in the governance of schools is a contemporary trend. This is reflected in the broadening of teacher power bases and of community power bases (the civil rights movement and other community groups) and the increased participation by other

governmental agencies. Pluralism is often stated as a goal rather than a reality.

5. *Organizational transition.* There is a movement on the part of many schools from organizational styles described as mechanistic (bureaucratic) to those described as organic (professional).

6. *Ability-authority dilemma.* Schools are witnessing increased attention to the distinction between the right to decide and the power and expertise to do. This dilemma is frequently referred to as hierarchical authority versus ability authority. Schools seem to be relying more heavily on ability authority.

7. *Federal participation in public education.* Activism by federal agencies to exert influence on and stimulate change in the planning and development of American education is increasing.

8. *Private participation in public education.* Activism by private corporations and foundations to exert influence on and stimulate change in the planning and development of American education is increasing.

9. *Innovations movement.* Related to a number of items above and below (see, for example, items 1, 7, 8, and 10); advocates consider the movement an attempt to increase drastically the effectiveness of American schools.

10. *Urban problems, rural problems, and civil rights.* This is a general trend which sums as simply the stark realization that American education has failed many of its constituents.

11. *Social science perspectives.* There is increased reliance by those who study and practice educational administration and supervision on concepts and ideas from the social sciences as stimulants of thought and as frameworks for action.

12. *The human school.* Our concern for the human school is evidenced by a realization (not too late, we hope) that American education must be characterized by, and indeed focus on, the human client, the human curriculum, the human organization, if it is to contribute persistently and dynamically to individual and society.

This book is written in reaction to the trends described above and is an attempt to map the changes which must take place in order to bring about supervisory effectiveness in modern schools. Our goal is the transformation of the American school into the human school. We believe that effective supervision can contribute to this goal. Newer patterns of action described in the book are referred to as *enlightened supervision,* as opposed to contemporary supervision (those patterns which describe prevailing supervisory practice) and classical-traditional supervision (those supervisory patterns which by now, we would hope, have been abandoned, at least in spirit if not in practice).

SUPERVISION: EXPANDED OR LIMITED

Supervision is described in Chapter 1 as attitudes, efforts, and behaviors on the part of one who is dependent upon and works through others in order to achieve school goals. Who the supervisor is and what he does are questions of tremendous complexity which preclude specific lists of titles, job descriptions, role expectations, and the like. Traditionally, supervision is considered the province of those responsible for instructional improvement. While we hold this view, we add to this instructional emphasis responsibility for all school goals which are achieved through or dependent upon the human organization of the school.

A number of statements, assumptions, and beliefs constitute the folklore of supervision. Many have ancient and treasured heritages, some are loved, and all are defended and passed down with tenderness. They are accepted and preserved without reflection and thus are rarely tested and examined for strength, purpose, or goodness of fit. Some examples of this folklore follow:

1. Supervision is for women.
2. Supervision is a staff function rather than a line function.
3. Supervision is a nonevaluative role.
4. Supervision is a limited role directed specifically at instructional improvement.
5. Supervision is a function more important to the elementary school than to the secondary school.
6. Supervision is visiting classrooms systematically.
7. Supervision is in-service education.
8. Supervision is working individually with teachers in order to improve their performance.
9. Supervision is curriculum development.
10. Supervisors need a curriculum or content orientation and background.

While each of these statements contains, like any decent folklore, elements of truth, they are relatively narrow views of the supervisory process and, if taken literally, may unnecessarily restrict school effectiveness.

SOME OTHER VIEWPOINTS

We do not intend to review what key authors see as critical components and concepts of supervision. We have, however, selected material from three books which we think provides an indication of the prevailing concept of supervision. We offer it without comment or interpretation.

1. Ben Harris defines *supervision* as:

What school personnel do with adults and things for the purpose of maintaining or changing the operation of the school in order to directly influence the attainment of the major instructional goals of the school. Supervision has its impact on the learner, then, through other people and things.[1]

2. Kimball Wiles views supervision as those activities which are designed to improve instruction at all levels of the school enterprise. He describes supervisors as follows:

They are the expediters. They help establish communication. They help people hear each other. They serve as liaison to get persons into contact with others who have similar problems or with resource people who can help. They stimulate staff members to look at the extent to which ideas and resources are being shared, and the degree to which persons are encouraged and supported as they try new things. They make it easier to carry out the agreements that emerge from evaluation sessions. They listen to individuals discuss their problems and recommend other resources that may help in the search for solutions. They bring to individual teachers, whose confidence they possess, appropriate suggestions and materials. They sense, as far as they are able, the feelings that teachers have about the system and its policies, and they recommend that the administration examine irritations among staff members. They provide expertness in group operation, and provide the type of meeting place and structure that facilitate communication. They are, above all, concerned with helping people to accept each other, because they know that when individuals value each other, they will grow through their interaction together and will provide a better emotional climate for pupil growth. The supervisor's role has become *supporting, assisting,* and *sharing,* rather than directing. The authority of the supervisor's position has not decreased, but it is used in another way. It is used to promote growth through assuming responsibility and creativity rather than through dependency and conformity.[2]

3. William Burton and Leo Brueckner, two pioneers in the area of supervision whose classic 1955 book, *Supervision: A Social Process,*[3] seems remarkably contemporary, identify certain principles which govern the operation of supervision as follows:

PRINCIPLES GOVERNING THE OPERATION OF SUPERVISION
1. Administration is *ordinarily* concerned with providing material facilities and with operation in general.
2. Supervision is *ordinarily* concerned with improving the setting for learning in particular.
3. Administration and supervision considered *functionally* cannot be separated or set off from each other. The two are co-ordinate, correlative, comple-

[1]Ben M. Harris, *Supervisory Behavior in Education,* Prentice-Hall, Englewood Cliffs, N.J., 1963.
[2]Kimball Wiles, *Supervision for Better Schools,* 3d ed., Prentice-Hall, Englewood Cliffs, N.J., 1967.
[3]William H. Burton and Leo J. Brueckner, *Supervision: A Social Process,* 3d ed., Appleton-Century-Crofts, New York, 1955.

mentary, mutually shared functions in the operation of educational systems. The provision of any and all conditions favorable to learning is the common purpose of both.

4. Good supervision is based on philosophy and science.

   a. Supervision will be sensitive to ultimate aims and values, to policies, with special reference to their adequacy.

   b. Supervision will be sensitive to "factness" and to law, with special reference to their accuracy.

   c. Supervision will be sensitive to the emergent, evolutionary, nature of the universe and of democratic society in particular, hence should be permeated with the experimental attitude, and engage constantly in re-evaluation of aims and values, of policies, of materials and methods.

5. Good supervision is (in the United States) based upon the democratic philosophy.

   a. Supervision will respect personality and individual differences between personalities, will seek to provide oppotunities for the best expression of each unique personality.

   b. Supervision will be based upon the assumption that educational workers are capable of growth. It will accept idiosyncrasies, reluctance to co-operate, and antagonism as human characteristics, just as it accepts reasonableness, co-operation, and energetic activity. The former are challenges; the latter, assets.

   c. Supervision will endeavor to develop in all a democratic conscience, that is, recognition that democracy includes important obligations as well as rights.

   d. Supervision will provide full opportunity for the co-operative formulation of policies and plans, will welcome and utilize free expression and contributions from all.

   e. Supervision will stimulate initiative, self-reliance, and individual responsibility on the part of all persons in the discharge of their duties.

   f. Supervision will substitute leadership for authority. Authority will be recognized as the authority of the situation and of the facts within the situation. Personal authority if necessary will be derived from group planning.

   g. Supervision will work toward co-operatively determined functional groupings of the staff, with flexible regrouping as necessary; will invite specialists when advisable.

6. Good supervision will employ scientific methods and attitudes in so far as those methods and attitudes are applicable to the dynamic social processes of education; will utilize and adapt to specific situations scientific findings concerning the learner, his learning processes, the nature and development of personality; will co-operate occasionally in pure research.

7. Good supervision, in situations where the precise controlled methods of science are not applicable, will employ processes of dynamic problem-solving in studying, improving, and evaluating its products and processes. Supervision either by scientific methods or through orderly thought processes will constantly derive and use data and conclusions which are more objective, more

precise, more sufficient, more impartial, more expertly secured, and more systematically organized than are the data and conclusions of uncontrolled opinion.

8. Good supervision will be creative and not prescriptive.

   a. Supervision will determine procedures in the light of the needs of each supervisory teaching-learning situation.

   b. Supervision will provide opportunity for the exercise of originality and for the development of unique contributions, of creative self-expression; will seek latent talent.

   c. Supervision will deliberately shape and manipulate the environment.

9. Good supervision proceeds by means of an orderly, co-operatively planned and executed series of activities.

10. Good supervision will be judged by the results it secures.

11. Good supervision is becoming professional. That is, it is increasingly seeking to evaluate its personnel, procedures, and results; it is moving toward standards and toward self-supervision.

PRINCIPLES GOVERNING THE PURPOSES OF SUPERVISION

1. The ultimate purpose of supervision is the promotion of pupil growth, and hence eventually the improvement of society.

2. A second general purpose of supervision is to supply leadership in securing continuity and constant readaptation in the educational program over a period of years; from level to level within the system; and from one area of learning experience and content to another.

3. The immediate purpose of supervision is co-operatively to develop favorable settings for teaching and learning.

   a. Supervision, through all means available, will seek improved methods of teaching and learning.

   b. Supervision will create a physical, social, and psychological climate or environment favorable to learning.

   c. Supervision will co-ordinate and integrate all educational efforts and materials; will supply continuity.

   d. Supervision will enlist the co-operation of all staff members in serving their own needs and those of the situation; will provide ample, natural opportunities for growth by all concerned in the correction and prevention of teaching difficulties, and for growth in the assumption of new responsibilities.

   e. Supervision will aid, inspire, lead, and develop that security which liberates the creative spirit.[4]

DEPARTURES

While the viewpoint expressed in this book has much in common with, and in fact utilizes and builds upon, contemporary supervision literature in education, there are several fundamental differences in emphasis. Three of these

[4]From *Supervision: A Social Process,* 3d ed. by William H. Burton and Leo J. Brueckner. Copyright © 1955 by Appleton-Century-Crofts, Inc. Reprinted by permission of Appleton-Century-Crofts, Division of Meredith Corporation. P. 85 and p. 88.

are reflected in the statements listed below and others will be apparent to the reader as he progresses through the book.

1. While instruction *is a major function* of supervision, it is not the only function of supervision and, in fact, *may not be the major function* of supervision.
2. Supervision needs to be defined and described broadly in terms of goals-and-means behavior manifestations rather than roles, incumbents, job descriptions, and tasks per se.
3. "Things" usually considered administrative may be supervisory and "things" usually considered supervisory may be administrative, depending upon how they are carried out.

In Chapter 1 we define and expand the basis for enlightened supervision and in Chapter 2 relate this foundation to a theory of supervisory effectiveness. The theory is expanded and applied to the human school in the remaining chapters of Part I.

Chapter One
PERSPECTIVES
FOR SUPERVISION

Supervision is a function which exists in various degrees and in various forms in any school organization. The process of supervision is viewed by teachers, students, and others on a continuum extending from outright hostility through indifference to outright enthusiasm. How one views supervision depends largely upon one's past experience with supervisory practices. A history of supervisory experiences characterized by frustration, control, denial, and competition will leave most teachers with attitudes of suspicion toward even the most enlightened supervisory environment. As such, enlightened supervisors may find that their actions and statements are subjected to a credibility gap which exists between what enlightened supervision promises to teachers and what is readily forthcoming from traditional supervisory patterns. Unpleasant experiences are difficult for teachers and other school personnel to repress.

This book is about supervisory effectiveness. It examines a variety of attitudes and assumptions held by those who supervise and those who are supervised and relates them to effective supervision. The focus of the book is on the human organization which exists within any school organization and which, in fact, determines the effectiveness of that school organization. The success of any school activity is largely determined by the well-being, skill, and motivation of the human side of the school. Managing the human organization is central to school administration in that other aspects of school success are dependent upon how well this is done.

THE NEED FOR SUPERVISION

Many educators feel that supervision is not only unnecessary in modern schools but is frequently an obstacle to school effectiveness. Usually, proponents of this view describe supervision as an appendage to classical management theories which emphasize control, compliance, and authority. Still others see supervision as a unidimensional concept associated with the office of supervisor and with an incumbent of this office who serves to regulate, systemize, enforce, and evaluate according to what he views to be the school's administrative requirements.

Newer patterns of supervision which appear to be emerging in the more effective modern schools, however, offer opportunities for increasing school effectiveness. They depend largely upon promoting the personal and professional growth of the entire staff as a means of effectively managing the school enterprise. Such enlightened schools enjoy personal, social, and intellectual enrichment not only of school employees but of school clients as well. Client enrichment is, after all, at the apex of any hierarchy of school purposes.

ASSUMPTIONS

It seems useful to distinguish between modes of behavior which can be described as supervisory and others which cannot. Deciding on what constitutes supervisory behavior helps us to realize the scope and breadth of supervision. Below are several statements which help to clarify the concept of supervision:

1. Supervision as a process is a more meaningful mode of analysis than viewing supervision as a role or the supervisor as a particular role incumbent.

   If supervision is viewed as a process, then all personnel who practice supervision in schools (superintendent, principals, librarians, staff personnel, department or division chairmen, classroom teachers, and others, including nonprofessional personnel) are supervisors at one time or another. Thus, successful management of the human organization of any school requires a commitment from the total school.

2. Supervision is a process used by those in schools who have responsibility for one or another aspect of the school's goals and who *depend directly upon others* to help them achieve these goals.

   A crucial aspect which differentiates supervisory behavior from other forms of organizational behavior is *action to achieve goals through other people*. A principal who works to improve the effectiveness of the educational program for students by helping teachers become more effective in the classroom is behaving in a supervisory way. A critical aspect of this relationship is that the principal is dependent upon the teacher as he attempts to increase program effectiveness.

3. Since behavior is a significant part of the supervisory process, it is often useful to focus on this aspect of supervision as a primary analytical method for increasing understanding of the process as a whole.

   While the supervisory process requires attention to the social, cultural, attitudinal, and behavioral ethos of the total supervisory environment, it is often analytically easier to discuss the process in terms of behavior. Thus supervisory behavior is an important staple of this book and, as such, forms the basis for analyzing other aspects of the supervisory process and their relationship to supervisory effectiveness.

4. Behavior by administrators and others in school organizations which is characterized by action toward achievement of school goals but is *not* dependent upon others for success is described as administrative rather than supervisory.

When administrators and others work with things and ideas rather than people as they pursue school goals, they tend to be operating in an administrative way rather than in a supervisory way. While work on the budget, the master schedule, or the program for a summer workshop and preparation of a memo for the superintendent may all be related to achieving or facilitating school purposes, the principal is often justified in carrying out these activities and responsibilities in a way which does not require his dependence upon others for success.

5. Depending upon the circumstances, one may choose to behave in an administrative way—directly—or in a supervisory way—through people —to achieve school goals.

Certain aspects of school goals are more effectively (and in some cases exclusively) accomplished through administrative behavior, while other aspects are more effectively accomplished through behavior described as supervisory. The choice between one and the other pattern of behavior is critical for decision making in school organizations. To be sure, as schools mature and develop as professional organizations, the supervisory way of behaving becomes the dominant pattern of operation for all school personnel. Figure 1-2 illustrates this relationship.

We need at this point to differentiate between working with and through people to achieve school goals and using people to achieve these goals. Using people is consistent with classical-traditional management styles

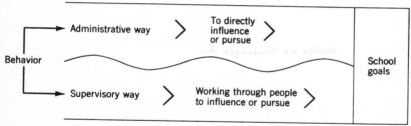

Figure 1-1. Behaving in an administrative way or supervisory way.

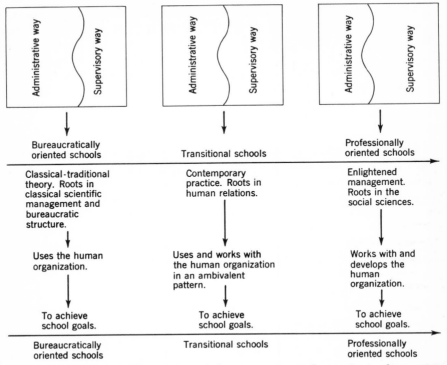

Figure 1-2. The relationship between behavior patterns and organizational maturity.

(and, to a lesser extent, contemporary management patterns), which considered people as appendages of administrators as they, the administrators, pursued school goals. Modes of operation consistent with this pattern are not effective in marshaling the human organization to work on behalf of the school's purposes. While such modes of operation may show signs of high performance efficiency, these results are usually short-term, with long-term results that are disastrous for the manager, the managed, the organization, and, in our case, the young clients who pass through the nation's schools.

6. When administrators and others choose to operate in an administrative way to achieve school purposes, their actions may or may not involve change; but when they choose to operate in a supervisory way, their actions invariably include some aspects of change in behavior.

A major effort of any supervisory act is the changing of some aspect of a person's concept of self, way of behaving, attitude set, or relationship to the school and within the school as an organization. Whether a supervisor is working to improve the performance of teacher A, the effectiveness of classroom B, the attitude of group C, or the direction of school D, each purpose requires fundamental attention to the nature of change, strategies for change, and resistance to change. When administrators and others decide to behave in a supervisory way, they adopt the perspective of change agent. Processes of change and their relationships to supervisory attitudes and behavior are explored in detail in later chapters.

SUMMARY

In this chapter we have discussed and described perspectives for understanding the concept of supervision. An effort has been made to differentiate between alternate ways of behaving in order to accomplish school goals. Actions on the part of school administrators, teachers, and others which involve and depend upon aspects of the human organization of the school in order to achieve these goals are described as *supervisory*. Actions on the part of administrators, teachers, and others which do not involve or depend upon aspects of the human organization to achieve school goals are described as *administrative*.

As schools progress toward professional maturity, the dominant pattern of behavior for all school personnel will be supervisory rather than administrative. Notice that supervisory ways of behaving are not the province of a particular person or a particular position (principal, science supervisor, teacher) but are natural modes of behavior for all who work with and are a part of the human organization of any school.

Chapter Two
A THEORY
OF SUPERVISION

Throughout this book a number of frameworks for thinking, analyzing, conceptualizing, and synthesizing about supervision and supervisory behavior are presented. Among them are Jacob Getzels's and Egon Guba's Social System formulation, Amatai Etzioni's compliance theory, Rensis Likert's System 4, Robert Blake and Jane Mouton's Managerial Grid, the leadership behavior formulations popularized for educators by Andrew Halpin, the Matthew Miles concept of organizational health, the conflict models proposed by Chris Argyris and Ronald Corwin, Gerald Hage's axiomatic theory of organizations, McGregor's theories X and Y, and so on.[1] Each of these modes of thought varies considerably in depth and breadth as well as focus of analysis, but each provides readers with "power concepts" which facilitate the explanation of organizational, administrative, and supervisory phenomena. This understanding forms the basis for improved supervisory performance. The frameworks, models, and schemata suggested in this introduction, as well as other theoretical formulations, are an integral part of the theory which follows and are discussed and applied in subsequent chapters. None of the formulations presently available to educators is extensive enough, however, to provide us with a general theory of supervision.

A SYNTHESIZING THEORY OF SUPERVISION

What follows in the form of a synthesizing theory of supervision represents a blueprint for the development of subsequent chapters as well as a basis for supervisory strategies which, it is hoped, will *be developed by the reader*. The theory proposed is one which depends heavily upon a number of borrowed formulations, concepts, and ideas which have been combined and related to provide an integrated and systematic effort toward improving supervisory effectiveness.

The theory identifies and describes three sets of variables. One set, the organizational success variables, represents the output which results from school efforts and activities. Another set, the initiating variables, represents those assumptions, actions, belief patterns, and modes of operation which are

[1] A bibliography for these authors appears at the end of Chapter 2.

best described as administrative and organizational. The third set, the mediating variables, constitutes the fabric of the human organization of any school.

While the list which follows is not inclusive or exhaustive, it provides samples of the variables which need to be considered in each of the three sets.

THE INITIATING VARIABLES

1. Assumptions which supervisors hold in reference to their peers, subordinates, and themselves.
2. Administrative and supervisory behavior patterns which are consistently displayed by management personnel.
3. Structural elements of organizations which exist in a state of interdependence and which, when viewed for a given school, compose the organizational style for that school. Examples of such elements are the extent to which a school exhibits:
    a. Formalization (uses rules and regulations).
    b. Stratification (relies on hierarchical status systems).
    c. Centralization (decisions made at higher levels).
    d. Productivity (the number, but not necessarily the quality, of units processed).
    e. Efficiency (cost in terms of material).
    f. Adaptability (responsiveness of the school to its external environment).
    g. Complexity (professional-personal specialization).
    h. Job satisfaction (organizational emphasis on job satisfaction as a legitimate goal).
4. The nature of the authority system which prevails in a school and the resulting strategies for compliance.
5. The nature of goals and directions for the school and patterns for the emergence of these goals.

MEDIATING VARIABLES

1. Attitudes which teachers and other employees have toward their jobs and toward their superiors, peers, and subordinates.
2. Levels of job satisfaction which exist for staff (security, social relations, esteem, autonomy, self-actualization).
3. The extent to which the staff is committed to school goals and purposes.
4. Levels of performance goals held by teachers and other educational workers.
5. Levels of group loyalty and group commitment which exist in the school.

6. The extent to which teachers have confidence and trust in themselves, their peers, and their superiors.
7. The extent to which teachers feel that they have control over their immediate work environment and can meaningfully influence the larger school environment.
8. The extent to which a facilitation for communications exists at all levels of the school enterprise and in all directions.

ORGANIZATIONAL SUCCESS VARIABLES

1. Performance levels of teachers and other employees.
2. Performance levels of students.
3. Growth levels of students.
4. The amount of increase in the worth of the human organization.
5. Absence and turnover rates of the staff.
6. Absence and dropout rates of the students.
7. Quality of school-community relations.
8. Quality of labor relations.

Traditional Supervisory Patterns

Much confusion results as one attempts to map the relationships which exist between variables of one set and those of other sets. Classical management theory, and to some extent contemporary supervisory practices, attempt to promote positive change in the organizational success variables through *consistent* and direct manipulation of one or another of the initiating variables. This approach rarely includes conscious and direct efforts to influence and change the mediating variables. As such, administrators and supervisors risk

Initiating _____→ School success
variables   variables

alienation or at best apathy from the human organization of the school as they attempt to work toward what they perceive to be school effectiveness.

Enlightened Supervision

Emerging patterns of supervision are based on the premise that consistent and long-term achievement of school success is dependent upon the positive presence of the mediating variables.

The human organization of schools, which includes the quality of communications, group loyalty, levels of job satisfaction, and commitment to task, for example, exerts a direct influence in determining the nature and quality of school success. In turn, these mediating variables are influenced and determined by the nature and quality of attitudes, practices, and conditions which compose the initiating variables.

Initiating ⟶ Mediating ⟶ School success
variables   variables   variables

The direct approach is illustrated by a principal who, in attempting to improve learning experiences for youngsters, wishes to adopt innovation A for his school. This principal may, by behaving in an administrative way, choose to use his hierarchical position and legal prerogative to require this change (he might proceed with the adoption over the summer recess and present the new teaching pattern, innovation A, to the teachers upon their return in the fall), or he may, by behaving in a supervisory way, approach the human organization concerning the problem of improving learning experiences for children, with an expectation of their professional response to this problem.

The first approach—the strategy which moves directly from the intervening variable set to the school success variables—risks apathy or alienation from the human organization. Teachers will tend not to identify with changes imposed on them from above. The effectiveness of the school therefore may actually be reduced rather than improved as originally intended by our fictitious principal. A well-meaning administrator who ignores the human organization often finds that his efforts are unappreciated as well as ineffectual in terms of school performance.

The theory suggests that the second alternative—working to effect change in the mediating variables—will *in the long run* increase the school's effectiveness. Consistent patterns of the first kind may bring short-term organizational success to the school (often being for a time more productive than patterns of the second kind), but in the long run they will corrode the effectiveness of the school. This phenomenon is illustrated by the now classic Morse and Reimer study[2] which analyzed the effectiveness (productivity and well-being of the human organization) of employees subject to two different styles of supervision. Group 1, subjected to a style of supervision described as hierarchical by the investigators, outdistanced group 2, subjected to a participatory style, in productivity but showed a commensurate decline in the quality of its human organization. Over time, corrosion of the human organization in hierarchically controlled environments takes its toll in performance. In commenting on this phenomenon, Likert notes that "the attitudes, loyalties, and motivation which improved the most in the participative program and deteriorated the most in the hierarchical controlled program are those which these studies have consistently shown to be most clearly related *in the long run* to employee motivation and productivity."[3]

Enlightened supervision, that which fully coordinates, develops, and uti-

[2]Nancy Morse and E. Reimer, "The Experimental Change of a Major Organizational Variable," *Journal of Abnormal and Social Psychology*, vol. 52, 1956, pp. 120–129.
[3]Rensis Likert, *New Patterns of Management*, McGraw-Hill, New York, 1961, p. 68.

lizes the resources of the human organization, requires an investment in time by school officials before appreciable results can be realized. As the mellowing process sets, school management's investment in its human organization will show improvement in each of the organizational success variables.

THE THEORY ILLUSTRATED

The accompanying flow chart (Table 2-1) suggests samples of alternate attitudes and ways of behaving for those who supervise in schools, as well as several organizational styles which schools may adopt. The potential effects of each of these initiating variables on a host of mediating variables are described, and finally, changes which can be expected to result in the school success variables are indicated. The theory, as illustrated in Table 2-1, forms the basis for Part I of this book, and each of the concepts which compose the theory is cross-referenced to later chapters. There the concepts will be illustrated, explained, and applied to supervision for better schools.

Supervisory Approaches

Administrative and supervisory attitudes and behaviors, organizational styles, and management belief systems (those actions, attitudes, and related phenomena which compose the initiating variable set) can be described on a conceptual continuum extending from classical-traditional through contemporary to enlightened. Classical supervisory styles, according to the theory, seem to have type 1 effects on the human organization and tend to result in low organizational performance. Contemporary approaches to supervision—those which encourage type 2 reactions from the human organization—encourage mediocre school performance. Type 3 reactions—those encouraged by enlightened approaches to supervision—result in higher organizational performance in schools for each of the organizational success variables.

Mediating Variables—Type 1 Reaction   *Classical-traditional*

Type 1 reactions—those promoted by classical-traditional supervisory patterns —are typically characterized by considerable teacher job dissatisfaction with working conditions, supervision, school policies, and administration. Further, dissatisfaction with job security, with interpersonal relations with peers and subordinates, and with superiors, status, and salary can be expected. Some of these factors are symptomatic of a managerial climate which encourages alienation of the teaching staff. No professional person charged with supervisory responsibilities works deliberately to cause a type 1 reaction from his staff. This reaction is usually an unanticipated consequence of a supervisor's—often one who is well-meaning—ignoring the human organization of the school. The type 1 reaction invariably results, over time, in lower levels of performance, resistance to change, higher turnover, antiorganizational informal

TABLE 2-1. A SYNTHESIZING THEORY OF SUPERVISORY EFFECTIVENESS

Initiating variables	Supervision			Mediating variables	Results: types 1-3	School success variables	Low / Med. / High
	Classical	Contemporary	Enlightened				
		Consistent choice					Overtime
							(p. 23)
1. Administrative and supervisory assumptions (McGregor)	Theory X (p. 74) ———	Theory Y ———		Type 1 (p. 19) ——→		Low	
				Type 3 (p. 23) ——→		High	
Management assumptions (Argyris)	Infancy assumptions (p. 78) ———	Growth assumptions ———		Type 1 ——→		Low	
				Type 3 ——→		High	
2. Administrative and supervisory orientation:							
Style propensity (Gibb)	Defensive (p. 87) ———	Participatory ———		Type 1 ——→		Low	
				Type 3 ——→		High	
Value system	School / Community / Society / Individual (p. 83)	Individual / Society / Community / School		Type 1 ——→		Low	
				Type 3 ——→		High	
3. Administrative and supervisory behavior:							
Social system (Getzels)	Nomothetic (p. 31) ———	Ideographic ———	Transactional ———	Type 1 ——→		Low	
				Type 2 (p. 23) ——→		Medium	
				Type 3 ——→		High	
Managerial grid style (Blake and Mouton)	9,1. (p. 91) ———	1,9. ———	9,9. ———	Type 1 ——→		Low	
				Type 2 ——→		Medium	
				Type 3 ——→		High	
LBDQ (Halpin)	IS + C− (p. 89) ———	IS − C+ ———	IS + C+ ———	Type 1 ——→		Low	
				Type 2 ——→		Medium	
				Type 3 ——→		High	

New patterns of management (Likert)

Man-to-man style of supervision (p. 179) ——→ Type 1 ——→ Low

Group supervision ——→ Type 3 ——→ High

4. Authority systems (Thompson)

Legally defined authority based on position-hierarchy ——→ Type 1 ——→ Low

Organizationally defined authority based on ability (p. 67) ——→ Type 3 ——→ High

Peabody formulation

Formal authority { Legitimacy, Position ——→ Type 1 ——→ Low

Functional authority { Competence, Person (p. 39) ——→ Type 3 ——→ High

Power base (French and Raven)

Legitimate, Coercive, Reward (p. 43) ——→ Type 1 ——→ Low

Expert, Referent ——→ Type 3 ——→ High

5. Compliance system (Etzioni)

Coercive ——→ Type 1 ——→ Low

Utilitarian (p. 47) ——→ Type 2 ——→ Medium

Normative ——→ Type 3 ——→ High

6. Nature of goals and direction

Decided by management (p. 107) ——→ Type 1 ——→ Low

Emerge from group action ——→ Type 3 ——→ High

Manifest only are legitimate ——→ Type 1 ——→ Low

Manifest and latent are legitimate (p. 101) ——→ Type 3 ——→ High

TABLE 2-1. A SYNTHESIZING THEORY OF SUPERVISORY EFFECTIVENESS (Continued)

Initiating variables	Supervision			Mediating variables	Results: types 1-3	School success variables {Low Med. High}
	Classical	Contemporary	Enlightened			→ Over time
7. Manifestation of organizational style, managerial emphasis on mechanistic or organic, bureaucratic or professional (Hage)	Mechanistic Formalization Stratification Centralization Production Efficiency ($) (p. 61)	Organic	Consistent choice	Type 1 —→		Low
			Adaptability Complexity Job satisfaction	Type 3		High
8. Management system (Likert)	System 1 System 2	System 3	System 4	Type 1 Type 2 Type 3		Low Medium High
9. Organizational climate (Halpin and Croft)	Closed ———————→		Open —→	Type 1 Type 3		Low High

group activity, and formal labor problems for the school. Those who evoke type 1 reactions from teachers tend not to supervise at all, by our definition. They rely heavily on administrative ways of behaving.

Mediating Variables—Type 2 Reaction *Contemporary approach*

The type 2 reaction to patterns of initiating variables generally revolves around a feeling of apathy insofar as the welfare of the school and the vigorous pursuit of school goals are concerned. Teachers are relatively relieved from job dissatisfaction, although they are not afforded opportunities for meaningful job satisfaction. Performance expectations are generally low, with supervisors emphasizing a shallow group life characterized by high morale, good feelings, and low tension.[4] Teachers are relatively protected from the pressure of work, and security is guaranteed. Yet teachers "feel" no compulsion to exert commitment, energy, and effort beyond that which is minimally required to carry on day by day. Little opportunity exists for teachers to grow personally and professionally and to enjoy deep satisfaction from their work.[5] Contemporary supervisory patterns which rely almost entirely on human relations perspectives evoke this response from subordinates. Supervisors who evoke type 2 reaction from teachers often fail to distinguish between using people and working with people to achieve school goals. This is a confused pattern characterized by ambivalence and uncertainty.

Mediating Variables—Type 3 Reaction *Enlightened*

Enlightened supervisory patterns—those which work to achieve school success variables through encouraging the growth and development of the human organization—evoke responses from subordinates which are labeled type 3. This type of response is characterized by high commitment to the work of the school, high loyalty to the school and to the membership subunit, high performance goals, and a desire, combined with an opportunity, for personal and professional growth. Job satisfaction centers around growth opportunities, achievement, recognition, responsibility, and advancement. The reward system which composes the type 3 response depends heavily upon achievement of the school success variables.[6] Supervisory behavior which evokes a type 3 response from the human organization automatically

[4]The evidence does not substantiate a link between morale—that is, satisfaction—and performance—that is, productivity—unless satisfaction is dependent upon performance. See, for example, Bernard M. Bass, *Organizational Psychology*, Allyn and Bacon, New York, 1965, p. 38.

[5]Type 2 response is characterized by the relative absence of dissatisfaction combined with little opportunity for achieving satisfaction. The phenomenon is discussed in detail in Chapter 8. See, for example, Frederick Herzberg, Bernard Mausner, and Barbara Synderman, *The Motivation to Work*, Wiley, New York, 1959.

[6]See footnote 4.

approaches school success. This pattern clearly characterizes supervisory ways of behaving.

SUMMARY

While many scholars have proposed theories and models which have potential for powerful use by those who supervise in the nation's schools, no one schema has been offered as a general theory of supervision. Chapter 2 builds upon the work of scholars from a variety of social science fields by integrating and relating their ideas into a synthesizing theory of supervisory effectiveness. The theory identifies and relates three sets of variables: initiating (administrative and organizational), mediating (human organization), and school success, which permit the conceptual mapping of effective supervision.

The concepts, models, and schemata which compose the initiating variables in the synthesizing theory are the focus of Chapters 3, 4, 5, and 6. Chapters 7 and 8 deal with the mediating variables and the school success variables.

SELECTED REFERENCES

Argyris, Chris: *Personality and Organization*, Harper, New York, 1957.

Blake, Robert, and Jane Mouton: *The Managerial Grid*, Gulf Publishing Company, Houston, 1966.

Corwin, Ronald: "Professional Persons in Public Organizations," *Educational Administration Quarterly*, 1965.

Etzioni, Amatai: *A Comparative Analysis of Complex Organizations*, Free Press, New York, 1961.

Getzels, Jacob W., and Egon G. Guba: "Social Behavior and Administrative Process," *The School Review*, Winter, 1957.

Hage, Gerald: "An Axiomatic Theory of Organization," *Administrative Science Quarterly*, 1967.

Halpin, Andrew W.: *Theory and Research in Administration*, Macmillan, New York, 1967.

Likert, Rensis: *The Human Organization: Its Management and Value*, McGraw-Hill, New York, 1968.

McGregor, Douglas: *The Human Side of Enterprise*, McGraw-Hill, New York, 1960.

Miles, Matthew B.: "Organizational Health: Figure and Ground," *Change Processes in the Public Schools*, Center for the Advanced Study of Educational Administration, University of Oregon, Eugene, Ore., 1965.

Chapter Three
THE NATURE
OF SCHOOL
ORGANIZATIONS

Stresses environment as a factor in supervision

Supervisory behavior takes place in a system of complexity which involves the interplay of initiating, human, and school success variables. Supervisory behavior has its roots in the initiating variables, visualizes its targets in the school success variables, and focuses on change in the human variables in order to approach its targets. The principal or superintendent, for example, operates (1) in an organizational environment, (2) from an authority base, (3) in a specific way, (4) in order to change staff attitudes or behaviors, and (5) with the goal of increasing some dimension of school effectiveness.

This chapter focuses on those initiating variables described as organizational (authority-compliance systems, status-hierarchical systems, organizational styles, and the like) as opposed to behavioral (attitudes and leadership manifestations) in the synthesizing theory presented in Chapter 2. The purpose of this chapter is to expose those who administer and supervise in our schools to the sociological environment for supervision. The best intentions and the most rational plans have little chance of success for those who ignore, misjudge, or cannot comprehend the environmental milieu of schools. The same fate awaits those who work to manipulate this environmental milieu for their own ends as opposed to those of the human organization or to those of the human school.

ORGANIZATIONAL PERSPECTIVE

We recognize, of course, that schools constitute organizational types which are significantly and uniquely different from other organizations. Nevertheless, much can be learned about schools by viewing them broadly as organizational entities in and of themselves. As such, organizations may be viewed as living organisms having a composite of characteristics much as people have a variety of personality traits. Like individuals, organizations need to identify and pursue goals, react to stress, seek homeostatis, adapt, maintain themselves internally, ensure survival, eliminate uncertainty, and grow in size, power, and experience if they are to function effectively.[1]

[1] An extended discussion of this theme appears in Fred D. Carver and Thomas J. Sergiovanni (eds.), *Organizations and Human Behavior: Focus on Schools*, McGraw-Hill, New York, 1969, p. 2.

Much human activity in schools and other organizations is motivated by administrative reaction to these and other organizational needs. As such, organizational change is often haphazard and, therefore, described as organizational drift. It appears that organizations evolve, adjust, and readjust, seemingly unaffected by conscious efforts of their members. An alternative to this reactive behavior is proactive behavior (planned change). Here organizational change takes place as a result of conscious efforts by individuals to control the organization rather than to be controlled by the organization. Planning and structuring the growth patterns and directions of schools, developing strategies to overcome or to live and grow with uncertainty, and establishing the nature and frequency of change (new homeostatic levels) are examples of proactive administrative behavior. Organizational needs are potent motivators of organizational movement as well as of organizational resistance to change. Proactive behavior by administrators and supervisors must operate within the limits set by organizational needs.

Cyert and March,[2] March and Simon,[3] and recently Thompson[4] suggest that a basic fallacy behind early attempts to study organizations has been our tendency to view them as rational structures. In this context, we have theoretically assumed that problem-solving activity in schools included carefully delineating *all* the alternative solutions to a given problem, anticipating the effects of these solutions, and weighing each of the alternatives systematically. The alternative with the highest score is then chosen as the best solution. This process represents a most formidable task, one which is beyond the capabilities of all but superhumans and superorganizations. Indeed, one needs to exercise caution when viewing schools as maximizing organizations. As man tends to seek not the best needle in a haystack, but rather one that satisfies the reason for his search, so schools tend to seek not maximizing solutions to their problems, but rather solutions which they can accept as satisfying current needs. *Organizations are notoriously satisfying as they follow their own impulses.*

Many educational administrators and supervisors are tempted to capitalize on the satisfying nature of schools, but while they may find personal comfort and security in such approaches, schools operating under such supervision do so at appreciably lower levels of effectiveness. As we add an enlightened human dimension to the organization, however, we introduce elements of rationality by identifying and establishing significant goals, by pursuing these goals, and, ultimately, by *attempting* to maximize this goal relationship.

[2]Richard M. Cyert and James G. March, *A Behavioral Theory of the Firm,* Prentice-Hall, Englewood Cliffs, N.J., 1963.
[3]James G. March and Herbert A. Simon, *Organizations,* Wiley, New York, 1958.
[4]James Thompson, *Organizations in Action,* McGraw-Hill, New York, 1968.

ORGANIZATIONAL REQUIREMENTS

Parsons[5] proposes four basic needs which all organizations as social systems seek to satisfy in order to survive as effective institutions. Since schools are no exception to general laws which describe organizational phenomena, the Parsonian criteria are illustrated below for schools. Examples are suggestive rather than exhaustive.

ORGANIZATIONAL NEEDS

Qua Organizations		*For Schools*
1. Adaptation to the organizational environment	1.	*a.* Being receptive to the changing needs of society at the local, national, and international levels.
		b. Professional innovation in technology and instruction.
		c. Dealing with multiple and often conflicting pressure groups. The adaptation function is performed largely by superintendents, a few specialists, and outside resource people. The school's greatest weakness may be its lack of concern, organizationally, with this function. Planning, research, experimentation, and development departments are still rare in educational organizations.
2. Achievement of organizational goals	2.	These are summarized in Chapter 2 as part of the school success variables which compose the last panel of the synthesizing theory. They include:
		a. Student achievement.
		b. Citizenship.
		c. Student self-actualization.

[5]Talcott Parsons, *Structure and Process in Modern Societies,* Free Press, Glencoe, Ill., 1960, pp. 16–96.

ORGANIZATIONAL NEEDS (*Continued*)

Qua Organizations		*For Schools*
		d. Favorable dropout rates.
		e. As a latent goal, teacher growth and development.
3. Integration of subunits into the larger organizational system	3. *a.*	Improving relationships with the school board and other agencies which operate at the boundary of the school.
	b.	Curricular coordination within a school and among schools which compose the school system.
	c.	Administrative and educational integration and articulation of departments, agencies, bureaus, and other semiautonomous units which make up any school and school system.
4. Maintenance of value patterns over time (pattern maintenance)	4. *a.*	Efforts directed at the cultivation and improvement of morale, cohesion, and loyalty.
	b.	The socialization of students and faculty to the general educational ethos and that which is unique for the school in question.
	c.	Counseling efforts to reflect and "impose" the organizational point of view on schools.

Argyris[5] proposes two critical requirements for all organizations: that they maintain themselves internally (items 3 and 4 in the Parsons formulation) and that at the same time they be externally adaptive (items 1 and 2 in Parsons). In each case, two organizational thrusts seem apparent. One thrust is an organizational increase in effort to serve society and to seek its approval (after Parsons' adaptation and achievement), and the other is an

[6] Chris Argyris, *Personality and Organization*, Harper & Row, New York, 1957; also, *Integrating the Individual Organization*, Wiley, New York, 1964.

Figure 3-1. Conceptual cycle of integration: a dual focus.

organizational effort to serve itself through integration and maintenance. Organizational tendencies, we have suggested, favor integration and maintenance, since adaptation and achievement result in upsetting homeostatic levels and introduce significant quantities of uncertainty and stress. Enlightened supervision (see Figure 3-1) recognizes the importance of providing for each of the organizational requirements and visualizes them on a manageable conceptual cycle of integration, Through enlightened supervision, as the school adapts and achieves it provides for integration and maintenance. As the school provides for integration and maintenance, its capabilities for adaptation and achievement increase, and so on. We illustrate this cycle of integration in subsequent chapters as we discuss the concept of organizational health, reward systems which are available to teachers, patterns of individual accommodation to organizational life, leadership concepts, and the concept of planned change.

The School as a Complex Organization

While romantic vestiges of the little red schoolhouse still exist in America, schools, like most organizations, have experienced phenomenal growth in terms of sheer size and area serviced and of professional complexity. The emergence and spread of the large high school, for example, has accelerated rapidly in the last decade to the point where this unit, in a variety of forms, dominates American secondary education. The operation of the large high school is usually characterized by conservation of technical resources, scientific staff utilization, computerized scheduling, diversity of program offerings and other student services, favorable time and space utilization for building use, and centralized supporting professional and nonprofessional staff. These characteristics have had strange and often unanticipated effects upon the education of school clients, upon the level and nature of job satisfaction available to teachers, and upon the school's ability to respond creatively to its environments. The contemporary elementary school is no exception in kind to the characteristics described above, but only in intensity.[7]

[7] See, for example, Ole Sand, "The School of the '70s—Amazing Changes Ahead," *The Family Weekly,* Sept. 1, 1968.

In addition to size, modern organizations are also characterized by a high degree of specialization. Schools are not unlike other organizations in this regard in that they have their share of contemporary experts (some imagined and some real) who claim ability monopolies over certain aspects of the management system (directors, vice-principals, division heads for instructional units, student personnel, administrators, finance experts, and so on) as well as the technical system (subject-matter specialists, hardware experts, early childhood-disadvantaged-compensatory education specialists, sociopsychological practitioners, and the like).[8] The number of new positions and functional roles which have appeared in the last decade in American education is overshadowed only by their variety.

Sheer size and wide specialization are ample symptoms of complexity. The facts that schools are often arranged into a series of interdependent subunits which compose a school system and that this system is often the largest enterprise in many American communities (with the largest share of tax dollars and the largest budget) are further evidence that the modern school is indeed a complex organization. In larger communities, the diversity of the school's mission, combined with the large number of personnel (clients and workers) included in the school organization, often makes it comparable in complexity with other organizations. It should be understood, however, that size in itself is not a sufficient criterion for identifying complexity. Schools are complex primarily because of the sophistication of their technology, the diversification of their mission, the varied nature of their task, and their patterns of structure.

THE SOCIAL MILIEU FOR SUPERVISION

In order for administrators, teachers, and other personnel who supervise in America's schools to behave in ways which increase school effectiveness, they must first come to understand and be able to work from an understanding of the sociological milieu for supervision. Crucial to this understanding is a comprehension of authority systems, compliance systems, and status systems which form the basis for administrative action. Power systems operate in an interaction arrangement between the bureaucratic tendencies of schools and the professional tendencies of schools. Systems of interaction invariably contain conflict. We consider conflict in schools from a number of perspectives, including the individual versus the organization; the management system versus the technical system; sources of ability versus

[8]Management and technical systems are used, after Parsons, to differentiate between the administrative sphere and the educo-technical sphere. See Talcott Parsons, "Some Ingredients of a General Theory of Organization," in Andrew W. Halpin (ed.), *Administrative Theory in Education*, Midwest Administration Center, University of Chicago, Chicago, 1958.

sources of authority; and bureaucratic inclinations of schools versus professional inclinations. We begin this discussion with an analysis of the school as a social system.

The Social System Formulation

Over the years a variety of frameworks have been offered for the study of administrative behavior. These "theories of administration" offer alternate windows through which the educational practitioner and educational researcher are able to view school problems and issues. While theories are not prescriptive, in terms of "how to do it," they are potent modes of understanding which, it is hoped, will lead to insightful prescription for administrative and supervisory action. We believe that the practitioner is the one qualified to build prescription from theory. This is simply a necessity in view of the uniqueness and complexity of the circumstances he faces. The educational researcher, theorist, and serious writer provides the practitioner with theoretical stimuli and a conceptual arsenal of insights through which and from which he, the practitioner, builds prescription.[9]

The most widely recognized and perhaps the most useful framework for studying and understanding administrative and supervisory behavior is the social systems analysis developed for educators by Jacob Getzels and Egon Guba.[10] This formulation is reviewed and modified for supervision below.

The social systems theorists[11] view administration as a social process and the context of administration as a social system. The administrative process and context can be examined, according to this view, from structural, functional, and operational perspectives. Structurally, administration is considered to be a series of superordinate-subordinate relationships within a social system. Functionally, this hierarchy of relationships (principal to teacher, teacher to student, and so on) is the basis for allocating and integrating roles, personnel, and facilities on behalf of the school goals. Operationally, the administrative process occurs in person-to-person interaction.

[9]The authors propose that the usefulness of this book for the practitioner depends upon his ability (as either a pre-service or in-service reader) to work through the book as a basis for his invention of practical strategies for supervision and an educational program unique to his circumstances.

[10]The following discussion is based on a number of sources. Documentation is loose in view of the general familiarity and acceptance of the Getzels and Guba social systems model. See, for example, J. W. Getzels, "A Psycho-sociological Framework for the Study of Educational Administration," *Harvard Educational Review*, vol. 22, Fall, 1952, pp. 235–246; J. W. Getzels and E. G. Guba, "Social Behavior and the Administrative Process," *The School Review*, vol. 65, 1957, pp. 423–441; J. W. Getzels, "Administration As a Social Process," in Andrew W. Halpin (ed.), *Administrative Theory in Education*, Midwest Administration Center, University of Chicago, Chicago, 1958; and more recently J. W. Getzels et al., *Educational Administration As a Social Process: Theory, Research, Practice*, Harper & Row, New York, 1968. Especially basic to this discussion is the Getzels and Guba 1957 article.

[11]Cf. Talcott Parsons, *The Social System*, Free Press, New York, 1951.

The term *social system* is used by Getzels and Guba in a conceptual rather than descriptive way. They conceive of this system as containing two interdependent but interacting dimensions. The first dimension consists of the *institution,* which is defined in terms of its *roles,* which are in turn defined in terms of *role expectations,* all of which are carefully designed to fulfill the goals of the institution.

Institution → Roles → Role expectations → Institutional goal achievement

All institutions have certain common characteristics and imperative functions:

1. *Institutions have purposes.* They are established to perform certain functions and are legitimized by client groups and societal groups on the basis of these functions. Purposes for schools are generally of two kinds: those which are manifest—the educational and custodial functions which win community and societal support—and those which are latent —the power gratification and growth rewards which members (teachers and administrators) seek.

2. *Institutions are structural.* Institutional goals are achieved through task diversification. As such, roles are established with appropriate role descriptions. Each role is assigned certain responsibilities and resources, including authority for implementing given tasks. The ideas are conceived and responsibilities allocated in terms of actors, as defined above, rather than of personalities.[12]

3. *Institutions are normative.* Roles serve as norms for the behavior of those who occupy the roles. Each actor or role incumbent is expected to behave in certain predetermined ways if he is to retain a legitimate position in the school. Teachers, for example, who adopt modes of behavior typical of the student culture have difficulty in maintaining their legitimate position in the eyes of other teachers, administrators, and perhaps even of students.

4. *Institutions are sanction-bearing.* Institutions have at their disposal appropriate positive and negative sanctions for ensuring compliance with established norms. Teachers who are rate-busters in the eyes of other teachers, for example, may be subject to a silent treatment or to a whisper campaign. Deviants in the eyes of the principal wait longer for school supplies, "earn" undesirable class assignments, and are swamped with classroom visitations.

---

[12]A survey of a typical kindergarten class on the first day of school will reveal reliable, even though stereotyped, descriptions of the role of principal as compared with the role of teacher.

Institutions are operationally defined and analyzed in terms of the subunit role. Roles represent the various positions, offices, and status prerogatives which exist within the institution and are themselves defined in terms of role expectations. Roles are generally institutional givens and, therefore, are not formulated to fit one or another personality. Behaviors associated with a given role are arranged on a conceptual continuum extending from required to prohibited. Certain behaviors are considered absolutely mandatory (that the teacher at least show up for school) and others are absolutely forbidden (that the teacher not become romantically involved with students). Between these extremes are other behavior patterns—some recommended, others disapproved, but all permissible. Roles are best understood when examined in relation to other roles. The student role helps us to understand the teacher role, and so on.

In the absence of individuals with complex and unique personalities, the organizational dimension described above provides for maximum organizational predictability. This aspect of the social system model is called the nomothetic dimension. The second aspect, the ideographic dimension, adds the human element to the social system formulation.[13] As the institutional dimension was analyzed in terms of role and expectation, so the individual dimension is similarly analyzed and defined operationally in terms of personality and need disposition.

Nomothetic dimension

Institution ———→ Roles ———→ Role expectations ———→ Institutional goal achievement

Individual ———→ Personality ———→ Need disposition ———→ Individual goal achievement

Ideographic dimension

The ideographic dimension is similar in format (but not in substance) to the nomothetic dimension in that individuals, like institutions, have goals which they express through their personalities and pursue according to their unique need dispositions.

[13]Guba describes the process by which the terms *nomothetic* and *ideographic* were chosen for the theory as follows: "The terms 'ideographic' and 'nomothetic' were picked from *Roget's Thesaurus* by me one wintry afternoon when I had nothing better to do than to try to find some new and interesting terms to use in our theory. We justified this at the time by claiming that we had to find terms 'untainted' by value connotations."—E. G. Guba, "Development, Diffusion and Evaluation," in T. L. Eidell and J. M. Kitchell (eds.), *Knowledge Production and Utilization in Educational Administration*, CASEA, 1968, p. 38.

The two dimensions of the social system are assumed to be in constant interaction. Nomothetically, the organization strives to socialize the individual to its own image and ends, while ideographically, the individual strives to socialize the organization to his own image and ends.[14] Behavior, then, in any social system is a function of the interaction between unique personalities and preestablished roles. Conformity to the institution, its roles, and expectation leads to organizational effectiveness, while conformity to the individual, his personality, and his need disposition leads to individual efficiency.

The Expanded Model

The expanded social systems model which appears as Figure 3-2 shows the relationship of school A to other institutions which constitute its reference group and to the human organization which composes and operationalizes the school. An alternate analysis can be made by introducing the concept of group to the model. This is a "switch hitter" concept in that groups can assume an institutional or nomothetic position in reference to a given individual, or a group may assume (as a composite of individuals) an individualizing position in reference to the institution.

Getzels and Guba identify a number of conflict situations which may potentially result from the organization's interaction with its human inhabitants. Among them are role-personality conflicts which result from a discrepancy between the pattern of expectations attached to a given role and the pattern of need dispositions of the role incumbent. An assistant principal with a high dependence orientation would find a role characterized by autonomous and independent action quite uncomfortable; teachers with a professional and technical need to interact with school policy makers who are defensive, authoritarian, and noncommunicative experience similar role-personality conflict. Multiple but conflicting expectations for the same role are another source of role conflict. Supervisors who are expected by some teachers to visit classes and by others to stay away experience conflict of this type. The young mother-teacher faces role conflict of this type as she struggles to justly fulfill two demanding roles. The school as an organization is frequently subject to "role conflict" of this type as it attempts to appease multiple and conflicting expectations from its many publics.

Administrative and supervisory behavior, according to this model, may follow one of four general patterns: the nomothetic style, the ideographic style, the compromise style, and the transactional style. While each of these styles is discussed in detail in Chapter 5, a brief description of each follows. Managerial grid numbers and style are also discussed in Chapter 5.

[14] E. W. Bakke, "Concept of the Social Organization," in Mason Haire (ed.), *Modern Organization Theory*, Wiley, New York, 1961, p. 60.

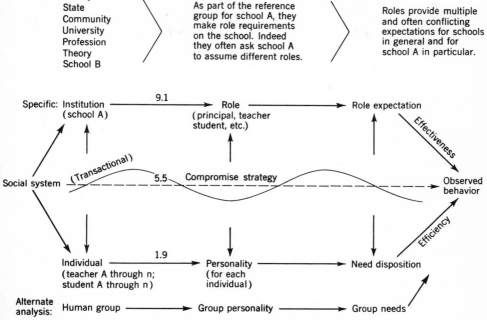

Figure 3-2. The expanded social system model. NOTE: (1) *Effectiveness* implies achievement of organizational goals. (2) *Efficiency* implies achievement of individual needs. (3) *Transactional* implies the integration of the two dimensions into a meaningful and mutually rewarding whole. This is a non-zero-sum relationship in that one dimension need not "lose" for the other to gain. (4) *Compromise* implies a give-and-take, zero-sum, bargaining relationship. (5) Managerial grid numbers (9,1., 1,9., 5.5., and 9,9.) are added to this model for future reference. See our discussion of supervisory style in Chapter 5. (6) *Human group* offers an alternative analysis for the model. The "group" can assume a position either on the organizational dimension in reference to individuals or as a composite of individuals in reference to the institution.

1. *Nomothetic style.* Administrative and supervisory behavior which focuses primarily on the institutional dimension as it seeks to achieve school goals (classical management—9,1. managerial grid style).

2. *Ideographic style.* Administrative and supervisory behavior which focuses primarily on the individual dimension as it seeks to achieve individual goals (human relations—1,9. managerial grid style).

3. *Compromise style.* Administrative and supervisory behavior which focuses "realistically" on achievement of school goals and individual goals in a satisfactory manner (gray flannel suit, organization man—5,5. managerial grid style).

4. *Transactional style.* Administrative and supervisory behavior which operates not from the assumption that the two dimensions are in conflict, but

rather from the position that they are interdependent. That is, achievement of school goals depends upon meaningful, individual need satisfaction. Meaningful need satisfaction, at least for professional and semiprofessional workers, depends upon achievement of school goals. This style seeks to optimize and expand achievement of school goals and individual goals.

A PERSISTENT SUPERVISORY DILEMMA

We have, for illustrative purposes, given the school life quite apart from that which results from those who live and work in the school. As the school becomes "alive" it takes on many of the characteristics of a human organism. As such, the school develops a unique organizational personality which is expressed by and, indeed, imposed upon those who come to live and work within its boundaries. Further, in the absence of more than token human direction and control, the school pursues a series of satellite goals which revolve around the simple but omnipresent need for growth and survival.[15] Within this context the school's goals are pursued in a mechanical way, with changes occurring only as the nature of growth and survival needs change. When changes do occur, they are seemingly unaffected by and reflect little interest in the wishes and requirements of the school's human inhabitants except as such concerns contribute to its growth and survival. If left to its own whims, the school evolves into a monolithic structure which captures and uses its human participants to accomplish its, rather than their, ends. This phenomenon is illustrated by the *natural* tendency of schools to adopt conservative perspectives, to exert a major emphasis on maintenance activities, to avoid change, and thereby to avoid controversy and conflict. School conservatism is illustrated by the now classic Mort studies, which showed a fifty-year gap between educational invention and widespread adoption of the educational practice.[16]

A fundamental concern of supervision is the question of whether schools use people to accomplish organizational ends or whether people use schools to accomplish human ends. This concern is placed in perspective by the following phrase from the *Cardinal Principles of Secondary Education 1918*: "The objectives must determine the organization or else the organiza-

[15]While *school growth* refers to extension of curricular offerings, school boundaries, size of staff, and the like, it also refers to increases in influence, status, and prestige. *Survival,* for schools, refers to continued community financial and moral support and the avoidance of conflict, controversy, and uncertainty, as well as guaranteed tenure for the present school establishment. Both can be maintained by giving only token attention to a quality educational program.

[16]The Mort studies are neatly summarized in Paul R. Mort, "Studies in Educational Innovation from the Institute of Administrative Research: An Overview," in Matthew B. Miles (ed.), *Innovation in Education,* Teachers College Press, New York, 1964, pp. 317–328.

tion will determine the objectives." We ask the reader to recall the countless times he found no reason or no record of origin for a particular policy, act, or way of behaving in the schools of his experience. How many administrators and other educational workers are prepared to provide an *educational rationale* for school policies—indeed, for their own behavior?

Supervisors work to exert the human dimension in schools. They are concerned with the appropriateness of school goals, the welfare and growth of school workers, and, indeed, the intellectual, social, and emotional self-actualization of school clients. Such human concerns require the school as an organization to serve its inhabitants, rather than traditional supervisory patterns, which required individuals to serve the school.

We have been discussing the problems of human-organizational interface—a persistent theme of this book and a persistent supervisory dilemma. For example, how do we compromise, on the one hand, the socializing tendencies of schools as they attempt to mold individuals (teachers, administrators, and students alike) into school images and, on the other hand, the individualizing tendencies of people as they attempt to mold the school into their respective individual images? Further, how do we work to shift school goals from mere organizational growth and survival to a dynamic model which permits the school to achieve its ends through the growth, development, and extension of its human participants?

Individual-organizational interface concerns are expressed in the treatment of four fundamental organizational needs proposed by Parsons. Indeed, working to achieve balance in direction and perspective between and among school achievement, adaptation, integration, and maintenance needs is the cornerstone of school effectiveness. The Getzels and Guba social system formulation portrays in detail the socializing tendency of schools (the nomothetic dimension) and the individualizing tendency of school inhabitants (the ideographic dimension) and suggests a number of behavior patterns which can form the basis for supervisory style. The interdependence of school and individual is illustrated by the transactional style. Here the enrichment of school goals and individual goals is maximized when one contributes to the other.

The persistent nature of the organizational-individual theme is illustrated in the next section as we consider authority systems in schools. As the school increases its control over people, formal authority systems are stressed. As individuals increase their control over the school, functional authority systems are emphasized. We begin by tracing the origin of organizational authority to Max Weber's classical formulation and end by discussing the bases of supervisory power.

AUTHORITY SYSTEMS IN SCHOOLS

Fundamental to administrative and supervisory action in any school is an understanding of the nature of authority—its many origins, its many forms, its operational feasibility, and its acceptance. As schools have matured into complex professional organizations, newer forms of authority have emerged in schools to challenge traditional authority sources. Entrepreneurial administrative behavior, the one-man show, hierarchical authority which rests largely in the position one occupies, and the "tyranny of bureaucratic rules" are being seriously challenged by professional authority, ability authority, and other sources.

Weber's Authority Types

Max Weber distinguishes among three types of authority[17] on the basis of their acceptance as a common value orientation for a particular group. They are described as follows:

> *Traditional*. This authority base is legitimized by the belief in the sanctity of tradition. On this base, a given person or caste of people, usually on the basis of heredity, is preordained to rule over the others. The divine right of kings is a classical example of traditional authority. In contemporary organizations, the management caste treasures and passes on traditional prerogatives which other employees are perceived not to have. This is particularly visible in patriarchal family business and in paternalistic schools.

> *Charismatic*. This authority base rests on a profession of faith which considers the pronouncements of a given leader to be inspired by supernatural powers. Disciples willingly follow the charismatic leader as they become converted to and champions of his cause. In contemporary organizations, the innovator, the champion of new educational and social movements, may be able to tap the charismatic power base. Charismatic movements eventually evolve into traditional or bureaucratic management systems.

> *Legal*. This authority base is legitimized by a formalistic belief in the supremacy of norms and laws. In legal systems, compliance occurs as a result of a body of impersonal and universal principles and rules rather than of loyalty to the traditional or charismatic leader. Legal authority forms the basis for the ideal bureaucratic organization.

The Weber formulation provides a background for most scholarly discussions of organizational authority and power. We have seen in recent years a fourth source of organizational authority—one based on professional norms and skill. Professional authority is similar to legal authority in that both are legitimized by codes, rules, and norms. This similarity is the major cause of conflict between the two. In schools organizational norms and rules

[17]Max Weber, *The Theory of Social and Economic Organization*, A. M. Henderson and Talcott Parsons, trans., Talcott Parsons (ed.), Free Press, Glencoe, Ill., 1947.

often conflict with educo-professional norms. One example of this conflict is supplied by the guidance counselor who feels it unethical or harmful to disclose test scores to parents but who is required to do so by the school code or by administrative decree. We begin our discussion by examining two general types of authority in schools—that which is formal and that which is functional.

Formal Authority versus Functional Authority

Peabody,[18] in summarizing the work of Weber, Urwick, Simon, Bennis, and Presthus, identifies four broad categories of authority: "(1) authority of legitimacy; (2) authority of position, including the sanctions inherent in position; (3) authority of competence, including both technical skills and experience; and (4) authority of person, including leadership and human relations skills." [19] The Peabody formulation appears in Table 3-1.

According to this formulation, bases of formal authority (hierarchical authority, legitimacy, position, and office) are distinguished from sources of functional authority. Examples of the latter are professional competence, experience, and human relations skills.

Peabody examined and compared perceptions of the bases for authority in three public service organizations: a police department, a welfare office, and an elementary school. A summary of his findings appears in Table 3-2.

An overview of Table 3-2 clearly indicates that teachers seem to value authority of competence over authority of person, position, or legitimacy. Peabody offers the following conclusion:

Perhaps the most striking contrast between these three public service agencies was the relative importance attached to authority of professional competence in the elementary school. Almost half of the twenty-member school staff singled out this basis as compared with 22 per cent of the welfare workers and only 15 per cent of the police officers. In part, this was related to the fact that 75 per cent of the school staff had had graduate training, including nine teachers with the equivalent of master's degrees or beyond. Furthermore, all school staff members except the secretary and the custodian belonged to two or more professional organizations, as compared with about half the members of the police department and about one-quarter of the welfare workers who belonged to one or more professional organizations. While the principal of this school played a more passive "democratic" leadership role than either the police chief or the district director, his position or the school administration as a whole was the next most frequently mentioned source of authority in the school. The diffusion of authority which seemed to characterize this school may be the dominant pattern of authority relations in such highly professionalized organizations as research institutions, psychiatric and medical clinics, and universities.[20]

---

[18]Robert L. Peabody, "Perceptions of Organizational Authority: A Comparative Analysis," *Administrative Science Quarterly,* vol. 6, no. 4, March, 1962.
[19]*Ibid.,* p. 466.
[20]*Ibid.,* pp. 480–481.

TABLE 3-1.   THE BASES OF AUTHORITY

	Formal authority		Functional authority	
	Legitimacy	Position	Competence	Person
Weber*	Legal		Rational authority	Traditional authority
	Legal order	Hierarchical office	Technical knowledge, experience	Charismatic authority
Urwick†		Formal, conferred by the organization	Technical, implicit in special knowledge or skill	Personal, conferred by seniority or popularity
Simon‡	Authority of legitimacy, social approval	Authority of sanctions	Authority of confidence (technical competence)	Techniques, persuasion (as distinct from authority)
Bennis§		Role incumbency	Knowledge of performance criteria	Knowledge of the human aspect of administration
Presthus¶	Generalized deference toward authority	Formal role or position	Technical expertise	Rapport with subordinates, ability to mediate individual needs

* Max Weber, *The Theory of Social and Economic Organization*, A. M. Henderson and Talcott Parsons, trans., Talcott Parsons (ed.), Free Press, Glencoe, Ill., 1947, pp. 328, 339.

† L. Urwick, *The Elements of Administration*, London, 1944, p. 42.

‡ Herbert A. Simon, "Authority," in Conrad M. Arensberg et al. (eds.), *Research in Industrial Human Relations*, New York, 1957, pp. 104–106; H. A. Simon et al., *Public Administration*, New York, 1950, pp. 189–201.

§ Warren G. Bennis, "Leadership Theory and Administrative Behavior: The Problem of Authority," *Administrative Science Quarterly*, vol. 4, 1959, pp. 288–289.

¶ Robert V. Presthus, "Authority in Organizations," *Public Administration Review*, vol. 20, 1960, pp. 88–91.

From Robert L. Peabody, "Perceptions of Organizational Authority: A Comparative Analysis," *Administrative Science Quarterly*, vol. 6, no. 4, March, 1962, p. 467.

Of similar significance is the strong showing, for elementary school teachers, of position authority as opposed to authority of person. To be sure, current supervisory trends do not substantiate this finding, and one can interpret the high teacher recognition of position authority as a vestige of classical and contemporary supervision. Enlightened supervision relies heavily on competence and person as sources of authority. While the bases of authority remain somewhat stable in enlightened supervisory environments, the authority actors change as function changes. Hartmann describes the fluid nature of functional authority as follows:

One of the most important characteristics of functional authority is its relativity. Authority of this kind is always dependent on the successful accomplishment of given ends. Performance is the immediate judge and executioner of such authority.

TABLE 3-2. PERCEPTIONS OF THE BASES OF AUTHORITY IN THREE PUBLIC SERVICE ORGANIZATIONS

Bases of authority	Police department, % (N = 33)	Welfare office, % (N = 23)	Elementary school, % * (N = 20)
Authority of legitimacy			
Generalized legitimacy	12	9	10
Law, state legislation, city ordinances, the state, county, city	15	17	15
Administrative codes, rules, regulations, manuals	0	17	0
Governing boards, policies of board	0	0	10
Authority of position			
Top external executive or executives, organization as a whole†	0	17	15
Top internal executive, ranking officers, administration as a whole‡	27	13	30
Immediate supervisor	9	39	0§
Inherent in position or job characteristics	30	26	15
Authority of competence			
Professional or technical competence, experience	15	22	45
Authority of person			
Personal characteristics or way in which authority is exercised	42	13	15
Other sources	6	4	0
No source specified	18	22	15

* Percentages total more than 100 percent because some respondents indicated more than one base of authority.

† The category of "top *external* executive" included the chief executives of the parent organizations, for example, the county manager, director of public welfare, city manager, and school superintendent.

‡ The category of "top *internal* executive" included the police chief, the district director, and the principal.

§ Coded as "top *internal* executive" in the case of the elementary school.

From Robert L. Peabody, "Perceptions of Organizational Authority: A Comparative Analysis," *Administrative Science Quarterly*, vol. 6, no. 4, March, 1962, p. 477.

He continues:

> Actually, the concept of functional authority makes it hard to understand why there should be hierarchies at all. The functional interplay of the productive process has an intrinsic order inasmuch as the specific contributions of all productive agents are geared to the exigencies of the over-all task. But there is nothing intrinsic to these functions (qua functions) to suggest that they should be ranked in such a way that some of these contributions should be subordinate to others.[21]

While the elimination of an educational hierarchy has some appeal, particularly to professionally oriented teachers, hierarchy does offer stability to schools and provides continuity over time. This is particularly important for schools in view of the high degree of turnover which characterizes the typical professional teaching staff. While enlightened supervision recognizes and supports legitimate and position authority, it stresses and attempts to develop competence and person authority. Mary Parker Follett captures the flavor of authority systems in enlightened supervisory environment as follows:

> Another corollary from this conception of authority and responsibility as a moment in interweaving experience is that you have no authority as a mere left-over. You cannot take the authority which you won yesterday and apply it today.... In the ideal organization authority is always fresh, always being distilled anew.[22]

The Erosion of Authority Bases for Administrators

We have argued that authority bases for those who administer and for those who supervise in our nation's schools are changing, shifting, and in many cases, diminishing. Particularly susceptible to change and erosion is the principal's position. Once the lord of his fief, the principal proudly possessed rather strong credentials as the legal and *legitimate* head of the school; as having broad powers by virtue of his *position* to impose sanctions and rewards; as displaying superior *competence* as super teacher; and as being a rather persuasive, if not paternal, *personality*.

As the technical structure (the teaching and educational program structure) increases in complexity and diversification, teachers by virtue of competence and person authority have assumed more responsibility for these areas. This increase in educational sophistication has required administrative arrangements beyond the traditional definition of the principal's role. Thus new positions and new policies are formed or added (legitimate and position-authority bases) above the principal position and located in the central office. The former trend is documented by growth of the teacher auton-

[21]Heinz Hartmann, *Authority and Organization in German Management,* Princeton University Press, Princeton, N.J., 1959, p. 284.
[22]Henry C. Metcalf and L. Urwick, *Dynamic Administration: The Collected Papers of Mary Parker Follett,* Harper, New York, 1942.

omy movement and the latter by phenomenal increases in central office staffs.

THE BASES OF SUPERVISORY POWER

Authorities tend not to agree on definitions of authority and power and what distinguishes one from another. For the purposes of this discussion, it seems useful to consider authority as a broad basis for action not directed at any one or another individual. Power, on the other hand, is derived from authority and administratively is directed at winning individual or group compliance on behalf of organizational "superiors."[23]

French and Raven identify and describe five bases for the social power which person O can exert over person P:

(a) reward power, based on P's perception that O has the ability to mediate rewards for him; (b) coercive power, based on P's perception that O has the ability to mediate punishments for him; (c) legitimate power, based on the perception by P that O has a legitimate right to prescribe behavior for him; (d) referent power, based on P's identification with O; (e) expert power based on the perception that O has some special knowledge or expertness.[24]

Reward power is a particular characteristic of benevolent but paternalistic administrative and supervisory environments in schools. Rewards, of course, need to be acceptable to teachers or to be desired by them. Pay increase, recognition, special favors, better schools, favorable work assignments and schedules, better equipment, and so on, are among the reward incentives available to administrators. Reward power may also provide relief from disagreeable circumstances. *Coercive power* is simply the ability to impose sanctions on teachers. Coercive power systems are the reverse of reward power systems. They often go hand in hand. If a department chairman complies with the wishes of the principal, his department budget is increased. If he defies the wishes of the principal, his department budget is cut, and so on.

Expert power, a concept very similar to the competence authority base, is the ability to command compliance on the basis of professional knowledge, information, and skills. Administrators and supervisors who are able to command the admiration and respect of others operate from a *referent power base.* While this power factor is often a result of expert power—that is, we

[23]This definition is not limited to compliance between and among superordinates and subordinates. Teacher A may have a powerful influence on teacher B and thus be assured of reliable compliance by teacher B on behalf of teacher A, yet both are officially at the same hierarchical level.
[24]J. R. P. French, Jr., and B. Raven, "The Bases of Social Power," in D. Cartwright and A. F. Zander (eds.), *Group Dynamics: Research and Theory,* 2d ed., Row, Peterson, Evanston, Ill., 1960, p. 612.

TABLE 3-3.　MEAN RATINGS OF BASES OF POWER *

Bases of power	Organizational settings				
	1 Branch offices	2 Colleges	3 Insurance agencies	4 Production work units	5 Utility company work groups
Legitimate	4.1	3.6	3.3	3.4	4.7
Expert	3.5	4.1	3.8	3.4	3.0
Referent	2.9	3.5	2.5	2.7	2.1
Reward	2.7	2.3	2.8	2.8	2.7
Coercive	1.9	1.6	1.8	2.3	2.5

* All ratings have been adjusted so that a value of 5.0 represents the highest possible rating and 1.0 represents the lowest possible rating. Respondents in organizational settings 1, 2, and 5 used a ranking procedure; those in settings 3 and 4 used a procedure that permitted independent ratings of the five bases of power.

From Jerald D. Bachman et al., "Bases of Supervisory Power: A Comparative Study in Five Organizational Settings," in A. S. Tannenbaum (ed.), *Control in Organizations*, McGraw-Hill, New York, 1968, p. 234.

respect and admire an individual's competence—referent power is nevertheless conceptually independent of expert power. Many supervisors gain the support of others simply because they are admired as people.

Legitimate power refers to an administrative prerogative of command and influence as a right of the office. When the new teacher meets the superintendent at the September orientation tea, be assured that the new teacher understands fully (and understandably exaggerates) the concept of legitimate power.

Bases of Supervisory Power, Satisfaction, and Performance

In an attempt to answer the question, Why do people comply with the requests of supervisors, and how are these reasons related to organizational effectiveness and individual satisfaction? Bachman, Bowers, and Marcus[25] examined the bases of supervisory power in five organizational settings. The investigators asked subordinates why they complied with their supervisor's wishes. Additional measurements were obtained for worker satisfaction and, in three of the organizations, for worker performance. Table 3-3 shows the mean ratings of bases of power for each of the five organizations on each of the five power variables. Note that power variables are adopted from French and Raven.

The investigators observe that the most important reason for complying with the wishes of superiors was response to legitimate power and expert power. Referent and reward power were cited less often, with coercive

[25]Jerald D. Bachman et al., "Bases of Supervisory Power: A Comparative Study in Five Organizational Settings," in Arnold S. Tannenbaum (ed.), *Control in Organizations*, McGraw-Hill, New York, 1968, p. 229.

TABLE 3-4.   CORRELATIONS WITH SATISFACTION MEASURES

| Bases of power | Organizational settings | | | | |
	1 Branch offices (N = 36)	2 Colleges (N = 12)	3 Insurance agencies (N = 40)	4 Production work units (N = 40)	5 Utility company work groups (N = 20)
Legitimate	−.57*	−.52	.04	.40†	−.35
Expert	.69*	.75*	.88*	.67*	.30
Referent	.75*	.67†	.43†	.57*	.11
Reward	−.57*	−.80*	.48*	.27	−.12
Coercive	−.31	−.70†	−.52*	.01	−.23

*$p < .01$, two-tailed.
†$p < .05$, two-tailed.

From Jerald D. Bachman et al., "Bases of Supervisory Power: A Comparative Study in Five Organizational Settings," in A. S. Tannenbaum (ed.), *Control in Organizations*, McGraw-Hill, New York, 1968, p. 235.

power the least likely reason for compliance. This trend seems more pronounced for organizations described as professional—the branch office, the college, and the insurance agency. Public schools would be expected to respond similarly.

Correlations between the five bases of supervisory power and measures of satisfaction with the supervisor or with the job appear in Table 3-4.

This table shows that expert power and referent power seem to provide the strongest and most consistent positive correlation with worker satisfaction. Coercive power, particularly for the educational organizations studied, draws the most negative correlation with satisfaction. The investigators summarize their findings as follows:

This summary of data obtained in five organizational studies has provided a number of fairly consistent findings. (1) Legitimate power was rated one of the two most important bases of power; however, it did not seem a consistent factor in organizational effectiveness, nor was it related significantly to total amount of control. (2) Expert power was the other very prominent basis of power, and it was strongly and consistently correlated with satisfaction and performance. Of the five bases, expert power was most positively related to total amount of control. (3) Referent power was of intermediate importance as a reason for complying with a supervisor's wishes, but in most cases it was positively correlated with criteria of organizational effectiveness. In two sites it was significantly and positively related to total amount of control. (4) Reward power was also of intermediate importance; in this case the correlations with organizational effectiveness and with total control were not consistent. (5) Coercive power was clearly the least prominent reason for compliance; moreover, this basis of power was often negatively related to criteria of effectiveness and in two cases negatively related to total amount of control.[26]

[26]*Ibid.*, p. 236.

TABLE 3-5. POWER, PERFORMANCE, AND SATISFACTION

Bases of manager's power	Mean standardized performance	Mean satisfaction with manager
Referent	.40*	.75*
Expert	.36*	.69*
Reward	− .55†	− .51†
Coercive	− .31	− .71†
Legitimate	− .17	− .57†

NOTE: Cell entries are product-moment correlation.

*$p < .05$, two-tailed.

†$p < .01$, two-tailed.

From Bachman et al., "Control, Performance, and Satisfaction: An Analysis of Structural and Individual Effects," in A. S. Tannenbaum (ed.), *Control in Organizations*, McGraw-Hill, New York, 1968.

In another study using the French and Raven formulation, Bachman, Smith, and Slesinger[27] examined the relationship among bases for social power and satisfaction and performance in a professional sales office.[28] Correlations among worker perception of office manager power, office mean performance scores, and office mean satisfaction scores are provided in Table 3-5.

Table 3-5 again suggests that referent power and expert power yield higher positive and significant correlations with performance and satisfaction, while reward, coercive, and legitimate power bases yield some significant but all negative correlations with performance and satisfaction. The investigators conclude as follows:

Total control, performance, and satisfaction with the office manager were all relatively high for the office manager whose leadership was perceived as resting largely upon his skill and expertise (expert power) and upon his personal attractiveness (referent power). Conversely, the less effective office manager was one who appeared to rely more heavily upon the use of rewards and sanctions (reward power and coercive power) and upon the formal authority of his position (legitimate power) as a formal description of his role might indicate. At the level of interoffice comparison, this overall relationship was substantial and highly consistent.[29]

In examining the relationship between influence and satisfaction in school organizations, Hornstein and his associates conclude:

These data, which are in full accord with the findings of previous studies, suggest that the effects of superior-subordinate relations in school systems are very much like those of various industrial, sales, and voluntary organizations. Teachers

[27]Jerald D. Bachman et al., "Control, Performance, and Satisfaction: An Analysis of Structural and Individual Effects," in Arnold S. Tannenbaum, *op. cit.*, p. 213.

[28]The salesmen in this study earned from $10,000 to $25,000 per year prior to 1961. Thirty-six branch offices of a national firm were used.

[29]Bachman et al., *op. cit.*, p. 225.

TABLE 3-6.   THE COMPONENTS AND CHARACTERISTICS OF ETZIONI'S COMPLIANCE THEORY *

Component	Type A	Type B	Type C
Goal	Order	Economic	Cultural
Power	Coercive	Utilitarian	Normative
Involvement	Alienative	Calculative	Moral
Task	Routine	Instrumental	Expressive

* *Order goals* are oriented toward control of actors in the organization. *Economic goals* refer to increasing or maintaining output at favorable cost to the organization. *Cultural goals* refer to the socializing, institutionalizing, preserving, extending, and applying of value systems and life systems. From Amatai Etzioni, *A Comparative Analysis of Complex Organizations*, Free Press, New York, 1961.

report greatest satisfaction with their principal and school system when they perceive that they and their principals are mutually influential, especially when their principal's power to influence emanates from their perceiving him as an expert. Moreover, this same principal-teacher relationship is associated with a perception of higher student satisfaction.[30]

It seems readily apparent that supervisory behavior which relies on functional authority and on expert and referent power bases will have positive effects on the human organization of the school. Such efforts should lead to positive effects on the school success variables which are outlined in the synthesizing theory of Chapter 2.

Compliance Theory (Etzioni)

While we have given emphasis to one or another base for supervisory action, a number of strategies, power bases, authority systems, and the like, may be appropriate, depending upon the nature of goals to be achieved and the tasks which compose action toward the goals. The "goodness of fit" of a given compliance or *power* strategy depends upon three major variables: *goals, involvement, and task.* The four components are arranged in a formulation of compliance theory by Etzioni.[31] The components and characteristics derived from his compliance theory are summarized in Table 3-6.

The appropriateness of a given compliance strategy will depend largely on organizational costs in relation to goal achievement. If, for example, the goal is order and the task routine, the most efficient compliance strategy is coercive. Yet, before one chooses this strategy he must be prepared to pay the price of alienated subordinates. If the price is worth the accomplishment of the goal, then the coercive strategy (at least within the limits of this for-

[30]Harvey A. Hornstein et al., "Influence and Satisfaction in Organizations: A Replication," *Sociology of Education*, vol. 41, no. 4, Fall, 1968, p. 389.
[31]Amatai Etzioni, *A Comparative Analysis of Complex Organizations*, Free Press, New York, 1961.

mulation) is legitimate. The key, of course, rests with the time variable. Any system can absorb short periods of alienation by subordinates, but over time, alienation results in a collapse of the system. Schools, for example, can hardly operate as dynamic learning institutions with alienated students, parents, or teachers.

We generally consider the goals of schools to be predominantly cultural in nature. The tasks of teachers and students are largely expressive in that they define, legitimize, and strengthen commitment to the cultural goals of the school. Expressive tasks and cultural goals require, according to this formulation, normative compliance strategies and obtain moral commitment from school inhabitants. One can argue for each of the three goals as being legitimate for schools. Enlightened supervision, however, although recognizing the occasional legitimacy of each, does not view them as equally balanced but shamelessly supports and emphasizes the cultural, normative, expressive, and moral compliance strategy.

STATUS SYSTEMS IN EDUCATIONAL ORGANIZATIONS

Status systems are closely related to power systems and authority systems and may, in fact, be considered as one component of any authority or power taxonomy. While status-free societies and status-free organizations may have intellectual and emotional appeal, most authorities[32] agree that some sort of reward or motivation should be present in the social structure to ensure that those who are capable of performing essential societal and organizational tasks do indeed perform them. Further, particularly in educational organizations at the elementary and secondary school levels, stratification provides stability over time and the protection of continuity for community clients and beneficiaries.

Status systems of different kinds and of varying degrees of complexity are found in all school organizations. That the range of elaborateness and detail among schools is great does not alter the presence of stratification. It appears in the administrative caste, the professional teaching staff, the nonprofessional worker group, and the student structure of the school. When each of these subsystems is taken as a whole, the stratification system is indeed quite large and elaborate. Consider, for example, the difference in status (and in organizational power and influence) between a high school freshman and the deputy superintendent of schools.

In describing the emergence of status systems in formal organizations, Barnard makes the following observations:

It may be asserted first of all that systems of status arise from the differential

[32]See, for example, K. Davis and W. E. Moore, "Some Principles of Stratification," *American Sociological Review,* vol. 10, 1945, pp. 242–249; also Talcott Parsons, *The Social System,* p. 69.

needs, interests, and capacities of individuals. I shall discuss these in five topical divisions as follows:

1. The differences in the *abilities* of individuals.
2. The differences in the *difficulties* of doing various kinds of work.
3. The differences in the *importance* of various kinds of work.
4. The desire for formal status as a social or organizational tool.
5. The need for protection of the integrity of the person.[33]

Surely each of the above is at one time or another a reasonably legitimate basis for status systems in schools. Yet, once erected and formalized, even the best-intended status systems run the risk of entrenchment and exaggeration. Barnard notes that "paradoxically, such (status) systems operate like principles of growth, necessary to attain maturity, but without a self-regulated control that prevents disproportionate development of parts, unbalance, and maladaption to the environment."[34] Barnard suggests the following as potential dysfunctional aspects of status systems:

1. The status system tends in time to distorted evaluation of individuals.
2. It restricts unduly the "circulation of the elite."
3. It distorts the system of distributive justice.
4. It exaggerates administration to the detriment of leadership and morale.
5. It exalts the symbolic function beyond the level of sustainment.
6. It limits the adaptability of an organization.[35]

The organizational dilemma which confronts those who administer and supervise in the nation's schools is, How does one live with a "necessary evil"? The key to solving the dilemma is the question of control—Does the human organization control the status system, or does the status system control the human organization? Symptoms of the latter situation are lack of flexibility, low responsiveness, infrequent or one-way communication patterns, low organizational commitment, teacher and student dissatisfaction, and low adaptiveness.

While teachers have made, and will continue to make, great strides in altering the status system in schools to their favor, students still feel quite distant from things that matter in the typical school. To be sure, exaggerated status systems still frustrate teachers and hinder school effectiveness, but the major dysfunction appears to occur for the schools' clients, the students. As we discuss in Part II of this book, a more equitable distribution of power, authority, and status is a prerequisite for success of the human curriculum and, in fact, the human school.

---

[33]Chester I. Barnard, "Functions and Pathology of Status Systems in Formal Organizations," Bobbs-Merrill reprint series in the Social Sciences, p. 53. Reprinted from William Foote Whyte (ed.), *Industry and Society*, McGraw-Hill, New York, 1946.
[34]*Ibid.*, p. 71.
[35]*Ibid.*

SUMMARY

In the next chapter we examine an emerging environment for supervision and contrast this with environments of the past and present. As we proceed with this analysis we build, describe, and apply two organizational models for schools—the bureaucratic and the professional. As part of this discussion, we deal again with the supervisory problem of organizational-individual (bureaucratic-professional) interface. Further, the content and flavor of the particular organizational style exhibited by a school—in a sense, its organizational personality—depend largely upon the prevailing authority system of the school. For example, bureaucratically oriented schools tend to rely on formal authority systems while professionally oriented schools tend to rely on functional authority systems.

SELECTED REFERENCES

Carver, Fred D., and Thomas J. Sergiovanni (eds.): *Organizations and Human Behavior: Focus on Schools,* McGraw-Hill, New York, 1969.

Getzels, Jacob W., James M. Lipham, and Roald F. Campbell: *Educational Administration As a Social Process,* Harper & Row, New York, 1968.

Tannenbaum, Arnold S.: *Control in Organizations,* McGraw-Hill, New York, 1968.

Chapter Four
MODERN ENVIRONMENT
FOR SUPERVISION

What does the word *bureaucracy* mean to you? Chances are, this word conjures up negative feelings and reactions from most Americans. If we were to suggest, as we most assuredly do, that schools are by and large bureaucracies, we would be sure to evoke a negative reaction from readers in education. The bureaucracy bias is an unfortunate one in that it limits and inhibits rational discussion of the positive and negative bureaucratic tendencies of schools. We perhaps contribute to this bias by designating schools as being either bureaucratically oriented or professionally oriented. We use the bureaucratic orientation for schools in a negative sense in that enlightened supervision will tend not to thrive there. Professional orientation for schools is used in a positive sense as an ideal environment for supervision. Yet underlying these perspectives, the authors recognize the fact that schools are realistically on a continuum extending from more bureaucratic to less bureaucratic. We also concede that, except for large high schools and for large school districts, schools, when compared with other community institutions, seem considerably less bureaucratic.

BUREAUCRATIC ELEMENTS AND TENDENCIES IN SCHOOLS

The man who is responsible for introducing the concept of bureaucracy, with its accompanying characteristics, to the political and social science literature is, of course, Max Weber. He believed that "the decisive reason for the advance of bureaucratic organization has always been its purely technical superiority over other forms of organization." [1] Weber's ideal bureaucracy is characterized as follows: (1) the use of a division of labor and of specific allocation of responsibility; (2) reliance on fairly exact hierarchical levels of graded authority; (3) administrative thought and action based on written policies, rules, and regulations; (4) an impersonal, universalistic application of the bureaucratic environment to all inhabitants; and (5) the development and longevity of administrative careers. [2]

[1] Max Weber, "Bureaucracy," in Hans Gerth and C. Wright Mills, *From Max Weber,* Oxford, New York, 1946, p. 214.
[2] Max Weber, *Theory of Social and Economic Organization,* trans. by A. M. Henderson and T. Parsons, Oxford, New York, 1947, pp. 333–336.

The extent to which schools follow the bureaucratic model varies, of course, from school to school. Yet all schools exhibit some bureaucratic tendencies.[3] A comparison of general bureaucratic characteristics and bureaucratic tendencies of schools follows.

CHARACTERISTICS OF BUREAUCRACY	APPLIED TO SCHOOLS
1. Organization tasks are distributed among the various positions as official duties. Implied is a clear-cut division of labor among positions which makes possible a high degree of specialization. Specialization, in turn, promotes expertness among the staff, both directly and by enabling the organization to hire employees on the basis of their technical qualifications.	1. The school organization has clearly been influenced by the need for specialization and the factoring of tasks. The division of the school into elementary and secondary units; the establishment of science, mathematics, music, and other departments within a school; the introduction of guidance programs and psychological services; indeed, the separation of the administrative function from the teaching function, all represent responses to this need.
2. The positions or offices are organized into a hierarchical authority structure. In the usual case this hierarchy takes on the shape of a pyramid wherein each official is responsible for his subordinates' decisions and actions as well as his own to the superior above him in the pyramid and wherein each official has authority over the officials under him. The scope of authority of superiors over subordinates is clearly circumscribed.	2. The school organization has developed a clearly defined and rigid hierarchy of authority. Although the term "hierarchy" is seldom used in the lexicon of the educational administrator, the practices to which it refers are commonly prevalent. The typical organization chart is intended specifically to clarify lines of authority and channels of communication. Even in the absence of such a chart, school employees have a clear conception of the nature of the hierarchy in their school systems. In fact, rigid adherence to hierarchical principles has been stressed to the point that failure to adhere to recognized lines of authority is viewed as the epitome of immoral organizational behavior.
3. A formally established system of rules and regulations governs offi-	3. The school organization has leaned heavily upon the use of general

[3]Any list of items which characterizes or describes bureaucracy in reference to "ideal type" is limited in that no one organization fits the description exactly.

CHARACTERISTICS OF BUREAUCRACY

cial decisions and actions. In principle the operations in such administrative organizations involve the application of these general regulations to particular cases. The regulations insure the uniformity of operations and, together with the authority structure, make possible the coordination of various activities. They also provide for continuity in operations regardless of changes of personnel, thus promoting a stability lacking, as we have seen, in charismatic movements.

4. Officials are expected to assume an impersonal orientation in their contacts with clients and with other officials. Clients are to be treated as cases, the officials being expected to disregard all personal considerations and to maintain complete emotional detachment, and subordinates are to be treated in a similar impersonal fashion. The social distance between hierarchical levels and that between officials and their clients is intended to foster such formality. Impersonal detachment is designed to prevent the personal feelings of officials from distorting their rational judgment in carrying out their duties.

5. Employment by the organization constitutes a career for officials. Typically an official is a full-time employee and looks forward to a lifelong career in the agency. Em-

APPLIED TO SCHOOLS

rules to control the behavior of members of the organization and to develop standards which would assure reasonable uniformity in the performance of tasks. Whether they have taken the form of policy manuals, rules and regulations, staff handbooks, or some other type of document, general rules have been used extensively to provide for the orderly induction of new employees into the organization and to eliminate capricious behavior on the part of all school personnel, including administrators and members of boards of education.

4. Despite frequent proclamations regarding togetherness and democracy, the school organization has made extensive application of Weber's principle of impersonality in organizational relationships. Authority has been established on the basis of rational considerations rather than charismatic qualities or traditional imperatives; interpersonal interactions have tended to be functionally specific rather than functionally diffuse; and official relationships have been governed largely by universalistic as contrasted with particularistic considerations. Thus, by operating in a spirit of "formalistic impersonality," the typical school system has succeeded, in part, in separating organizational rights and obligations from the private lives of individual employees.

5. Employment in the educational organization has been based upon technical competence and has constituted for most members a professional career. Promotions have

CHARACTERISTICS OF BUREAUCRACY	APPLIED TO SCHOOLS

ployment is based on the technical qualifications of the candidate rather than on political, family, or other connections. Usually such qualifications are tested by examination or by certificates that demonstrate the candidate's educational attainment—college degrees for example. Such educational qualifications create a certain amount of class homogeneity among officials, since relatively few persons of working-class origins have college degrees, although their number is increasing. Officials are appointed to positions, not elected, and thus are dependent on superiors in the organization rather than on a body of constituents. After a trial period officials gain tenure of position and are protected against arbitrary dismissal. Remuneration is in the form of a salary, and pensions are provided after retirement. Career advancements are "according to seniority or to achievement or both."[5]

been determined by seniority and by achievement; tenure has been provided; and fixed compensation and retirement benefits have been assured.[4]

Examples of Unanticipated Consequences

While Weber's concept of bureaucracy provides a framework for prescribing administrative action, much that is intended by administrators and supervisors may result in unanticipated reactions from the human organization and dysfunctional consequences for the school. It is difficult to conceive of any school administrator willfully acting on behalf of school dysfunction. When school dysfunction does occur, his actions are undoubtedly well intended but he may be unaware of the possibilities of unanticipated results.

We discuss in detail in the last section of this chapter the nature of dysfunction which contributes to teacher militancy, student militancy, and other symptoms of general disengagement between and among teachers,

[4]Max G. Abbott, "Hierarchical Impediments to Innovation in Educational Organizations," in M. G. Abbott and John Lovell (eds.), *Change Perspectives in Educational Administration,* School of Education, Auburn University, 1965, pp. 44–45.
[5]Peter M. Blau and W. Richard Scott, *Formal Organizations: A Comparative Approach,* Chandler Publishing Company, San Francisco, 1962, pp. 32–33. Copyright © 1962 by Chandler Publishing Company.

administrators, and students. Here, our discussion will be limited to only one aspect of the problem—what we intend to accomplish and do not intend to accomplish as we work to increase control over the achievement of school goals through an emphasis on *reliability, delegation* of authority, and the use of *universal impersonal* rules.[6] Each of these variables is a crucial component of the ideal bureaucracy.

Emphasis on Reliability

As school administrators, teachers, and others with supervisory responsibility attempt to increase control over the school's goals as they perceive them (at a very simple level, for example, maintaining student attention in class; at an abstract level, preparing better citizens), they frequently attempt to increase reliability in decision-making processes and in behavior by teachers and students. This is often accomplished by instituting and implementing policies, standard operating procedures, rules, and regulations to guide behavior within the human organization. Uniformity of behavior is seen as a powerful means to move large numbers of people toward goals with a minimum amount of confusion and conflict.

Merton describes organizational and client reaction to an emphasis on reliability of behavior in Figure 4-1.[7]

The client and supervisory roles in Figure 4-1 are interchangeable for teachers in that they may be supervisors in relation to clients or students and clients in relation to supervisors or principals. Parents and other "beneficiaries" of the school may also be considered clients at one time or another.

The intended result of reliability through rules is, of course, uniform and programmed decision making. This in turn decreases the search for alternatives to problems and results in more rigid behavior on the part of supervisors. The entire system also provides the supervisor with a potent weapon which permits him to escape personal accountability for his actions. Presumably, students will vent hostility on the rules, the system, or the establishment rather than on the teacher, as he enforces dress codes, gum-chewing regulations, marking policies, and other characteristics of the "tyranny of rules." Administrators optimistically work under the same assumption as they apply the rules to teachers.

The unanticipated consequences[8] of a reliability emphasis are described

---

[6]This discussion relies heavily on James G. March and Herbert A. Simon's discussion of the Merton, Selznick, and Gouldner formulations which appears in *Organizations,* Wiley, New York, 1958, pp. 36–47.

[7]This model and the three which follow are adapted from that which appears in March and Simon, *op. cit.,* pp. 36–47.

[8]We do not suggest, and Merton clearly does not suggest, that unanticipated consequences always occur. Such consequences may or may not occur, depending upon a number of contingency variables. In this case, where egalitarian values are strong, clients will resent increases in visible power by superordinates. Where egalitarian values are not strong, the unanticipated consequences are less likely to occur. The same caution applies as well to the Selznick and Gouldner formulations which follow.

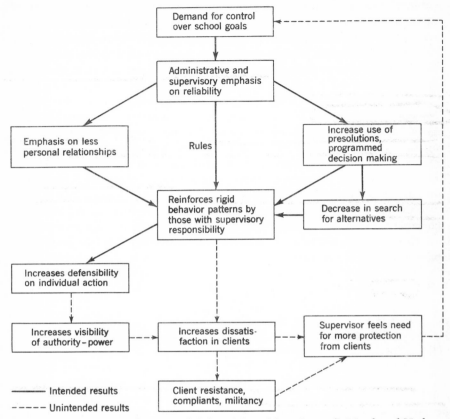

Figure 4-1. Merton: Emphasis on reliability. Adapted from James G. March and Herbert A. Simon, *Organizations*, Wiley, New York, 1958, pp. 36–47.

by Merton as (1) increases in the visibility of power and authority which supervisors have by virtue of position; (2) increases in levels of dissatisfaction and frustration by clients; (3) resistance, complaints, militancy, and conspiracy by clients as a result of this dissatisfaction and frustration; (4) a felt need by supervisors for more protection from client hostility; which (5) results in an increase in control; and so the cycle continues. This is an example of a school "getting better" and "getting worse" at the same time.

Emphasis on Delegation

Schools have been formally characterized by a division of labor since the introduction of the graded system. As professional and technical skill expands, the division of tasks becomes eclipsed by personal and professional specialization. Both represent a form of delegation of authority in that division carries with it some autonomy and responsibility for action. The rationale for delegation is an increase in competency and utilization of the specialist in order to increase his performance and thus close the gap between performance and school goals. In the large high school the typical form of delegation is found in departmentalization. Selznick describes organizational and client reaction to an emphasis on delegation of authority and division of labor in Figure 4-2.

The danger of departmentalization, delegation, and division is the emergence of subgoals for the newly formed subgroups. As these subgoals (sometimes referred to as *means goals*) become internalized, they tend to assume priority over the total school mission. Some of this is natural, of course, particularly at budget time; but over the long run such goal conflict actually lowers performance on behalf of the total school goals. A number of variables tend to increase or decrease the possibility of unanticipated consequences of delegation as described by Selznick. If total school goals, for example, are so remote or are beyond operationalizing, teachers tend to focus on their own department or grade-level goals as they seek guides to their professional performance.

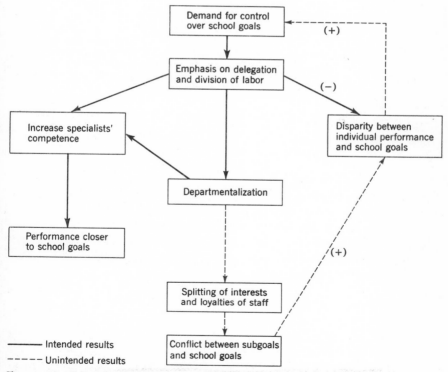

Figure 4-2: Selznick: Emphasis on delegation. Adapted from James G. March and Herbert A. Simon, *Organizations*, Wiley, New York, 1958, pp. 36–47.

High school departments, grade levels in elementary schools, bureaus in the central office, special teacher groups, the new academic and vocational division units (divisions of humanities, social science, physical science, vocational education, and so on) appearing as substitutes for departments in many high schools, schools within the school, teaching teams, and the like, all run the risk of negative consequences as described by Selznick.

Emphasis on General and Impersonal Rules

The literature is nearly unanimous in suggesting to administrators and others that the legitimacy of their supervisory role, as perceived by subordinates, is largely a function of low visibility of power (nonauthoritarianism) and low levels of interpersonal tension. As a result of this tendency, those in authority tend to rely on the use of general and impersonal rules in order to regulate or modify the behavior of subordinates. This phenomenon and its interesting potential consequence are described by Gouldner in Figure 4-3.

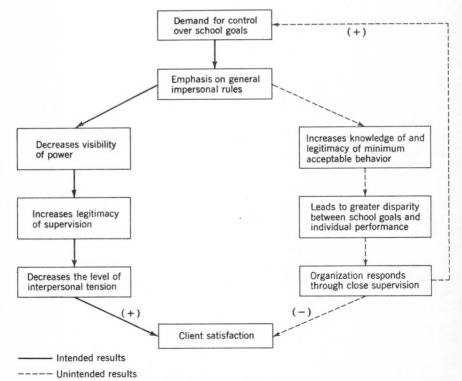

Figure 4-3. Gouldner: Emphasis on general and impersonal rules. Adapted from James G. March and Herbert A. Simon, *Organizations*, Wiley, New York, 1958, pp. 36–47.

Gouldner's model portrays the inherent dangers in relying on universal-general-impersonal rules. It suggests that as supervisors attempt to decrease power visibility and interpersonal tension, in order to obtain satisfaction and compliance in teachers, through the use of general rules, they obtain results the opposite of those intended. When one wishes to regulate the behavior of a few through the use of rules which apply to all, he announces and legitimizes for all minimum organizational expectations. This in turn may lead to modification in performance from maximizing to satisfying efforts. Any reduction in performance is sure to receive an organizational response in the form of close supervision. Close supervision tends to increase power visibility and interpersonal tension. This tends to decrease the legitimacy of supervision, particularly in egalitarian cultures such as ours, and decreases teacher satisfaction. The model works remarkably well when applied to classroom management with students as clients.

The likelihood of the Gouldner reaction is considerably reduced if members have high commitment and loyalty to the school and have largely internalized the goals of the school. One of the dangers of presenting a section on unanticipated consequences of bureaucratic behavior is that readers will assume that what we describe as simple images of thought are indeed complex mirrors of reality. We do not intend to replicate the complexity of organizational behavior in schools in a tidy model (simply because we cannot), but rather we hope to capture for the reader the nature of this complexity and to provide him with clues which will allow him meaningful entry. As such, there are numerous variables—many still undiscovered—which have an effect upon whether one or another of the models presented will "come out" as we have described. Perhaps in summary it is sufficient to caution that seemingly simple administrative-supervisory acts, however well intended, have complex and often negative ramifications in the human organization of the school and in the school itself.

PROFESSIONAL ELEMENTS AND TENDENCIES IN SCHOOLS

We have discussed earlier the emergence of the school as a complex organization, and we have described how the school has increased in specialization as its mission has become more diversified and its tasks more varied. The human organization has had concurrent and related development and growth in that it, too, is characterized by human complexity and personal specialization.

Professional organizations, or more appropriately those which are professionally oriented, tend to differ from other organizations primarily in the nature of their authority and power systems. This type of organization is characterized by the development and application of a pluralistic power structure which is (1) dispersed throughout the organization on the basis of ability and competence, (2) dynamic, in the sense that it shifts from person to person and from time to time on the basis of task, (3) interdependent, in that usually coalitions of individuals are needed to marshal sufficient competence to command authority at a given time, and (4) functional, in that it tends not to keep well in storage but needs to be constantly examined for "goodness of fit" in terms of competence and task. The professionally oriented organization tends to rely on task-oriented rather than people-oriented power bases.[9]

At the risk of gross simplification—after all, books have been written on the topic[10]—the professionally oriented person is one who is characterized by (1) considerable advanced formal preparation, (2) skills not readily available in others, including other professionals, (3) a commitment to his profession, discipline, or area which often assumes priority over a commitment to his place of employment, and (4) an interest in a reward system which emphasizes growth and development, achievement, and responsibility but does not ignore "bread and butter" items such as security, salary, and the like.

Perhaps the major administrative weakness facing schools today is the gap which exists between the growth and development of the human organization and the growth and development of the structural organization. We maintain that teachers have outdistanced schools in moving toward professionalization. As such, we are confronted with a large number of professionally oriented employees who are expected to operate and grow in schools which are by and large bureaucratically oriented. In the next section we explore in detail this gap as a basis for describing conflict in schools. Galbraith, in describing similar changes which are taking place in the business world, captures the flavor of the problem in education and removes it from the stereotype of the special case. The techno-structure which Galbraith describes is not unlike the emergence of a professional organization within the traditional school structure.

In the past, leadership in business organization was identified with the entrepreneur—the individual who united ownership or control of capital with capacity for organizing the other factors of production and, in most contexts, with a further capacity for innovation. With the rise of the modern corporation, the emergence of the organization required by modern technology and planning and the divorce of the owner of the capital from control of the enterprise, the en-

---

[9]Like any "rule" or "truism," this one has exceptions. As competency becomes established in a person—that is, as his professional reputation increases—his authority base may shift to himself as a person (who he is rather than what he can contribute) or may include himself as a person (who he is and what he can contribute). At the group level, if one pessimistically applies "Michel's iron law of oligarchy" to this process, he is led to conclude that what starts as ability authority soon turns into status authority.

[10]See Myron Lieberman, *Education As a Profession,* Prentice-Hall, Englewood Cliffs, N.J., 1956.

trepreneur no longer exists as an individual person in the mature industrial enterprise. Everyday discourse, except in the economics textbooks, recognizes this change. It replaces the entrepreneur, as the directing force of the enterprise, with management. This is a collective and imperfectly defined entity; in the large corporation it embraces chairman, president, those vice presidents with important staff or departmental responsibility, occupants of other major staff positions and, perhaps, division or department heads not included above. It includes, however, only a small proportion of those who, as participants, contribute information to group decisions. This latter group is very large; it extends from the most senior officials of the corporation to where it meets, at the outer perimeter, the white and blue collar workers whose function is to conform more or less mechanically to instruction or routine. *It embraces all who bring specialized knowledge, talent or experience to group decision-making. This, not the management, is the guiding intelligence—the brain—of the enterprise.* There is no name for all who participate in group decision-making or the organization which they form. I propose to call this organization the Technostructure.[11] [Italics ours.]

AN AXIOMATIC THEORY OF ORGANIZATIONS

Several formulations have been offered in attempting to capture the scope and breadth of interaction which takes place in organizations. One formulation in particular seems appropriate to schools in that it has the ability to describe the professionally oriented school, contrast it with the bureaucratically oriented school, and describe an organizational system of interaction which helps to map the sociological environment of schools for supervision. This rather ambitious framework, developed and articulated by Hage,[12] is called *an axiomatic theory of organizations.*

The Structural-Functional System

The axiomatic theory revolves around the identification and interaction of eight key components, found in schools and other organizations, which when taken together compose the structural-functional system of that organization. The key components are arranged in a means-ends dichotomy as follows:

STRUCTURAL-FUNCTIONAL SYSTEM

Organizational means	Organizational ends
Complexity (specialization)	Adaptiveness (flexibility)
Centralization (hierarchy of authority)	Production (effectiveness)
Formalization (standardization)	Efficiency (cost)
Stratification (status)	Job satisfaction (emphasis on manifest goal)[13]

[11]John K. Galbraith, *The New Industrial State,* Houghton Mifflin, Boston, 1967, pp. 70–71.

[12]This discussion is based primarily on Gerald Hage, "An Axiomatic Theory of Organizations," *Administrative Science Quarterly,* vol. 10, no. 3, December, 1965, pp. 289–320.

[13]*Ibid.,* p. 293.

Each of these components may be arranged propositionally in two-variable relationships. Hage expresses them as follows:

THE HAGUE PROPOSITIONS

> I. The higher the centralization, the higher the production.
> II. The higher the formalization, the higher the efficiency.
> III. The higher the centralization, the higher the formalization.
> IV. The higher the stratification, the lower the job satisfaction.
> V. The higher the stratification, the higher the production.
> VI. The higher the stratification, the lower the adaptiveness.
> VII. The higher the complexity, the lower the centralization.[14]

The variables and propositions which compose the theory are not new with Hage but are reminiscent of material we have discussed earlier in this chapter. Propositions I, II, and III are derived from Weber's bureaucracy model[15]; propositions IV, V, and VI are from Barnard's work with status systems[16]; and proposition VII is borrowed from Thompson's formulation dealing with specialization.[17]

The School Context

Many of the variables which compose the axiomatic theory have already been defined and discussed. The theory summarizes these variables and arranges them in a conceptual system which provides additional potency for understanding and guidelines for practice. Yet, like any general theory, when we apply it specifically—for example, to schools—we encounter problems in operationalizing the variables to fit the specific case.

The variable *complexity*, which has been discussed at some length, primarily because of its contemporaneousness as a crucial variable in schools, refers to how specialized the school is organizationally and administratively as well as the degree of professional and technical specialization which exists in the professional teaching staff. *Centralization* describes the extent to which levels of decision making correspond to elaborate hierarchical authority systems. If decision making (responsibility and authority) is dispersed throughout the school, this suggests low centralization. If decision making is primarily the prerogative of the central office and perhaps the principal, this suggests high centralization. *Formalization* describes the extent to which a school relies on standardized rules and regulations to increase reliability in performance. Linked with centralization, high formalization in schools pro-

---

[14]*Ibid.*, pp. 297–299.
[15]Max Weber, *The Theory of Social and Economic Organization.*
[16]Chester I. Barnard, "Functions and Pathology of Status Systems in Formal Organizations," Bobbs-Merrill reprint series in the Social Sciences, quoted in William Foote Whyte (ed.), *Industry and Society,* McGraw-Hill, New York, 1946.
[17]Victor A. Thompson, *Modern Organization,* Knopf, New York, 1961, pp. 3–113.

grams decision making by teachers and students (and sometimes building administrators) and funnels upward any decision situations which are varied or which cannot be accounted for by the rules. *Stratification,* also linked with centralization and formalization, implies considerable status differences between and among hierarchical levels in the school. The operational basis for stratification is legitimate authority rather than functional authority. These variables constitute the organizational means by which the school arranges itself in order to achieve certain ends.

The variable *production* suggests to us the most difficult operational problem in applying the axiomatic theory to schools. Hage defines the variable in terms of the "number of units" processed by the organization. To us this means the number of students graduated, the dropout rate, the number of students off to college, and the like. Quality—to us, how well a student has learned as opposed to how much—is not included in definitions of the production variable. *Efficiency* refers to cost per unit of output. Cost includes money, utilization of staff, time, material and space utilization, and so on. The school's means variables of centralization, formalization, and stratification are likely to increase school production and efficiency, so the theory goes, while the school's means variable of complexity is likely to result in lower production and efficiency. *Adaptiveness* is a variable which describes a school's ability to respond and its emphasis on responding to its professional and societal environments. Does the school utilize the most advanced professional and technical know-how, and is the educational program of the school relevant to the needs of its clients? These are questions which test the adaptability of schools. *Job satisfaction* describes the extent to which schools focus on the worth of the human organization as a manifest goal of the school enterprise. Need fulfillment and professional and personal growth and development of the teaching staff are, for schools that focus on job satisfaction, perceived as legitimate school goals and enjoy a ranking with student learning, and so on. Providing for student need, growth, and development is already (at least, according to the literature) a legitimate school goal. The two, to us, seem inseparable and interdependent; thus success for the latter depends upon success for the former, and vice versa. The axiomatic theory proposes that complexity is the means by which schools achieve adaptiveness and job satisfaction, while centralization, formalization, and stratification tend to retard achievement of these goals.

The Bureaucratic-Professional Transition in Schools

The variables which constitute the structural-functional system of the school seem to sort themselves into two constellations. The larger constellation consists of centralization, formalization, stratification, school production, and school efficiency, while the smaller constellation includes complexity, adaptability, and job satisfaction. (See Figure 4-4.)

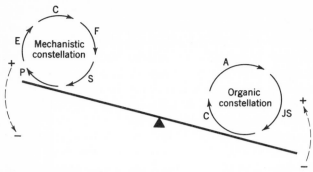

Figure 4-4. The relationship between mechanistic and organic constellations as alternate themes for school organization.

We call the larger group the *mechanistic constellation* and the smaller group the *organic constellation*.[18]

When one variable in the mechanistic constellation is increased, each of the other variables in the same constellation increases while variables in the organic constellation decrease. A decrease in any one of the mechanistic variables leads to similar decreases in the other four but to increases in the three organic variables. The theory proposes similar relationships for changes in the organic constellation. The mechanistic constellation tends to describe the bureaucratically oriented school, while the organic constellation tends to describe the professionally oriented school.

Mechanistic model
(Bureaucratically oriented schools)

L complexity	L adaptiveness
H centralization	H production
H formalization	H efficiency
H stratification	L job satisfaction

Organic model
(Professionally oriented schools)

H complexity	H adaptiveness
L centralization	L production
L formalization	L efficiency
L stratification	H job satisfaction

("L" = Lower; "H" = Higher.)

The Ideal School Types Summarized

Schools which approach the mechanistic model in structure and orientation tend to be precise in defining roles, obligations, duties, rights, and relations

[18]Our use of the words *mechanistic* and *organic* in describing organizational structures is adopted from Hage, *op. cit.* They come "originally" from Tom Burns and G. M. Stalker, *The Management of Innovation*, Tavistock Publications, London, 1961. Mechanistic schools tend to be bureaucratically oriented while organic schools tend to be professionally oriented.

(high formalization and high stratification); are detailed in prescribing rules and regulations as they seek to program decision making for teachers and clients (high formalization); seek to funnel decision making which is varied and unpredictable to the top while standardizing decision making at lower levels (high centralization); and are concerned with processing the largest number of students at the least cost in terms of personnel, money, equipment, space, and the like (high production and high efficiency). Since all of the structural features of schools are interdependent, a change in one variable results in changes in other variables. Thus, mechanistic schools, while increasing in formalization, centralization, and the like, display a low tolerance for innovativeness and change (low adaptiveness); for permitting power to be diffused to lower organizational levels and thus encouraging authority based on ability rather than simply position (low complexity); and for providing teachers with meaningful reward systems which will permit them to function as respected, autonomous, and responsible professionals (low job satisfaction).

The ideal professional type of school stresses adaptiveness rather than production and is characterized by its complexity and the level of job satisfaction available to its members. The emergence and spread of professionally oriented organizations in education are a reflection of four closely related trends in teaching as an occupation: (1) the increased specialization of semi-professional and professional workers; (2) the quality and sophistication of their academic and professional training; (3) the knowledge explosion which has occurred in virtually all the curriculum areas, the teaching fields, and the educational technologies; and (4) the belief (real or imagined) that schools as they are presently functioning have not met their commitment in providing all school clients with an intellectual, social, and emotional experience appropriate for growth in a society as we know it today or in the years ahead. These are confounded by a prevalent mood for autonomy which seems to permeate every aspect of our society from the unionization of vineyard workers in California to the emergence of an underground student newspaper in a Maine high school.

The professionally oriented large school, for example, is one which seeks to accommodate the need for expression which professional workers require. It is complex (in terms of its administrative diversification as well as the degree of personal specialization which exists in the staff) and highly innovative and provides teachers, students, and other members with opportunities for their personal as well as professional fulfillment. This type of school tends also to be wasteful and expensive;[19] it ignores or circumscribes hierarchically defined status and authority systems; and it defies more than a minimum use of rules and other forms of programmed decision making.

[19]The professionally oriented school is a poor loser in the efficiency category when the same standards of the bureaucratically oriented school are applied. In terms of quality of output, however, the professionally oriented school seems immeasurably more able.

Advocates of the professional model argue that the production emphasis of the mechanistic model is incompatible with providing quality education for youth and is in fact damaging and demoralizing to educational workers and students.

It is readily apparent to even the most casual observer that schools are shifting from orientations we describe as bureaucratic to orientations we describe as professional. That the trend is being realized at different rates for different schools, school systems, and communities should not be allowed to mask the long-term trend. To be sure, the human organization seems to be in the forefront of this transition phenomenon, with the school as an organization lagging somewhat behind.

SUPERVISORY CONFLICT

The focus of this chapter has been in an area not typically of concern to those with supervisory responsibilities. Yet supervisors are invariably charged with some aspect of change and are required to work on this behalf in constant interaction with the structural-functional system of the school. To be sure, the focus of supervision is people and program. Supervisors work with other professionals through an educational program to effect positive change in students. Success largely depends upon the realization that this work does not take place in a vacuum. Realism requires that the supervisor does not ignore the organizational context of schools. Enlightened supervision is most assuredly dependent upon a realistic appraisal and understanding of the school as an organization.

The organizational context has revealed a number of sources of conflict for schools. In this final section organizationally derived conflict is summarized and synthesized in the form of the supervisory dilemma.

1. *Professional and bureaucratic role dilemma.* Some evidence seems to exist that contemporary organizations in American society are undergoing a process of simultaneous professionalization and bureaucratization.[20] Corwin[21] suggests that this is indeed the case for schools. He observes that administrators hold primarily bureaucratic expectations for behavior in

---

[20]Litwak, for example, proposes several models of bureaucracy, one of which is the professional model which combines Weberian concepts with those of the human relations movement. He maintains that this model is most effective where jobs deal with both uniform and nonuniform events or with social skills as well as the traditional knowledge area. Eugene W. Litwak, "Models of Bureaucracy which Permit Conflict," *The American Journal of Sociology,* vol. 67, September, 1961, pp. 177–184.

[21]Ronald Corwin, "Professional Persons in Public Organizations," *Educational Administration Quarterly,* vol. 1, no. 3, Autumn, 1965, pp. 1–23.

schools while teachers hold primarily professional expectations. This comparison is presented in Table 4-1.

In an analysis of school conflict identified through research based on this comparison, Corwin makes the following observation:

Approximately forty-five per cent of all the incidents involved teachers in opposition to members of the administration; about one-fifth of these disputes were "open" discussions involving direct confrontations of parties in an argument or "heated" discussions (as judged by content analysis), or "major incidents" including a third party in addition to those teachers and administrators initially involved; this is a larger number of open conflicts than reported among teachers themselves. About one-half of all incidents involved *groups* of teachers (teacher's organizations in seven per cent of the cases).

Twenty-four per cent of all conflict incidents fell in the categories of classroom control, curriculum management, and authority in the school; these incidents embraced such issues as the use of proper teaching techniques and procedures, changing the curriculum and selection of textbooks. About half of these involved administrators. Of the 159 incidents that were in the open, about one-fourth were with the administration over these issues of authority.[22]

The higher the professional orientation of teachers, according to Corwin's findings, the higher the rates of conflict. He concludes, "The weight of evidence from this very limited sample suggests that there is a consistent pattern of conflict between teachers and administrators over the control of work, and that professionalization is a militant process."[23] The dilemma for the supervisor is, of course, reconciling for himself and on behalf of the human curriculum and its beneficiaries the increasing bureaucratization and professionalism which Corwin and others see as two simultaneous but conflicting thrusts for schools.

2. *The ability-authority dilemma.* This is a result of a contemporary distinction being emphasized in schools between the right to decide and the power and expertise to do. This dilemma is related to our previous discussions comparing hierarchical authority and ability authority. Teachers have, on the basis of ability authority, successfully co-opted many functions previously reserved for administrators. Administrative reaction to increased teacher authority is generally mixed with pessimism and often with fear. Most of what administrators have yielded deals with curriculum and teaching matters, although it should be understood that no administrative responsibility is immune from co-optation on the basis of ability authority.

The dilemma, of course, is how do those who administer and supervise as part of their legal responsibility maintain control over school developments? Enlightened supervision offers clues to solving the dilemma in that it

[22]*Ibid.*, p. 12.
[23]*Ibid.*, p. 15.

TABLE 4-1. CONTRASTS IN THE BUREAUCRATIC- AND PROFESSIONAL-EMPLOYEE PRINCIPLES OF ORGANIZATION

Organizational characteristics	Bureaucratic-employee expectations	Professional-employee expectations
Standardization		
Routine of work	Stress on uniformity of clients' problems	Stress on uniqueness of clients' problems
Continuity of procedure	Stress on records and files	Stress on research and change
Specificity of rules	Rules stated as universals; and specific	Rules stated as alternatives; and diffuse
Specialization		
Basis of division of labor	Stress on efficiency of techniques; task orientation	Stress on achievement of goals; client orientation
Basis of skill	Skill based primarily on practice	Skill based primarily on monopoly of knowledge
Authority		
Responsibility for decision making	Decisions concerning application of rules to routine problems	Decisions concerning policy in professional matters and unique problems
Basis of authority	Rules sanctioned by the public	Rules sanctioned by legally sanctioned professions
	Loyalty to the organization and to superiors	Loyalty to professional associations and clients
	Authority from office (position)	Authority from personal competence

From Ronald Corwin, "Professional Persons in Public Organizations," *Educational Administration Quarterly*, vol. 1, no. 3, Autumn, 1965, p. 7.

advocates the development and extension of ability monopolies for adminis-trators. These ability monopolies will be, not in instructional and curriculum areas, but in the management, growth, and development of the human organ-ization of the school. The distinction which Parsons makes between the management system and the technical system in organizations seems useful here.[24] As ability monopolies, administrators and supervisors, on the basis of ability authority, contribute to school goals through the management system, while teachers, on the basis of ability authority, contribute to school goals through the technical system. While enlightened supervision does not en-dorse organization apartheid,[25] in that it does recognize and respect the legiti-macy of a number of sources of authority, it focuses primarily on ability au-thority.

3. *The autonomy-coordination dilemma.* As teachers become more sophisticated and specialized in terms of professional and academic train-ing, interests, and performance, and as personal specialization and ability bases expand, teachers increase their demands for autonomy from adminis-trators. Yet, as the personal specialization phenomenon increases, teachers become more dependent upon others in order to achieve school goals. The typical organizational reaction to interdependence among specialists is one of coordination.[26] However, coordination of professional specialists imposes limits on their autonomy and is a threat to their ability monopolies. The supervisory dilemma can be reduced to this: how to cope with a situation in which teachers are becoming more autonomous as they become less auton-omous.

Pusic portrays the drama of professional specialization versus coordination as follows:

Professional specialization leaves the specialist in possession of the necessary knowledge and skill to perform complex and meaningful activities. He is much less in danger of being separated from the meaning of his work and, therefore, much more independent. He knows his work and does not need to wait for others to assign tasks to him. Still the work of the individual specialist has to be coordinated and integrated into larger contexts. An individual physician in a hospital, a social worker in an agency, a scientist in a laboratory, a teacher in a school, an administrator in an office can make their full contribution only as

---

[24]*Management* and *technical systems* are used here, after Parsons, to differentiate between the administrative sphere and the educo-technical sphere in schools. See Tal-cott Parsons, "Some Ingredients of a General Theory of Organization," in Andrew W. Halpin (ed.), *Administrative Theory in Education,* Midwest Administration Center, University of Chicago, Chicago, 1958.
[25]Complete separateness of the two destroys one of the valid and beneficial distinctions which schools enjoy when compared with other institutions.
[26]The phenomenal growth of directors, staff assistants, and other coordinators in schools seems to document this trend.

their work is brought into rational relationships with the work of others. The very independence of their individual activities, however, makes co-ordination both more necessary and more difficult. The classical school of administrative science early became aware that the span of control—the number of people to be co-ordinated by one superior—was in inverse proportion to the professional level of the work co-ordinated.[27]

While recognizing the importance of coordination to administrators and to the organization, Pusic sees dangers in overemphasis. Addressing himself to welfare agencies, he makes the following comments:

> The methods of co-ordination practiced within the traditional structure of organization seem to be ill adapted to the task of tying together the work of professional specialists. The work of individuals is co-ordinated within an organization by a hierarchy of superiors who are responsible for the allocation of work tasks to those below them as well as for the control and necessary correction of their work performances. With the increasing complexity of organizations and of the work done by their individual members the hierarchical method of co-ordination requires more and more of everybody's time. The flow of directives down the line and of reports up the line becomes more abundant. More time is spent in meetings and other forms of face-to-face contact. More writing and reading for purposes of co-ordination have to be done at all levels. Administrative procedures become more involved, formalities more numerous as the organizational system tries to counteract the centrifugal tendencies of specialization. This increase of co-ordinating activities, however, has to find its place within the fixed time-budget at the disposal of the organization. Co-ordination can ultimately expand only at the expense of the main activity, which is the initial social reason for the existence of the system. More co-ordination means less health work, less social welfare services, less education, less research by the respective organizations. The point of diminishing returns can be clearly seen: it is the moment when the balance between co-ordination and basic activity becomes so unfavorable that organization will no longer be the socially most economical method of human co-operation.[28]

While a number of additional supervisory dilemmas derived from the organizational context of schools can be identified and discussed, we limit ourselves to the three discussed above and charge the reader with responsibility for further delineation.

In the next chapter we consider the components of supervisory practice. These, along with the organizational dimensions of schools discussed in this chapter, form the basis of organizational behavior. We discuss three interrelated themes in Chapter 4: (1) how administrators and supervisors behave, (2) what assumptions administrators have for themselves and for others, and (3) what is the focus for supervisory leadership. While Chapters 3 and 4

[27]Eugen Pusic, "The Political Community and Future of Welfare," in John Morgan (ed.), *Welfare and Wisdom,* University of Toronto Press, Toronto, 1967, p. 67.
[28]*Ibid.,* p. 68.

explore the organizational variables of the synthesizing theory, Chapter 5 considers supervisory assumptions and behavior. Together, they constitute the initiating variable set of the synthesizing theory.

SELECTED REFERENCES

Bennis, Warren G.: *Changing Organizations,* McGraw-Hill, New York, 1966.

Blau, Peter M. and W. Richard Scott: *Formal Organizations: A Comparative Approach,* Chandler Publishing Co., San Francisco, 1962.

Thompson, Victor A.: *Modern Organizations,* Knopf, New York, 1961.

Chapter Five
THE COMPONENTS
OF SUPERVISORY PRACTICE

We now turn to the components of supervisory practice, one basis for organizational behavior. Administrative and supervisory behavior variables complement those variables described as organizational (authority-compliance patterns, status-hierarchical systems, and organizational styles) in the synthesizing theory, and together they constitute the initiating variable set. While the focus of this chapter is on administrative and supervisory behavior in schools, we also examine supervisory assumptions and operational orientations of supervisors which provide the basis for this behavior. We ask, What assumptions do supervisors and others make about the nature of man and, particularly, his behavior in his world of work? How do these assumptions affect the supervisor's behavior? What are the effects of this behavior on the human organization of the school? What are the predominant behavioral orientations that supervisors and others bring to school problems? How do these orientations affect supervisory behavior? And, again, how does this behavior affect the human organization of the school? Enlightened supervision is vitally concerned with the worth, growth, and development of the human organization, for it is on this growth that the success of the school enterprise depends. It is within this framework that supervisory assumptions, orientations, and predominant behavior patterns are of crucial importance to school success.

PROBLEMS IN DEFINITION

In the 1964 yearbook of the National Society for the Study of Education, Lipham[1] carefully differentiates between behavior he considers administrative and that which he describes as leadership. After Hemphill,[2] Lipham defines leadership as "the initiation of a new structure or procedure for accomplishing an organization's goals and objectives or for changing an organization's goals or objectives."[3] On the other hand, the administrator "may be

[1]James Lipham, "Leadership and Administration," in National Society for the Study of Education, *Behavioral Science and Educational Administration*, 1964 Yearbook, Chicago, 1965, pp. 119–141.
[2]James K. Hemphill, "Administration As Problem Solving," in Andrew Halpin (ed.), *Administrative Theory in Education*, Midwest Administration Center, University of Chicago, Chicago, 1958, p. 98.
[3]Lipham, *op. cit.*, p. 122.

identified as the individual who utilizes existing structures or procedures to achieve an organizational goal or objective."[4] The emphasis for leadership, according to Lipham, is on newness or change, while administration is primarily concerned with maintaining and using existing structures. Both behavioral modes are directed toward the achievement of school goals, and the appropriateness of one or the other depends upon the uniqueness of circumstances.[5] Moreover, both leadership and administrative behavioral patterns use the same organizational and individual variables as they work toward school goals.

While this differentiation between leadership and administrative behavior is not entirely consistent with our definition[6] of supervisory ways of behaving as opposed to administrative ways of behaving, the two are not contradictory. The Hemphill-Lipham definition of leadership is more likely to emerge as a result of behaving in a supervisory way (by our definition, supervisory ways of behaving invariably involve change in one or another aspect of the human organization), although it may also occur in schools as a result of administrative ways of behaving. For example, a high school department chairman divides a class into two sections according to ability and thus alters teacher A's assignment and the work flow of the department. If he makes this decision independently of his colleagues, he has initiated change but in an administrative way. If at another level as a teacher, independently of his young clients, he alters class goals or procedures, he displays leadership according to the Lipham description, but nevertheless he has chosen not to operate in a supervisory way. While modes of behavior described above as administrative may be appropriate or not, depending upon the circumstances, we caution that, as *consistent* behavioral patterns, they run the risk of having negative effects on the human organization and, subsequently, the success of the school.

MANAGEMENT PHILOSOPHY AND SUPERVISORY ASSUMPTIONS

Whatever a person does makes sense to him. This explains why two educators, with similar supervisory responsibilities, in similar schools, with similar goals, and with similar personnel, when confronted with an identical

---

[4]*Ibid.*

[5]To be sure, however, both administrative and leadership styles are essential to the school, and although the question of correct mix is complex, schools need to maintain themselves internally and to balance this maintenance with appropriate external adaption.

[6]We do not embark on this adventure without being realistically aware of the limitations inherent in the concept of leadership as we presently know it. As Warren Bennis observes, "Of all the hazy and confounding areas in social psychology, leadership theory undoubtedly contends for top nomination. And ironically, probably more has been written and less is known about leadership than about any other topic on the behavioral sciences." See his "Leadership Theory and Administrative Behavior," *Administrative Science Quarterly,* vol. 4, December, 1959, pp. 259–260.

problem may operate in dramatically dissimilar ways. Each perceives that his method of operation is perhaps the only one suitable to his task and circumstances. How do supervisors, principals, teachers, and others come to establish styles of supervision?[7] These are partly the result of management philosophies and of supervisory assumptions which individuals have accumulated or learned over the years.

Teachers, for example, whose classrooms are characterized as "open" have learned to consider students differently from their counterparts with "controlled" classrooms. These teachers have different management philosophies and different expectations for their roles and the roles of their students. So, too, with principals who operate open as opposed to closed schools.[8] Interestingly, in each case the client group responds to the supervisor's expectations in such a way that they prove him correct. As such, this simply reinforces his use of a given supervisory style. This self-fulfilling prophecy is crucial to understanding the relationship between management philosophy and supervisory behavior.[9] In the next section we present and discuss Douglas McGregor's comparison of two ideal-type management philosophies, along with supervisory assumptions which emerge from these philosophies.[10] He describes them as theories X and Y in order to minimize semantic and value confusion.

Theory X and Schools

While McGregor's language may seem more descriptive of non-school environments, his ideas have wide application to schools.[11] Examine his assump-

---

[7]By *supervisory* or *leadership style* we refer simply to predominant patterns of behavior associated with a given person, role, or school. Any given style permits and absorbs occasional departures in behavior provided that they do not alter the prevailing or basic behavior pattern.

[8]*Open* and *closed* are used here within the framework of the Organizational Climate Description Questionnaire. See Andrew Halpin and John Croft, *The Organizational Climate of Schools*, Midwest Administration Center, University of Chicago, Chicago, 1963.

[9]An interesting application of the self-fulfilling prophecy is in the operation of controlled-environment examinations. When heavy cheating is expected, elaborate controls are implemented, and the cheating rate will tend to rise. The rate declines as expectations for cheating decline and controls are minimized. For an extensive treatment of the self-fulfilling prophecy as it applies to teacher expectations for student performance, see Robert Rosenthal and Lenore Jacobson, *Pygmalion in the Classroom*, Holt, New York, 1968.

[10]An ideal type represents a conceptualization of a number of interrelated ideas in a polarized fashion. While the risk of stereotyping is present in the use of ideal types, they are nevertheless most useful in describing and grouping phenomena. As such, while no one individual or case may provide a mirror image for any ideal type, and while it is recognized that ideal descriptions tend to overstate their arguments, such individuals or cases may be usefully described as approximating one or another type.

[11]This discussion is based largely on Douglas McGregor, *The Human Side of Enterprise*, McGraw-Hill, New York, 1960. Also, Warren G. Bennis and Edgar H. Schein (eds.), *Leadership and Motivation, Essays of Douglas McGregor*, Massachusetts Institute of Technology Press, Cambridge, Mass., 1966.

tions and propositions below first in reference to school executives and their subordinates, and then in reference to the teacher and his class.

MANAGEMENT PROPOSITIONS—THEORY X

1. Management is responsible for organizing the elements of productive enterprise—money, materials, equipment, people—in the interest of economic [educational] ends.
2. With respect to people, this is a process of directing their efforts, motivating them, controlling their actions, modifying their behavior to fit the needs of the organization.
3. Without this active intervention by management, people would be passive—even resistant—to organizational needs. They must therefore be persuaded, rewarded, punished, controlled—their activities must be directed. This is management's task—in managing subordinate managers or workers. We often sum it up by saying that management consists of getting things done through other people.

SUPERVISORY ASSUMPTIONS—THEORY X

Behind this conventional theory are several additional beliefs—less explicit, but widespread:

4. The average man is by nature indolent—he works as little as possible.
5. He lacks ambition, dislikes responsibility, prefers to be led.
6. He is inherently self-centered, indifferent to organizational needs.
7. He is by nature resistant to change.
8. He is gullible, not very bright, the ready dupe of the charlatan and the demagogue.[12]

While McGregor argues that his description fits the human side of economic enterprise, we cannot avoid noticing similar school tendencies toward the pessimistic assumptions of theory X. In answering the question of whether this pessimistic image of man is correct or not, McGregor suggests that human behavior in organizations is indeed approximately what management perceives it to be. Nevertheless, social scientists who have confirmed management's theory X suspicions are sure that this behavior is not a consequence of man's inherent nature. For schools, such behavior on the part of students or teachers is a consequence of our administrative, supervisory, and educational philosophy, policy, and practice. The concentrated approach of theory X is based on mistaken notions of what is cause and what is effect.

Fundamental to theory X is a philosophy of direction and control. This philosophy is administered in a variety of forms—hard, soft, firm, fair, and the like—and rests upon a theory of motivation which is inadequate for

[12]These assumptions are quoted from McGregor's essay, "The Human Side of Enterprise," which appears in Bennis and Schein, *op. cit.*, p. 5. The essay first appeared in *Adventure in Thought and Action,* Proceedings of the Fifth Anniversary Convocation of the School of Industrial Management, Massachusetts Institute of Technology, April 9, 1957. We added the word *educational* to item 1 in McGregor's list. The article has been reprinted in *The Management Review,* 1951, vol. 46, no. 11, pp. 22–28.

most adults, particularly professional adults, and indeed is quickly outgrown by young school clients.[13] Theory X assumptions are clearly in opposition to those which form the bases for enlightened supervision.

Theory Y and Schools

An alternate management philosophy based on more adequate assumptions of human nature is needed in order for schools to meet their professional growth commitment to teachers and to improve the intellectual, social, and emotional welfare of their young clients. After McGregor, this optimistic philosophy is called theory Y. Its main components are outlined below.

PHILOSOPHY AND ASSUMPTIONS—THEORY Y

1. Management is responsible for organizing the elements of productive enterprise—money, materials, equipment, people—in the interest of economic [educational] ends.
2. People are *not* by nature passive or resistant to organizational needs. They have become so as a result of experience in organizations.
3. The motivation, the potential for development, the capacity for assuming responsibility, the readiness to direct behavior toward organizational goals are all present in people. Management does not put them there. It is a responsibility of management to make it possible for people to recognize and develop these human characteristics for themselves.
4. The essential task of management is to arrange organizational conditions and methods of operation so that people can achieve their own goals *best* by directing *their* own efforts toward organizational objectives.[14]

Indeed, there are formidable obstacles which stand in the way of full implementation of this theory in every cubic inch of our nation's schools. We have made strides in this direction, even if it has been slow, but additional modifications will need to be made in the attitudes of the school establishment, its publics, administrators, teachers, and students alike.

Another way of saying this is that Theory X places exclusive reliance upon external control of human behavior, whereas Theory Y relies heavily on self-control and self-direction. It is worth noting that this difference is the difference between treating people as children and treating them as mature adults. After generations of the former, we cannot expect to shift to the latter overnight.[15]

While we are essentially in agreement with McGregor's comments, enlightened supervision argues that even children do not wish to be treated like "children" in the management sense. As part of the normal road to ma-

[13]We discuss the motivational assumptions which are the bases for theories X and Y in a later chapter. See A. H. Maslow, *Motivation and Personality*, Harper, New York, 1954.
[14]McGregor in Bennis and Schein, *op. cit.*, p. 15. Again we add the word *educational* to item number 1.
[15]*Ibid.*, p. 19.

turity, they, too, need and require more opportunities for responsibility over their own destiny. After all, the road to maturity is what schools are all about.

Infancy Management Assumption

A perhaps harsher analysis of assumptions inherent in management is offered by Argyris.[16] He notes that the ordinary worker (in the school's case, at two levels of analysis—teacher and student) is considered to have little substantial ability for self-direction and self-discipline. Further, he largely prefers to be told what to do rather than to think for himself, and when he does have ideas, they are generally naive or unrealistic. Gellerman, in interpreting the Argyris position, makes the following comments:

> Most organizations, especially at the lower levels, are geared for men who make a very childlike adjustment to life: They leave very little leeway for choosing, for using discretion, or for adapting rules to fit circumstances. Most employees are expected to do just as they are told and leave the thinking to the foreman, whose capacity for doing so is a perennially moot point among the people he supervises. In any case millions of grown men are required to spend forty hours a week suppressing their brainpower in order to maintain a system that is not nearly as efficient as it looks.[17]

The Argyris position is essentially that the human personality is not given sufficient opportunity to mature in most formal organizations. To be sure, schools in general do offer relatively more opportunities for personal growth of their inhabitants than most other organizations. Yet proportionally—that is, when one considers that schools are essentially human organizations—*our record on this matter is less than impressive.*

In noting the distinction between the mature and immature personality, Argyris lists seven processes that normally occur as the infant grows into the young adult, as the young adult grows into the man, and as the man increases his capabilities and effectiveness over the course of his lifetime. The seven dimensions and directions of human growth[18] follow.

First, the healthy human being tends to develop from a state of passivity as an infant to a state of activity as an adult. He moves from being stimulated, motivated, or disciplined to relying on self-initiative and self-determination. As he matures, he relies less on supervision (teacher's, principal's, or

[16]This discussion is based largely on Chris Argyris, *Personality and Organization,* Harper & Row, New York, 1957. See also, "Individual Actualization in Complex Organizations," *Mental Hygiene,* vol. 44, no. 2, April, 1960, pp. 226–237, and *Integrating the Individual and Education,* Wiley, New York, 1964.

[17]Saul Gellerman, *Motivation and Productivity,* American Management Association, New York, 1963, p. 73.

[18]Our discussion of the seven directions and dimensions of the mature personality follows closely that which appears in Chris Argyris, "Individual Actualization in Complex Organizations," *op. cit.,* pp. 226–227.

parent's) to control him. Given clear expectations and the opportunity to develop commitment, the mature adult acts on his own.

Second, he moves as an infant from a state of dependence upon others to an adult state of relative independence and finally to interdependence. He is able to stand on his own feet and yet to acknowledge healthy dependencies. As part of this development, he internalizes a set of values which become the bases of his behavior.

Third, he tends to develop from being capable of behaving in only a few ways as an infant to being capable of behaving in many different ways as an adult. He actually prefers to vary his style and does not care for fixed or rigid job assignments. He prefers to develop his own means to achieve ends rather than to be limited by the *best* way as defined by the organization.

Fourth, he tends to develop from unpredictable, shallow, casual interests of short term as an infant to deeper interests as an adult. The mature personality is characterized by an endless series of challenges, and reward comes from doing something for its own sake. He needs a work environment which is challenging to skill and creativity.

Fifth, he tends to develop from having a short-term perspective as an infant—one in which the present largely determines his behavior—to a much larger time perspective as an adult—one in which behavior is affected by past events and future hopes. As such, he remembers the pains and frustration of organizational life (a reference to the long-term consequences of administrative and supervisory behavior which alienates the human organization of a school) but is also willing to make enormous sacrifices and to postpone gratification for future success as an individual and as a member of an effective organization.

Sixth, he tends to develop from being in a subordinate position in the family and society as an infant to aspiring to occupy an equal and/or superordinate position in reference to his peers. He is willing to accept leadership from others if he perceives it as legitimate, but he finds being "bossed" offensive.

Seventh, he tends to develop from a lack of awareness of self as an infant to an awareness of and control over self as an adult. He is sensitive of his concept of self and aware of his individuality. He therefore experiences with displeasure attempts to lessen his self-worth. As such, he cannot be expected to simply do the work that is put before him. He needs to experience ego-involvement in his work.

School assumptions which require teachers and others to behave in ways which tend toward the infancy end of the Argyris continuum usually have negative consequences for the human organization and ultimately retard school effectiveness. Such assumptions are reflected administratively in the formal organizational structures of the school (for example, the mechanistic or bureaucratically oriented school described in Chapter 3), in directive leadership (we discuss this in forms of supervisory styles in later sections), and in managerial control through budget, incentive systems, inspection and review procedures, and the like. Argyris describes the effects of "infancy" managerial assumptions as follows:

> Healthy human beings (in our culture) tend to find dependence, subordination and submissiveness frustrating. They would prefer to be relatively independent, to be active, to use many of their deeper abilities; and they aspire to positions equal with or higher than their peers. Frustration leads to regression, aggression, and tension. These in turn lead to conflict (the individual prefers to leave but fears doing so). Moreover, it can be shown that under these conditions, the individual will tend to experience psychological failure and short-time perspective.[19]

While our focus in this discussion has been on adults in school organizations who may be required to behave in ways which approximate the infancy half of Argyris's continuum, the analogy is perhaps more importantly applicable for students. Argyris has captured the very function of American schools—to earnestly and tenderly move youngsters from infancy to maturity, intellectually, socially, and emotionally. Let us examine some of the alternatives that teachers on the one hand and students on the other have as they adapt to school environments which frustrate their mature development.[20]

Some writers maintain that what Argyris criticizes so vehemently is exactly what workers in organizations want. Dubin, for example, argues:

> The fact of the matter is this. Work for probably a majority of workers, and even extending into the ranks of management, may represent an institutional setting that is not a central life interest for its participants. The consequence of this is that while participating in work, a general attitude of apathy and indifference prevails. The response to the demands of the institution is to satisfy the minimum expectations of required behavior without reacting affectively to these demands.[21]

What Dubin fails to add is that this reaction is learned as a result of one's experience with organizations. People are not inherently removed from organizational life. Reactions by teachers and students similar to those described by Dubin should be interpreted as symptoms of school failure.

[19]*Ibid.*
[20]The list which follows is an adaptation of one which appears in Argyris, "Individual Actualization in Complex Organizations," *op. cit.*, p. 227.
[21]Robert Dubin, "Person and Organization," William Greenwood (ed.), *Management and Organizational Behavior Theories,* South-Western Publishing Company, Cincinnati, 1965, p. 487. See also George Strauss, "Some Notes on Power-Equalization, in Harold J. Leavitt (ed.), *The Social Science of Organizations,* Prentice-Hall, Englewood Cliffs, N.J., 1963, pp. 45–59.

FOR TEACHERS	FOR STUDENTS
1. Leave the school. Absence and turnover.	1. Same.
2. Climb the organizational ladder into administration.	2. Submit and "play ball' with the system. Company-union approach.
3. Become defensive, daydream, become aggressive, nurture grievances, regress, project, feel low self-worth.	3. Same.
4. Become apathetic, disinterested, non-ego-involved in the school and its goals.	4. Same.
5. Create informal groups for mutual protection from the organization.	5. Same.
6. Formalize into militant associations and unions.	6. Go underground—dissent, newspapers, organized demonstration, student unions.
7. Deemphasize in one's own mind the importance of self-growth and creativity and emphasize the importance of money and other material rewards.	7. Deemphasize intrinsic learning goals and other values and emphasize grades, credits, and the like, to beat the system.
8. Accept the above-described ways of behaving as being proper for their lives outside the organization.	8. The sickness of this cycle of events is that youngsters may accept socialization into the value system of infancy management and thus reinforce and perpetuate the system for another generation.

Value Assumptions and Decision Making

More fundamental than one's assumptions in regard to management philosophy is the very value system which contributed to these assumptions. Since decision making is the very essence of administration and supervision, and since decisions have fundamental effects on people, organizations, institutions, time, and events, the question of values cannot be ignored. Education is particularly susceptible to attention in the value domain by virtue of its position and function in society.

At the simplest level, and at some risk, let us view values, not as the scholar-philosopher does, but less gracefully as what one with supervisory responsibility considers as he is confronted with a decision-making problem.

Further, as he establishes criteria for decision making, what priorities does he place on one or another criterion? Four general areas of consideration confront educators as they work in schools toward the identification and achievement of school goals. One area concerns the school itself and includes its growth, its survival, its control mechanisms, and other manifestations of the school as an organization. A second area focuses on the local benefactors and beneficiaries of the school—the community. A third area relates to the broader society in which we live. The fourth, so significant to the *literature* of education, is the individual and his welfare.

School professionals consider, of course, elements of each as they perform their work. In a scarce decision-making situation, however, which receives priority over others? The choices made vary with who the decision maker is and what his circumstances are. Yet each of us, consciously or not, has developed value styles within each and among all the four value areas. These styles are one of the more important and influential bases for supervisory behavior. Educators surely value each of the four areas, but nevertheless they must necessarily make choices among them. A principal who values control as well as justice and human dignity may, if control is of higher priority to him, be required to forsake justice and human dignity. Another principal may ignore community wishes—something he values—in order to protect a teacher's right to dissent or a student's right to dress in a specific way if the principal values these more than the former.

Traditional supervisory practices have tended to focus on a hierarchical value pattern which places the school at the highest level of priority, followed in turn by the community, society, and, finally, the individual (see Table 5-1). Guided by such a pattern, decisions are made on the basis of individual values only if they do not conflict with societal, community, and school values. Decisions are made on behalf of social values only if they do not conflict with community and school values, and so on.

Enlightened supervisory practices are also based on a hierarchical value pattern, but one which is the inverse of that for traditional supervision. Following this pattern, enlightened supervision places highest priority on the individual, then on society, the community, and finally the school.[22] Contemporary supervisory practices are based on an ambivalent hierarchical pattern which is characterized by search, contradiction, and conflict. A good deal of the unrest which characterizes American education (as exhibited by teachers, students, and many community and societal segments) can be attributed to this value confusion.

Our discussion of assumptions about work in schools and about people

---

[22]We are tempted to say, "And last but not least, the school." To be sure, the maintenance of the school as an organization is of great importance and one that should not be ignored or set aside unless such emphasis violates values inherent in one of the other three areas.

TABLE 5-1.   *THE VALUE HIERARCHY—GUIDE TO SUPERVISORY DECISION MAKING*

	Supervision					
	Traditional		Contemporary		Enlightened	
Priority	Decision criteria	Goals, objectives	Decision criteria	Goals, objectives	Decision criteria	Goals, objectives
High I	The school	Welfare of the system Survival Growth Control Elite satisfaction			The individual	Individual welfare
II	Community	Welfare of benefactors Community service Pressure groups Community need	Transitional period characterized by search, ambivalence, and conflict		Society	Social welfare
III	Society	Social welfare Culture Civilization Order Justice			Community	Welfare of benefactors
IV Low	The individual	Individual welfare Freedom Opportunity Self-realization Human dignity			The school	Welfare of the system

Adapted and extended from a model for management decisions which appears in Wilmar Bernthal, "Value Perspective in Management Decisions," *Academy of Management Journal*, December, 1962, pp. 190–196.

who work in schools is incomplete without self-analysis by the reader. Indeed, each of us needs to be aware of and concerned about our assumptions, values, and beliefs regarding the nature of work, the nature of man, and how these relate to the function of schools in our society. This last concern is of critical importance in that faulty supervisory assumptions, and subsequently faulty school climates, are able to penetrate classroom doors. Thus, they take their toll from our young school clients and from classroom learning environments. A principal who holds growth goals for students but denies growth opportunities to teachers inadvertently denies them to students. We believe that teachers will withhold from students that which schools withhold from teachers.

In the next section we move closer to descriptively linking supervisory assumptions, value systems, and belief systems with supervisory behavior as we examine some determinants of supervisory practice. Three supervisory forces are identified—each is a screen through which the supervisor must travel as he prepares for decision making. We follow this discussion with an analysis of defensive and open leadership patterns as a prelude to examining dimensions of leadership behavior.

DETERMINANTS OF SUPERVISORY PATTERNS

The focus of this chapter is on values, assumptions, and management philosophies which are a part of the supervisor's concept of self. As these dimensions are internalized and become a part of one's life style, they largely determine dominant supervisory behavior patterns. Other forces, however, such as those which exist within the client and those which exist in the environment, contribute to prevailing supervisory style. These forces are delineated and described in the following sections.[23]

Forces in the Supervisor

As a supervisor faces a problem, his approach, behavior, or style is largely, if not unconsciously, affected by each of the following internalized forces.

1. *His value system.* How strongly does he feel that individuals should have a share in making the decisions which affect them? Or, how convinced is he that the official who is paid to assume responsibility should personally carry the burden of decision making? . . . his behavior will also be influenced by

---

[23]This discussion follows Robert Tannenbaum and Warren Schmidt, "How to Choose a Leadership Pattern," *Harvard Business Review*, vol. 36, no. 2, 1958, pp. 95–101. Tannenbaum identifies three forces which managers should consider in deciding how to manage: (1) forces in the manager, (2) forces in the subordinates, and (3) forces in the situation. See also Tannenbaum and Fred Massarick, "Participation by Subordinates in the Managerial Decision-making Process," *Canadian Journal of Economics and Political Science*, August, 1950, pp. 413–418.

the relative importance that he attaches to organizational efficiency, personal growth of subordinates and company profits.

2. *His confidence in his subordinates.* Managers differ greatly in the amount of trust they have in other people generally, and this carries over to the particular employees they supervise at a given time. In viewing his particular group of subordinates, the manager is likely to consider their knowledge and competence with respect to the problem. A central question he might ask himself is: "Who is best qualified to deal with this problem?" Often he may, justifiably or not, have more confidence in his own capabilities than in those of his subordinates.

3. *His own leadership inclinations.* There are some managers who seem to function more comfortably and naturally as highly directive leaders. Resolving problems and issuing orders come easily to them. Other managers seem to operate more comfortably in a team role where they are continually sharing many of their functions with their subordinates.

4. *His feelings of security in an uncertain situation.* The manager who releases control over the decision-making process thereby reduces the predictability of the outcome. Some managers have a greater need than others for predictability and stability in their environment. This "tolerance for ambiguity" is being viewed increasingly by psychologists as a key variable in a person's manner of dealing with problems.[24]

While such an impressive list of internalized forces may provoke feelings of helplessness in supervisors, each of these dimensions can be altered and modified. A first step toward this end is awareness and understanding. As one with supervisory responsibility in schools comes to understand the nature of his values, prejudices, and management style which have become a part of his conscious or unconscious self, he begins to construct the very foundation for meaningful change.

Forces in the Supervisory Environment

The organizational forces which we have described in Chapter 3 are a major influence on supervisory style. The organizational style of the school, the school's normative culture, its role expectations, its belief pattern, and its authority and power systems serve as boundaries which often delimit choice of supervisory action. Further, the nature of the problem, the consequences of the task, and the character of the goal are additional determiners of appropriate supervisory behavior. A teacher, for example, may be required by default to consult with students when class activities are varied and complex, but such consultation is little more than perfunctory when activities are routine and simple.

---

[24]Tannenbaum and Schmidt, *op. cit.* While the label "manager" tends to have negative connotations to many school people, the descriptions are equally appropriate if one substitutes the word *supervisor* for *manager*.

Forces in the Clients

The extent to which school supervisors may permit their respective clients to exercise more freedom and control over their own destiny and that of the school depends largely on the following conditions:

1. If the subordinates have relatively high needs for independence. (As we all know, people differ greatly in the amount of direction that they desire.)
2. If the subordinates have a readiness to assume responsibility for decision making. (Some see additional responsibility as a tribute to their ability; others see it as "passing the buck.")
3. If they have a relatively high tolerance for ambiguity. (Some employees prefer to have clear-cut directives given to them; others prefer a wider area of freedom.)
4. If they are interested in the problem and feel that it is important.
5. If they understand and identify with the goals of the organization.
6. If they have the necessary knowledge and experience to deal with the problem.
7. If they have learned to expect to share in decision making. (Persons who have come to expect strong leadership and are then suddenly confronted with the request to share more fully in decision making are often upset by this new experience. On the other hand, persons who have enjoyed a considerable amount of freedom resent the boss who begins to make all the decisions himself.)[25]

The danger in suggesting this—that choice of one supervisory pattern over another is partly a function of forces in the client to be supervised—is that this rationale provides a convenient "out" for those whose dominant supervisory patterns are less than enlightened.

Enlightened supervision recognizes that forces in the client may require the supervisor to behave in a variety of ways. Highly dependent teachers will need paternalistic supervisory environments and noncommitted students will require close-controlled supervisory environments. Enlightened supervisors, however, are not resigned to these patterns in that they do not accept dependency in teachers as being natural or inherent; they do not accept noncommittedness in students as being natural or inherent. Dependency by teachers and lack of commitment by students (and vice versa) are perceived as symptoms of client immaturity and/or perhaps supervisory immaturity and organizational immaturity. With this perception, the enlightened supervisor works to end client dependency and to increase client commitment, for these are the means to positively affect the school success variables in the synthesizing theory.

We shall now discuss and explore alternate supervisory behavior—leadership behavior patterns and examine their effects on the school and the human organization which constitutes the school.

[25]*Ibid.*

LEADERSHIP AND SUPERVISORY BEHAVIOR OBSERVED

Jack Gibb, in writing for the American Association for Higher Education 1967 Yearbook, *In Search of Leaders,* identifies and describes two ideal types of leadership style used by school administrators. The emergence of one or another of these styles for a given individual largely depends upon how that individual feels about himself (in terms of adequacy) and about others (in terms of trust).

Gibb classifies the first view, sometimes described as authoritarian, paternalistic, or conservative, as defensive. "Dynamically the view defends the administrator against his own fears and distrusts and against perceived or anticipated attack from the outside."[26] In this view, defensive leadership patterns are based on fear and distrust, thrive on the distortion of information, and use strategies of persuasion and high control.

The alternative to defensive supervisory practices is described by Gibb as being participatory. The key to this leadership style is high trust and confidence in people. "The self-adequate person tends to assume that others are also adequate and, other things being equal, that they will be responsible, loyal, appropriately work-oriented when work is to be performed, and adequate to carry out jobs that are commensurate with their levels of experience and growth."[27]

The two ideal types of supervisory behavior described by Gibb are not without substantial support from the literature of leadership-supervisory styles. While the Gibb analysis depends heavily on the forces within the supervisor which determine his behavior, we move now to examining this behavior and its effects on the school. In order to do this, we need to shift our focus from an evaluative level to a descriptive level. Our concern then will be with how leaders behave. This is decidedly different from how we think leaders should behave.

The Dimensions of Leadership

Dimensions of leadership tend to sort themselves into two general categories. One category is concerned with people and the other category is concerned with getting the job done. The notion of two primary leadership dimensions is a popular one which is amply supported in the literature of administration. In Table 5-2 we summarize leadership dimensions of supervisory behavior.

The researchers and theorists, from top to bottom in Table 5-2, see the primary or theme dimensions of leadership behavior as work facilitation and

[26]Jack R. Gibb, "Dynamics of Leadership," in American Association for Higher Education, *In Search of Leaders,* National Education Association, Washington, D.C., 1967, p. 56.
[27]*Ibid.,* p. 62.

TABLE 5-2. SUMMARY OF LEADERSHIP DIMENSIONS

	Concern for people	Concern for getting job done
Bowers and Seashore	Interaction facilitation	Work facilitation
Hemphill and Coons (1957)	Group-interaction facilitation behavior	Objective attainment behavior
Halpin and Winer (1957)	Consideration	Initiating structure
Katz et al. (1950)	Employee orientation	Production orientation
Kahn (1958)	Providing need satisfaction	Enabling goal achievement
Mann (1962)	Human relations skills	Adminstrative skills; technical skills
Likert (1961)	Principle of supportive relationships	Technical knowledge, planning, scheduling
Cartwright and Zander (1960)	Group maintenance functions	Goal-achievement functions
Getzels and Guba (1957)	Ideographic	Nomothetic
Brown (1966)	Person orientation	System orientation
Blake and Mouton (1966)	Concern for people	Concern for production

Adapted and extended from David G. Bowers and Stanley E. Seashore, "Predicting Organizational Effectiveness with a Four-factor Theory of Leadership," *Administrative Science Quarterly*, vol. 2, September, 1966, p. 248.

interaction facilitation, goal-oriented behavior and group-interaction behavior, initiating structure and consideration, production-centered and employee-centered, providing for organizational needs and providing for individual needs, management skills and human relations skills, high performance goals and group-supportive relationships, goal achievement and group maintenance, behaving in a nomothetic way and behaving in an ideographic way, system orientation and person orientation, and concern for production and concern for people.[28]

Upon analysis, this literature is overwhelming in suggesting, not that the two dimensions of leadership behavior, focusing on people and focusing on the job, are at opposite ends of the same continuum, but that the dimensions are more appropriately described as being mutually exclusive. By this we mean that effective leadership-supervisory style is not an either/or proposition but is dependent upon the presence of both dimensions. Much of the work in leadership theory and research is directed at identifying the exact

[28]This discussion follows that which appears in Thomas Sergiovanni, Richard Metzcus, and Larry Burden, "Toward a Particularistic Approach to Leadership Style: Some Findings," *American Educational Research Journal*, January, 1969.

mix of the two dimensions which is most appropriate for given school circumstances.

The Ohio State Leadership Studies

Studies in education dealing with dimensions of leadership behavior have tended to rely heavily on the Ohio State Leadership Studies and the instrument which emerged from these studies, the Leadership Behavior Description Questionnaire (the LBDQ). This instrument identifies initiating structure and consideration as the two fundamental leadership dimensions.[29] Halpin describes the two dimensions as follows:

Initiating Structure refers to the leader's behavior in delineating the relationship between himself and members of the work-group, and in endeavoring to establish well-defined patterns of organization, channels of communication, and methods of procedure. Consideration refers to behavior indicative of friendship, mutual trust, respect, and warmth in the relationship between the leader and the members of his staff.[30]

The two leadership dimensions may be viewed schematically in Figure 5-1.

Each of the four quadrants represents a distinct leadership style. Quadrant 1 describes leaders who emphasize both initiating structure and consideration. The literature suggests that leaders of this type are perceived as being most effective. Quadrant 2 describes leaders who emphasize initiating structure rather than (and often at the expense of) consideration. Leaders of this type emphasize the task and getting the job done. They are surprisingly effective in times of tension, when work is routine, and in all cases for very short periods of time. Over time, however, particularly when jobs are of a professional nature, treating people in mechanical ways or perhaps not treating them at all has negative organizational consequences. Quadrant 3 emphasizes consideration of members at the expense of initiating structure. This is generally a shortsighted strategy, since meaningful satisfaction in teachers' work comes from the achievement of worthwhile school purposes.[31]

[29]The Leadership Behavior Description Questionnaire was developed by the Personnel Research Board at Ohio State University and is published by the Bureau of Business Research at that university. See John K. Hemphill and Alvin E. Coons, *Leader Behavior Description,* Personnel Research Board, The Ohio State University, Columbus, Ohio, 1950.
[30]Andrew Halpin, *Theory and Research in Administration,* Macmillan, New York, 1967, p. 86. Halpin's efforts with the LBDQ and education are pioneering. See his *The Leadership Behavior of School Superintendents,* Midwest Administration Center, University of Chicago, Chicago, 1959. Also "The Leader Behavior and Leadership Ideology of Educational Administrators and Aircraft Commanders," *Harvard Educational Review,* vol. 25, Winter, 1955, pp. 18–32.
[31]This observation seems particularly appropriate for professionally oriented workers such as teachers.

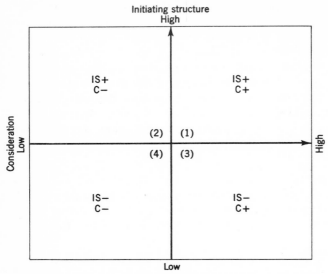

Figure 5-1. Halpin: The leadership quadrant. Adapted from
Andrew Halpin, "The Superintendent's Effectiveness
As a Leader," *Administrators Notebook*, vol. 7, no. 2,
October, 1958.

Thus, the consideration dimension alone tends not to be a potent enough
means for leaders to express authentic consideration toward members. Quadrant 4 is a distorted leadership style which emphasizes neither initiating
structure nor consideration. This style is generally perceived as being least
effective of the four.

In summarizing work[32] with the LBDQ in educational organizations,
Halpin notes that the evidence clearly indicates that initiating structure and
consideration are fundamental dimensions of leadership behavior.[33] Further,
effective leadership is generally associated with high performance on both
dimensions. Halpin further notes, however, that there is some tendency for
superiors and subordinates to consider opposite dimensions of leadership as
being most critical to effectiveness, with superiors favoring initiating structure and subordinates consideration. Halpin also suggests that high initiating
structure combined with high consideration is associated with favorable attitudes in group members.

[32]This discussion follows that which appears in Halpin, *Theory and Research in
Administration*, pp. 97–98.
[33]Recent work with Stogdill's new LBDQ XII, reported by Brown, is consistent with
the pattern of two leadership dimensions. Although the LBDQ XII purports to measure
twelve dimensions of leadership behavior, Brown found that six of the dimensions load
on factor 1 (systems orientation, a concept close to initiating structure) and six load
on factor 2 (person orientation, a concept close to consideration). See Alan Brown,
"Reactions to Leadership," *Educational Administration Quarterly*, Winter, 1967.

When asked to describe ideal leadership behavior in principals, teachers tend to express a preference for the integrated style which combines both initiating structure and consideration. This preference seems to hold even though teachers may vary in terms of personality or need orientations. This observation lends support to the optimistic assumptions which comprise the McGregor-Argyris management philosophy. That is, teachers, seem able to describe ideal leadership behavior as emphasizing task—the organizational and structural aspects of the school—as well as providing for individual needs, regardless of their own personality shortcomings or strengths. Enlightened supervision maintains that providing for needs of mature teachers is dependent upon efforts toward achieving school goals: the two dimensions then are interdependent, since goal achievement over time is dependent upon provision for teacher need, and teacher need over time is dependent upon the achievement of school goals.

THE MANAGERIAL GRID

A more descriptive attempt to conceptualize the task dimension and the people dimension of supervisory behavior has resulted in a formulation referred to as the *managerial grid*.[34] The grid focuses on five "ideal type" theories of supervisory behavior, each based on the two dimensions which we have identified and discussed as crucial variables found in organizations: (1) task and (2) people. Blake and Mouton, the proposers of the grid formulation, show the relationship between the two variables and present the five ideal-type combinations of style in Figure 5-2.

Notice that the horizontal axis, concern for production, is strikingly similar to the Halpin concept of initiating structure, and that the vertical axis, concern for people, more than resembles Halpin's consideration dimension. By locating degree of intensity for each of these two dimensions (from 1 to 9), the grid has potential for generating eighty-one different styles.

Our focus in this discussion will be on the five ideal types which are numbered by degree of intensity of concern as 1,9., 9,9., 5,5., 1,1., and 9,1. We need again to caution that while no one supervisor is perfectly described by these ideal types, the types serve as useful bench marks to show tendencies toward one or another of the ideal types. Further, descriptions of the ideal types serve as a basis for self-evaluation of style orientation and provide clues as to how one may evaluate and shift his own supervisory behavior patterns. We now describe each of the five managerial grid styles.[35]

[34]Robert Blake and Jane Mouton, *The Managerial Grid,* Gulf Publishing Company, Houston, Tex., 1964.
[35]This discussion is adapted and extended (without too much violence, we hope) from Chaps. 3 through 7 in Blake and Mouton, *op. cit.*

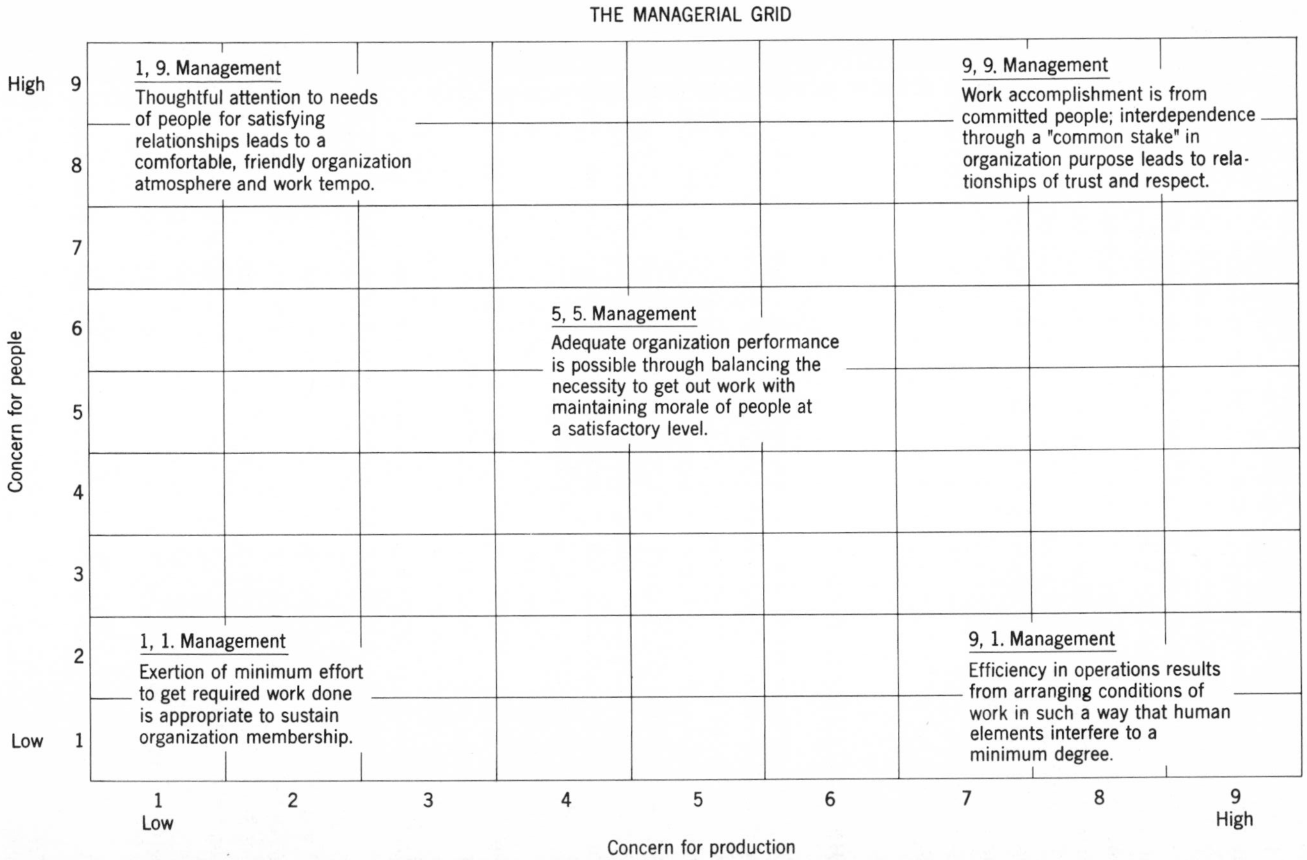

THE MANAGERIAL GRID

Concern for people

High

9

1, 9. Management
Thoughtful attention to needs of people for satisfying relationships leads to a comfortable, friendly organization atmosphere and work tempo.

8

7

6

5

5, 5. Management
Adequate organization performance is possible through balancing the necessity to get out work with maintaining morale of people at a satisfactory level.

4

3

2

1, 1. Management
Exertion of minimum effort to get required work done is appropriate to sustain organization membership.

1

9, 9. Management
Work accomplishment is from committed people; interdependence through a "common stake" in organization purpose leads to relationships of trust and respect.

9, 1. Management
Efficiency in operations results from arranging conditions of work in such a way that human elements interfere to a minimum degree.

Low

| 1 | 2 | 3 | 4 | 5 | 6 | 7 | 8 | 9 |
| Low | | | | | | | | High |

Concern for production

Figure 5-2. The managerial grid. From Robert Blake and Jane Mouton, *The Managerial Grid*, Gulf Publishing Company, Houston, Tex.

The 9,1. Supervisory Orientation

Supervisors whose behavior approximates the 9,1. style place heavy emphasis on getting the job of the school done but at the same time need to be on top of things. The 9,1. supervisor has pessimistic assumptions about his subordinates. Further, he has a strong need to be in control of the flow and direction of work. As such he accepts fully the blame for failure and the praise for success. He relies heavily on formal authority and expects compliance on the basis of the position he occupies. He uses standardized methods and engages in relatively close supervision (Table 5-3).

TABLE 5-3. THE 9,1. SUPERVISORY STYLE

Assumptions	Theory X—Pessimistic man
Orientations	Self—Needs to be in control
Authority system	Formal—Legitimate and hierarchical
Control strategy	Close—Standardized procedures
Supervisory emphasis	Task—Accomplishment

Interestingly, many writers see the 9,1. supervisor as one who places top priority on the goals of the school and their achievement. While this may be his manifest intent, the 9,1. supervisor seems driven by a desire for control primarily as a means of protection from threats of others. He would be crushed upon returning to the school, after a semester's leave, to find that it indeed can thrive without him. He tends to be self-oriented internally and task-oriented externally.

The 1,9. Supervisory Orientation

Outward appearances of a 1,9. supervisory environment suggest a state of bliss and happiness. To be sure, the 1,9. supervisor works hard to eliminate dissatisfaction in the work environment and makes few demands upon subordinates in terms of performance. He relies on personal diplomacy and hopes to obtain compliance because he is a nice guy and his subordinates owe it to him. Human relationships are important for their own sake and group harmony is the key to organizational success.

The 1,9. supervisor believes that inherent conflict exists between people and work and he sides with people against the harsh demands of the organization. He relies on friendship and favors in order to get compliance and uses very general, gentle, and particularistic methods of control.

The good-guy 1,9. supervisor is often assumed to be naturally oriented to others. While this may be the net effect of his behavior, the 1,9. is driven by a powerful desire to be accepted and loved by others. To support himself

TABLE 5-4. THE 1,9. SUPERVISORY STYLE

Assumptions	Inherent conflict between people and work; sides with people.
Orientations	Self-oriented. Needs to be accepted and loved by others.
Authority system	Friendship; bribe, loyalty.
Control strategy	General, low-power, particularistic.
Supervisory emphasis	People-oriented.

in this regard, he will go to bat against impossible odds for his subordinates. Interestingly, his lack of emphasis in achieving school goals deprives subordinates of the route to meaningful satisfaction.

The 1,1. Supervisory Style

This style is characterized by low concern for achievement of school goals coupled with low concern for the human organization of the school. The 1,1. style is an unnatural style which comes to those who have accepted defeat. As such, low involvement reduces the risk of deeper frustration and additional defeat. Students who have learned failure early become 1,1.[s], as do teachers who over the years have not, or feel that they have not, kept up with the mainstream of their profession. The educator who has been passed up for promotion for the third time may also retreat to the 1,1. perspective.

A major function of enlightened supervision is the salvaging and restructuring of 1,1.[s] (particularly among teachers) found in schools—to the extent that this is possible, and we are not tremendously optimistic here—as well as working to prevent this tragic development.

The 5,5. Supervisory Style

The 5,5. supervisor is the proud product of typical university programs which prepare people (teachers, principals, and others) to assume supervisory positions in our nation's schools. Students, too, become socialized to the 5,5. management philosophy, partly at home and partly in school, so that

TABLE 5-5. THE 1,1. SUPERVISORY STYLE

Assumptions	People and organization are both no good.
Orientations	Aloof-defensive-survival.
Authority system	Legal—but minimum enforcement.
Control strategy	Limited to direction, but no follow-up or commitment.
Supervisory emphasis	Low concern for both dimensions.

TABLE 5-6.   THE 5,5. SUPERVISORY STYLE

Assumptions	Inherent conflict between organization and man
Orientations	Bureaucratic
Authority system	Combination—ability within legal
Control system	Compromise, realistic appeasement
Supervisory emphasis	Half and half, balanced

they reinforce and confirm these practices by educators. *Realism, satisfying,* and *compromising* are the key words which describe and excuse 5,5. supervisory behavior patterns.

The 5,5. supervisor believes that emphasis on school goals and emphasis on the welfare of people are equally important, and he works to maintain a balance between the two. With this foundation, his solutions are generally always acceptable, satisfactory, and workable but rarely outstanding. In our view, he has introduced mediocrity into the school as a professional management system and into the classroom as a learning system. The 5,5. supervisor believes that there is inherent conflict between organization and man, but, rather than standing for one or the other, he works to appease both through compromise. His orientation is generally bureaucratic in that he relies on ability and competence only to the extent that they do not seriously compromise the formal authority system.

The 5,5.[s] supervisory style is characterized by a series of paradoxes. For example, the 5,5.[s] supervisor's policy may be to communicate enough to give people a feeling of what is going on but withhold enough so that they cannot substantially influence policy. The use of buzz sessions as a symptom of "democratic" administration is typical of the focus of 5,5. supervisory behavior. Here subordinates are given an opportunity to fully and freely offer suggestions. Each suggestion is carefully recorded and acknowledged by the 5,5. supervisor. Subordinates leave (at least according to the 5,5. ethos) with a feeling of maximum involvement and participation, while the supervisor retires to his chambers to make the final decision. While the 5,5. supervisor wishes to be considerate by permitting participation, he still does not trust subordinates entirely, and thus he feels the necessity (after all, the school and its children are at stake) to make a private decision.

The 9,9. Supervisory Style

The establishment of 9,9. supervisory patterns in schools will result, at least initially, in difficult and demanding adjustments for the school as an organization, for those with supervisory responsibility, and for other school inhabitants. Yet it is precisely through 9,9. patterns that schools will be able to actualize themselves and their most important young clients.

TABLE 5-7. THE 9,9. SUPERVISORY STYLE

Assumptions	Theory Y—no inherent conflict between work and people
Orientations	The achievement of school goals
Authority system	Functional authority—competence
Control system	Self-direction—commitment
Supervisory emphasis	Integrated

The 9,9. supervisor does not see an inherent conflict between the goals of the school and the goals of its inhabitants. Rather, he sees each being dependent upon the achievement of the other. He relies heavily on commitment and self-control. He does not view making the best decision as part of his job but rather sees it as part of his job to make sure that the best decision is made. He believes that when people have a stake in something, they assume responsibility for its success.

The adoption of 9,9. behavior patterns begins with modifying forces within the supervisor. The 9,9. style requires that certain attitudes and assumptions be present in the supervisor. He then needs to work with subordinates, clients, colleagues, and superintendents so that they, too, move to adopt this perspective. The environment for enlightened supervision requires a complementary interdependence of internal, external, and situational forces.

We have described the phenomenon of leadership as an important dimension of supervisory behavior from the perspective of assumptions and beliefs which generate the process and the styles of behaving which manifest the process. In the next chapter we examine the direction and focus of leadership by answering the question, Leadership in supervision for what purpose?

SELECTED REFERENCES

Blake, Robert, and Jane Mouton: *The Managerial Grid,* Gulf Publishing Company, Houston, Tex., 1964.

Fiedler, Fred: *A Theory of Leadership Effectiveness,* McGraw-Hill, New York, 1968.

Halpin, Andrew: *Theory and Research in Administration,* Macmillan, New York, 1967.

McGregor, Douglas: *The Human Side of Enterprise,* McGraw-Hill, New York, 1960.

National Society for the Study of Education, *Behavioral Science and Educational Administration,* 1964 Yearbook of the Society, Chicago, 1965.

Chapter Six
THE FOCUS
OF EDUCATIONAL
LEADERSHIP

In Chapter 5 we considered the process of leadership in terms of assumptions and philosophies which form the process and the behavioral styles which implement the process. We need now to consider the question of direction for leadership-supervisory behavior in order to place this phenomenon in perspective. While we have traditionally accepted the notion of instructional leadership as being central to supervision, this concept is being challenged by other roles and functions. The change-agent concept for supervision is a fairly popular one, as is that which considers supervision as coordination. Still other viewpoints substitute developing the human organization for instructional leadership as the new plan for supervision. While we endorse and accept the newer conceptions of the supervisor's role, we do not see them as replacing or supplementing his instructional responsibilities, but rather as enhancing this function.

INSTRUCTIONAL LEADERSHIP

The basic issue in regard to instructional leadership is simply: How do we reconcile the gap which frequently exists between the authority for leadership (by virtue of position) which supervisors have and the ability for leadership (by virtue of professional expertness) which subordinates have? More bluntly, how can we expect an elementary school principal to supervise kindergarten and first-grade teachers and to conduct curriculum development at this level when he clearly may not be qualified for this work by virtue of his professional orientation, preparation, and experience? This is the kind of persuasive argument which diminishes the role of instructional leadership for those who are incumbents of hierarchical roles in schools.

The argument sticks if we view supervisory control as directing the functioning of schools in the traditional-classical management sense. However, if we view supervisory control as assuming responsibility for the establishment and pursuit of meaningful school goals, then the question of who does what, when, and where is clearly not relevant, provided that what happens moves the school closer to its goals.

Enlightened supervision views instructional leadership as a process which does not forbid the supervisor to contribute his professional expertise as an educator but does not limit him to this function. Rather, the focus of instructional leadership is to see that the process (instructional leadership) indeed does emerge, regardless of who the leader is, and that leadership efforts are consistent with the school's purposes. As this process takes place, the supervisor on one occasion assumes the client role and looks to his staff as consultants who can provide him with help and information (usually in the educo-technical areas), and on another occasion assumes the consultant role (usually in the broader educo-professional and in the coordinator-management areas) to his staff, who become the client group. Instructional leadership then occurs in a dynamic system of *interchanging roles,* with teachers, students, supervisors, administrators, and others assuming one role (client) or the other role (consultant) depending upon the uniqueness of circumstances.

The Expanded Leadership Role

While instructional leadership is still at the core of the supervisor's role, the focus is less on who assumes the role and more on whether it is indeed assumed. We have suggested that the supervisor may display instructional leadership directly or by working to see that leadership does emerge within the teaching staff. Fundamental to this position is the belief that a major aspect of the supervisor's job is to provide the circumstances, environment, and climate for leadership. Some directions for achieving this purpose are presented below as we consider the Matthew Miles[1] concept of organizational health and the Andrew Halpin and Don Croft[2] concept of organizational climate.

ORGANIZATIONAL CLIMATE AND SCHOOLS

It is often useful to view schools as being on a conceptual climate continuum that extends from open to closed.[3] This framework is not unlike that which considers individual personalities as being on a continuum from open-mindedness to closed-mindedness. At a very simple level, *organizational climate* refers to the feeling which exists in a given school and the variabil-

---

[1]Matthew Miles, "Planned Change and Organizational Health: Figure and Ground," *Change Processes in the Public Schools,* Center for the Advanced Study of Educational Administration, The University of Oregon, Eugene, Ore., 1965, pp. 11–34.
[2]Andrew Halpin and Don Croft, *The Organizational Climate of Schools,* Midwest Administration Center, University of Chicago, Chicago, 1963. For a condensed version see Halpin's *Theory and Research in Administration,* Macmillan, New York, 1967, pp. 131–249.
[3]The Halpin climate "continuum," as measured by the Organizational Climate Description Questionnaire, moves from open through autonomous, controlled, familiar, and paternal to closed.

ity in this feeling as one moves from school to school. Halpin, in describing climate, notes that "as one moves to other schools, one finds that each has a 'personality' of its own. It is this 'personality' that we describe here as the 'organizational climate' of the school. Analogously, personality is to the individual what organizational climate is to the organization."[4]

The Organizational Climate Description Questionnaire was developed by Halpin and Croft as a means to measure and chart the difference in "feel" which characterizes individual schools. The instrument examines eight dimensions of organizational climate, four of which focus on teacher behavior and four on the behavior of the principal. These are presented in Table 6-1.

TABLE 6-1. THE EIGHT DIMENSIONS OF ORGANIZATIONAL CLIMATE

	Intensity scale	
	Open	Closed
Teachers' Behavior		
1. *Disengagement* refers to the teachers' tendency to be "not with it." This dimension describes a group which is "going through the motions," a group that is "not in gear" with respect to the task at hand. It corresponds to the more general concept of *anomie* as first described by Durkheim.* In short, this subtest focuses upon the teachers' behavior in a task-oriented situation.	−	++
2. *Hindrance* refers to the teachers' feeling that the principal burdens them with routine duties, committee demands, and other requirements which the teachers construe as unnecessary "busywork." The teachers perceive that the principal is hindering rather than facilitating their work.	−	+
3. *Esprit* refers to morale. The teachers feel that their social needs are being satisfied, and that they are, at the same time, enjoying a sense of accomplishment in their job.	++	− −
4. *Intimacy* refers to the teachers' enjoyment of friendly social relations with each other. This dimension describes a social-needs satisfaction which is not necessarily associated with task-accomplishment.	+	+
Principal's Behavior		
5. *Aloofness* refers to behavior by the principal which is characterized as formal and impersonal. He "goes by the book" and prefers to be guided by rules and policies rather than to deal with the teachers in an informal, face-to-face situation. His behavior, in brief, is universalistic rather than particularistic; nomothetic rather than idiosyncratic. To maintain this style, he keeps himself—at least, "emotionally"—at a distance from his staff.	−	+

[4]Andrew Halpin, *Theory and Research in Administration*, p. 131.

TABLE 6-1.   THE EIGHT DIMENSIONS OF ORGANIZATIONAL CLIMATE
(Continued)

	Intensity scale	
	Open	Closed
6. *Production Emphasis* refers to behavior by the principal which is characterized by close supervision of the staff. He is highly directive and plays the role of a "straw boss." His communication tends to go in only one direction, and he is not sensitive to feedback from the staff.	−	+
7. *Thrust* refers to behavior by the principal which is characterized by his evident effort in trying to "move the organization." Thrust behavior is marked not by close supervision, but by the principal's attempt to motivate the teachers through the example which he personally sets. Apparently, because he does not ask the teachers to give of themselves any more than he willingly gives of himself, his behavior, though starkly task-oriented, is nonetheless viewed favorably by the teachers.	+ +	−
8. *Consideration* refers to behavior by the principal which is characterized by an inclination to treat the teachers "humanly," to try to do a little something extra for them in human terms.	+	−

* Emile Durkheim, *Le Suicide*, Libraire Felix Alcan, Paris, 1930, p. 277. *Anomie* describes a planlessness in living, a method of living which defeats itself because achievement has no longer any criterion of value; happiness always lies beyond any present achievement. Defeat takes the form of ultimate disillusion—a disgust with the futility of endless pursuit.
+ + Very high emphasis
  + High
  − Low
− − Very low

From Andrew Halpin, *Theory and Research in Administration*, Macmillan, New York, 1967, pp. 150–151. The intensity scale is our addition to the original Halpin table.

Each of the eight dimensions of climate is represented in the instrument as a subtest.[5] Various combinations of emphasis on each of the subtests, as perceived by the teachers responding to the instrument, reveal for the school a climate similarity score which determines the relative position of the school on the open-to-closed continuum. The school with an open climate, for example, is characterized by low disengagement, low hindrance, very high esprit, high intimacy, low aloofness, low production emphasis, very high thrust, and high consideration. The closed school exhibits very high disengagement, high hindrance, very low esprit, high intimacy, high aloofness, high production emphasis, low thrust, and low consideration. Open and closed school climates are described by Halpin as follows:

The Open Climate depicts a situation in which the members enjoy ex-

[5]*Ibid.*, p. 150. The dimension which seems to have the strongest relationship to open climate is esprit.

tremely high *Esprit*. The teachers work well together without bickering and griping (low disengagement). They are not burdened by mountains of busywork or by routine reports; the principal's policies facilitate the teachers' accomplishment of their tasks (low Hindrance). On the whole, the group members enjoy friendly relations with each other, but they apparently feel no need for an extremely high degree of Intimacy. The teachers obtain considerable job satisfaction, and are sufficiently motivated to overcome difficulties and frustration. They possess the incentive to work things out and to keep the organization "moving." Furthermore, the teachers are proud to be associated with their school.[6]

The Closed Climate marks a situation in which the group members obtain little satisfaction in respect to either task-achievement or social-needs. In short, the principal is ineffective in directing the activities of the teachers; at the same time, he is not inclined to look out for their personal welfare. This climate is the most closed and the least genuine climate that we have identified.[7]

It seems obvious to us that the work of the school needs to be accomplished within the framework of open climates. Attention to climate is particularly crucial, as we have argued earlier, in that the classroom door does not provide a sufficient buffer of immunity to protect the classroom from the prevailing school climate. Closed climates organizationally breed closed learning climates, while open climates organizationally breed open learning climates. A significant direction for leadership-supervisory behavior is toward the development and maintenance of a climate most conducive to dynamic instructional leadership.

ORGANIZATIONAL HEALTH: A SUPERVISORY GOAL

A similar but broader approach to understanding the prevailing flavor, attitude, sentiment, and orientation of a given school is that which Miles proposes as the concept of organizational health. Miles describes the healthy school as one which exhibits reasonably clear and reasonably accepted goals (goal focus), relatively distortion-free communication vertically, horizontally, and across boundary lines (communication adequacy), equitable distribution of influence to all levels of the organization (optimal power equalization), and effective and efficient use of inputs both human and material (resource utilization). The healthy school likewise reflects mutually satisfying vectors of influence between the inhabitants and the school (cohesiveness), a feel-

---

[6]Halpin, *Theory and Research in Administration*, pp. 174–175.
[7]*Ibid.*, p. 180. We should caution at this time that the OCDQ was developed for use with elementary schools. While some controversy seems to exist over whether the instrument can be used in other school settings, the instrument tends not to be valid for large secondary schools and perhaps (in our opinion) even for large elementary schools. As schools increase in size and/or complexity, the referent-point principal needs to be changed to someone closer to the teachers. See J. Foster Watkins, "The OCDQ —an Application and Some Implications," *Educational Administration Quarterly*, vol. 4, Spring, 1968, pp. 46–60. Also, Fred D. Carver and T. Sergiovanni, "Some Notes on the OCDQ," *Journal of Educational Administration*, vol. 7, no. 1, May, 1969.

ing of well-being among the staff (morale), self-renewing properties (innovativeness), and an active response to its environment (autonomy and adaptation). Finally, the healthy school maintains and strengthens its problem-solving capabilities (problem-solving adequacies).

Each of the ten dimensions of health is described in detail below. They should be examined carefully, for we believe they form a major share of the content which composes the process of supervision. From Miles, they are:

1. *Goal focus.* In a healthy organization, the goal (or more usually goals) of the system would be reasonably clear to the system members, and reasonably well accepted by them. This clarity and acceptance, however, should be seen as a necessary but insufficient condition for organization health. The goals must also be *achievable* with existing or available resources, and be *appropriate*—more or less congruent with the demands of the environment.

2. *Communication adequacy.* Since organizations are not simultaneous face-to-face systems like small groups, the movement of information within them becomes crucial. This dimension of organization health implies that there is relatively distortion-free communication "vertically," "horizontally," and across the boundary of the system to and from the surrounding environment. That is, information travels reasonably well—just as the healthy person "knows himself" with a minimum level of repression, distortion, etc. In the healthy organization, there is good and prompt sensing of internal strains; there are enough data about problems of the system to insure that a good diagnosis of system difficulties can be made. People have the information they need, and have gotten it without exerting undue efforts, such as those involved in moseying up to the superintendent's secretary, reading the local newspaper, or calling excessive numbers of special meetings.

3. *Optimal power equalization.* In a healthy organization the distribution of influence is relatively equitable. Subordinates (if there is a formal authority chart) can influence upward, and even more important—as Likert has demonstrated—they perceive that their boss can do likewise with his *boss*. In such an organization, intergroup struggles for power would not be bitter, though intergroup conflict, (as in every human system known to man) would undoubtedly be present. The basic stance of persons in such an organization, as they look up, sideways and down, is that of collaboration rather than explicit or implicit coercion.

4. *Resource utilization.* We say of a healthy person, such as a second-grader, that he is "working up to his potential." To put this another way, the classroom system is evoking a contribution from him at an appropriate and goal-directed level of tension. At the organization level, "health" would imply that the system's inputs, particularly the personnel, are used effectively. The overall coordination is such that people are neither overloaded nor idling. There is a minimal sense of strain, generally speaking (in the sense that trying to do something with a weak or inappropriate structure puts strain on that structure). In the healthy organization, people may be working very hard indeed, but they feel that they are not working against themselves, or against the organization. The fit between people's own dis-

positions and the role demands of the system is good. Beyond this, people feel reasonably "self-actualized"; they not only "feel good" in their jobs, but they have a genuine sense of learning, growing, and developing as persons in the process of making their organizational contribution.

5. *Cohesiveness.* We think of a healthy person as one who has a clear sense of identity; he knows who he is, underneath all the specific goals he sets for himself. Beyond this, he *likes himself;* his stance toward life does not require self-derogation, even when there are aspects of his behavior which are unlovely or ineffective. By analogy at the organization level, system health would imply that the organization knows "who it is." Its members feel attracted to membership in the organization. They want to stay with it, be influenced by it, and exert their own influence in the collaborative style suggested above.

6. *Morale.* The implied notion is one of well-being or satisfaction. Satisfaction is not enough for health, of course; a person may report feelings of well-being and satisfaction in his life, while successfully denying deep-lying hostilities, anxieties, and conflicts. Yet it still seems useful to evoke, at the organization level, the idea of morale: a summated set of individual sentiments, centering around feelings of well-being, satisfaction, and pleasure, as opposed to feelings of discomfort, unwished-for strain, and dissatisfaction.

7. *Innovativeness.* A healthy system would tend to invent new procedures, move toward new goals, produce new kinds of products, diversify itself, and become more rather than less differentiated over time. In a sense, such a system could be said to grow, develop, and change, rather than remaining routinized and standard.

8. *Autonomy.* The healthy person acts "from his own center outward." Seen in a training or therapy group, for example, such a person appears nearly free of the need to submit dependently to authority figures, *and* from the need to rebel and destroy symbolic fathers of any kind. A healthy organization, similarly, would not respond passively to demands from the outside, feeling itself the tool of the environment, and it would not respond destructively or rebelliously to perceived demands either. It would tend to have a kind of independence from the environment, in the same sense that the healthy person, while he has transactions with others, does not treat their responses as *determinative* of his own behavior.

9. *Adaptation.* The notions of autonomy and innovativeness are both connected with the idea that a healthy person, group, or organization is in realistic, effective contact with the surroundings. When environmental demands and organization resources do not match, a problem-solving, restructuring approach evolves in which *both* the environment and the organization become different in some respect. More adequate, continued coping of the organization, as a result of changes in the local system, the relevant portions of the environment, or more usually both, occurs. And such a system has sufficient stability and stress tolerance to manage the difficulties which occur during the adaptation process.

10. *Problem-solving adequacy.* Finally, any healthy organism—even one as theoretically impervious to fallibility as a computer—*always* has problems, strains, difficulties, and instances of ineffective coping. The issue is not the presence or absence of problems, therefore, but the *manner* in which the

person, group, or organization copes with problems. Argyris has suggested that in an effective system, problems are solved with minimal energy; they stay solved; and the problem-solving mechanisms used are not weakened, but maintained or strengthened. An adequate organization, then, has well-developed structures and procedures for sensing the existence of problems, for inventing possible solutions, for deciding on the solutions, for implementing them, and for evaluating their effectiveness.[8]

Each of the dimensions of organizational health for any school operates in a system of dynamic interaction characterized by a high degree of interdependence. Clear goal focus, for example, depends upon the extent to which the school communicates its goals and permits inhabitants to modify and rearrange them. At another level, a high degree of organizational health encourages school adaptiveness, while school adaptiveness contributes to and is essential to organizational health.

THE SUPERVISOR'S WORK

What does the supervisor do? To respond simply that he is responsible for instructional leadership begs the issue. Instructional leadership, if it is to be at all significant, depends upon optimal presence of each of the ten dimensions of organizational health, that is, upon an open school climate. As instructional leaders, enlightened supervisors exert major efforts toward health and climate goals for schools because they recognize that instructional leadership efforts in less than healthy and open school environments stand little chance of succeeding.

The synthesizing theory requires that supervisors assess the effects of the initiating variables (those discussed here as well as in Chapters 3, 4, and 5) on those mediating variables which compose the school's human organization. School effectiveness depends upon appropriate responses from the human organization. In Chapter 7 we begin to intensify our focus on the human organization. We do this by examining four management systems. While our analysis does not purely isolate the mediating variables for analysis, we see within each management system human reaction to alternative organizational styles, authority systems, management assumptions, and supervisory behavior.

SELECTED REFERENCES

Halpin, Andrew: *Theory and Research in Administration,* Macmillan, New York, 1967.

Miles, Matthew: "Planned Change and Organizational Health: Figure and Ground," *Change Processes in the Public Schools.* The University of Oregon, Center for the Advanced Study of Educational Administration, Eugene, Ore., 1965.

[8]Matthew Miles, *op. cit.,* pp. 18–21.

Chapter Seven
SYSTEM 4—
AN INTEGRATED APPROACH
TO SCHOOL SUPERVISION

We depart somewhat from the synthesizing theory to present a parallel approach to school supervision. This approach summarizes the intervening variables we discussed in Chapters 3, 4, and 5 and relates them to the mediating variables which compose the human organization. We deal more specifically with the school's human organization in Chapter 8. This chapter is adapted entirely from an integrated approach to supervision developed at the Institute for Social Research, University of Michigan. While the original model was not developed with schools in mind, the potency of ideas and the strong conceptual basis for the model permit its wide application to a number of settings, including schools.

In 1961 *New Patterns of Management*,[1] by Rensis Likert, appeared as part of the general literature in supervision. The book made a significant and widespread impact in noneducational settings, and a small but nevertheless significant inroad was made in the literature and in the practice of educational supervision. The significance of this book to educational supervision is that it offered for the first time an integrated research-based system of supervision applicable to schools. This system is based on the development of highly effective work groups who are committed to the goals of the school and who work toward this end as a means to professional growth and development and personal self-fulfillment. These groups are linked together in an overlapping pattern which permits them to function, on the one hand, as relatively small and cohesive primary groups and, on the other hand, as dynamic contributors to and influencers of the total school enterprise.

A highly effective school work group is described as one which: (1)

[1]Rensis Likert, *New Patterns of Management*, McGraw-Hill, New York, 1961. Rensis Likert is Director, Institute for Social Research at the University of Michigan. The institute is composed of three centers, the Survey Research Center, the Research Center for Group Dynamics, and the Center for Research on the Utilization of Scientific Knowledge. In the early chapters of *New Patterns of Management*, Professor Likert summarizes, synthesizes, and articulates hundreds of studies performed through the institute which have relevance to supervision. In the remaining chapters, Likert uses this mass of findings to evolve and support a theory of supervision based on three fundamental principles: (1) the principle of supportive relationships, (2) the principle of group decision making and group supervision, and (3) the principle of high performance goals for individuals, groups, and the organization.

members perceive as supportive and which builds and maintains their sense of personal worth, (2) has high performance goals which are consistent with those of the school and/or the profession, (3) uses group decision making, and (4) is linked to other school groups through multiple and overlapping group structures.

THE HUMAN ORGANIZATION

The year 1967 witnessed the appearance of another Likert book, *The Human Organization, Its Management and Value*,[2] which further describes, extends, supports, and integrates the initial supervisory theory. As Likert develops the initial theory, he identifies and classifies organizational variables into three types: causal, intervening, and end-result, as follows:

The "causal" variables are independent variables which determine the course of developments within an organization and the results achieved by the organization. These causal variables include only those independent variables which can be altered or changed by the organization.

The "intervening" variables reflect the internal state and health of the organization, e.g., the loyalties, attitudes, motivations, performance goals, and perceptions of all members and their collective capacity for effective interaction, communication, and decision making.

The "end-result" variables are the dependent variables which reflect the achievements of the organization, such as its productivity, costs, scrap loss, and earnings.[3]

This classification of variables resembles the framework for the synthesizing theory presented in Chapter 2. We referred to the three classes as initiating variables, mediating variables, and school-success variables.

All the variables which compose the Likert theory are presented in the profile of organizational characteristics which appears as Table 7-1. Next to each variable is an intensity index which indicates the nature of the variable and the amount of the variable present in a given organization. It would be helpful if the reader would take a moment to respond to the profile presented in Table 7-1 in accordance with Likert's directions.

Please think of the *most* productive (effective) department, division, or organization you have known well. Then place the letter *h* on the line under each organizational variable in the following table to show where this organization would fall. Treat each item as a continuous variable from the left extreme of System 1 to the right extreme of System 4.[4]

---

[2]Rensis Likert, *The Human Organization: Its Management and Value*, McGraw-Hill, New York, 1967.
[3]*Ibid.*, p. 29.
[4]*Ibid.*, p. 3. Numerous other uses of the form are apparent. Ideal management system can be compared with real management system. Superordinates' perceptions of *ideal* or *real* can be compared with subordinates' perceptions of *ideal* or *real*, and so on.

The reader may also wish to respond to the form a second time placing an *l* at the point which describes the least effective educational unit or school organization for each of the organizational variables.[5]

Respondents generally perceive high-performing departments, units, and organizations as being toward the right end of the table on each of the organizational variables, with low-performing units toward the left. Likert reports research which supports these perceptions and notes that as organizations move toward system 4, they are more productive, are characterized by high-performing work groups, have lower costs, have more favorable attitudes, and display improved labor-management relationships, with system 4 organizations achieving excellent records on each of these dimensions. The converse seems to be true for organizations displaying management systems well toward system 1.[6] We would, of course, expect similar responses from educators and similar findings in educational organizations.

SHIFTING MANAGEMENT SYSTEMS

The management systems described in Table 7-1 are composed of individual characteristics and tendencies, each dependent upon the appearance of others of similar kind and intensity. As a result of this interdependence among the organizational variable types, it is not likely that a given school can be described as possessing some characteristics of system 1, others of system 2, and still others of system 4. Typically, a pattern of response to Table 7-1 would emerge for a given school which would clearly type the school into one or another system category. In explaining this phenomenon Likert observes:

> The communications processes of System 1 are compatible with all other aspects of System 1 but are not compatible with any aspect of System 3 or System 4. The same is true of the decision-making processes and the compensation plans. *The Management system of an organization must have compatible component parts if it is to function effectively.*[7]

It is not likely that enduring changes can be made, for example, in the commitment level of teachers in terms of school goals without substantial changes in supervisory assumptions. As one alters his supervisory assumptions, he should expect to see this reflected in each of the mediating varia-

[5]Table 7-1 is a reproduction of Appendix II of Rensis Likert's *The Human Organization, Its Management and Value,* pp. 197–211. It appears here with only minor modifications in format. Appendix II is a combination of Tables 3-1 and 7-1 of the same book. We are grateful to Professor Likert and to McGraw-Hill Book Company for permitting us to reproduce material which is so fundamental to their book. Table 7-1, of course, may not be reproduced in any way without permission from the publisher.

[6]*Ibid.;* see, for example, pages 13–46.

[7]*Ibid.,* p. 123.

TABLE 7-1. PROFILE OF ORGANIZATIONAL CHARACTERISTICS

Organizational variable	System 1	System 2	System 3	System 4	Item no.
1. Leadership processes used					
a. Extent to which superiors have confidence and trust in *subordinates*	Have no confidence and trust in subordinates	Have condescending confidence and trust, such as master has in servant	Substantial but not complete confidence and trust; still wishes to keep control of decisions	Complete confidence and trust in all matters	1
b. Extent to which subordinates, in turn, have confidence and trust in *superiors*	Have no confidence and trust in superiors	Have subservient confidence and trust, such as servant has in master	Substantial but not complete confidence and trust	Complete confidence and trust	2
c. Extent to which superiors display supportive behavior toward others	Display no supportive behavior or virtually none	Display supportive behavior in condescending manner and situations only	Display supportive behavior quite generally	Display supportive behavior fully and in all situations	3
d. Extent to which superiors behave so that subordinates feel free to discuss important things about their jobs with their immediate superior	Subordinates do not feel at all free to discuss things about the job with their superior	Subordinates do not feel very free to discuss things about the job with their superior	Subordinates feel rather free to discuss things about the job with their superior	Subordinates feel completely free to discuss things about the job with their superior	4

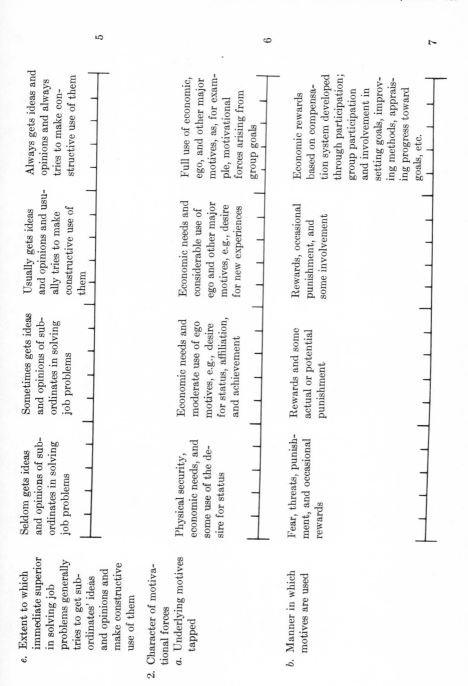

e. Extent to which immediate superior in solving job problems generally tries to get subordinates' ideas and opinions and make constructive use of them	Seldom gets ideas and opinions of subordinates in solving job problems	Sometimes gets ideas and opinions of subordinates in solving job problems	Usually gets ideas and opinions and usually tries to make constructive use of them	Always gets ideas and opinions and always tries to make constructive use of them
2. Character of motivational forces				
a. Underlying motives tapped	Physical security, economic needs, and some use of the desire for status	Economic needs and moderate use of ego motives, e.g., desire for status, affiliation, and achievement	Economic needs and considerable use of ego and other major motives, e.g, desire for new experiences	Full use of economic, ego, and other major motives, as, for example, motivational forces arising from group goals
b. Manner in which motives are used	Fear, threats, punishment, and occasional rewards	Rewards and some actual or potential punishment	Rewards, occasional punishment, and some involvement	Economic rewards based on compensation system developed through participation; group participation and involvement in setting goals, improving methods, appraising progress toward goals, etc.

TABLE 7-1. *PROFILE OF ORGANIZATIONAL CHARACTERISTICS (Continued)*

Organizational variable	System 1	System 2	System 3	System 4	Item no.
c. Kinds of attitudes developed toward organization and its goals	Attitudes usually are hostile and counter to organization's goals	Attitudes are sometimes hostile and counter to organization's goals and are sometimes favorable to the organization's goals and support the behavior necessary to achieve them	Attitudes usually are favorable and support behavior implementing organization's goals	Attitudes are strongly favorable and provide powerful stimulation to behavior implementing organization's goals	8
d. Extent to which motivational forces conflict with or reinforce one another	Marked conflict of forces substantially reducing those motivational forces leading to behavior in support of the organization's goals	Conflict often exists; occasionally forces will reinforce each other, at least partially	Some conflict, but often motivational forces will reinforce each other	Motivational forces generally reinforce each other in a substantial and cumulative manner	9
e. Amount of responsibility felt by each member of organization for achieving organization's goals	High levels of management feel responsibility; lower levels feel less; rank and file feel little and often welcome opportunity to behave in ways to defeat organization's goals	Managerial personnel usually feel responsibility; rank and file usually feel relatively little responsibility for achieving organization's goals	Substantial proportion of personnel, especially at higher levels, feel responsibility and generally behave in ways to achieve the organization's goals	Personnel at all levels feel real responsibility for organization's goals and behave in ways to implement them	10

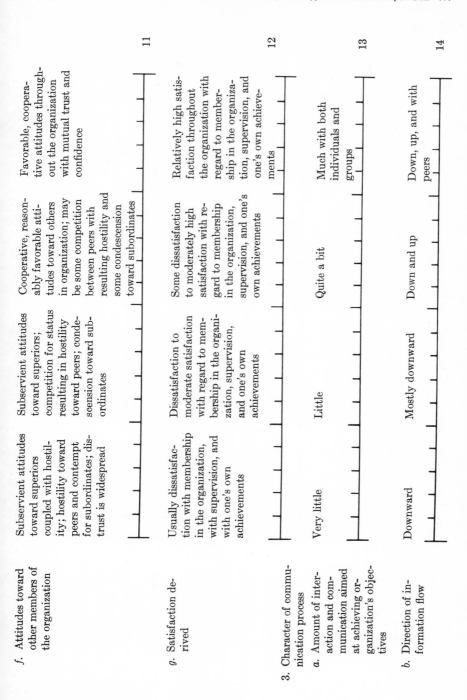

	System 1	System 2	System 3	System 4	
f. Attitudes toward other members of the organization	Subservient attitudes toward superiors coupled with hostility toward peers and contempt for subordinates; distrust is widespread	Subservient attitudes toward superiors; competition for status resulting in hostility toward peers; condescension toward subordinates	Cooperative, reasonably favorable attitudes toward others in organization; may be some competition between peers with resulting hostility and some condescension toward subordinates	Favorable, cooperative attitudes throughout the organization with mutual trust and confidence	11
g. Satisfaction derived	Usually dissatisfaction with membership in the organization, with supervision, and with one's own achievements	Dissatisfaction to moderate satisfaction with regard to membership in the organization, supervision, and one's own achievements	Some dissatisfaction to moderately high satisfaction with regard to membership in the organization, supervision, and one's own achievements	Relatively high satisfaction throughout the organization with regard to membership in the organization, supervision, and one's own achievements	12
3. Character of communication process					
a. Amount of interaction and communication aimed at achieving organization's objectives	Very little	Little	Quite a bit	Much with both individuals and groups	13
b. Direction of information flow	Downward	Mostly downward	Down and up	Down, up, and with peers	14

TABLE 7-1. PROFILE OF ORGANIZATIONAL CHARACTERISTICS (Continued)

Organizational variable	System 1	System 2	System 3	System 4	Item no.
c. Downward communication					
(1) Where initiated	At top of organization or to implement top directive	Primarily at top or patterned on communication from top	Patterned on communication from top but with some initiative at lower levels	Initiated at all levels	15
(2) Extent to which superiors willingly share information with subordinates	Provide minimum of information	Give subordinates only information superior feels they need	Give information needed and answers most questions	Seek to give subordinates all relevant information and all information they want	16
(3) Extent to which communications are accepted by subordinates	Viewed with great suspicion	Some accepted and some viewed with suspicion	Often accepted but, if not, may or may not be openly questioned	Generally accepted, but if not, openly and candidly questioned	17
d. Upward communication					
(1) Adequacy of upward communication via line organization	Very little	Limited	Some	A great deal	18

	System 1	System 2	System 3	System 4	
(2) ... feeling of responsibility for initiating accurate upward communication	...ally communicates "filtered" information and only when requested; may "yes" the boss	...gree of responsibility to initiate accurate upward communication		...sibility felt and much initiative; group communicates all relevant information	19
(3) Forces leading to accurate or distorted upward information	Powerful forces to distort information and deceive superiors	Many forces to distort; also forces for honest communication	Occasional forces to distort along with many forces to communicate accurately	Virtually no forces to distort and powerful forces to communicate accurately	20
(4) Accuracy of upward communication via line	Tends to be inaccurate	Information that boss wants to hear flows; other information is restricted and filtered	Information that boss wants to hear flows; other information may be limited or cautiously given	Accurate	21
(5) Need for supplementary upward communication system	Great need to supplement upward communication by spy system, suggestion system, and similar devices	Upward communication often supplemented by suggestion system and similar devices	Slight need for supplementary system; suggestion systems may be used	No need for any supplementary system	22
e. Sideward communication, its adequacy and accuracy	Usually poor because of competition between peers, corresponding hostility	Fairly poor because of competition between peers	Fair to good	Good to excellent	23

TABLE 7-1. *PROFILE OF ORGANIZATIONAL CHARACTERISTICS (Continued)*

Organizational variable	System 1	System 2	System 3	System 4	Item no.
f. Psychological closeness of superiors to subordinates (i.e., friendliness between superiors and subordinates)	Far apart	Can be moderately close if proper roles are kept	Fairly close	Usually very close	24
(1) How well does superior know and understand problems faced by subordinates	Has no knowledge or understanding of problems of subordinates	Has some knowledge and understanding of problems of subordinates	Knows and understands problems of subordinates quite well	Knows and understands problems of subordinates very well	25
(2) How accurate are the perceptions by superiors and subordinates of each other?	Often in error	Often in error on some points	Moderately accurate	Usually quite accurate	26
4. Character of interaction-influence process					
a. Amount and character of interaction	Little interaction and always with fear and distrust	Little interaction and usually with some condescension by superiors; fear and caution by subordinates	Moderate interaction, often with fair amount of confidence and trust	Extensive, friendly interaction with high degree of confidence and trust	

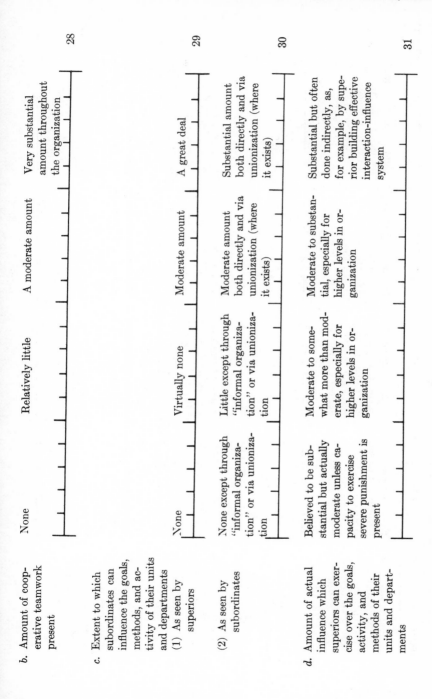

	None	Relatively little	A moderate amount	Very substantial amount throughout the organization	
b. Amount of cooperative teamwork present					28
c. Extent to which subordinates can influence the goals, methods, and activity of their units and departments	None	Virtually none	Moderate amount	A great deal	
(1) As seen by superiors					29
(2) As seen by subordinates	None except through "informal organization" or via unionization	Little except through "informal organization" or via unionization	Moderate amount both directly and via unionization (where it exists)	Substantial amount both directly and via unionization (where it exists)	30
d. Amount of actual influence which superiors can exercise over the goals, activity, and methods of their units and departments	Believed to be substantial but actually moderate unless capacity to exercise severe punishment is present	Moderate to somewhat more than moderate, especially for higher levels in organization	Moderate to substantial, especially for higher levels in organization	Substantial but often done indirectly, as, for example, by superior building effective interaction-influence system	31

TABLE 7-1. *PROFILE OF ORGANIZATIONAL CHARACTERISTICS (Continued)*

Organizational variable	System 1	System 2	System 3	System 4	Item no.
e. Extent to which an effective structure exists enabling one part of organization to exert influence upon other parts	Effective structure virtually not present	Limited capacity exists; influence exerted largely via vertical lines and primarily downward	Moderately effective structure exists; influence exerted largely through vertical lines	Highly effective structure exists enabling exercise of influence in all directions	32
5. Character of decision-making process					
a. At what level in organization are decisions formally made?	Bulk of decisions at top of organization	Policy at top, many decisions within prescribed framework made at lower levels but usually checked with top before action	Broad policy decisions at top, more specific decisions at lower levels	Decision making widely done throughout organization, although well integrated through linking process provided by overlapping groups	33
b. How adequate and accurate is the information available for decision making at *the place where the decisions are made?*	Information is generally inadequate and inaccurate	Information is often somewhat inadequate and inaccurate	Reasonably adequate and accurate information available	Relatively complete and accurate information available based both on measurements and efficient flow of information in organization	34

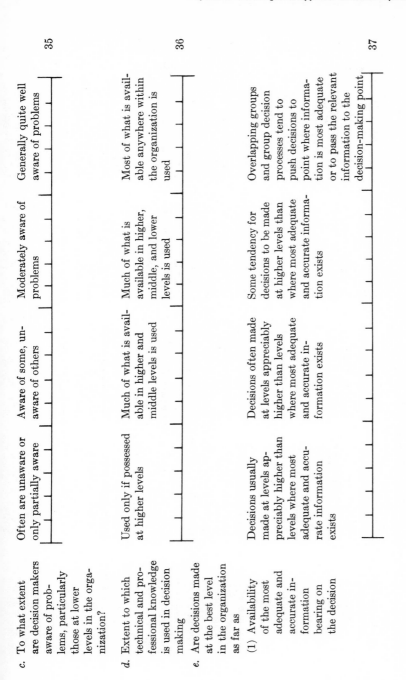

	Often are unaware or only partially aware	Aware of some, unaware of others	Moderately aware of problems	Generally quite well aware of problems	
c. To what extent are decision makers aware of problems, particularly those at lower levels in the organization?					35
d. Extent to which technical and professional knowledge is used in decision making	Used only if possessed at higher levels	Much of what is available in higher and middle levels is used	Much of what is available in higher, middle, and lower levels is used	Most of what is available anywhere within the organization is used	36
e. Are decisions made at the best level in the organization as far as (1) Availability of the most adequate and accurate information bearing on the decision	Decisions usually made at levels appreciably higher than levels where most adequate and accurate information exists	Decisions often made at levels appreciably higher than levels where most adequate and accurate information exists	Some tendency for decisions to be made at higher levels than where most adequate and accurate information exists	Overlapping groups and group decision processes tend to push decisions to point where information is most adequate or to pass the relevant information to the decision-making point	37

TABLE 7-1. PROFILE OF ORGANIZATIONAL CHARACTERISTICS (Continued)

Organizational variable	System 1	System 2	System 3	System 4	Item no.
(2) The motivational consequences (i.e., does the decision-making process help to create the necessary motivations in those persons who have to carry out the decision?)	Decision making contributes little or nothing to the motivation to implement the decision, usually yields adverse motivation	Decision making contributes relatively little motivation	Some contribution by decision making to motivation to implement	Substantial contribution by decision-making processes to motivation to implement	38
f. To what extent are subordinates involved in decisions related to their work?	Not at all	Never involved in decisions; occasionally consulted	Usually are consulted but ordinarily not involved in the decision making	Are involved fully in all decisions related to their work	39
g. Is decision making based on man-to-man or group pattern of operation? Does it encourage or discourage teamwork?	Man-to-man only, discourages teamwork	Man-to-man almost entirely, discourages teamwork	Both man-to-man and group, partially encourages teamwork	Largely based on group pattern, encourages teamwork	40

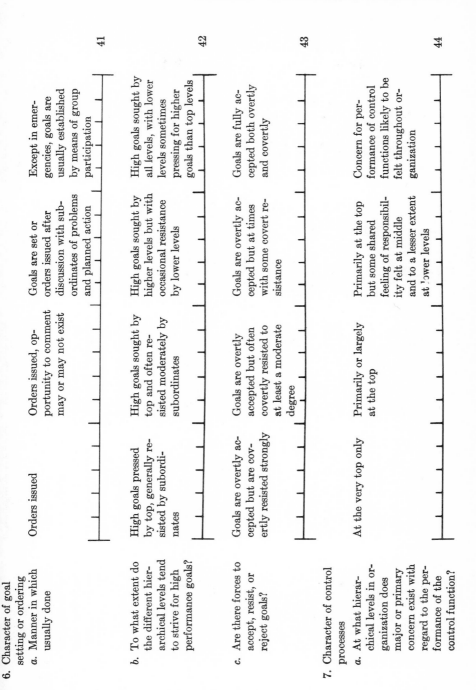

	System 1	System 2	System 3	System 4
6. Character of goal setting or ordering *a.* Manner in which usually done	Orders issued	Orders issued, opportunity to comment may or may not exist	Goals are set or orders issued after discussion with subordinates of problems and planned action	Except in emergencies, goals are usually established by means of group participation
b. To what extent do the different hierarchical levels tend to strive for high performance goals?	High goals pressed by top, generally resisted by subordinates	High goals sought by top and often resisted moderately by subordinates	High goals sought by higher levels but with occasional resistance by lower levels	High goals sought by all levels, with lower levels sometimes pressing for higher goals than top levels
c. Are there forces to accept, resist, or reject goals?	Goals are overtly accepted but are covertly resisted strongly	Goals are overtly accepted but often covertly resisted to at least a moderate degree	Goals are overtly accepted but at times with some covert resistance	Goals are fully accepted both overtly and covertly
7. Character of control processes *a.* At what hierarchical levels in organization does major or primary concern exist with regard to the performance of the control function?	At the very top only	Primarily or largely at the top	Primarily at the top but some shared feeling of responsibility felt at middle and to a lesser extent at lower levels	Concern for performance of control functions likely to be felt throughout organization

41   42   43   44

TABLE 7-1. PROFILE OF ORGANIZATIONAL CHARACTERISTICS (Continued)

Organizational variable	System 1	System 2	System 3	System 4	Item no.
b. How accurate are the measurements and information used to guide and perform the control function, and to what extent do forces exist in the organization to distort and falsify this information?	Very strong forces exist to distort and falsify; as a consequence, measurements and information are usually incomplete and often inaccurate	Fairly strong forces exist to distort and falsify; hence measurements and information are often incomplete and inaccurate	Some pressure to protect self and colleagues and hence some pressures to distort; information is only moderately complete and contains some inaccuracies	Strong pressures to obtain complete and accurate information to guide own behavior and behavior of own and related work groups; hence information and measurements tend to be complete and accurate	45
c. Extent to which the review and control functions are concentrated	Highly concentrated in top management	Relatively highly concentrated, with some delegated control to middle and lower levels	Moderate downward delegation of review and control processes; lower as well as higher levels perform these tasks	Review and control down at all levels with lower units at times imposing more vigorous reviews and tighter controls than top management	46
d. Extent to which there is an informal organization present and supporting or opposing goals of formal organization	Informal organization present and opposing goals of formal organization	Informal organization usually present and partially resisting goals	Informal organization may be present and may either support or partially resist goals of formal organization	Informal and formal organization are one and the same; hence all social forces support efforts to achieve organization's goals	47

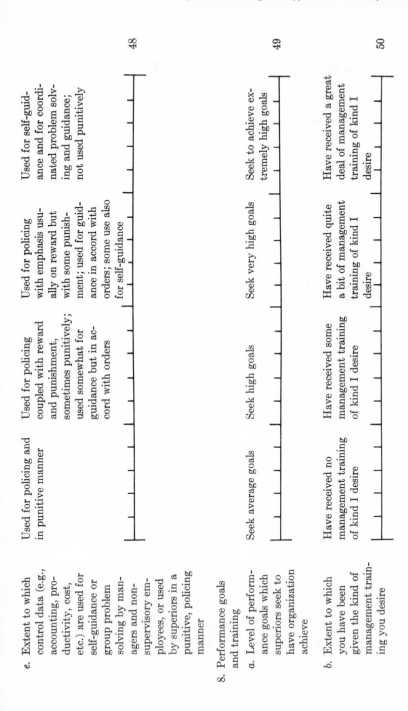

e. Extent to which control data (e.g., accounting, productivity, cost, etc.) are used for self-guidance or group problem solving by managers and non-supervisory employees, or used by superiors in a punitive, policing manner

48

| Used for policing and in punitive manner | Used for policing coupled with reward and punishment, sometimes used punitively; used somewhat for guidance but in accord with orders | Used for policing with emphasis usually on reward but with some punishment; used for guidance in accord with orders; some use also for self-guidance | Used for self-guidance and for coordinated problem solving and guidance; not used punitively |

8. Performance goals and training

a. Level of performance goals which superiors seek to have organization achieve

49

| Seek average goals | Seek high goals | Seek very high goals | Seek to achieve extremely high goals |

b. Extent to which you have been given the kind of management training you desire

50

| Have received no management training of kind I desire | Have received some management training of kind I desire | Have received quite a bit of management training of kind I desire | Have received a great deal of management training of kind I desire |

TABLE 7-1. PROFILE OF ORGANIZATIONAL CHARACTERISTICS (Continued)

Organizational variable	System 1	System 2	System 3	System 4	Item no.
c. Adequacy of training resources provided to assist you in training your subordinates	Training resources provided are only fairly good	Training resources provided are good	Training resources provided are very good	Training resources provided are excellent	51

The table above can be used for other purposes by appropriate modifications in the instructions:

Form S Instructions:

On the line below each organizational variable (item), please indicate the kind of organization you are trying to create by the management you are providing. Treat each item as a continuous variable from the extreme at one end to that at the other. Place a check mark on each line to show the kind of management you are using and the kind of organization you are creating.

Form D Instructions:

On the line below each organizational variable (item), please indicate by a check mark where you would *like* to have your organization fall with regard to that item. Treat each item as a continuous variable from the extreme at one end to that at the other.

NOTE: When the Profile of Organizational Characteristics is used as a survey instrument, responses to certain items selected at random are reversed.

From Rensis Likert, *The Human Organization: Its Management and Value.* Copyright © 1967 by McGraw-Hill, Inc. Used with permission of McGraw-Hill Book Company. No further reproduction or distribution authorized without permission of McGraw-Hill.

bles (Likert's intervening variables), including commitment levels of teachers. As a further illustration, it is not likely that supervisory efforts to improve the problem-solving capabilities of staff will have much payoff if each of the other variables which compose this system (which are interdependent with problem-solving capabilities) is ignored. The hard facts of the matter suggest that a system 2 supervisor who wishes to adopt one dimension of system 4 will not have success without adopting each of the other dimensions. By the same token, a supervisor who tries to adopt all of the system 4 dimensions with the exception of one or two (for example, he still lacks confidence and trust in subordinates—a system 1 characteristic) will experience failure.[8]

Systems 1 and 2

System 1 is referred to as exploitive-authoritarian and system 2 as benevolent-authoritarian. While differences between the two exist, they are close enough to be described together. Supervisors (principals, teachers, and others) who adopt system 1 or system 2 perspectives[9] rely on high-control methods, hierarchical pressures and authority, theory X assumption in regard to subordinates, domination, regulation, and distortion of communication channels, and programmed, delimited, and centralized decision making as they work to achieve school goals.

Systems 1 and 2 supervisors can expect from subordinates (administrators, teachers, students, and others) less group loyalty, lower performance goals, less cooperation, more conflict, less teamwork and mutual assistance among peers, more feeling of unreasonable pressure, less favorable attitudes toward supervisors and the school, and lower motivational potential for performance.[10] This response from the human organization of the school takes its toll in poor performance on each of the school-success variables.

Systems 3 and 4

System 3 is described as consultive while system 4 is labeled participative. System 3 is somewhat descriptive of supervisory practice which characterizes schools well on their way toward developing professional organization. It is a

[8]This failure will tend to reinforce his belief that you cannot trust people anyway, and that system 1 is better after all. He will have evidence to support this contention in that he did give system 4 a try, but it just does not work.

[9]We do not portray educators of this configuration as bad guys because often they are well-intending and have high performance expectations for themselves, the school, and its inhabitants. Some do, indeed, adopt systems 1 and 2 as a result of their own inadequacies. These systems permit supervisors to behave defensively and ensure that they will remain immune from a relatively hostile interpersonal world. See Jack Gibb, "Dynamics of Leadership," American Association for Higher Education, *In Search of Leaders,* National Education Association, Washington, D.C., 1967.

[10]Likert, *The Human Organization: Its Management and Value,* p. 76.

transitional management system which is often characterized as being better than "before" but still clings to many of the features of "before." While system 3 fails in attempting to maximize the achievement of school goals, student actualization, and teacher self-fulfillment, it at least performs satisfactorily in each of these pursuits while maintaining dimensions and features which are organizationally and administratively familiar.

While one can settle for a satisfactory automobile or other material product, educational institutions are by default committed to maximizing relationships. System 4 has the potential to maximize. It supplies to students the opportunity for optimal personal, social, and intellectual growth; to teachers, professional opportunities for self-actualization; and to schools, opportunities to contribute dynamically and meaningfully to society.

System 4 is indeed close to our concept of enlightened supervision. Administrators, teachers, and others who adopt this perspective rely on the principle of supportive relationships, on group methods of supervision, on theory Y assumptions, on self-control methods, on ability authority, and on other principles of system 4. The human organization of the school reacts to this perspective by displaying greater group loyalty, high performance goals, greater cooperation, more teamwork and sharing, less feeling of unreasonable pressure, more favorable attitudes toward the supervisor and the school, and higher levels of motivation for performance.[11] The result, of course, is increases in the dimensions of school success.

PRESCRIPTIONS FOR ENLIGHTENED SUPERVISION

Careful study of the profile of organizational characteristics in Table 7-1 provides operationally defined descriptions of four supervisory-management systems. Their usefulness in prescribing supervisory behavior in detail and in an integrated way is enormous. System 4, for example, paints an extensive portrait of a major segment of enlightened supervision. Each of the four systems is able to describe the supervisory environment of not only teachers in relation to administrators, supervisors, and others, but teachers as supervisors in relation to their young clients.

Table 7-1 can also serve as a guideline for measuring organizational position on the management continuum and movement along the continuum. This instrumentation can also serve as a target-setting device by measuring (1) where a school or educational subunit is on the continuum, (2) where it would like to be, and (3) progress at intervals toward this goal. Basic to this discussion is the concept that change toward system 4 tends not to occur on a random broken-front basis, but as a total assault on all the variables which compose the system. The system 4 conceptualization is funda-

11*Ibid.*, p. 76.

mental to the development of enlightened supervisory practices in our nation's schools.

We believe that the Likert approach, as illustrated in Table 7-1, offers an operational definition of the supervisor's job, provides a practical means for generating and ordering supervisory goals, and serves as a useful tool for measuring supervisory effectiveness. Further, we argue that the human curriculum, with its emphasis on student self-actualization, depends upon a system 4 supervisory environment for success. In the next chapter we focus more intensively on the school's human organization as we return again to the synthesizing theory.

SELECTED REFERENCES

Likert, Rensis: *The Human Organization: Its Management and Value,* McGraw-Hill, New York, 1967.

————: *New Patterns of Management,* McGraw-Hill, New York, 1961.

Chapter Eight
THE HUMAN
ORGANIZATION OF SCHOOLS

The human organization of the school represents the connecting link—in the synthesizing theory, the set of mediating variables—between how supervisors think, believe, and behave and school progress toward achievement of its goals. Both the dynamics of schools as organizations and the organizational milieu which patterns behavior in schools are also connected, for better or for worse, to the achievement of school goals by the human organization.

As an illustration, whether Johnny learns X or not depends largely upon how Johnny feels about learning X. Teachers as supervisors affect Johnny's learning by affecting Johnny's feelings. While we are the first to agree that our explanation of Johnny's learning suffers from lack of detail in outlining the complexities and contingencies of the matter, our point should be clear nevertheless. Johnny's learning of X or of anything else is largely affected by his concept of self, his levels of aspiration, his unique motivational orientation, the perceived relevancy to his need structure of what is being offered for learning, his level of commitment, his previous experience with similar learning situations, his level of maturation, his value-belief system, and his interpersonal entanglements and commitments to others.

Teachers also believe in certain things, behave in certain ways, and perform at certain levels for largely the same reasons. While material presented in this chapter has undiluted relevance to all who compose the human organization of the school, we focus on the teacher. We are interested in how teachers react to various stimuli from the initiating variable set and the effect that this human reaction has on school success.

TEACHERS AND THEIR WORLD OF WORK

The world of work has enormous potential for providing individuals with enrichment, challenge, and self-development. This observation is particularly true for professionally oriented occupations. Teaching clearly qualifies in this regard on two counts, the nature of the work of the teacher and the uniqueness of the school's mission in society. Theoretically, the schools function with the intent to provide students with enrichment, challenge, and self-development on intellectual, social, and psychological dimensions.

If one accepts the premise that educators (at least initially) seek meaningful satisfaction from work and wish to view themselves as competent, significant, and worthwhile contributors to society, then it is easy to understand why, when confronted with work environments characterized by distrust, arbitrariness, passivity, conformity, and paternalism, they often look to recreation, hobbies, and fraternal or social groups for this satisfaction. Some seek more militant alternatives as they attempt to increase their control over the reward-granting structures of schools. Still another group chooses to play the "organizational game" in hopes that they may be promoted to positions which afford more potential for meaningful satisfaction.[1]

Teachers face two quite different levels of decisions in the course of their organizational lives in schools.[2] At the first level a teacher decides to become a member and remain a member of a school faculty. In exchange for this membership and its rewards, such as job security, income, position, a sense of belonging, and the like, the teacher is expected to give satisfactory performance, to display at least minimal loyalty, to abide by the rules, and to do in a satisfactory manner what is otherwise reasonably asked of him. If he decides to participate, he is generally regarded as being a rather solid, good teacher who is conscientious about meeting school commitments and requirements. We view teachers who have made this decision as loyal participants in the school enterprise.

A decision by teachers at the second level requires an exchange of services and rewards which, although more difficult to achieve and more subtle to describe, is much more rewarding for both teacher and school. What teachers do beyond that which is required in order to maintain membership as a participant in the school suggests the flavor of the second-level decision. This enormous increase in commitment is exchanged for rewards such as recognition of competency and autonomy, opportunities for assuming responsibility and participating in decision making, and opportunities for experiencing success. This relationship is illustrated in Figure 8-1.

Schools which are deficient in providing rewards associated with teacher decisions at the first level are characterized by high turnover (for students, high dropout rates) and, at best, marginal membership. Schools which are deficient in providing rewards associated with teacher decisions at the second level are characterized by gradual decreases in performance. This second phenomenon generally goes unnoticed. As administrators and supervisors, we tend not to notice performance which is less than extraordinary because of our preoccupation with identifying, avoiding, and sanctioning performance which is less than satisfactory.

Many traditional supervisors have assumed that as long as teachers are

[1]Fred D. Carver and Thomas J. Sergiovanni (eds.), *Organizations and Human Behavior: Focus on Schools*, McGraw-Hill, New York, 1969, p. 185.
[2]This discussion follows that which appears in Thomas J. Sergiovanni, "New Evidence on Teacher Morale," *North Central Association Quarterly*, vol. 42, no. 3, 1968, pp. 259–266.

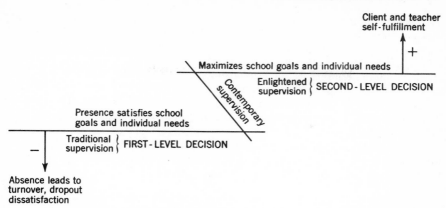

Figure 8-1. Teacher decision levels, reward systems, and organizational performance.

doing a decent job and are meeting commitments to the school (a first-level decision), we should not expect more from them. This seems to disregard the notion that teachers would like to give more if afforded the opportunity[3] to do so. The extent of commitment teachers make, the decision level, is largely dependent upon manifestation of variables which constitute the initiating variables in the synthesizing theory. Ultimately the quality of the school is largely dependent upon the decision level for which most teachers opt.

The Concept of Self

Fundamental to an understanding of human motives and human behavior is the concept of self. Why do people behave the way they do? Why does this behavior invariably make sense to them but often not to us? How can I meaningfully influence your behavior and you mine? Although answers to these questions will travel many routes, they eventually arrive at the concept of self for analysis. Recent literature in supervision contains some perceptive statements about the concept of self. Of those offered below, the first three are from the 1962 yearbook of the Association for Supervision and Curriculum Development,[4] and the remainder are quotations from Saul Gellerman[5] as he applies the concept of self to supervision.

[3]By *opportunity* we mean to avoid the casual observation that "they can give as much as they wish." This observation implies that teachers receive nothing more or *more of the same* in exchange for their further effort. Opportunity to us means substantially altering the reward system in kind and intensity so that an equitable exchange for service at the second level is available. We believe that this applies to students as well.
[4]Association for Supervision and Curriculum Development, *Perceiving, Behaving, Becoming, a New Focus in Education,* National Education Association, Washington, D.C., 1962. The Arthur Coombs quotation appears on page 84, the Earl Kelly quotation on page 65, and the Abraham Maslow quotation on page 83.
[5]Saul Gellerman, *Motivation and Productivity,* American Management Association, New York, 1963. Quotations appear on pages 184, 185, and 186.

The self-concept, we know, is learned. People learn who they are and what they are from the ways in which they have been treated by those who surround them in the process of growing up. This is what Sullivan called learning about self from the mirror of other people. [Combs]

One of the most revealing facts about perception is that it is *selective*. We do not see everything in our surroundings. There are thousands of coincidences in the situation to which we find ourselves at any point of time. To perceive them all would cause pandemonium. We therefore *choose* that which the self feeds upon. [Kelly]

This inner core, or self, grows into adulthood only partly by (objective or subjective) discovery, uncovering and acceptance of what is "there" beforehand. Partly it is also a creation of the person himself. [Maslow]

Gellerman comments on the concept of self and its relationship to supervision as follows:

The average individual is not particularly well acquainted with himself, so to speak, but he remains quite faithful to his not-so-accurate image of himself and thereby acquires consistency.

Throughout his life he is motivated—highly motivated—by the desire to behave in a manner consistent with the symbolic role he has accepted as "himself."

There is a sense, in other words, in which we all become creatures of our own ideas about ourselves and of our compulsion to behave consistently with these ideas.

Anyone who places himself athwart someone else's self-concept is likely to find that cooperation is given grudgingly, if at all.

. . . it can be just as devastating to leave a self-concept unsupported as it is to oppose it.

Here lies the nub of the problem of supervision. An adult self-concept has a high degree of inertia; neither the supervisor's perceptions nor the general opinion of the rest of society is likely to change it very much. It preserves itself, and the individual's sanity with it, by perceiving the world in its own way and by assuming, when necessary, that the rest of the world is out of step. People insist stubbornly on being themselves, and managing them can be quite an exasperating process if their work requires that they "be" something other than themselves. But because self-concepts vary so greatly there is no single set of needs that all workers want to find satisfaction for at work. Therefore, no single supervisory style will lead to optimum effort from all workers.

The self-concept provides a conceptual background for our development and discussion of teacher needs, teacher motivation, and teacher job satisfaction and dissatisfaction which follow. While we support Gellerman's refusal to endorse a single supervisory style, the prevailing style of enlightened supervision permits optimum development of self. We accept the concept of self as a formidable determinant of behavior, but this writing would not take place if we felt that teachers and students were without the potential for changing defensive self-concepts into more open and fulfilling self-concepts.

HUMAN MOTIVATION AND TEACHERS

A common-sense approach to the identification and discussion of characteristics which compose human needs would undoubtedly reveal a list of factors not unlike that which we will develop in this section. Our common-sense list would probably include such universal human needs as air, water, shelter, food, protection, love, acceptance, importance, success, recognition, control, and the like. This approach reveals a somewhat random and undifferentiated list which requires significant effort to condense into guidelines for supervisory behavior. Abraham Maslow,[6] a distinguished psychologist at Brandeis University, proposed a theory of human motivation which integrates the common-sense approach to human needs. His theory forms an operational basis for supervisory behavior.[7]

The Maslow Theory

The Maslow theory differs from other motivational formulations in that it does not consider an individual's motivation on a 1-to-1 basis or as a series of independent drives. Each of the human needs which compose the theory are examined in relationship to others and are classified and arranged into a hierarchy of prepotency. Thus before need B can be satisfied, one must first satisfy need A, and so on.

As a preface to his theory of human motivation, Maslow offers the following propositions. Each is to be considered as an assumption basic to his theory and as a statement of criteria by which the adequacy of motivation theory is evaluated.

1. The integrated wholeness of the organism must be one of the foundation stones of motivation theory.
2. The hunger drive (or any other physiological drive) was rejected as a centering point or model for a definitive theory of motivation. Any drive that is somatically based and localizable was shown to be atypical rather than typical in human motivation.
3. Such a theory should stress and center itself upon ultimate or basic goals rather than partial or superficial ones, upon ends rather than means to these ends. Such a stress would imply a more central place for unconscious than for conscious motivations.
4. There are usually available various cultural paths to the same goal. Therefore conscious, specific local-cultural desires are not as fundamental in motivation theory as the more basic, unconscious goals.

[6]Abraham H. Maslow, *Motivation and Personality*, Harper, New York, 1954.
[7]Maslow describes the origins of his theory as follows: "This theory is, I think, in the functionalist tradition of James and Dewey, and is fused with the holism of Wertheimer, Goldstein, and Gestalt Psychology, and with the dynamism of Freud and Adler. This fusion or synthesis may arbitrarily be called a 'general-dynamic' theory." Maslow, "A Theory of Human Motivation," *The Psychological Review*, vol. 50, 1943, pp. 370–396.

5. Any motivated behavior, either preparatory or consummatory, must be understood to be a channel through which many basic needs may be simultaneously expressed or satisfied. Typically an act has more than one motivation.
6. Practically all organismic states are to be understood as motivated and as motivating.
7. Human needs arrange themselves in hierarchies of prepotency. That is to say, the appearance of one need usually rests on the prior satisfaction of another, more prepotent need. Man is a perpetually wanting animal. Also no need or drive can be treated as if it were isolated or discrete; every drive is related to the state of satisfaction or dissatisfaction of other drives.
8. Lists of drives will get us nowhere for various theoretical and practical reasons. Furthermore any classification of motivations must deal with the problem of levels of specificity or generalization of the motives to be classified.
9. Classifications of motivations must be based upon goals rather than upon instigating drives or motivated behavior.
10. Motivation theory should be human-centered rather than animal-centered.
11. The situation or the field in which the organism reacts must be taken into account but the field alone can rarely serve as an exclusive explanation for behavior. Furthermore the field itself must be interpreted in terms of the organism. Field theory cannot be a substitute for motivation theory.
12. Not only the integration of the organism must be taken into account, but also the possibility of isolated, specific, partial or segmental reactions.[8]

With each of the twelve propositions in mind, Maslow then developed a hierarchy of needs consisting of five levels. Specific need dimensions which compose each of the five levels are bound together by similarities in description, but more importantly, by similarities in potency potential. Essentially, the most prepotent need occupies, and to a certain extent monopolizes, an individual's attention, while less prepotent needs are minimized. When a need is fairly well satisfied the next prepotent need emerges and tends to dominate the individual's conscious life. Gratified needs, according to this theory, are not active motivators of behavior. Douglas McGregor describes each of the five Maslow levels and the prepotency feature of the theory simply and concisely as follows:

PHYSIOLOGICAL NEEDS

Man is a wanting animal—as soon as one of his needs is satisfied, another appears in its place. This process in unending. It continues from birth to death.

Man's needs are organized in a series of levels—a hierarchy of importance. At the lowest level, but pre-eminent in importance when they are thwarted, are his *physiological needs.* Man lives for bread alone, when there is no bread. Unless the circumstances are unusual, his needs for love, for status, for recognition are inoperative when his stomach has been empty for a while. But when he eats

[8]Abraham H. Maslow, "A Preface to Motivation Theory," *Psychosomatic Medicine,* vol. 5, 1953, pp. 85–92.

regularly and adequately, hunger ceases to be an important motivation. The same is true of the other physiological needs of man—for rest, exercise, shelter, protection from the elements.

A satisfied need is not a motivator of behavior! This is a fact of profound significance that is regularly ignored on the conventional approach to the management of people. Consider your own need for air: Except as you are deprived of it, it has no appreciable motivating effect upon your behavior.

SAFETY NEEDS

When the physiological needs are reasonably satisfied, needs at the next higher level begin to dominate man's behavior—to motivate him. These are called *safety needs.* They are needs for protection against danger, threat, deprivation. Some people mistakenly refer to these as needs for security. However, unless man is in a dependent relationship where he fears arbitrary deprivation, he does not demand security. The need is for the "fairest possible break." When he is confident of this, he is more than willing to take risks. But when he feels threatened or dependent, his greatest need is for guarantees, for protection, for security.

The fact needs little emphasis that, since every industrial employee is in a dependent relationship, safety needs may assume considerable importance. Arbitrary management actions, behavior which arouses uncertainty with respect to continued employment or which reflects favoritism or discrimination, unpredictable administration of policy—these can be powerful motivators of the safety needs in the employment relationship at *every level,* from worker to vice president.

SOCIAL NEEDS

When man's physiological needs are satisfied and he is no longer fearful about his physical welfare, his *social needs* become important motivators of his behavior—needs for belonging, for association, for acceptance by his fellows, for giving and receiving friendship and love.

Management knows today of the existence of these needs, but it often assumes quite wrongly that they represent a threat to the organization. Many studies have demonstrated that the tightly knit, cohesive work group may, under proper conditions, be far more effective than an equal number of separate individuals in achieving organizational goals.

Yet management, fearing group hostility to its own objectives, often goes to considerable length to control and direct human efforts in ways that are inimical to the natural "groupiness" of human beings. When man's social needs—and perhaps his safety needs, too—are thus thwarted, he behaves in ways which tend to defeat organizational objectives. He becomes resistant, antagonistic, uncooperative. But this behavior is a consequence, not a cause.

EGO NEEDS

Above the social needs—in the sense that they do not become motivators until lower levels are reasonably satisfied—are the needs of greatest significance to management and to man himself. They are the *egoistic needs,* and they are of two kinds:

1. Those needs that relate to one's self-esteem—needs for self-confidence, for independence, for achievement, for competence, for knowledge.

2. Those needs that relate to one's reputation—needs for status, for recognition, for appreciation, for the deserved respect of one's fellows.

Unlike the lower needs, these are rarely satisfied; man seeks indefinitely for more satisfaction of these needs once they have become important to him. But they do not appear in any significant way until physiological, safety, and social needs are all reasonably satisfied.

The typical industrial organization offers few opportunities for the satisfaction of these egoistic needs to people at lower levels in the hierarchy. The conventional methods of organizing work, particularly in mass-production industries, give little heed to these aspects of human motivation. If the practices of scientific management were deliberately calculated to thwart these needs, they could hardly accomplish this purpose better than they do.

SELF-FULFILLMENT NEEDS

Finally—a capstone, as it were, on the hierarchy of man's needs—there are what we may call the needs for *self-fulfillment*. These are the needs for realizing one's own potentialities, for continued self-development, for being creative in the broadest sense of that term.

It is clear that the conditions of modern life give only limited opportunity for these relatively weak needs to obtain expression. The deprivation most people experience with respect to other lower-level needs diverts their energies into the struggle to satisfy those needs, and the needs for self-fulfillment remain dormant.[9]

While McGregor's analysis forces the needs into specific steps, Maslow considered all of them as being somewhat interdependent and, in fact, overlapping. It is nevertheless useful, at least conceptually, to consider human needs as being arranged into fairly delimited prepotency levels.

The Importance of Autonomy

Some controversy exists as to whether needs which are at the lower levels of the hierarchy are ever activated enough to be considered work motivators. Porter,[10] for example, in adopting the Maslow hierarchy of needs for his research, has eliminated physiological needs from the list. Presumably, Porter feels that in our society this category lacks the prepotency to motivate behavior for most people. He substitutes instead a category of needs labeled *autonomy*. The Porter modification seems to have particular relevance to education, for while physiological needs have tended to depreciate in importance,[11] teachers and students have expressed a demand for control over their work environment and, indeed, over their destiny. The need for autonomy which many educational participants express is based on the principle of self-government, self-control, and self-determination. Teachers, in

[9]Douglas McGregor, *The Human Side of Enterprise*, McGraw-Hill, New York, 1960, pp. 36–39.
[10]Lyman Porter, "Attitudes in Management: Perceived Deficiencies in Need Fulfillment as a Function of Job Level," *Journal of Applied Psychology*, vol. 46, 1962, p. 375.
[11]Basic provision for needs at this level seems largely guaranteed in our society.

Figure 8-2. The hierarchy of needs: a motivational focus for supervision.

particular, display formidable credentials in terms of professional expertness as justification for expression of this need.

In Figure 8-2 we use Porter's revision of the Maslow categories to illustrate the hierarchical relationships which constitute the theory of human needs.

Lower-order and Higher-order Needs

As we look to the needs hierarchy as a framework for prescribing the scope and content of supervisory behavior, it is helpful to visualize needs as falling into two categories: those which we describe as lower-order needs (security, social, and, to some extent, esteem), and those which we describe as higher-order (esteem, autonomy, and self-actualization). The lower-order needs are those which are available to teachers as they make first-level decisions in schools. The school exchanges money, benefits, position, friendship, protection, interpersonal gratification, and the like, for satisfactory membership by teachers. Surely these are fundamental needs which must be supplied in order for teachers to function adequately as persons. Increasingly, however, teachers view rewards of this kind as given. They feel entitled to security and social need fulfillment by virtue of their membership in the school. From this point of view, the school should expect little in return for that which teachers automatically expect and, in fact, demand. Supervisors who rely on reward structures characteristic of the lower-order needs are by and large tapping shallow motivational levels in teachers. The adequacy of these relationships is presented in Figure 8-3.

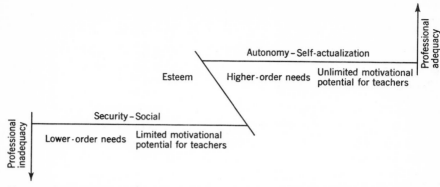

Figure 8-3. The order of needs: professional adequacy and inadequacy.

The higher-order needs are those whose fulfillment is exchanged for service which teachers give to the school and its clients as a result of decisions at the second level. We should clearly state that for decisions at the second level the first-level decision by teachers is a prerequisite. Further, teachers will tend not to be concerned with the pursuit of higher-order needs without consistent and considerable satiation of the lower-order needs. Since meaningful satisfaction of the esteem, autonomy, and self-actualization variety is intimately imbedded in performance, teachers will need to earn rewards of this kind through efforts toward the achievement of school goals. While teachers consider it perfectly fair and proper to be accepted by the school simply because they are there, many recognize that fulfillment of the higher-order needs is rightfully earned through performance. Supervisors who rely on reward structures characteristic of the higher-order needs are by and large tapping often virgin, but always potent, motivational levels in teachers.

The motivational base for enlightened supervision consists of needs of each of the five levels but focuses on those which we describe as higher-order. As Figure 8-2 indicates, the limited motivational basis for traditional and, to some extent, contemporary supervision is totally inadequate for providing personal- and professional-growth opportunities which we believe professionally oriented teachers seek.

Competence and Achievement: Professional Motives

While the Maslow approach provides an integrated and interdependent view of need structures, some scholars have tended to focus on one need, often to the exclusion of other needs. Two of these efforts seem to have particular relevance to understanding teacher behavior and teacher need. One effort explores in detail the competence motive—the desire for mastery—and the other, the achievement motive—the desire for success. The first effort, developed and popularized by Robert White,[12] presumes that people wish to understand and control their environment and wish to be active participants in this environment. This need is traced by White to early infancy and childhood experiences and is observed in the seemingly random and endless searching, feeling, tinkering, exploring, and investigating which characterize this age. White claims that the years six to nine are critical ones in developing this motive. If early experiences prove successful, one is likely to continue developing and extending his competence motive. As an adult, he behaves in ways which permit him to test and reconfirm the adequacy of his competence. The competence test reoccurs as successes are compiled, and further, each new test is usually at a level which is more challenging than that of his previous success.[13]

Many individuals have lost the capacity to strive for competence largely because of a history of failure. In this situation, they are less ready to try something new, to undertake a more difficult assignment, or the like, for fear of additional failure. Schools and school clients benefit by the developing and encouraging of the competence motive, since teachers and other professional workers readily express a desire for job mastery and professional growth. A useful exercise for readers is to identify those aspects of the curriculum, the classroom management system, and the school management system which prohibit, delimit, or otherwise frustrate the opportunity for school inhabitants to develop, express, and confirm the competence motive. When this motive is reinforced in teachers, personal satisfaction for the human organization and extraordinary performance for the human school are reaped.

The second need, the achievement motive, is one studied intensively by David C. McClelland.[14] Gellerman describes people who are "blessed" or "afflicted" with high need for achievement as follows:

He tries harder and demands more of himself, especially when the chips are down. Consequently, he accomplishes more. We find, for example, that college students who have a strong achievement drive will usually get better grades than equally bright students with weaker needs for achievement. Executives "on their way up" in their companies are usually driven by stronger achievement needs than those who do not rise so quickly. The stronger the achievement drive, the greater the probability that the individual will demand more of himself.

Perhaps the most fascinating aspect of the achievement motive is that it seems to make accomplishment an end in itself. If anything, it is the person who

[12]Robert W. White, "Motivation Reconsidered: The Concept of Competence," *Psychological Review,* vol. 66, no. 5, 1959, pp. 297–333.
[13]As one perceives of himself as becoming increasingly competent, he evokes the self-fulfilling prophecy.
[14]David C. McClelland et al., *The Achievement Motive,* Appleton-Century-Crofts, New York, 1953. Also, David C. McClelland, *The Achieving Society,* Van Nostrand, Princeton, N.J., 1961.

has little achievement motivation who expects a tangible reward for greater effort. While the achievement-motivated person does not spurn tangible rewards and even has a rather unexpected use for them, they are not really essential to him, either. He takes a special joy in winning, in competing successfully with a difficult standard; this means more to him than money or a public pat on the back. He is not an altruist: He simply finds enough delight in doing difficult things that he does not need to be bribed to do them.[15]

The person with a high need for achievement, as one can readily see, has much to give to organizational productivity. He displays an entrepreneurial behavior pattern which McClelland characterizes as containing: (1) moderate risk taking as a function of skill rather than chance, (2) energetic or novel instrumental activity, (3) individual responsibility and accountability for behavior, (4) the need for knowledge of results—or money as a *measure of success,* and (5) anticipation of future possibilities.[16]

While an individual with high need for achievement has much to give to a school, his demands in return are great. He needs an opportunity to display the behavior manifestations which McClelland describes above and resists attempts to limit this behavior. If he cannot express his achievement need within the good graces of the organization, he seeks this expression (1) organizationally in a "negative" fashion, (2) extra-organizationally in teacher associations, unions, and the like, or (3) in noneducational organizations and institutions. While the teacher with a high need for achievement can be troublesome for many administrators and supervisors, he has the potential to give fully and in a spirit of excellence to the school and its efforts. A major problem for educational administration and supervision is how to change existing educational structures to accommodate the larger number of people with seemingly high needs for achievement who are entering the field of education.

MOTIVATING TEACHERS: SOME EVIDENCE

What do teachers want from their jobs? What do teachers need in order to be stimulated to extraordinary performance? Do needs and wants vary as the years go by? Do teachers at different career stages, different age levels, and of opposite sex vary in their perception of needs? Is there an "overkill' concept in need fulfillment—that is, do we provide teachers with too much of one or another kind of satisfaction? What is the relationship between needs and wants and job satisfaction and job dissatisfaction? Are these related to increases or decreases in performance? Can the reward system presently available to teachers adequately provide for their needs? These and other questions are considered as we examine some evidence which relates to the

[15]Gellerman, *op. cit.,* p. 124.
[16]McClelland, *The Achieving Society, op. cit.,* p. 207.

important topic of satisfaction and need fulfillment in teaching. Our treatment of this phenomenon is far less than definitive. We suspect that more questions are raised than answered. Nevertheless, our hope is that supervisors will come to better understand the problems of human motivation as they relate to teachers and students.

The Need Deficiency Concept

As those who supervise approach the problem of motivation through the Maslow need hierarchy, an early concern or question that comes to mind is the identification of the present level of focus or operation for most teachers.[17] Which levels are adequately provided for teachers, and where do the largest gaps exist?

One attempt to measure need levels of educators asked teachers and administrators in one school district to report on perceptions of need deficiencies in their work environment.[18] The educators responded to a thirteen-item need deficiency questionnaire which was modeled after the Maslow theory. For each item respondents were asked to indicate: (1) how much of the particular characteristic was presently available in their jobs (*actual*), and (2) how much of this same characteristic they thought should be available in their school positions (*ideal*). Responses were given on a seven-point scale with the item's need deficiency score determined by subtracting *actual* response from *ideal* response. Thus an *actual* response of three to the social-need item "the opportunity to develop close friendships in my school position" subtracted from an *ideal* response of five yields a need deficiency score of two. Table 8-1 gives sample items for each of the five need categories.

We assume that the larger the perceived need deficiency for an item or for a need level, the higher the index of dissatisfaction. Smaller scores, on the other hand, indicate relative satisfaction with the level of need fulfillment for that item. Some of the findings from the study are presented in Table 8-2. This table presents mean need deficiency scores for each of the Maslow-type need levels by age group of respondents and again by sex of respondents.

Note that in every case except one (the forty-five-and-over age group)

---

[17] The concept of individual differences, particularly as it relates to needs, applies as well to teachers as it does to students. While the concept is often ignored for both groups, we seem particularly negligent in applying it to teachers. We believe that teachers as a group tend to focus on one level primarily (the esteem level), but we recognize that teachers at one time or another span the Maslow hierarchy. The Maslow theory suggests that as esteem needs become more easily satiated, teachers will focus increasingly on autonomy and self-actualization need levels.

[18] Francis M. Trusty and Thomas J. Sergiovanni, "Perceived Need Deficiencies of Teachers and Administrators: A Proposal for Restructuring Teacher Roles," *Educational Administration Quarterly*, vol. 2, Autumn, 1966, pp. 168–180.

TABLE 8-1. NEED DEFICIENCY INDEX: SAMPLE ITEMS

Category	Item
Security	The feeling of security in my school position
Social	The opportunity, in my school position, to give help to other people
Esteem	The prestige of my school position inside the school (that is, the regard received from others in the school)
Autonomy	The opportunity, in my school position, for participation in the setting of goals
Self-actualization	The opportunity for personal growth and development in my school position

The items which constitute the Need Deficiency Index are adapted from those developed by Lyman Porter for use with business management personnel. See his "Job Attitudes in Management: I. Perceived Deficiencies in Need Fulfillment as a Function of Job Level," *Journal of Applied Psychology*, vol. 46, December, 1963, pp. 375–384.

the esteem level accounts for the largest need deficiencies. In all cases, for both age and sex categories, esteem, autonomy, and self-actualization items account for larger need deficiencies than items which compose the security and social need levels. Fulfillment at the social level, for example, seems not to be of concern to educators at all.[19] If one views deficiencies in need as measurements of job satisfaction, then supervisors must work to restructure reward systems in schools so that they focus more adequately at the levels where the largest deficiencies exist.

Two other observations can be made in reference to the data reported in Table 8-2. The age data suggest a deficiency curve with smallest deficiencies reported by educators in the twenty-to-twenty-four age group and largest deficiencies in the twenty-five-to-thirty-four age group; a tapering trend is noticed in the thirty-five-to-forty-four age group, with moderate need deficiencies reported by those forty-five or over. A similar satisfaction age curve is reported by Herzberg in his 1957 comprehensive review of job satisfaction research. He notes that employees (from a variety of occupational groups) under twenty are relatively satisfied, with greatest dissatisfaction reported by those in the twenty-to-twenty-nine age group. The curve tapers for the thirty-to-thirty-nine group, with those forty and over reporting as relatively more satisfied than others.[20] Nancy Morse observes that "in general,

[19]This observation may very well represent an indictment against a seeming overemphasis on human relations of the sticky variety and against our concern for "groupiness" and togetherness in schools.

[20]Frederick Herzberg et al., *Job Attitudes: Review of Research and Opinion*, Psychological Service of Pittsburgh, Pittsburgh, 1957, pp. 5–13. Herzberg further comments as follows:

From a lifetime of diverse learning, successive accomplishment through the various academic stages, and periodic reinforcement of efforts, the entrant to our modern com-

TABLE 8-2. PERCEIVED NEED DEFICIENCIES OF EDUCATORS

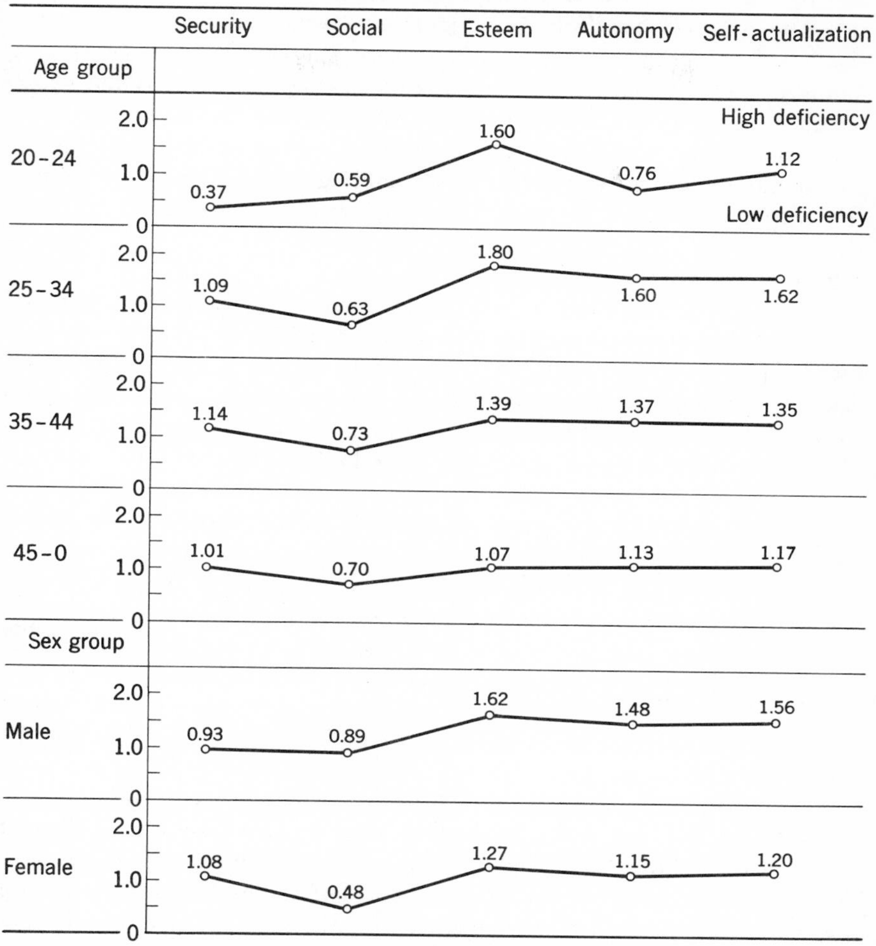
Security
Social
Esteem
Autonomy
Self-actualization
Age group
High deficiency
Low deficiency
20-24
0.37
0.59
1.60
0.76
1.12
25-34
1.09
0.63
1.80
1.60
1.62
35-44
1.14
0.73
1.39
1.37
1.35
45-0
1.01
0.70
1.07
1.13
1.17
Sex group
Male
0.93
0.89
1.62
1.48
1.56
Female
1.08
0.48
1.27
1.15
1.20
2.0
1.0
0

the shorter the time the employee has been with the company the more satisfied he is with his salary and his chances for progress in it."[21]

Generally speaking, women educators seem more satisfied with their school jobs than men. Table 8-2 shows that, except for the security level, women perceive smaller need deficiencies. Each of these cases can be

panies finds that, rather than work providing an expanding psychological existence, the opposite occurs; and successive amputations of his self-conception, aspirations, learning, and talent are the consequences of earning a living.

"The Motivation-Hygiene Concept and Problems of Manpower," *Personnel Administration,* vol. 27, no. 1, January-February, 1964, pp. 3–7.

[21]Nancy Morse, *Satisfactions in the White Collar Job,* University of Michigan Press, Ann Arbor, Mich., 1953, p. 68.

explained by differences in levels of aspiration and differences in individual and professional expectations which people face or feel as a result of age or sex. The twenty-five-to-thirty-four age group seems well aware that promotions and advancements occur at this point in their careers. As chances diminish, they rationalize job wants and needs—lower aspirations and expectations—and accept the available and prevalent reward system. By and large, men seem to have higher levels of aspiration than women and, indeed, receive more external expectations for advancement than women. As a result, they are more difficult to please in terms of job wants and needs.[22]

Secondary School Teachers

As part of a larger study which investigated relationships between and among innovativeness, complexity, and job satisfaction in thirty-six large high schools (with between 1,500 and 2,500 students), 1,593 high school teachers responded to the Maslow-type need deficiency index described earlier.[23] The mean need deficiency scores for this group for each of the five levels of the Maslow-type hierarchy are given in Table 8-3.

TABLE 8-3. PERCEIVED NEED DEFICIENCIES OF HIGH SCHOOL TEACHERS

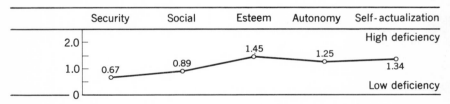

These findings suggest again that, while teachers are generally well satisfied with the two lower-order needs, they express appreciably less satisfaction with respect to the three higher-order needs. While the trend in need deficiency tends to follow that proposed by Maslow, the least satisfaction for these high school teachers was reported for esteem. The investigators conclude as follows:

Relatively, the opportunity for higher-order need satisfaction is not available to teachers to the same extent as lower-order need satisfaction. While this observation does not speak to the expected or observed relationship it suggests that teachers (as a professional group) are ready to move up the Maslow-type needs hierarchy and derive satisfactions from the positions themselves. Further, the mean satisfaction scores suggest that immediately the most pressing need of

[22]James G. March and Herbert A. Simon offer a classic discussion of the relationship between aspiration, expectation, and satisfaction in *Organizations,* Wiley, New York, 1958, pp. 83–111. See particularly their model of adaptive motivated behavior.

[23]Fred D. Carver and Thomas J. Sergiovanni, "The School as a Complex Organization: An Analysis of Three Structural Elements," Department of Educational Administration, University of Illinois, June, 1968. (Mimeographed)

teachers is the need for esteem—internal and external to the high school. We would hypothesize that as esteem needs are met, perhaps as a result of increased salary and benefits derived through flexing of teacher organization muscles, teachers will move to satisfy autonomy and self-actualization needs. The implication for administrators is clear—provide teachers with opportunities to make independent educational decisions and encourage personal and professional development.[24]

JOB SATISFACTION AND JOB DISSATISFACTION

While the concept of need has conceptual potency, its utility rests in operationalizing needs in terms of job satisfaction and job dissatisfaction factors. The usefulness of these factors, in turn, depends upon the extent to which they are derived from and related to individual wants and needs. An assumption basic to present thinking about teacher satisfaction is that factors which contribute to job satisfaction and factors which contribute to job dissatisfaction of teachers are arranged on a conceptual continuum. Thus under this assumption, a factor identified as a source of dissatisfaction is also likely to be a source of satisfaction. For example, if teachers are dissatisfied with the present policy of filing lesson plans or with the length of the school day, improving these conditions will move them to the satisfaction end of the continuum. The continuum assumption is illustrated in Figure 8-4.

Negative or absent—Job factors—Positive or present

Dissatisfaction ◄────────────────────────────────────► Satisfaction

Figure 8-4. The continuum assumption. From Thomas J. Sergiovanni, "Factors Which Affect Satisfaction and Dissatisfaction of Teachers," *Journal of Educational Administration,* vol. 5, no. 1, May, 1967.

By the same token, factors which contribute to job satisfaction, if removed, lead to job dissatisfaction. The supervisory prescription based on the continuum assumption is that if a factor accounting for dissatisfaction is altered or eliminated, job satisfaction will result. Or, failure to maintain a condition which contributes to satisfaction will result in teacher dissatisfaction.

The Herzberg Hypothesis

Frederick Herzberg has proposed a satisfaction and dissatisfaction theory[25] which suggests that factors which contribute to job satisfaction and factors

[24]*Ibid.*

[25]The Herzberg theory is one of the most controversial yet most studied theories of job satisfaction. About as many studies support the theory as do not. When investigators use methods similar to Herzberg's (depth interview and content analysis), results tend to support the hypothesis; but when they use questionnaires and other "objective" devices, the hypothesis tends not to be supported. Samples of educational studies which support the Herzberg thesis are: Ralph M. Savage, "A Study of Teacher Satisfaction and Attitudes: Causes and Effects" (unpublished doctoral dissertation, Department of

which contribute to job dissatisfaction are *not* arranged on a conceptual continuum but are mutually exclusive. Herzberg's hypothesis is that some factors are satisfiers when present but not dissatisfiers when absent; other factors are dissatisfiers, but when eliminated as dissatisfiers the result is not positive motivation. The Herzberg hypothesis is illustrated in Figure 8-5.

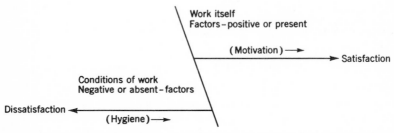

Figure 8-5. Herzberg hypothesis: Satisfaction factors and dissatisfaction factors are mutually exclusive. Adapted from Thomas Sergiovanni, "Factors Which Affect Satisfaction and Dissatisfaction of Teachers," *Journal of Educational Administration*, vol. 5, no. 1, May, 1967, p. 67.

Herzberg comments on the unipolar phenomenon in satisfaction as follows:

The opposite of job satisfaction would not be job dissatisfaction, but rather *no* job satisfaction; and similarly the opposite of job dissatisfaction is *no* job dissatisfaction—not job satisfaction. The statement of the concept is awkward and may appear at first to be a semantic ruse, but there is more than a play with words when it comes to understanding the behavior of people on jobs.[26]

Herzberg further suggests that factors which satisfy are related to the work itself, while factors which dissatisfy are related to the environment of work. Herzberg's research with over two hundred accountants and engineers from Pittsburgh industry tends to confirm the existence of the satisfier-and-dissatisfier phenomenon. He found that five factors (achievement, recognition, work itself, responsibility, and advancement) tended to affect job attitudes in only a positive direction. The absence of these factors did not necessarily result in job dissatisfaction. The presence of these factors tended to contribute to increases in performance. In the case of most of the eleven

Educational Administration, Auburn University, 1967), and J. Warren Adair, "Keeping Teachers Happy," *The American School Board Journal*, vol. 54, January, 1968, pp. 28–29. Our discussion of the Herzberg hypothesis, the Herzberg study, and the motivation-hygiene theory which emerges is based on and follows that which appears in Frederick Herzberg, Bernard Mausner, and Barbara Snyderman, *The Motivation to Work*, Wiley, New York, 1959.

[26]Frederick Herzberg, "The Motivation-Hygiene Concept and Problems of Manpower," *op. cit.*

remaining factors, if the factor was not present, its absence led to employee dissatisfaction. The presence of these factors tended not to lead to employee satisfaction, nor did they lead to noticeable increases in performance. The factors in the two subcategories appear as Table 8-4.

TABLE 8-4. THE SATISFACTION AND DISSATISFACTION FACTORS

Satisfiers (Found in the work itself)	Dissatisfiers (Found in the environment of work)
Achievement	Salary
Recognition	Possibility of growth
Work itself	Interpersonal relations (subordinates)
Responsibility	Interpersonal relations (superiors)
Advancement	Interpersonal relations (peers)
	Supervision—technical
	Company policy and administration
	Working conditions
	Personal life
	Status
	Job security

The factors were identified and reported by Herzberg in F. Herzberg et al., *The Motivation to Work*, New York, 1959.

The Herzberg findings are summarized in Figure 8-6. Factors to the right of the zero line contribute predominantly to satisfaction and factors to the left of this line contribute predominantly to dissatisfaction. The longer the line associated with a factor, the more often respondents cited this factor as contributing to job feelings. The larger the width of the line—diagrammatically, the box—the longer the duration of the attitude. Thus while respondents cited achievement more often than responsibility as a source of high job feelings, when responsibility was cited, the feeling lasted longer than in the case of achievement.

The Herzberg Hypothesis and Teachers

A test of the Herzberg hypothesis with teachers as respondents revealed similar findings.[27] The sixteen Herzberg factors listed in Table 8-4 were used. Eight showed significant differences for teachers. The contributors to job satisfaction were achievement, recognition, and responsibility. These needs, if not met (or if absent), tended not to contribute to job dissatisfaction. The factors cited as sources of considerable dissatisfaction for teachers, but not satisfaction, were interpersonal relations with students, teachers, and peers, technical supervision, school policy and administration, and personal life. These factors and others which composed the sixteen used are presented in

[27]This discussion follows that which appears in Thomas J. Sergiovanni, "Factors Which Affect Satisfaction and Dissatisfaction of Teachers," *Journal of Educational Administration*, vol. 5, no. 1, May, 1967.

Figure 8-6. Comparison of satisfiers and dissatisfiers. From Frederick Herzberg et al., *The Motivation to Work,* Wiley, New York, 1959, p. 81.

Table 8-5. In the table, percentages for each factor are presented which represent the proportion of attitudes (high or low) which were accounted for by this factor. Achievement, for example, accounted for 30 percent of the 142 high-attitude responses collected from the seventy-two teachers in the sample but only 9 percent of the 142 low-attitude responses. The P column shows those factors which contributed more significantly to high attitudes than to low or more significantly to low attitudes than to high. Where no significance level is provided, the factor may tentatively be considered as a contributor to both satisfaction and dissatisfaction.[28]

[28]With the exception of work itself, other nonsignificant factors simply were not mentioned by teachers with enough frequency to adequately test for significance.

TABLE 8-5. *PERCENTAGES FOR THE FREQUENCY WITH WHICH JOB FACTORS CONTRIBUTED TO HIGH ATTITUDES AS COMPARED WITH LOW ATTITUDES FOR TEACHERS*

Job factors	Percentage of highs NR = 142	Percentage of lows NR = 142	P
1. Achievement	30*	9	.01
2. Recognition	28*	2	.001
3. Work itself	11	8	
4. Responsibility	7*	1	.05
5. Advancement	0	1	
6. Salary	2	3	
7. Possibility of growth	6	2	
8. Interpersonal relations (subordinates)	7	20*	.01
9. Interpersonal relations (superiors)	3	4	
10. Interpersonal relations (peers)	1	15*	.001
11. Supervision—technical	1	10*	.01
12. School policy and administration	2	13*	.01
13. Working conditions	2	6	
14. Personal life	0	5*	.05
15. Status	0	0	
16. Security	0	1	

N = 72 teachers; NR = Number of responses
*Significant factor.

When responses of subgroups of teachers were compared, it was found that sources of job satisfaction and job dissatisfaction tended not to differ. Men teachers did not respond differently from women teachers, elementary teachers tended not to respond differently from secondary teachers, and tenure teachers tended not to respond differently from nontenure teachers.[29]

THE MOTIVATION-HYGIENE THEORY

A fundamental problem which becomes apparent as a result of the Herzberg studies is our failure in education to distinguish between human avoidance needs and human approach needs. At the avoidance level, a human tendency exists which stimulates individuals to protect themselves against physical and psychological hardship, danger, and discomfort. At the approach level, mature, fully functioning individuals build upon fulfillment of their avoidance needs by seeking adventure, stimulation, newness, variety, challenge, and the like. The psychologically healthy person (one with a rela-

---

[29]In the tenure-nontenure analysis, it was found that tenure teachers were somewhat more dissatisfied with interpersonal relations with superiors than nontenure teachers, while the nontenure group was more dissatisfied with interpersonal relations with peers than the tenure group. Nontenure teachers were also more dissatisfied with the security factor.

tively mature personality) has two commitments to himself: (1) a hygiene commitment which requires him to seek satisfaction at the avoidance level—of his lower-order needs; and (2) a motivational commitment which requires him to seek fulfillment at the approach level—of his higher-order needs. Our hygienic concerns are those which protect us from trouble and which help us to maintain ourselves as we are. Our motivator concerns are those which urge us to seek, to search, to move on, and to establish new psychological boundaries and new homeostatic levels. Teachers express this latter concern in their desire for personal and professional growth.

The job factors which we have identified as being dissatisfiers rather than satisfiers are avoidance in nature and are labeled hygienic. Herzberg describes them as follows:

> They act in a manner analogous to the principles of medical hygiene. Hygiene operates to remove health hazards from the environment of man. It is not a curative; it is, rather, a preventive.[30]

Adequate presence of the hygienic factors—those which focus on the conditions of work—seems essential if teachers are to avoid dissatisfaction, frustration, unpleasantness, and the like. These are the factors which make work tolerable, which help us to continue our participatory agreement with the school. These factors, however, are lacking in motivational potential in terms of achieving school goals. Teachers expect fair and adequate supervision, supportive school policies and administrative directives, friendly interpersonal relationships, pleasant working conditions, and the like.

The job factors which we have identified as being satisfiers rather than dissatisfiers are approach in nature and are described as motivators. These are intrinsic factors which can be earned only through performance on the job. For teachers the motivation to work depends upon a reward system which indeed provides for one's hygienic needs but focuses on one's motivational needs. From this point of view, supervisors work to provide a job environment characterized by adequate communications, good interpersonal feelings, fair and honest technical supervision, sensible and practical policies, pleasant working conditions, status, and security, for these are the things which will relieve teachers of the burdens of dissatisfaction. To stop here, however, is to leave untapped a tremendous reservoir of effort available in the teaching staff, as well as a meaningful reservoir of satisfaction available for teachers. Enlightened supervision builds upon this effort by providing opportunities for teachers to experience a work environment characterized by opportunities for achievement—success, recognition for these efforts, meaningful responsibility, professional advancement, and work-itself satisfaction. This goal is accomplished only when human participants in schools are given the opportunity to own full shares in the school enterprise.

[30]F. Herzberg et al., *The Motivation to Work*, p. 113.

In Figure 8-7 we show the delicate balance which exists in education as a result of supervisory emphasis on human avoidance tendencies as opposed to human approach tendencies, on lower-order needs as opposed to higher-order needs, on failure avoidance as opposed to success seeking, on hygiene orientation as opposed to motivation orientation, and, operationally, on the job dissatisfiers as opposed to the job satisfiers.

Contemporary supervisory practices, with their emphasis on practical human relations but still immersed in the control assumptions and belief systems of traditional supervision, at best play one emphasis against another. We view this approach as that which is "practical-realistic" (or perhaps easy) and as that which results in mediocre, satisfying results for man, organization, and client. Enlightened supervision works to push the balance in favor of our approach tendencies, our higher-order needs, our potential to seek success, and our motivation orientation. We should remember that this is a balance of *focus* and does not imply abandoning the hygienic dimension but rather uses this dimension as a springboard to the motivation dimension.

An Individual Approach

By now, readers have probably identified a number of exceptions among people they know and work with to the motivation perspective described here. Indeed, this is as it should be. A faulty assumption would be that all teachers focus at the same level of the Maslow need hierarchy or seek the same success or satisfaction from their jobs. By and large, however, it does appear that most teachers are ready, willing, and able to respond to more intrinsic reward systems in schools if given a genuine opportunity to do so. Another group of teachers would like to respond similarly if they had the confidence to do so. Enlightened supervision, therefore, must help these teachers function more adequately as individuals, in order to develop in

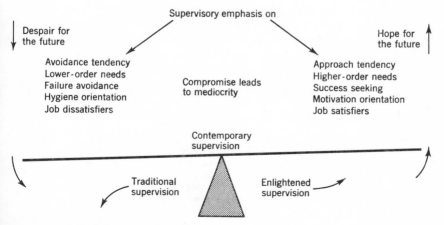

Figure 8-7. The balance in education.

them the necessary independence and desire for mature enrichment. A third group, quite small we think, simply cannot and probably will not respond to supervisory styles which emphasize the motivation orientation. These people are not approaching the fully functioning concept and have lost the potential to do so. Their emotional immaturity classes them as psychological cripples. A few teachers come to the school with this orientation, but far too many learn this life style, this behavioral orientation, as a result of less than rewarding organizational lives.

Herzberg,[31] Hamlin and Nemo,[32] and Haywood and Dobbs[33] have attempted to measure the extent to which a person focuses on matters of hygiene as opposed to matters motivational, and vice versa, by an instrument we call the Choice Motivator Scale. As part of a larger study, an improved version of the Choice Motivator Scale[34] was used to determine the relative need orientation of 227 elementary and secondary school teachers. An analysis of responses to this instrument revealed that two-thirds of the teachers tended toward the motivation orientation and one-fourth of the teachers tended toward the hygiene orientation, with the remainder falling at a point between the two orientations. This frequency relationship did not change when responses of respondents were compared by sex, by teaching level (elementary-secondary), or when teaching sisters were compared with nonreligious teachers. These need data were gathered as part of a study which investigated the relationship between need orientation of teachers and their perception of ideal supervisory style. Hygiene-oriented teachers and motivation-oriented teachers seemed to agree that the ideal style is that which emphasizes both system orientation (initiating structure) and person orientation (consideration), and that the climate of this orientation is described as optimizing as opposed to controlling. While it is comforting to know that teachers by and large agree on descriptions of ideal supervisory style, it is nevertheless unclear what style type they feel is *best for them*. It seems reasonable to assume that a hygiene-oriented teacher may give a description of how a supervisor should behave that is contradictory to the behavior he finds safe and comfortable. One who fears responsibility, for example, may recognize that, ideally, "good" supervisors emphasize shared responsibility.

[31]Frederick Herzberg, *Work and the Nature of Man*, World Publishing, New York, 1966.
[32]Roy Hamlin and Robert Nemo, "Self Actualization in Choice Scores of Improved Schizophrenics," *Journal of Clinical Psychology*, vol. 19, 1961.
[33]Carl Haywood and Virginia Dobbs, "Motivation and Anxiety in High School Boys," *Journal of Personality*, vol. 32, no. 3, September, 1964.
[34]The improved version consisted of twenty-two pairs of vocational titles, each pair matched in terms of social status and required educational training. Teachers were asked to make one vocational choice for each pair and to select a reason for their choice from ten reasons that were provided. A need orientation score was derived from the reasons selected for choices made. See Thomas J. Sergiovanni, Richard Metzcus, and Larry Burden, "Toward a Particularistic Approach to Leadership Style: Some Findings," *American Educational Research Journal*, vol. 6, no. 1, January, 1969.

The topic of teacher motivation, so important in the literature of education as it applies to children, has been virtually ignored in the literature of supervision. Indeed, teacher motivation, need, and satisfaction ought to be fundamental concerns of any supervisory program. They form the basis for understanding the school's human organization. Since the school achieves its purposes through the human organization, this emphasis cannot be overstated. One thing seems clear: school clients grow and mature as the professional staff develops. Self-fulfillment for students is little more than an educational pipe dream if we deny self-fulfillment to teachers.

MORE THAN HUMAN RELATIONS

We endorse much of what educational administrators, supervisors, and teachers have absorbed from the human relations movement.[35] This emphasis, however, has been in making subordinates *feel* part of the school and in making them *feel* important as individuals, as opposed to incorporating subordinates as actual shareholders in the educational enterprise. We have tended to use human relations concepts and ideas without altering previous assumptions about people or previous concepts and ideas about management. Under traditional supervision, for example, control (compliance) is obtained through legitimate authority. Contemporary supervision, by incorporating human relations ideas, deviates from this pattern only slightly. Here supervisors seek control (compliance) *normatively* by working to improve morale. It is presumed that subordinates who are treated well will show appreciation for this state of happiness by responding to supervisory cues. Participation, in contemporary supervision, is used to give people a sense of belonging, a feeling of involvement, an expression of the fact that we care about them. As morale increases, resistance to compliance with formal authority is presumably lowered.

As a contrast to traditional and contemporary patterns, enlightened supervision holds two fundamental assumptions: (1) meaningful satisfaction comes from the work itself and (2) the basis for control rests in self-discipline and self-direction. As such, enlightened supervision does not work to make people feel important, useful, or wanted, but rather provides opportunities for people to experience these feelings. Participation, for example, is used to improve the quality of educational decision making, *not* to promote good feelings. Indeed, as this quality increases, meaningful satisfaction is experienced by all participants.

---

[35]Educational administrators and supervisors have not absorbed the total package but seem to have taken those elements of human relations which could be adopted into existing organizational-administrative structures and traditions. This operational human relations package is what we criticize rather than the original human relations movement. As some put it, we bought something other than what was being offered for sale by the human relations people.

Human Relations or Human Resources?

Raymond Miles[36] illustrates two approaches to supervision, the human relations approach and the human resources approach. He compares the two approaches on three dimensions: (1) attitudes, (2) participation, and (3) expectations, in his "Two Models of Participative Leadership," which appears here as Table 8-6.

Miles clearly indicates that human relations are simply not potent enough to provide for satisfaction of one's higher-order needs and, more

TABLE 8-6. TWO MODELS OF PARTICIPATIVE LEADERSHIP

	Human relations	Human resources
Attitudes toward people	1. People in our culture share a common set of needs—to belong, to be liked, to be respected.	1. In addition to sharing common needs for belonging and respect, most people in our culture desire to contribute effectively and creatively to the accomplishment of worthwhile objectives.
	2. They desire individual recognition, but more than this, they want to feel a useful part of the company and their own work group or department.	2. The majority of our work force is capable of exercising far more initiative, responsibility, and creativity than their present jobs require or allow.
	3. They will tend to cooperate willingly and comply with organizational goals if these important needs are fulfilled.	3. These capabilities represent untapped resources which are presently being wasted.
Kind and amount of participation	1. The manager's basic task is to make each worker believe that he is a useful and important part of the department "team."	1. The manager's basic task is to create an environment in which his subordinates can contribute their full range of talents to the accomplishment of organizational goals. He must attempt to uncover and tap the creative resources of his subordinates.
	2. The manager should be willing to explain his decisions and to discuss his subordinates' objections to his plans. On routine matters, he should encourage his subordinates to participate in planning and choosing among alternative solutions to problems.	2. The manager should allow, and encourage, his subordinates to participate not only in routine decisions but in important matters as well. In fact, the more important a decision is to the manager's department, the greater should be his effort to tap the department's resources.

[36]Raymond E. Miles, "Human Relations or Human Resources?" *Harvard Business Review,* vol. 43, no. 4, July–August, 1965, especially exhibits I and II.

TABLE 8-6.   TWO MODELS OF PARTICIPATIVE LEADERSHIP (Continued)

	Human relations	Human resources
	3. Within narrow limits, the work group or individual subordinates should be allowed to exercise self-direction and self-control in carrying out p'ans.	3. The manager should attempt to continually expand the areas over which his subordinates exercise self-direction and self-control as they develop and demonstrate greater insight and ability.
Expectations	1. Sharing information with subordinates and involving them in departmental decision making will help satisfy their basic needs for belonging and for individual recognition.	1. The overall quality of decision making and performance will improve as the manager makes use of the full range of experience, insight, and creative ability in his department.
	2. Satisfying these needs will improve subordinate morale and reduce resistance to formal authority.	2. Subordinates will exercise responsible self-direction and self-control in the accomplishment of worthwhile objectives that they understand and have helped establish.
	3. High employee morale and reduced resistance to formal authority may lead to improved departmental performance. It should at least reduce intra-department friction and thus make the manager's job easier.	3. Subordinate satisfaction will increase as a by-product of improved performance and the opportunity to contribute creatively to this improvement.

NOTE: It may fairly be argued that what I call the *human relations* model is actually the product of popularization and misunderstanding of the work of pioneers in this field. Moreover, it is true that some of the early research and writings of the human relationists contain concepts which seem to fall within the framework of what I call the *human sources* model. Nevertheless, it is my opinion [that of Miles] that while the early writers did not advocate the *human relations* model as presented here, their failure to emphasize certain of the *human resources* concepts left their work open to the misinterpretations which have occurred.

From Raymond E. Miles, "Human Relations or Human Resources?" *Harvard Business Review*, vol. 43, no. 4, July–August, 1965.

importantly, not potent enough to marshal the necessary professional coalition to improve educational decision making. His human resources model is clearly consistent with our conception of enlightened supervision.

Indeed, teachers adapt for use in the classroom the prevailing school model, whether it be human relations, human resources, or some other. While the human relations model for learning seems infinitely superior to authoritarian or high-control models, teachers still use students to achieve teacher goals. The human resources model permits subordinates (be they teachers or students) to become junior, equal, or senior partners in the educational enterprise. Partnership arrangements fluctuate, of course, as problems change and in accordance with what individuals can contribute to problem solving. The human resources model supports the interchangeable supervisory-client role relationship which characterizes enlightened supervision.

In the final chapters of Part I we branch out from the synthesizing theory, proposed earlier in the book, as we consider the nature of creativity and the problem of planned change, as well as supervisory group process and communications skills.

SELECTED REFERENCES

Gellerman, Saul: *Management by Motivation,* American Management Association, New York, 1968.

————: *Motivation and Productivity,* American Management Association, New York, 1963.

Herzberg, Frederick: *Work and the Nature of Man,* World Publishing, New York, 1966.

———— et al.: *The Motivation to Work,* New York, Wiley, 1959.

Maslow, Abraham: *Motivation and Personality,* Harper, New York, 1954.

Miles, Raymond: "Human Relations or Human Resources?" *Harvard Business Review,* vol. 43, no. 4, July, 1965.

Neff, Walter S.: *Work and Human Behavior,* Atherton Press, New York, 1968.

Sergiovanni, Thomas J.: "Factors Which Affect Satisfaction and Dissatisfaction of Teachers," *Journal of Educational Administration,* vol. 5, no. 1, May, 1967.

Chapter Nine
THE INTERACTION SYSTEM: CREATIVE SUPERVISION, PLANNED CHANGE, AND COMMUNICATIONS

Teaching requires enormous creative effort. The potential for creative expression is widely distributed in the population. Effective administration and supervision involve processes thoroughly dependent upon creative acts. Change for change's sake is an incredible educational slogan. While we expect youngsters to exhibit some creative promise in school, we generally work against creative expression. Further, we tend not to expect much creative expression from teachers. In this chapter we explore concepts of creativity and planned change from the perspective of educational supervision. We have listed some assumptions which are fundamental to this discussion and we add one other to this list. Creativity should not be viewed solely as a means to some educational end, but indeed is itself an educational end. We elaborate on each of these assumptions below and describe characteristics of creativity as they apply to the individual and to the school. We then examine the concept of planned change in relation to supervision and conclude with a discussion of communications. Creativity, planned change, and communications are essential components of the action system for supervision.

SOME ASSUMPTIONS

Teaching requires enormous creative effort. We more appropriately modify this statement by suggesting that effective teaching—that which works to develop fully the unique intellectual, social, and emotional capabilities of each school client—requires enormous creative effort. Moreover, an important goal of teaching is, indeed, to develop the creative capacities of students.[1] Such a goal for students *requires* similar expression from teachers and the school. Appropriate interchange of ideas between teacher-media-school and student requires that the process of teaching continually reshape learning environments, circumstances, methods, and devices to accommodate youngsters. These are not new ideas, but they are ideas which require creative effort for success.

---

[1] As Maslow suggests, the best way to teach a future engineer to be an engineer (or presumably to teach a student to be anything) is to teach him to be a creative person. A. H. Maslow, "The Need for Creative People," *Personnel Administration*, vol. 28, no. 3, 1965, p. 4.

The potential for creativity expression is widely distributed in the population. We believe that this statement is not contradicted by impressive evidence which indicates that a relatively small number of people account for most creative contributions. While frequency of creative expression is not widely or evenly distributed in the population, the potential for this expression enjoys widespread distribution. Creativity, in this sense, is much like intelligence.[2] While potential for both is relatively widespread, full expression requires proper nurturing. The parsimonious expression of creativity in schools, particularly among young students in elementary and secondary classes, can be attributed only to a creativity vacuum in schools as organizations and to a parallel vacuum in the leadership of these schools. Creative educational supervision does not work to instill creativity in teachers and students, but rather works to encourage the creativity which is already in people to emerge. A parallel focus, of course, is on developing a climate for creativity in the school.

Effective administration and supervision involve processes thoroughly dependent upon creative acts. Few occupations can rival educational management's dependence upon creativity for success. Modern large high schools, for example, are characterized by extremely complex goals, fully diversified clients, highly professional workers, pluralistic internal and external influence systems, sophisticated professional knowledge, and specialized educational technology. The successful accomplishment of school goals in this keenly professional and complex educational environment is dependent upon creative administration and supervision.

"Change for change's sake" is an incredible educational slogan. The popular and widespread use of this slogan in education is the cause of much unjustified apprehension about creative expression in American education. Indeed, there is always reason for change![3] A principal, for example, may propose a change to increase personal control or status, to improve efficiency, to hurt a rival school faction, to increase potential in achieving school goals, and so on, but never for the sake of change. Reasons for change generally fall into three categories—those which focus on self, those which focus on task, and those which focus on person or maintenance. One who advocates change to increase his own status, for example, is motivated by self-interest. If he advocates change because he believes that it will add needed perspec-

[2]The link between intelligence and creativity is not clear. Steiner notes that while measures of general intelligence fail to predict creativity, more creative individuals score higher on tests of flexibility, fluency, complexity, and originality. Gary A. Steiner (ed.), *The Creative Organization,* The University of Chicago Press, Chicago, 1965, p. 7. Much additional work needs to be done in identifying, mapping, and classifying the many modes of expression which exist for both intelligence and creativity.

[3]Those in education who charge "Change for change's sake" often mean that they do not like a given change or that they see no link between the change and increased effectiveness in achieving school goals.

tive to an educational problem, his focus is on task. He may also advocate change in a teaching format in order to permit newer school members opportunities to participate and thus accumulate shares in the school enterprise. In this case he is motivated by person considerations.[4]

While we expect youngsters to exhibit some creative promise in schools, we generally work against creative expression. Further, we tend not to expect much creative expression from teachers. These strange events are best evidenced by schools which attempt to achieve ambitious "creativity" objectives through techniques of control and regulation. Schools and classrooms, for example, which are organizationally characterized by high stratification, formalization, and centralization and which emphasize efficiency and production can provide little more than lip service to creativity objectives.

Creativity should not be viewed solely as a means to some educational, end, but is indeed itself an educational end. While many educators readily identify with seeking creative solutions to educational problems, they fail to see relevancy in schools' achieving a creative mind set. Carl Rogers describes this mind set as follows:

In the world which is already upon us, the goal of education must be to develop individuals [schools] who are open to change, who are flexible and adaptive, who have *learned how to learn,* and are thus able to learn continuously. Only such persons [schools] can constructively meet the perplexities of a world in which problems spawn much faster than their answers. The goal of education must be to develop a society in which people can live more comfortably with *change* than with *rigidity.* In the coming world the capacity to face the new appropriately is more important than the ability to know and repeat the old.

The word *schools* is added to the Rogers quote to dramatize the fundamental concept of interdependency between the creative individual and the creative school. We believe that achieving goals of openness and creative expression for youngsters in schools depends upon achieving these goals for the school itself.

CREATIVE INDIVIDUALS AND SCHOOLS

In supervision, creativity is operationally defined as expressions which include proposing, developing, and implementing new and better solutions to educational problems. We view innovation as one kind of creativity, rather than vice versa. Not all forms of creative expression need involve

---

[4]Whether such changes improve immediate educational effectiveness or not is generally not of concern in this instance. Shareholding, however, inevitably increases identification and commitment. These in turn result in performance effectiveness. This professional partnership is a powerful motivating strategy.

[5]Carl R. Rogers, "A Plan for Self-directed Change in an Educational System," *Educational Leadership,* vol. 24, no. 8, May, 1967, p. 717.

invention. Using in new ways ideas and concepts already available and synthesizing materials from a variety of sources as one seeks fresh perspective are also expressions of creativity. While creativity is often seen as seeking and developing *new* goals and emphasis, schools more often use creative energy to improve that which the school is already doing.

Certain characteristics distinguish the creative school from others and creative individuals from others. These distinguishing characteristics are similar to each other. This similarity suggests that creativity in individuals and creativity in schools form an interdependent relationship. Therefore the creative capacity of a given school depends largely upon creative expression of school inhabitants. And increasing creative expression among students, teachers, and administrators depends upon a certain propensity for creativity in the school as an organization. In Table 9-1 we summarize characteristics of the creative school and contrast these with characteristics of creative individuals.

Our theme has been that supervisors interested in developing creative expression in youngsters will need to emphasize a broader creative emphasis for the entire school. Developing creativity in schools requires making available for the human organization large amounts of uncommitted money, time, skill, and goodwill. A creative atmosphere is an indulgent one, not only in the availability of material resources, but in its psychological richness and its freedom from external pressure. In schools with this atmosphere the reward emphasis is on intrinsic satisfaction and esteem from knowledgeable peers. Hierarchical evaluation is largely replaced by feedback. When evaluation does occur, it comes from one's peer group. Power is readily dispersed throughout the school, and students and teachers have opportunities to influence the school. Further, the school is tolerant of mistakes and encourages risk taking.[6]

More Than Ideas

We do not limit creativity to invention. Indeed, creative action—that which broadens and implements good ideas—is the heartbeat of the school. New ideas are simply not enough! They need to be applied and extended to multiple school problems and then converted into practical solutions and strategies. Must everyone in the school express *inventive* creativity? We think not. We do believe, however, that creative action (the application and implementation of creative ideas) is a professional prerequisite to school success. While creativity deals with invention, synthesis, and application of educa-

[6]Victor Thompson, "The Innovative Organization," in Fred D. Carver and Thomas J. Sergiovanni (eds.), *Organization and Human Behavior: Focus on Schools*, New York, McGraw-Hill, 1969, pp. 392–403. In describing the creative person, Van Miller uses the locomotive wheel analogy. Indeed, the creative person is somewhat different (off center), but, like the train wheel with its off-center drive linkage, the organization cannot run without him.

TABLE 9-1.   CHARACTERISTICS OF CREATIVITY

The creative individual	The creative school
He has conceptual fluency and is able to produce a large number of ideas quickly. He is usually intelligent, but is not limited by logic and rationality.	Has idea men, open channels of communication, and encourages maximum internal and external contact.
He displays originality and generates unusual ideas. He is inquisitive and is generally dissatisfied with the status quo.	Has an open personnel policy which permits a variety of personality types, including locals and cosmopolitans, specialists and generalists. Assigns nonspecialists or cross-specialists to problems for fresh perspective.
He evaluates and analyzes ideas on the basis of merit, not source. He is motivated by interest in the problem itself and is primarily intrinsically oriented and dedicated to work.	Has an objective, fact-finding approach which emphasizes problem solving and not who solves problems. Ideas are evaluated on merit, not the status of the originator.
He suspends judgment until he has adequate evidence. He is much less dogmatic and certain about things and spends more time in analysis and exploration.	The school does not overcommit itself to one best approach to education. Specialized buildings—for example, those which "lock in" a given educational program—are avoided. Emphasis is on planning and development. The school willingly tries an idea before judging it. Everything gets a chance.
He is less authoritarian and takes a flexible, realistic view of life. He has a broad, yet deep, understanding of himself. He is self-accepting.	The school is more decentralized, more complex, and more diversified. Lines of authority are not always clear. The school is able to more readily absorb errors, live with ambiguity, and move in multiple directions. It tolerates risk taking and expects to take calculated chances.
He relies on independence of judgment and is less conforming. He sees himself as being different.	The school is autonomous and independent. Further, it expects similar independence in its departments and divisions. It seeks original and different approaches and tolerates internal diversity as it works to achieve educational ends. The school tries not to be another "X."
He has a rich, "bizarre" fantasy life and a superior perspective on reality.	The school recognizes and accepts creative expression as an end in itself. Nevertheless, it works to operationalize this expression in facilitating educational problem solving.

Adapted from Gary A. Steiner (ed)., *The Creative Organization,* University of Chicago Press, Chicago, 1965 pp. 16–18. Ideas from Scott are also incorporated. William E. Scott, "The Creative Individual," *Academy of Management Journal,* September, 1965, pp. 211–219.

tional ideas, *planned change* refers to the systematic dissemination of these ideas. How do we expose teachers to new ideas? What motivates teachers to adopt or reject a new idea? How can we systematically work to improve teacher performance? What change techniques are available to supervisors? These are concerns of planned change in educational supervision. Many of these concerns are related to creativity, while still others are the means to bring the fruits of creative effort to improved teaching and learning.

PLANNED CHANGE

One of the fundamental assumptions to this writing is that supervisory ways of behaving involve some aspect of change. While we wish to avoid stereotyping the supervisor as a change agent per se, the act of supervision invariably involves a human interaction directed at improving (and thus changing) some aspect of professional performance—the schools' work and/or the schools' goals. Therefore, although a supervisor may not be a full-time change agent, he indeed assumes the change posture, along with administrators, teachers, and others, when he behaves in a supervisory way. In this section we examine some of the issues which permeate change in education as well as some of the conditions which help and hinder educational change. We do not, however, provide engineering models for change. Indeed, such models are important, and many useful ones exist.[7] Our hope is that strategies for change, based on the synthesizing theory and our concept of enlightened supervision, will emerge as readers and classes use this book. Indeed, applied change models developed within the context of local and specific school problems and environments but based on enlightened theoretical foundations offer the school practitioner, at least for the present, the most promise for promoting educational change. We continue with considerations which may be helpful in inventing effective and "creative" change strategies.

Some Value Questions

Changing teacher behavior, educational program, and school direction on the one hand and avoiding the charge of manipulation or social engineering on the other have provided supervisors with an ambiguous work environment. Supervisors are assumed to be committed to educational change but are expected not to perform as manipulators. These expectations come from a variety of overlapping sources. MacDonald describes the problem as follows:

> Morally, we face the dilemma of deciding whether we should approach the

[7]For example, David L. Clark and Egon G. Guba, "An Examination of Potential Change Roles in Education," Seminar on Innovation in Planning School Curricula, Indiana University, October, 1965, and Egon G. Guba, "Development, Diffusion and Evaluation," in Terry L. Eidell and Joanne M. Kitchel (eds.), *Knowledge Production and Utilization in Educational Administration,* Center for the Advanced Study of Educational Administration, University of Oregon, 1968.

changing of teacher behavior with some criterion which lies outside the person of the teacher (e.g., pupil learning) as a basis for change, and, theoretically we do not agree upon how to proceed with the business of changing behavior.

These dilemmas, at this time, can only be resolved by some statement of premises or propositions upon which an in-service program can be built. This writer believes the following premises are justified.

1. Teaching is a complex integration of behaviors and single behavior chains cannot profitably be grafted onto the teacher's behavioral system.
2. It is morally wrong to set out to change teacher behavior unless the change sought has been rationally selected by the teacher from among a range of known alternatives.
3. Learning is an individual matter and how something is learned is determined primarily by the internal structure of needs, perceptions, readiness, motivations, etc., of the individual—not by the external conditions of an outside person desiring change.[8]

MacDonald accepts the change agent role for supervisors provided that they accept and work within the framework of certain fundamental principles relating to democratic change ethics and the dignity and worth of the change client. Indeed, we would be "out of business" if we were to conclude that adopting change agent perspectives is inherently contrary to democratic principles. We flirt with danger, however—to ourselves, change clients, school clients, and, indeed, schools—if we are unaware of the possibilities of compromising our democratic traditions as we participate in and evoke the change process. We need to identify a series of principles which will serve to guide change behavior and provide the supervisor with methodological norms. "It follows also that the best guarantee of the ethical operation of social engineers [in our context, supervisors] is that their basic training be focused in a methodology of planned change which unites the norms of democratic operation, relevant understandings of change processes and social structures, and skills in stimulating, inducing and stabilizing changes in persons and groups."[9]

Benne proposes a set of basic democratic norms which, if adopted by the supervisor, assures that the process of change is acceptable:

1. The engineering of change and the meeting of pressures on a group or organization toward change must be collaborative.
2. The engineering of change must be educational for the participants.
3. The engineering of change must be experimental.
4. The engineering of change must be task oriented, that is, controlled by the requirements of the problem confronted and its effective solution, rather than

[8]James B. MacDonald, "Helping Teachers Change," in James Raths and Robert R. Leeper (eds.), *The Supervisor: Agent for Change in Teaching*, The Association for Supervision and Curriculum Development, Washington, D.C., 1966, p. 3.
[9]Kenneth D. Benne, "Democratic Ethics and Social Engineering," *Progressive Education*, vol. 27, no. 7, May, 1949, p. 204.

oriented to the maintenance or extension of the prestige or power of those who originate contributions.[10]

As *collaboration,* enlightened supervision presumes that the change agent and the client form a change partnership (supervisor-teacher, teacher-student, superintendent-staff, and so on), with each being fully aware of the intentions of others. As *educational,* enlightened supervision presumes that the focus for change is at least two-dimensional. On the one hand, the supervisor works to implement change in some aspect of the school enterprise; on the other hand, he focuses on the process of change. He engages in a weaning process with the client group aimed at decreasing their dependence upon him. Indeed, as each change cycle is completed, clients are now better able to identify school problems, search for alternative solutions, choose among them, and implement their choice. The enlightened supervisor works for his own extinction while traditional supervisory patterns assume eternal client dependence upon the supervisor. As *experimental,* enlightened supervision presumes that all social arrangements, educational changes, and the like, exist in a malleable state rather than having been cast in stone. There is nothing sacred in the current best means of teaching reading or of providing feedback to teachers. As new conditions warrant and as new evidence is gathered, planned change requires that present conditons be reformed. Further, if a change proves ineffective or inappropriate, it should be discarded with relative ease. As *task-oriented,* enlightened supervision presumes that the motivation for change is authentic and, indeed, related to conscious efforts toward school improvement. In contrast, self-oriented change is that which focuses on the improvement of the status and welfare of the change agent rather than of the client group or the school.[11] Educational change can no longer remain a win-lose proposition for people but must be considered as a problem-solving method which increases educational effectiveness.

Environmental and Interpersonal Conditions for Change

We have argued that highest payoff for educational change comes from supervisory efforts which are directed toward improving susceptibility to change. Schools which are characterized by a high degree of centralization, formalization, status differential, efficiency, and the like, will tend to frustrate meaningful educational change. Such schools, however, are geared to make rather rapid superficial change. They can move swiftly to adopt all of the trappings (books, hardware, etc.) of modern math, for example, except

[10]*Ibid.,* pp. 205 and 206.
[11]Rensis Likert, for example, found that frequency of meetings was related to supervisors being perceived as promotable by superordinates. Rensis Likert, *New Patterns of Management,* McGraw-Hill, New York, 1961. School supervisors who engage in group activity primarily as a means to improve visibility and chance for promotion violate an important democratic norm.

enlightened teaching of modern math. Significant change is that which occurs at lower levels of the school organization or that which is accepted at lower levels. A school which emphasizes professional complexity, job satisfaction, decentralization, and the like, as well as a deemphasis of formalization, stratification, and efficiency, is more capable of nurturing meaningful educational change.[12] Related to this organizational framework are the establishment and maintenance of an open school climate and of adequate school health.[13]

At the performance improvement level, supervisors work as educational technicians in bringing newer developments to teachers and as professional developers in working to help teachers approach the fully functioning ideal.[14] As educational technicians they can do much to help teachers move "off zero" from satisfaction with present performance to search for alternate performance patterns. Moving from satisfaction to search, of course, means that teachers become dissatisfied with present performance levels.

The traditional means to bring about dissatisfaction of teachers with their present performance levels is the lesson evaluation. Under this system someone in authority, and therefore presumably someone who "knows" more, observes the teacher teaching. A conference typically follows, and the super-teacher points out to the regular teacher his strengths and weaknesses. He then prescribes and suggests to the regular teacher alternative teaching patterns. Contemporary means are similar to the traditional pattern except that regular teachers are permitted to discuss the lesson "more freely" with the superteacher, the hope being that together they may come to realize those deficiencies observed by the superteacher. Enlightened supervision relies less on evaluation as a means to bring about teacher dissatisfaction with present performance (and subsequent search for new teaching patterns) and rather emphasizes reality-testing or feedback techniques.

Essentially, reality testing is a means for the supervisor to help teachers see what they are actually doing while he attempts to hold supervisory value judgments to a minimum. The Amidon and Flanders interaction analysis[15] method is an example of a reality-testing feedback system. It is premised upon the belief that "programs organized for helping teachers to understand and to plan behavior change must have provision for an effective feedback system."[16]

In using the Flanders system, an observer (supervisor or other teacher)

---

[12]Note our discussion of Hage's axiomatic theory of organizations in Chap. 3.
[13]Concepts of climate and health for schools and supervisors are discussed in Chap. 4.
[14]In Chap. 6 we discussed and presented a professional development map which serves to help supervisors bring about the fully functioning phenomenon.
[15]Edmund J. Amidon and Ned A. Flanders, *The Role of the Teacher in the Classroom: A Manual for Understanding and Improving Teachers' Classroom Behavior*, Paul S. Amidon and Associates, Inc., Minneapolis, Minn., 1963.
[16]*Ibid.*, p. 4.

sits in the classroom and records, at three-second intervals, a category number which describes the kind of interaction he observes. The interaction categories are as follows:

Teacher talk		
Indirect	1.	Accepts feelings
	2.	Praises or encourages
	3.	Accepts or uses ideas of student
	4.	Asks questions
Direct	5.	Lectures
	6.	Gives directions
	7.	Criticizes students or justifies authority
Student talk		
	8.	Response to teacher
	9.	Initiates discussion
	10.	Silent or confused

From Edmund J. Amidon and Ned A. Flanders, *The Role of the Teacher in the Classroom: A Manual for Understanding and Improving Teachers' Classroom Behavior,* Paul S. Amidon and Associates, Inc., Minneapolis, Minn., 1963.

The observer can now provide the teacher with an interaction map of his lesson. The Amidon and Flanders book shows how this interaction map can be converted into a simple interaction matrix which indicates the percentage of time spent in teacher talk, in student talk, and the like. This objective description of behavior forms the basis for change.

In addition to the Flanders method, the supervisor may use other data collection devices. Among them are the Indiana State University Teacher Classroom Activity Profile (TCAP) and the Cooperative Educational Research Laboratories' Verbal-Behavior Classification System (CVC). "Homemade" devices, such as a rating-observation device patterned after the Bloom Taxonomy of Educational Objectives, for example, are also useful. Tape recorders and video tape television devices are other means of obtaining information as to what's happening in the classroom.[17]

Success of the reality-testing feedback strategy is largely dependent upon the nature and quality of the relationship which exists between client and change agent. The nature and quality of relationship for enlightened supervision are characterized by mutual determination of goals, a spirit of inquiry, mutual interaction, a voluntary change relationship with either party free to terminate, and a mutual influence system.[18]

---

[17]While we do not give detailed attention to the educo-technical methods and skills of supervision, we believe them to be of fundamental importance to supervisors. Sources for this important topic are provided at the end of this chapter.

[18] Warren G. Bennis, *Changing Organizations,* McGraw-Hill, New York, 1966, Chap. 5.

RESISTANCE TO CHANGE

We have discussed change which occurs in educational organizations at two levels: (1) at the performance level for individuals and groups, and (2) at the organizational level for adopting alternate educational program features, administrative arrangements, organizational structures, and the like. As supervisors work at each of these levels, they need to be aware of the obstacles to change they are likely to encounter. We attempt to catalog some reasons or causes of resistance to change below. The list suffers from overlap and from failure to differentiate between levels of changes. The usefulness of the list will increase if readers examine themselves, their professional colleagues, and their respective schools in relation to change resistance.

1. Limited identification: Individuals and groups in a particular school may not identify with school ends but rather hang tightly to rather local school means. Thus, if ends are to be improved by changing certain means, the person may be blind to the ends as he clings to the means.
2. Fear: A common cause of resistance to something new is simply fear. New teaching methods are resisted because a teacher does not know how to use them and wishes to avoid failure. Inadequate and distorted knowledge about a particular change increases fear.
3. Overspecialization: A modern cause of change resistance in schools is overspecialization. A teacher or administrator who specializes heavily bets on his unique skills being in demand for a long time. A Russian history teacher, for example, is likely to resist social studies core movements and other interdisciplinary ventures because they endanger his limited, but extensive, ability monopoly.
4. Dependence: Power centralization and other bureaucratic features of schools often leave teachers with a feeling of powerlessness in terms of educational programs and other educo-technical matters.[19] Having little opportunity to participate in school developments at the policy level, teachers become dependent upon others to decide and announce the next change. Dependence leads to uncertainty, and uncertainty is a cause of change resistance.
5. Status and position: Changes are often perceived as altering the formal and informal status hierarchy systems of a school. Thus, those with something to lose in this regard often play it safe and resist change.

[19] We are aware of the Gerald Moeller and W. W. Charters study which links bureaucratically oriented schools with increased sense of power for teachers. Power references in that study are largely in terms of student contact, protection from parents, and the like. We refer to educational program decision making. Gerald Moeller and W. W. Charters, "Relation of Bureaucratization to Sense of Power among Teachers," *Administrative Science Quarterly*, vol. 10, 1966, pp. 444–465.

6. Tradition: Individuals and groups often resist change because changes endanger cherished and accustomed ways of doing things. Indeed, the more threatening a change is to the social-cultural core of a given school, the more likely it is to be resisted.

7. Uncertainty: Although we referred to uncertainty in paragraph 4, we repeat it here because of its fundamental link with change resistance. The capacity to deal with uncertainty and ambiguity varies substantially among individuals. To some, exchanging the tried and true (no matter how inadequate it may be) for something new and strange is traumatic. Nevertheless, we note that when most writers describe the fully functioning person—the mature individual—they include a reference to his tolerance for ambiguity and his ability to cope with uncertainty.

8. Intelligent conservatism: All organizations and societies benefit from those who wish to have a second look before they leap. Intelligent conservatism is a plus for schools, hospitals, and other societal institutions which pay heavily in cost to clients and to society for professional misjudgments. Intelligent conservatism should not, however, provide *defensive* resistors to educational change with a respectable rationalization. Intelligent conservatism implies caution perhaps more than it does resistance.[20]

9. Administrative maintenance obligation: The status quo seems to have natural appeal to administrators primarily because of their legal responsibilities toward the maintenance of organizational stability. A first consideration for change for an administrator is: Can the new be assimilated into existing organizational structures? As such he supports piecemeal change, spaced over a long period of time.

Organizational control is another of his major goals, and this requires a high degree of conformity unless different members and parts of the organization are to go off in all directions at the same time. Innovation is a natural enemy of conformity, and the administrator must hold innovation within digestible limits unless he is to lose control and simply become the figurehead for a free-wheeling organization.[21]

[20]John Dewey describes three alternatives available to educators as we approach change.

Educators may act so as to perpetuate the present confusion and possibly increase it. That will be the result of drift, and under present conditions to drift is in the end to make a choice. Or they may select the newer scientific, technological, and cultural forces that are producing change in the old order; may estimate the direction in which they are moving and their outcome if they are given free play, and see what can be done to make the schools their ally. Or educators may become intelligently conservative and strive to make the schools a force in maintaining the older order intact against the impact of new forces.

John Dewey, *The School Frontier*, May, 1937, reproduced in *Progressive Education*, vol. 27, no. 1, Ocotber, 1949. While Dewey endorses some intelligent conservatism, he goes on to express his belief that educators should choose the second direction.

[21]Ray E. Brown, *Judgment in Administration*, McGraw-Hill, New York, 1966, p. 186.

As administrators continue direct efforts to seek control over people, they enjoy organizational security in terms of position, power, and the like. The unanticipated consequence of this phenomenon is that they ensure organizational mediocrity in terms of achieving school goals. Administrators who practice enlightened supervision seek organizational control over the accomplishment and extension of school goals, not over people.

In examining forces which teachers perceive as influencing the innovative process and the diffusion of classroom practice Lippitt finds that the innovative practice itself, the physical and temporal arrangements of the school, the social structure and authority system of the school, and attitudes of teachers are significant in helping and hindering change. He catalogs these "facilitating" and "hindering" forces in Table 9-2.

TABLE 9-2. FORCES RELEVANT TO THE FACILITATION AND HIN-DRANCE OF INNOVATION AND DIFFUSION OF TEACHING PRACTICES

	Facilitating forces	Hindering forces
1. Characteristics of the practice	A. Relevant to universal student problems	A. Does not meet the needs of a class
	B. Can be done a little at a time	B. Requires a lot of energy
	C. Consultant and peer help available, needed skills are clearly outlined	C. Requires new skills
	D. Clearly aids student growth	D. Requires change in teacher values
	E. A behavioral change with no new gimmicks	E. Requires new facilities
	F. Built-in evaluation to see progress	F. Won't work
	G. Innovation has tried a new twist	G. Not new
	H. Student, not subject, oriented	H. Not for my grade level or subject
	I. No social practice can be duplicated exactly	I. Effectiveness reduced if practice gains general use
2. Physical and temporal arrangements	A. Staff meetings used for professional growth, substitutes hired to free teacher(s) to visit other classrooms, lunchtime used for discussions, students sent home for an afternoon so teachers can all meet together	A. No time to get together
	B. Extra clerical help provided	B. Too many clerical duties to have time to share ideas
	C. Staff meetings for everyone to get together, occasionally; grade level or departmental meetings	C. Classrooms are isolated
	D. Meetings held in classrooms	D. No rooms to meet in

TABLE 9-2. *FORCES RELEVANT TO THE FACILITATION AND HIN-DRANCE OF INNOVATION AND DIFFUSION OF TEACHING PRACTICES* (*Continued*)

	Facilitating forces	Hindering forces
3. Peer and authority relations	A. Sharing sessions or staff bulletins become a matter of school routine	A. Little communication among teachers
	B. Public recognition given to innovators and adapters; innovation-diffusion seen as a cooperative task	B. Competition for prestige among teachers
	C. Sharing ideas is expected and rewarded; norms support asking for and giving help; regular talent search for new ideas	C. Norms enforce privatism
	D. Area team liaison supports new ideas	D. Colleagues reject ideas
	E. Principal or superintendent supports innovation-diffusion activity	E. Principal is not interested in new ideas
	F. Principal helps create a staff atmosphere of sharing and experimentation	F. School climate doesn't support experimentation
	G. Staff meetings used as two-way informing and educating sessions	G. Principal doesn't know what's going on
	H. Teachers influence the sharing process	H. Teacher ideas don't matter
4. Personal attitudes	A. Seeking new ways	A. Resisting change
	B. Seeking peer and consultant help	B. Fearing evaluation and rejecting failure
	C. Always open to adapting and modifying practices	C. Dogmatism about already knowing about new practices
	D. Public rewards for professional growth	D. Feeling professional growth not important
	E. See groups as endemic and relevant for academic learning	E. Negative feelings about group work
	F. Understand connection between mental health and academic learning	F. Mental health is "extra"
	G. Optimism	G. Pessimism
	H. Test ideas slowly	H. Afraid to experiment
	I. Suiting and changing practice to fit one's own style and class	I. Resistance to imitating others

From Ronald Lippitt et al., "The Teacher as Innovator, Seeker, and Sharer of New Practices," in Richard I. Miller (ed.), *Perspectives on Educational Change.* Copyright © 1967, Meredith Corporation. Reprinted by permission of Appleton-Century-Crofts.

Lippitt's table should serve as a useful checklist for supervisors as they scan educational problems dealing with change. As one examines creative supervision and planned change, the process of communications emerges as a critical skill for supervisors and staff. Communication theory is not unique to the change process but serves as the core of the action system of the school as it gives life to and unites the variables which make up the synthesizing theory. We conclude this chapter with a consideration of the supervisor and the process of communications.

COMMUNICATIONS

Culbertson, Jacobson, and Reller[22] identify six concepts which they believe are essential in describing and explaining the communications process. These are purpose, communicator, medium, channel, content, and receiver.[23] To this list we add *frequency* and *negotiations*. Each of these concepts applies to two-person communication, group communication, and organizational communication. For brevity, however, we use the singular receiver to refer to all. Further, as we discuss these concepts, each should be considered in relation to the others. The eight, as components of an interdependent system, form the process of communication.

As we describe the eight concepts, visualize them as a means to evaluate the effectiveness and adequacy of past supervisory efforts in your school, particularly as they relate to communication, and as a basis for developing future supervisory strategies. For example, use the concepts as a means to describe existing patterns of communication in your school and build upon them as you develop ideal communications patterns. The difference which exists in this analysis between "is" and "ought" will provide a rough index of communications adequacy for a given school.

Purpose

The reason for a given communication often determines who the communicator is, the channel direction, the media of transmission, the content, the frequency of contact, and the amount of mutual influence which results from negotiation. Two levels of purposes always exist for a communication attempt—manifest and latent. At the manifest level, purposes relate to some aspect of task or school functioning. At the latent level, purposes relate to some aspect of self or of need expressed or felt by the communicator. High communicators, for example, seem motivated by strong needs for exhibition, dominance, and aggression.[24]

---

[22]This discussion follows that which appears in Jack Culbertson et al., *Administrative Relationships: A Casebook,* Prentice-Hall, Englewood Cliffs, N.J., 1960, pp. 380–384.
[23]*Ibid.,* p. 380.
[24]Charles Mader, "Analysis of the Relationship between the Involvement of the Supervisor in the Structure of School Organization and Measures of His Personality Characteristics." Unpublished doctoral dissertation, Department of Educational Administration, University of Illinois, 1969.

The receiver needs to know if there is a single or multiple purpose for the communication. For example, is the purpose general or specific? Does it apply to one or to all? The more information a receiver has about the purpose of a communication, the more acceptable it will be to him. Indeed, the more information the sender has about the purposes of a communication (manifest and latent), the more effective he, the sender, will be.

While latent purposes are *never* absent from any communication, they need to be placed in perspective in relation to manifest purposes. As one becomes aware of the double nature of purposes, his ability to control latent tendencies increases. He is then able to more clearly delineate and articulate manifest purposes to receivers.

Communicator

The communicator is the person who sends the message. In formal school settings he generally transmits decisions or information and feelings which contribute to or evaluate decision making. How receivers perceive the communicator is crucial in determining communication effectiveness. For example, the source of authority for what a sender has to say is an important variable in determining receiver acceptance. Is the receiver expected to listen and comply because the sender has superior professional knowledge, is well liked, is legally authorized, occupies a superordinate position, or has the power to evoke positive and negative sanctions? What about the sender's character: Is he perceived as being generally trustworthy, honest, and authentic?[25] Is his previous communication record good? Are his purposes perceived as legitimate by receivers? Who the communicator is, what his perceived intent is, and the basis upon which he expects attention and compliance are important variables which influence communication effectiveness in the classroom, the corridor, the teacher's lounge, the committee setting, and so on.

Channel

Communications channels are the road networks which carry messages throughout the school. We classify channels broadly as upward, downward, and horizontal. Upward channels link members at lower organizational levels (students and teacher) with those at upper levels of the school (principals, central office, school board). Downward channels flow in the opposite direction. Horizontal channels are those which connect people at the same organizational level (teacher-teacher, student-student).

Downward channels are more easily established and used because they rely on existing formal organizational structures and traditional hierarchical

---

[25] Many schools, as senders, have image trouble as they communicate with the public, with teachers, or with students. This image trouble is not unlike the "credibility gap" which many perceive as existing in relation to the federal government and foreign policy.

arrangements. Organizationally, these are more "natural" communication networks, particularly for bureaucratically oriented schools. Upward channels, on the other hand, are more threatening to bureaucratic structures and therefore are more difficult to establish and maintain.[26] While it is perfectly natural and proper, for example, for the superintendent or his agents to send weekly notices to teachers, it is less than natural and proper for teachers to reciprocate with weekly notices to the superintendent. Further, while teachers read daily official notices to students, students must rely on less formal (often "underground") means to communicate with the school.

Most authorities deplore the virtual smothering of upward channels by heavy school emphasis on downward channels, yet we have surprisingly little research in this area. A recent British study of communication patterns in teaching hospitals adequately states the case for a better balance between upward and downward channels. The Manchester College of Science and Technology researchers[27] found that in hospitals with high nursing-staff turnover and slower patient recovery rates, communications channels tended to flow mainly downward. Further, student nurses and junior staff members found communications in such organizations to be virtually unintelligible. Hospitals with low nursing-staff turnover and faster patient recovery rates tended to have communication channels which formed an upward-downward loop. The junior staff in hospitals with this communication pattern felt that the senior staff considered them as junior partners in the enterprise. The researchers concluded that the quality of communication affects the quality of learning for student nurses, with the upward-downward loop being more conducive to learning than the downward flow. We would, of course, expect similar findings in elementary and secondary schools and in other educational institutions.

Effective horizontal communication channels are as important to supervision as is the upward-downward loop. Professionals in schools need opportunities for mutual exchange of information and ideas. Simply, teachers need to talk with teachers. This interaction is the lifeblood of professional growth and of educational program development. Students, too, need opportunities for mutual exchange as well as meaningful entry to the upward-downward communication loop of the school.[28]

---

[26]In desperation, teachers have learned to fight bureaucratic fire with bureaucratic fire in communicating. The emergence of elaborate grievance procedures and the like gives evidence of this.

[27]R. W. Revans, *Standards for Morale: Cause and Effect*, Oxford, London, 1964. This study is summarized in Saul Gellerman, *Management by Motivation*, American Management Association, New York, 1968.

[28]We hypothesize that schools which fail to provide students with adequate horizontal and upward communication channels are characterized by more student unrest, militancy, turnover, and dropout than schools which do provide these communication opportunities.

Medium

By *medium* we refer to the method of transmission. At the broadest level we classify media into oral and written categories. Notices, handbooks, bulletin boards, memos, and the like, are examples of written media. Meetings, polls, conferences, telephones, and television are examples of oral media. In an extensive study (of 969 principals in large high schools throughout the United States), McCleary inventoried methods and media used by principals as they communicated to their faculty as a whole and to individual faculty members.[29] He found that general faculty meetings, department meetings, principal's cabinet meetings, and meetings of department chairmen (in descending order) were most often used to bring the entire staff or significant parts of the staff together. In communicating with individual staff members, principals generally relied on classroom visits, individual conferences, and small-group meetings. Of these, the principal rated individual conferences as being most helpful. More than one hundred principals commented that increases in staff size and school complexity precluded their maintaining an "open door" policy for staff members. Principals relied almost exclusively on regular bulletins and special announcements or written communication devices. Intercom or P.A. systems were most often used as electronic means of communication. In McLuhan's mass-media age, it is distressing to note that little creativity is evidenced by the media used by principals to communicate with staff. Ninety-two percent of the principals, for example, have never used the medium of closed-circuit television, 89 percent the medium of video tape, 93 percent radio, and 65 percent voice tape to communicate with the memberships of the school.

Enlightened supervisors are increasing their reliance on media which permit nonevaluative feedback as they communicate with teachers.[30] These include group analysis techniques, interaction analysis, microteaching, and the like.

Communication Content

Information, facts, attitudes, feelings, and values that are transmitted to receivers compose the content of a communication. While the sender deliberately intends cognitive content, messages are always accompanied by affective content. Often, the unintended affective content determines the acceptance of a message. A student, for example, who is given good advice by a teacher he dislikes does not accurately perceive the message. The affective

[29]Lloyd E. McCleary, "Communications in Large Secondary Schools—A Nationwide Study of Practices and Problems," *The Bulletin, National Association of Secondary School Principals*, vol. 52, no. 325, February, 1968, pp. 48–61.
[30]Nonevaluative feedback techniques are not without pitfalls. Among the most serious problems is that a technique such as the Flanders interaction analysis may be nonevaluative at the manifest level *but most evaluative,* in the mind of the supervisor, at the latent level.

content, operating in this case as a reverse halo, obscures or contaminates the good advice. Our teacher is bewildered by the student's lack of acceptance of such obviously good counsel. This happens because he is unaware of affective content and therefore focuses entirely on the cognitive content. Indeed, the two send messages to each other which are quite different from those received. Affective content is sometimes included as an aspect of nonverbal communications. This is a broader content area which includes messages sent via facial expression, posture, hand gesture, and the like.

The Receiver

The receiver is the person, group, or organization for whom the communication is intended.

The meaning that results from a particular communication is highly dependent upon the basic motivations and personality patterns of the communicatee [receiver]. What are his interests? What does he expect from the communicator and the situation in which he finds himself? What is his attitude toward his peers? For what is he striving? Is he highly intelligent and keenly critical, or is he less intelligent and less critical? Such queries suggest that the communicatee is a significant element in communication.[31]

Frequency

Frequency refers to the number of contacts a communicator makes either with a given person or with a number of persons over a period of time. We have generally assumed that supervisors who communicate more frequently with teachers are more effective. Number of contacts per se, however, may not be an adequate index of effectiveness. In a recent study Mader found that high communication contact for supervisors in high school was positively associated with the supervisors' need for exhibition, dominance, and aggression but negatively associated with their need for succorance, nurturance, and change.[32] In summarizing his findings, Mader notes that the

[31]Culbertson et al., *op. cit.*, p. 383.
[32]Mader, *op. cit.* Frequency of contact for supervisors was compared with their responses to the Edwards Personal Preference Inventory. Behavior samples associated with exhibition, high dominance, and aggression on the Edwards scale are:
1. *Exhibition*—to say witty and clever things, to tell amusing jokes and stories, to talk about personal adventures and experiences, to have others notice and comment upon one's appearance, to say things just to see what effect it will have on others, to talk about personal achievements, to be the center of attention, to use words that others do not know the meaning of, to ask questions others cannot answer.
2. *Dominance*—to argue for one's point of view, to be a leader in groups to which one belongs, to be regarded by others as a leader, to be elected or appointed chairman of committees, to make group decisions, to settle arguments and disputes between others, to tell others how to do their jobs.
3. *Aggression*—to attack contrary points of view, to tell others what one thinks about them, to criticize others publicly, to make fun of others, to tell others off when disagreeing with them, to get revenge for insults, to become angry, to blame others when things go wrong, to read newspaper accounts of violence.

supervisor with high communication contact is "one who tends to be the 'organizational man' type who meets his own needs by compliance with organizational demands, and who is likely to be more institution-oriented than person-oriented."[33]

Low communicators, on the other hand, exhibit opposite need manifestations and behavior tendencies. Indeed, supervisors who are low communicators simply forfeit much good that they can do in school. Yet, as Mader's finding suggests, high communicators seem to have lost control over the balance between manifest and latent purposes for communicating with latent purpose (those which are largely self- rather than other- or task-oriented) predominating. Perhaps the relationship between frequency of communication and supervisor effectiveness is better described as curvilinear. Perhaps supervisors with high contact and those with low contact are both ineffective, even if for different reasons.

While frequency of contact is a useful concept in understanding communications theory, its potency depends upon a simultaneous analysis of other communication concepts.[34] Indeed, quality of content, authenticity, receiver perception of the sender, and perceived legitimacy of purpose may be more important that just frequency.

Negotiation

The concept of mutual influence—or, as some prefer, negotiations—is most fundamental to understanding communication. Through communicating the sender hopes to influence his receiver. For this to happen, *the receiver must in turn influence the sender.* The sender cannot hope for undiluted acceptance of his message if he and the receiver are to interact through this message. As a result of any communication interaction, the message assumes a new form. Indeed, the message reflects having been meaningfully absorbed by the receiver. This absorption results in message modification, and message modification is evidence of communications effectiveness.[35] Gellerman summarizes the concept of influence as follows:

Here is the nub of the entire communication problem: The sender, to be certain that his message will be accepted by the receiver, must be prepared to let the receiver influence him. He must even be prepared to let the receiver alter

---

[33]*Ibid.*, p. 89.

[34]For example, frequency provides us with relatively neutral data. That this tendency may be linked to latent-communication purpose which primarily serves the self-interest of the communicator is important. We should not assume, however, that *all* high communicators are self-oriented. We leave unexplored the question of supervisors' receptivity and availability to contact by subordinates. We believe that high contact of this type will have a positive effect on the school and its human organization.

[35]Perhaps the important point is that the receiver perceives he can change, alter, or modify the message. This perception of influence may be more important than actual modification. Thus the receiver negotiates when he chooses but otherwise accepts the message, understanding that he has the power of influence, of negotiation.

or modify the message in ways that make it more acceptable to the receiver. Otherwise it may not be understood, or it may not be accepted, or it may simply be given lip service and ignored.

In this sense there is a certain aspect of negotiation, or at least the possibility of negotiation, inherent in any effective communication. The message is communicated best in the context of communicating something else as well: the sender's willingness to consider the receiver's reaction to his message as relevant. The message is much less likely to get through if it comes in the context of another attitude: that the receiver should content himself with being a consumer, not a critic, of ideas.[36]

Persuasion or Problem Solving

Communications is an overlapping concept which applies to each of the three classes of variables—initiating, mediating, and school success—we outlined in the synthesizing theory. Supervisors, for example, have certain assumptions about communications which are related to more basic assumptions they have about management and people. These assumptions determine the supervisor's style of communication as he uses the eight concepts we have just discussed. The cycle is completed as receivers react positively, negatively, or neutrally to supervisory communication patterns. This reaction in turn affects their performance as they pursue school goals.

Gibb[37] identifies two views of the communication processes which he feels determine supervisor behavior patterns and subsequent response from the human organization. One view, the persuasion approach, assumes that it is the responsibility of school management to regulate the flow of information in order to ensure message transmission throughout the school. Another view, the problem-solving approach, assumes that effective communication is an outgrowth of effective work, authentic interpersonal relationships, and efficient problem solving. Gibb contrasts the two approaches to communication as follows:

The persuasion manager tends to see communication as primarily an influence process through which people can be changed, controlled, guided, or influenced. Communication becomes education, propaganda, leadership or guidance. Managers try to sell ideas, or to motivate others to work harder, feel better, have higher morale, and be more loyal.

The problem-solving manager sees communication primarily as a necessary adjunct of the process of doing work or solving problems. In order to solve the problem or get the job done certain information must be obtained, certain feelings must be expressed, and a certain amount of interpersonal perceptions must be exchanged in order for a team to be a healthy work or problem-solving unit. Job demands or team maintenance demands determine the amount and kind of communication that is necessary. Communication *is* problem solving.

[36]Gellerman, *op. cit.*, p. 46.
[37]Jack R. Gibb, "Communication and Productivity," *Personnel Administration*, vol. 27, no. 1, 1964, pp. 8–13 and 45.

The difference in the two approaches is one of *focus*. Communication is *both* influence and problem solving. The emphasis and the approach are the significant things. Persuasive communication tends to produce resistance, distrust, circumvention, or counter-persuasion. It is seen by the worker or subordinate as "news management," as propaganda, or as an effort to get him to do what he may not want to do. Research has shown persuasion-centered communications programs to be discouragingly ineffective in accomplishing management goals.

Problem-solving communication is subordinate to the demands of the job or the problem. The nature of the job or the problem calls forth certain bits of information, feelings or perceptions that are relevant to job accomplishment or problem solution. In general, the research shows that when conditions are created which produce relevant *emergent* communications out of the work situation, communications problems are reduced. Thus, face-to-face communications in small groups tend to be superior to other forms of communication because there is a greater likelihood that communications will emerge from interactive job and problem demands.[38]

Indeed, communicating is a human process rather than a management campaign, and in enlightened supervisory environments the *focus* of communication is on problem solving rather than on persuading. As such, messages are always incomplete, always slightly distorted, and always modified. Human weaknesses in communicating are at the same time strengths in that a true exchange of ideas requires that participants come to own shares in these ideas. Message modification, for example, permits this joint ownership.

Some Barriers to Communication

Carl Rogers has proposed that the greatest barrier to communication is our tendency to judge, to evaluate, and, indeed, to approve or disapprove prematurely. Often the affective content of the communication, or our perception of the communicator's purpose, contributes to this tendency. Premature evaluation serves also as a defense for our own ideas, our position, and, indeed, our psychological security. An example of this is our tendency to listen for what we "expect" the communicator to say and thus to miss what he actually says. Because we expect conservatism from an educational conservative or liberalism from our educational liberal, we categorize and distort his message to fit our expectation. This permits us, then, to more comfortably accept or reject his ideas.

Semantic problems are other barriers to communication. Schools are sometimes characterized by a multilingual situation. Students speak one language and teachers another; teachers one and administrators another; educationists one and the lay public another. Communicators simply cannot assume that the meaning they associate with a word is the same for receivers. Davis notes that there are an average of twenty-eight separate meanings

---

[38]*Ibid.*, p. 11.

in the *Oxford Dictionary* for each of the 500 most-used words in the English language.[39] Scholz observes that "since Shakespeare's time, the number of words in the English language has quintupled, increasing from about 140,000 to somewhere between 700,000 and 800,000. Only between 500 and 800 of these words are basic to simple conversation, but these words have more than 14,000 meanings."[40]

An organizational barrier to communication is the filtering and translating that takes place at the boundary of the school. As information moves into the school, it is received at the boundary by appropriate experts. They, in turn, (1) translate this information into general language and channel it into the school, or (2) decide that the information is not important to the school and reject it. Much information is lost or "absorbed" by translation or rejection at the school's boundary. The reading specialist, for example, decides whether to forward a commercial reading program advertisement to the principal or to discard it. If he decides to pass the advertisement on, he is expected to translate its content so that it is readily consumable by an understandably busy principal. *Translation involves evaluation, and evaluation requires absorption of information.*

We use the problems of absorption, evaluation, and semantics as examples of communication barriers. To be sure, there are more—Scholz lists some forty "obstacles" to communication.[41] Readers would better profit from examining communication patterns in their schools and, in the light of this discussion, identify strengths and weaknesses and, indeed, develop and formulate a prescription for improvement. We believe that supervision is, first and foremost, communication.[42]

We have argued that communication processes assume a central position in any comprehensive theory of supervision. Indeed, such processes compose the interlocking network which forms the effective group. Groups, on the other hand, are the building blocks of an effective school. Emerging patterns of supervision rely increasingly on highly effective professional work groups in the development of curriculum, the teaching of students, the "evaluation" of teachers, the administration of educational programs, and the development of educational policy. These groups are usually coalitions of interdependent expert professionals who work together in solving professional problems and in pursuing school goals.[43]

[39]Keith Davis, *Human Relations at Work*, McGraw-Hill, New York, 1962, p. 353.
[40]William Scholz, *Communication in the Business Organization*, Englewood Cliffs, N.J.: Prentice-Hall, 1962, p. 38.
[41]*Ibid.*
[42]Van Miller, *The Public Administration of American School Systems*, Macmillan, New York, 1965, p. 475. Miller's comment is, "Administration is first and foremost communication."
[43]Coalitions based on expertness and specialization are a function of the complexity of modern professional practice in education. See our discussion of the techno-structure in education which appears in Chap. 3.

In the next and final chapter of Part I we examine the concept of group, the process of group supervision, and methods of group analysis.

EDUCO-TECHNICAL SUPERVISION REFERENCES

Allen, Dwight W., and Richard J. Clark: "Micro-teaching: Its Rationale," *High School Journal,* vol. 51, November, 1967, pp. 75–79. (This entire issue is devoted to microteaching.)

Amidon, Edmund, and Elizabeth Hunter: *Improving Teaching: An Analysis of Classroom Verbal Interaction,* Holt, Rinehart and Winston, New York, 1966.

Biddle, Bruce J., and William Ellena (eds.): *Contemporary Research on Teacher Effectiveness,* Holt, Rinehart and Winston, New York, 1964.

"The CVC System," A CERLI Self-teaching Text, Cooperative Educational Research Laboratory, Inc., Northfield, Ill., July, 1968.

Educational Leadership, vol. 24, November, 1966. (Several articles on assessment.)

Evaluation as Feedback and Guide, 1967 Yearbook, Association for Supervision and Curriculum Development. Washington, 1968.

Howsam, Robert B.: *Who's a Good Teacher?* California Teachers Association, Burlingame, Calif., 1960.

Sharpe, Donald M.: "Notes on Teacher Classroom Activity Profile (TCAP)," Division of Teaching, Indiana State University, 1966.

SELECTED REFERENCES

Bennis, Warren, et al.: *The Planning of Change,* 2d ed., Holt, Rinehart and Winston, New York, 1969.

Culbertson, Jack, et al.: *Administrative Relationships: A Case Book,* Englewood Cliffs, N.J., Prentice-Hall, 1960.

Gibb, Jack R.: "Communication and Productivity," *Personnel Administration,* vol. 27, no. 1, 1964.

Miller, Richard (ed.): *Perspectives on Educational Change,* New York, Appleton-Century-Crofts, 1966.

Rogers, Carl: "A Plan for Self-directed Change in an Educational System," *Educational Leadership,* May, 1967.

Steiner, Gary A. (ed.): *The Creative Organization,* The University of Chicago Press, Chicago, 1965.

Chapter Ten
GROUP SUPERVISION: AN EMERGING PATTERN

As an initial impression, it appears that the work of the school is accomplished by accumulations of individual, often random, efforts of students, administrators, teachers, supervisors, and other school personnel. The casual school observer notes that administrative work, for example, is done in the absence of teachers, and that, indeed, administrators are often thankful for that quiet work time they have the first hour or two after classes begin. Further, he observes that students are expected to work alone and that cooperative effort is often discouraged and punished. Moreover, he is immediately aware that teachers work alone as he observes their daily dispersion to their respective cubicles of learning—isolated classrooms.[1]

Of course, there are many opportunities for teachers and other school members to function in groups. Formal-group opportunities include grade-level meetings, curriculum councils, department meetings, and ad hoc committees. "Coffee klatches," "smokers," "old guard," and "newcomers" suggest the multitude of less formal but nevertheless potent groups that may appear in a given school. As a matter of fact, group life is a natural, necessary, and integral part of the organizational life of schools. Indeed, while the day-by-day role performance of teachers may take place in relative isolation, for many teachers the character, content, and quality of this performance are directly related to their organizational group life.

GROUP SUPERVISION

The man-to-man pattern of supervision has been the predominant supervisory method since the beginning of schooling in America. Indeed, this pattern has been accepted by default through virtue of the "role performance invisibility" of teachers. Since teachers usually work alone and in physical environments which encourage isolation, the supervisor functions on a man-to-man basis as he moves from class to class and from teacher to teacher.

---

[1]Teachers tend to function in their professional roles by themselves, thus having little direct opportunity to display their skills and techniques before colleagues. Miles refers to this phenomenon as "role performance invisibility." Matthew Miles, "Planned Change and Organizational Health, Figure and Ground," in Richard Carlson et al., *Change Processes in the Public Schools,* Center for the Advanced Study of Educational Administration, University of Oregon, Eugene, Ore., 1965, p. 24.

Two major flaws exist in man-to-man supervision: (1) this pattern resembles an inspectoral system and, as such, typically evokes negative responses from teachers,[2] and (2) this pattern "locks in" a one-way client-consultant relationship with teachers always assuming the role of client and supervisors always assuming the role of consultant. Group patterns of supervision minimize power visibility as they replace inspection with problem solving. Further, the supervisory relationship is considered an interchangeable one, with actors assuming client or consultant roles as circumstances warrant and as funcional authority changes.

Emerging supervisory practices are characterized by an increased emphasis on professional work groups. In enlightened supervisory environments supervisors work with teachers, teachers work with teachers, and teachers work with students in problem solving, feedback, evaluation, and decision-making relationships which focus on improving the educational program and increasing teaching-learning effectiveness. As a simple illustration, in group supervision the emphasis shifts from supervisor A working to improve the teaching of reading by teacher B to teachers of reading working to improve the teaching of reading. Supervisor A may be included or not, depending upon a number of factors, including his potential contribution to the group's problem. As this group examines its present practices, goals, and objectives in reading instruction and evaluates its effectiveness, it may decide to scan and search for additional teaching materials and goals, adopt alternatives, gather feedback on these changes, and so on. As this group assumes some control over and influence on the supervisory process, teacher B (as well as other participants in the group) is more likely to engage in self-evaluation and to work independently or cooperatively to improve his performance.

The concept of group supervision is threatening to many supervisors and other school officials. This is particularly true for those who feel they need to rely on formal authority and established hierarchical arrangements as means to protect their interests and position in the school and to maintain control over subordinates. In our estimation, denying group supervision to the school is extremely costly in that this in turn denies to the staff the maximum opportunity for personal and professional growth, frustrates the improvement of the educational program, and decreases the potential for student self-actualization. The cost of maintaining present man-to-man supervisory patterns is high.

Enlightened supervisors use group methods because they depend upon

[2]While teachers may recognize and accept a hierarchy and thus attribute power and prerogatives to supervisors, our egalitarian culture and professional norms insist that such power be displayed only minimally. High power visibility evokes negative responses from the human organization. See our discussion of "Gouldner's model" in Chap. 4, where we consider unanticipated consequences of bureaucratic behavior.

voluntary efforts rather than coercion to do the work of the school. They believe that neither creativity nor cooperation can for long be commanded.[3] Further, they realize that increases in teacher professionalism, personal specialization, sophistication of teaching methods, and curriculum content have increased the complexity of educational decision making. Complex problems require coalitions of professionals with a variety of expertness for their solution. Improving reading instruction and counseling student militants are tasks much too complex for a committee of one. Indeed, professional interdependence is a concept fundamental to group supervision. Further, a shift from emphasis on hierarchical evaluation to an emphasis on feedback replaces the "superteacher" halo of supervisors with one of professional colleague. This collegial relationship mellows in the group setting as professionals engage in client-consultant interchange in the process of educational problem solving.

"Group" Defined

Cattell describes a *group* as "an aggregate of organisms in which the existence of all is utilized for satisfaction of the needs of each."[4] Bass defines a group as a collection of persons which is mutually reinforcing.[5] Groups are characterized by the extent to which participants find group membership rewarding. In return for some form of need satisfaction, group members are expected to provide the group with loyalty, effort, and interest. An awareness of the relationship between rewards and investments is fundamental to understanding groups. Individual group participants will tend to become marginal group members or to withdraw from the group when their rewards cease or become out of proportion to their contributions to the group. Further, some individuals abandon group membership when the group is no longer potent enough to provide the kind of need satisfaction that they require. This relationship is not a balanced one. The investor must perceive that the rewards he earns as a result of his active membership exceed his investment in the group.[6] As we indicate in Figure 10-1, he needs to get more out of group membership than he puts into the relationship.

[3]Gordon L. Lippitt and Edith Seashore, *The Leader and Group Effectiveness,* Association Press, New York, 1962. From Warren Schmidt's introduction, p. 6.
[4]Raymond Cattell, "New Concepts for Measuring Leadership in Terms of Group Syntality," *Human Relations,* vol. 4, 1951, pp. 161–184.
[5]Bernard Bass, *Leadership, Psychology and Organizational Behavior,* Harper & Row, New York, 1960. See Chap. 3.
[6]Homans refers to this phenomenon as the "theory of distributive justice." See, for example, Leonard Sayles and George Strauss, *Human Behavior in Organizations,* Prentice-Hall, Englewood Cliffs, N.J., 1966, p. 99. The theory works in either direction—the group ceases its reward-granting behavior when it no longer values or requires the commitment of individuals, and the individual ceases his commitment when rewards, in his view, are not sufficient to warrant his commitment.

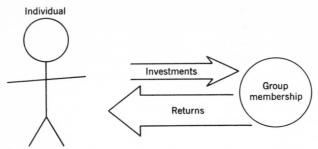

Figure 10-1. The investment exchange. Active group membership ceases (or becomes marginal) when investments in the group are equal to or exceed
returns for members.

PROPOSITIONS ABOUT GROUP FUNCTIONING

We discuss the nature of reward systems available to individuals as a result
of group membership in a later section of this chapter. Let us consider several general propositions and assumptions which are basic to understanding
groups.

1. Groups exist because they have to exist. Group life is a natural form of
   social organization for human beings. We influence groups and are
   influenced by groups throughout our lives. In the long run, more harm
   is done when schools work to frustrate and discourage group activity
   (among teachers *and* students) than when schools allow groups free
   expression.
2. Groups are neutral. In and of themselves, groups are neither good nor
   bad. While school groups can be powerful forces which work to achieve
   school goals, they can be equally powerful in working against school
   goals. For example, a teaching faculty with high morale may obtain satisfaction by working to frustrate school goals—and perhaps by "canning"
   the principal in the bargain—or by working to enhance school goals.
   Indeed, many student groups receive satisfaction in their dedication to
   frustrate the school's operation while others are equally satisfied working
   for or with the school.
3. Groups have unique "personalities" which are conceptually similar to
   individual personalities. This group personality stems from and is composed of characteristics which individuals bring to the group. Thus, two
   school faculties or two departments with similar goals differ markedly
   because their membership differs.
4. As part of the group's personality, a group culture emerges which
   includes norms of behavior and a value system or belief pattern which

are unique to the group. This belief pattern provides the cement which holds the group together and which regulates group behavior. We refer to the belief pattern as the group's *dynamic center*. A zone of freedom exists which permits members to stray somewhat from the dynamic center but still maintain group membership.

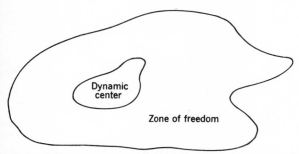

Figure 10-2. The group and its boundaries. From Harold Wilson et al., "The Group and Its Leaders," unpublished manuscript, Center for Educational Administration, Department of Education, Ohio State University, Columbus, Ohio, 1963.

When group members move beyond the zone of freedom, they cross the group's boundary and forfeit membership. The closer a group member is to this dynamic center, the more influential he will be. Goals closer to the dynamic center are more easily achieved if they are simply stated. Indeed, if they are stated at a level of abstraction which denies definition, they are accepted because of their ability to promote group harmony. School faculties, for example, who squabble over instructional technique, educational program focus, technology, and the like, find common ground in "educating youngsters for democratic life." In Figure 10-3 we show various positions of group membership and levels of agreement in relation to the group's dynamic center.

One who holds marginal membership in a group can improve his position by adopting more of the group's culture, thus moving closer to the dynamic center, or by moving the dynamic center of the group closer to him. This second strategy is difficult in that those who are removed from the dynamic center are often perceived as low influentials by other group members.

5. Individuals behave differently when they assume roles as group members from the way they behave when they operate as free agents. Groups influence people. As a result of this influence, people behave differently— they react to group pressure. This phenomenon is dramatized by Heron

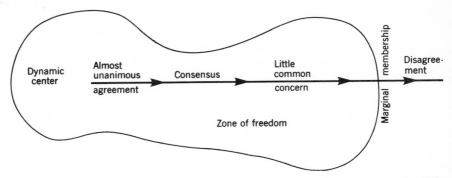

Figure 10-3. Group membership and movement. From Harold Wilson et al., "The Group and Its Leaders," unpublished manuscript, Center for Educational Administration, Department of Education, Ohio State University, Columbus, Ohio, 1963.

as he contrasts the actions and demands of workers as groups with their desires as individuals:

> The opinion polls almost always show that the most prominent desires of the individual employee relate to the most important thing in the world—*himself,* his personality, his recognition, his security, and his progress. He wants recognition, for his skills, his suggestions, his attention and energy, his performance and production.
>
> But when he gets together with his fellow workers—who want exactly the same things—they agree almost unanimously to demand standard wage rates for all workers on the same job, the prohibition of piecework and incentives, and uniform increases in all wage rates.
>
> He wants fair treatment, as an individual, in job assignments and promotions. He resents favoritism or any process of selection which seems to overlook his abilities and gives the foreman job to someone less competent. He wants to be rewarded for his merit.
>
> But in united action with his fellow workers he will demand that in promotions, layoffs, or rehirings, the principles of seniority shall strictly apply. He will stand on this demand with almost emotional devotion.[7]

As a result of this phenomenon, one may conclude that group pressures result in group conformity. Conformity in turn stifles creativity and individual expression. Therefore, as this argument develops, groups have negative and frustrating effects on individuality. We agree that groups do have enormous potential for applying pressure to individuals. Further, these pressures require conformity from group members. We believe, however, that conformity is the strength in groups that supervisors should seek. As such, we do not believe that conformity is inherently

[7] Alexander Heron, *Why Men Work,* Stanford University Press, Stanford, Calif., 1948, p. 20.

bad. Indeed, a group norm may be one of creative expression by its members. Thus members conform by expressing their individuality. This position is effectively argued by Cartwright and Lippitt as follows:

It is important, first, to make a distinction between conformity and uniformity. A group might have a value that everyone should be as different from everyone else as possible. Conformity to this value, then, would result not in uniformity of behavior but in nonuniformity. Such a situation often arises in therapy groups or training groups where it is possible to establish norms which place a high value upon "being different" and upon tolerating deviant behavior. Conformity to this value is presumably greater the more cohesive the group and the more it is seen as relevant to the group's objectives.[8]

6. Goals held for the group but not by the group tend to be rejected by the group. The zone of freedom for a group is similar to the concept of self for individuals. A behavioral change for individuals is best accompanied by broadening one's concept of self to include the change. Groups change by broadening zones of freedom to include new alternatives. Even the most forceful leadership is frustrated if it overlooks this important concept.

GROUP EFFECTIVENESS

In this section we present characteristics which describe the ideal group, and following this, a description of the components of group effectiveness. The ideal model should serve as a goal for supervisors to pursue as they work with school groups, and the effectiveness model suggests how this ideal might be accomplished.

Bradford and Mial suggest that an aggregate of individuals become a group:

When it knows why it exists.
When it has created an atmosphere in which work can be done.
When it has evolved acceptable ways of making decisions.
When it has established conditions under which each member can make his special contribution.
When it has achieved real communication among members.
When it has made it possible for members freely to give and freely to receive help.
When it can manage conflict as a potential source of creative problem solving.
When it has learned how to diagnose its processes and its "maintenance" problems in order to repair and improve them.[9]

[8]Dorwin Cartwright and Ronald Lippitt, "Group Dynamics and the Individual," *International Journal of Psychotherapy*, vol. 7, no. 1, January, 1957, p. 95.
[9]Leland P. Bradford and Dorothy Mial, "When Is a Group?" *Educational Leadership*, vol. 21, December, 1963, pp. 147–148.

This group maximizes its effectiveness, according to Likert, when it is characterized as follows:

1. The members are skilled in all the various leadership and membership roles and functions required for interaction between leaders and members and between members and other members.
2. The group has been in existence sufficiently long to have developed a well-established, relaxed working relationship among all its members.
3. The members of the group are attracted to it and are loyal to its members, including the leader.
4. The members and leaders have a high degree of confidence and trust in each other.
5. The values and goals of the group are a satisfactory integration and expression of the relevant values and needs of its members. They have helped shape these values and goals and are satisfied with them.
6. Insofar as members of the group are performing linking functions, they endeavor to have the values and goals of the groups which they link in harmony, one with the other.
7. The more important a value seems to the group, the greater the likelihood that the individual member will accept it.
8. The members of the group are highly motivated to abide by the major values and to achieve the important goals of the group.
9. All the interaction, problem-solving, decision-making activities of the group occur in a supportive atmosphere.
10. The group is eager to help each member develop to his full potential. It sees, for example, that relevant technical knowledge and training in interpersonal and group skills are made available to each member.
11. Each member accepts willingly and without resentment the goals and expectations that he and his group establish for themselves.
12. When necessary or advisable, other members of the group will give a member the help he needs to accomplish successfully the goals set for him. Mutual help is a characteristic of highly effective groups.
13. The supportive atmosphere of the highly effective group stimulates creativity. The group does not demand narrow conformity as do the work groups under authoritarian leaders.
14. There is strong motivation on the part of each member to communicate fully and frankly to the group all the information which is relevant and of value to the group's activity.
15. There is high motivation in the group to use the communication process so that it best serves the interests and goals of the group.
16. Just as there is high motivation to communicate, there is correspondingly strong motivation to receive communications.
17. In the highly effective group there are strong motivations to try to influence other members as well as to be receptive to influence by them.[10]

---

[10]Abridged from Rensis Likert, *New Patterns of Management*, McGraw-Hill, New York, 1961, p. 166. Likert's list is much more illustrative and comprehensive than that which we list here.

It seems useful to differentiate between two major sources of rewards for group members. One reward source is the mutual satisfaction or reinforcement that individuals get from interacting with other individuals. The more satisfaction for group members as a result of this interaction, the higher the interaction effectiveness of the group. Another source of rewards for group members comes from actual implementation of the group's purposes. The more satisfaction for group members as a result of doing the task, the higher the task effectiveness of the group. Task effectiveness and interaction effectiveness compose group effectiveness. The more satisfaction for group members as a result of interaction effectiveness and task effectiveness, the higher the group effectiveness.[11]

The Components of Group Effectiveness

Interaction effectiveness refers to the quality of group sentiment which exists for a given group. It includes such evasive concepts as morale, cohesiveness, communication ease, and so on. Bass suggests that this dimension of group effectiveness can be assessed by (1) the amount of harmony present and the absence of conflict, (2) the amount of satisfaction for members as a result of interaction, and (3) the perceived congruence between actual and expected relations among group members.[12]

Interaction effectiveness is facilitated by a number of variables, each having strength to increase the potential for group members to interact. For example, collections of individuals about the same age, with similar educational backgrounds, and with similar interests will tend to have high interaction potential. Or, the more homogeneous the group, the higher the interaction potential of the group. Exposure to contact, size, and pressures to participate are other variables affecting interaction potential.[13] Perhaps most inclusive in considering interaction potential is mutual predictability among group members. That is, a given group member is able to predict what other group members will do. The higher the mutual predictability among group members, the higher the interaction level of the group.

Consider, for example, a group of special teachers in an elementary school. One would predict that this group, being somewhat homogeneous,

---

[11]The notion of group effectiveness containing a task dimension and an interaction dimension is borrowed from Bernard Bass. Bass feels that *either* dimension or both dimensions may result in group effectiveness. Our view is that *both* dimensions are necessary for group effectiveness. Bernard Bass, *Leadership, Psychology and Organizational Behavior,* Harper & Row, New York, 1960, Chap. 3. This discussion follows that which appears in Thomas Sergiovanni, "Group Effectiveness: Human Relations Is Not Enough," *Illinois Elementary Principal,* September, 1967, pp. 15–17.

[12]Bass, *op. cit.,* p. 46.

[13]See James G. March and Herbert A. Simon, *Organizations,* Wiley, New York, 1958, pp. 68–71, for an interesting and comprehensive discussion of factors which affect frequency of interaction.

manageable in size, having frequent opportunities for mutual exposure, and possessing common sentiments in terms of educational philosophy and school organization, would enjoy high interaction effectiveness. It is more difficult, however, to predict whether this group—or any other school group, for that matter—will use its energies, its power, its pressures, and its unique reward system on behalf of the school's purposes. Perhaps this group of special teachers will harness its energies to provide the very best services that it can to the school. Or perhaps this same group may decide that it is more rewarding to be a thorn in the principal's side. Another possibility is that this group may simply enjoy its unique informal reward system at the expense of doing more than a minimum job, if it does a job at all.[14]

The direction and orientation of a school group hinge on another aspect of group effectiveness, the accomplishment of task. *Task effectiveness* refers to activity which promotes, defines, clarifies, pursues, and accomplishes relevant school goals. It is described in terms of the rewards that group members get from doing or completing a task. Challenging work, responsibility, intrinsic satisfaction, autonomy, feelings of success, achievement, and competence, recognition for task efforts, bolstering of self- and group esteem, and individual and group status are words and phrases which best describe the flavor of the reward system that characterizes task effectiveness.

A group whose primary reward system rests with task effectiveness will have at its disposal an arsenal of weapons to encourage, to motivate, and perhaps even to pressure group members to work on behalf of the school and its purposes. On the other hand, a group deprived of the reward system resulting from task effectiveness may divert its efforts away from work-centered activities and tend to concentrate on seeking satisfaction solely from the interaction effectiveness domain. The group, not the job, becomes the focus of an individual's attention. Group norms which conflict with the purposes of the school may be established. Conformity to the group and its norms becomes necessary if one wishes to benefit from the group's reward system. This conformity may require that teachers do not exert more than a minimum effort in their jobs.[15] Such groups take a passive, rather than negative, stand in relation to school purposes and tasks. They expend energies, talents, and efforts primarily to maintain the group as a source of personal

[14]Dubin discusses subversive, cooperative, and neutral groups in his analysis of informal organization. Robert Dubin, *Human Relations in Administration*, 2d ed., Prentice-Hall, Englewood Cliffs, N.J., 1961, pp. 84–87.

[15]The rate-buster phenomenon and the sanctions which follow have been well documented in industry. We suspect that the analogy works for education, too. For example, elementary school teachers often mentioned that too much effort, too many displays, noticeable project work, elaborate bulletin boards, taking work home, and other signs of "rate busting" frequently result in informal and formal sanctions from the group.

enjoyment for members. We conclude that groups high in interaction effectiveness but low in task effectiveness not only tend to be lacking in function, but may indeed be dysfunctional.

Interaction effectiveness and task effectiveness need not be at opposite ends of a continuum. A group may be highly successful in its task endeavors and actually use its interaction potential on behalf of the task. Such a group would tend to reap rewards (acceptance, affiliation, belonging, and security, for example) while at the same time deriving satisfaction from getting a job done. This combination would best describe group effectiveness.

The Supervisor as Key

The supervisor is frequently in a position to make group effectiveness a reality. His position is unique in that he affects *both* task and interaction effectiveness. He can foster interaction effectiveness by recognizing informal groups, by helping to open and promoting interaction patterns within and between groups, and by planning formal groups in terms of their interaction potential. Much can be done by deliberately linking subgroups so that together they constitute an identifiable whole and develop a sense of cohesiveness as a faculty.[16]

Interaction effectiveness tends not to be potent enough, however, to provide the kinds of rewards that nourish professional individuals. Professionals tend to need and actively seek the kinds of satisfaction that only task effectiveness can bring.[17] Admittedly there are exceptions to this tendency. Some teachers tend not to be professionally oriented and may seek only relatively shallow levels of need fulfillment. These types would be quite content with the limited rewards available from interaction effectiveness. Other teachers and teacher groups may focus on interaction effectiveness by default—that is, this is the only source of rewards left open to them.

The implementation of group task effectiveness requires that supervisors encourage groups, formal and informal, to identify with and accept the school, its tasks, and its purposes. Task identification appears to be related to the extent to which individual teachers and groups of teachers are given responsibility and autonomy for participating in decision making and for participating in the development and implementing of teaching programs. Further, task identification appears to be related to the extent to which individuals perceive that they have opportunities to develop their professional skills. These variables are likely to increase opportunities for individual, group, and

---

[16]Rensis Likert, *op. cit.*, proposes a plan of organization which is characterized by overlapping work groups, linked together by individuals who serve the original group but are also represented in groups at the next level. Likert's notion represents a proposal for organizing schools and other agencies on the basis of group structure.
[17]See our discussion of the motivation-hygiene theory which appears in Chap. 6.

professional success.[18] Promoting task identification requires that supervisors, principals, and others be committed to faculty and student involvement and collaborative management and that they willingly appreciate the authority which teachers and other school members bring to the school.

Group Effectiveness Summarized

The relationship between interaction effectiveness and task effectiveness in school groups is initially one of dependence. The consistent accomplishment of group tasks requires the establishment of interaction effectiveness. Once initial group effectiveness is achieved and the cycle reoccurs, the relationship changes to one of interdependence. That is, task effectiveness over time depends upon sustained interaction effectiveness, and sustained interaction effectiveness depends upon task effectiveness. We summarize the components of group effectiveness in Figure 10-4.

Interaction effectiveness, according to the model, is largely dependent upon communication frequency. The more homogeneous the group, the more opportunities for group member contact; and the greater the mutual predictability among group members, the greater the frequency of communication. It should be noted that when creativity is valued as a group goal,

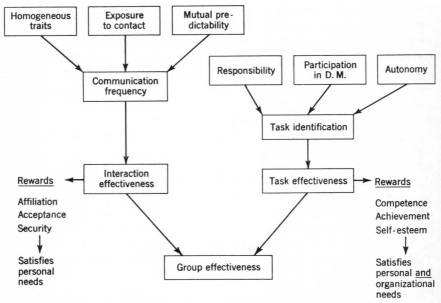

Figure 10-4. Basic components of the concept of group effectiveness.

[18]March and Simon, *op. cit.*, p. 77.

more heterogeneity will need to be introduced, even at some loss to interaction frequency.[19] The rewards available to teachers through interaction effectiveness are feelings of affiliation, acceptance, and security. These rewards tend to focus on personal need satisfaction but tend not to directly effect organizational need satisfaction.

The key component of task effectiveness is task identification. As group members identify with the task goals of the group, performance increases. March and Simon suggest that the greater the amount of perceived autonomy and responsibility of group members, and the more opportunities that exist for participation by group members, the greater the task identification of the group. Rewards available to teachers through task effectiveness are feelings of competence and achievement and the bolstering of group and individual self-esteem. This reward system is unique in that the basis for personal need satisfaction is through satisfying organizational needs. Task effectiveness and interaction effectiveness compose group effectiveness.

GROUPS IN ACTION

Here we examine the group in action. We begin this examination by describing phases which groups must transcend if they are to successfully accomplish their work. This is followed by an analysis of leadership functions as they apply to groups. We then present a taxonomy and description of roles which may be assumed by group members, and we conclude our discussion with suggestions as to how supervisors and other educators may gather feedback data on groups in action.

Group Phases

It is useful to visualize the group as having certain fundamental interpersonal needs much like those associated with the individual personality. Groups and individuals must provide for these needs before they can function properly. Schutz identifies group and individual needs as follows: "There are three fundamental interpersonal needs—*inclusion, control,* and *affection*—and in order for an individual to function optimally he must establish and maintain a satisfactory relation in all three areas."[20] Individuals need to include others and to be included, to control others and to be con-

---

[19]Heterogeneous groups are preferred when tasks are extremely complex, when time is plentiful, when the consequences of error in judgment are grave, and when creativity is desired. Homogeneous groups are preferred when time is scarce, when production is important, when tasks demand cooperation, and when problems are routine. See Bernard Bass, *Organizational Psychology,* Allyn and Bacon, Boston, 1965, pp. 204–213.

[20]William Schutz, "The Ego, FIRO Theory and the Leader As Completer," in Luigi Petrullo and Bernard Bass (eds.), *Leadership and Interpersonal Behavior,* Holt, New York, 1961, p. 57.

trolled, to love others and to be loved, with the exact mix of needing to express or wanting each of these variables differing for each person. Indeed, inclusion, control, and affection are phases through which groups must successfully pass if they are to be characterized by sustained effectiveness in accomplishing their goals. The phases are arranged into a relatively loose hierarchy with first attention by the group being given to inclusion, followed next by control and finally by affection. Problems associated with each of these are never solved by the group but are at least reasonably settled. This settling is not unlike a simmering pot, which is characterized by relative stability but subject to periodic eruption of bubbles. The phases, indeed, overlap (Figure 10-5), with the group generally moving forward but occasionally vacillating from one phase to another.

Conceptually, we examine each of the phases separately below:

Inclusion. A group needs to define its boundaries and to work to include people within them. The inclusion phase requires that the group know who is in the group and who is not. Further, in view of the group's dynamic center, the group must communicate and delineate to members an expression of required behavior and forbidden behavior. Part of this phase includes identifying and articulating group goals and subsequently testing members to see if they are in agreement with these goals. The group works to win commitment from its members or excludes those who express disinterest in its goals. This exclusion may be physical, if possible, or mental, if necessary.

Control. Once the inclusion phase of group activity has been relatively settled, the group turns its attention to matters of control. Members need to decide problems of leadership, solve status arrangements, assign and agree upon roles to be played, distribute and consolidate power, provide for a workable and acceptable "chain of command," and otherwise arrange themselves. While the control phase may not solve manifest control problems, hidden agenda, and other interpersonal problems, it works to solve them for

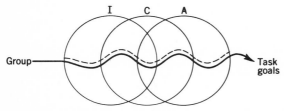

Figure 10-5. Natural group phases: inclusion, control, and affection.

the moment—to contain them. Whether such problems stay solved or not depends upon a group climate which is supportive, open, cooperative, and honest.

Affection. The inclusion and control phases of group activity are seldom characterized by tranquillity. Defining the dynamic center of a group and delineating its borders require a great deal of interpersonal expenditure. The control phase seems always characterized by tension. People are hurt as a result of the inclusion and control phases, and the group must heal its wounds if it is to function properly. The affection phase, then, is characterized by working to build a cohesiveness based on acceptance, forgiveness, and love.

The Hidden Agenda

Much of the group's activity, as it works through the inclusion, control, and affection phases, can be scheduled on the group's agenda and carried out through formal or overt procedures. A substantial amount of this activity, however, takes the form of an undercurrent which permeates the group's life. The official reasons for people coming together to form a group—the publicly stated and agreed-upon tasks to be accomplished—are referred to as the group's *public agenda.*[21] Beneath the public agenda there are a number of hidden agendas, often ignored but nevertheless most powerful, which are not openly recognized. Such private agendas are held by group members, group leaders, and, indeed, the "group" itself. Bradford describes the hidden agenda as follows:

> Unlabeled, private and covered, but deeply felt and very much the concern of the group, is another level. Here are all of the conflicting motives, desires, aspirations and emotional reactions held by the group members, subgroups, or the group as a whole that cannot be fitted legitimately into the accepted group task. Here are all of the problems which, for a variety of reasons, cannot be laid on top of the table.[22]

While hidden agendas are an issue in each of the phases of group activity, we believe their influence to be most strongly felt in the control phase. Hidden agendas need to be dealt with in one way or another. At one extreme they can be smothered or steamrolled by "strong" leadership, and at the other extreme they can be brought to the surface and "understood" as in human encounter or sensitivity groups.

Bradford offers a number of suggestions for supervisors as they confront

[21]This discussion follows that which appears in Leland P. Bradford, "The Case of the Hidden Agenda," *Adult Leadership,* September, 1952, pp. 3–7.
[22]*Ibid.,* p. 3.

the problem of handling hidden agendas. Among them are: (1) to be aware of, to look for, and to recognize hidden agendas—those of the supervisor and those of other group participants; (2) to recognize that the group works continuously and simultaneously at both levels—hidden and public; (3) to work to bring hidden agenda to the surface; but (4) to be sensitive to the group's readiness to force some hidden agenda items, for many have potential for hurting the group more if they are made public; (5) to accept hidden agendas without evoking self-guilt; (6) to help the group work out methods of solving or settling hidden agendas just as they develop methods of handling their surface agenda; and (7) to help the group evaluate its progress in handling hidden agendas.[23]

FUNCTIONAL ROLES OF GROUP MEMBERS

The question of leadership is one that cannot be avoided for long as groups are examined. Traditionally, we look to the group leader as the key determiner of a group's effectiveness. A "good" leader, according to this view, is one who points direction for group activity, clarifies goals, makes relevancy judgments as he guides group discussion, keeps people on the track, is the agenda watchdog, pushes for full participation, and forces decisions. The good leader gets things done! His tools are his official role as chairman, an acceptable agenda, group know-how, and guided discussion.

Enlightened supervision requires that designated group leaders (teachers, chairmen, supervisors, consultants, principals, and so on) come to conceive of their role as one of providing service rather than direction to the group.[24] For example, while traditional supervisory patterns require that the leader get things done (presumably by using the group and its resources), enlightened supervisors work to help the group accomplish its tasks. Within this context, the leader does not solve the group's problems but focuses on the group solving its problems; he does not move the group forward but helps the group as it moves forward. We have not solved the problem of leadership in groups as it is traditionally conceived. Somebody must get the group going, must initiate discussion, define problems and goals, evaluate, summarize, monitor, provide information, and the like. Indeed, the group will not accomplish its goals without these and other leadership roles being fulfilled. Enlightened supervisors are vitally concerned with these roles but hold no monopoly on them. *Leadership functions are considered to be the responsibility of the entire group—not just of the designated leader.* Our discussion is focused on leadership and other group roles which are assumed in

[23]*Ibid.*, p. 7.
[24]See, for example, George M. Prince, *Creative Leadership*, Harper & Row, New York, (in press at this writing), for a lengthy presentation of this view.

effective groups rather than on who should assume what role. Roles are best assumed by those most capable of assuming them.[25] Further, the effective group provides continuous "in-service" education to group members as they are encouraged to assume a variety of constructive group roles without fear of embarrassment or sanction.

Group roles are often classified into three broad categories: depending upon whether they support group task effectiveness, support group interaction effectiveness, or are expressed solely for the satisfaction of the role incumbent. The first category, group task roles, includes expressions which facilitate and coordinate the selection and definition of a common group problem and help in solving this problem. The second category, group-building or -maintenance roles, includes expressions which are oriented to the functioning of the group as a group. The third category, individual roles, includes expressions not primarily directed at enhancing the group or the task but at enhancing the individual participant.

Each of these roles is further described and illustrated below as we present Kenneth Benne and Paul Sheats's now classic taxonomy of functional roles for group members.

GROUP TASK ROLES

The following analysis assumes that the task of the discussion group is to select, define, and solve common problems. The roles are identified in relation to functions of facilitation and coordination of group problem-solving activities. Each member may, of course, enact more than one role in any given unit of participation and a wide range of roles in successive participations. Any or all of these roles may be played at times by the group "leader" as well as by various members.

a.   The *initiator-contributor* suggests or proposes to the group new ideas or a changed way of regarding the group problem or goal. The novelty proposed may take the form of suggestions of a new group goal or a new definition of the problem. It may take the form of a suggested solution or some way of handling a difficulty that the group has encountered. Or it may take the form of a proposed new procedure for the group, a new way of organizing the group for the task ahead.

b.   The *information seeker* asks for clarification of suggestions made in terms

[25]At least two kinds of "capabilities" must be considered in deciding who assumes leadership in a given situation. Indeed, first and foremost is expert capability. Enlightened supervision requires that ability authority be a prime consideration in the leadership decision. Another important dimension, particularly in reference to assigned or legitimate leaders as opposed to ad hoc or informal leaders, is the personality inclination or leadership propensity, given certain circumstances. Certain situations, for example, require one style of leadership and other situations another style. Who can best provide the needed leadership style for a given situation is an interesting and intriguing question. We consider this question later in the chapter when we discuss formal leadership in groups.

of their factual adequacy, for authoritative information and facts pertinent to the problem being discussed.

c. The *opinion seeker* asks not primarily for the facts of the case but for a clarification of the values pertinent to what the group is undertaking or of values involved in a suggestion made or in alternative suggestions.

d. The *information giver* offers facts or generalizations which are "authoritative" or relates his own experience pertinently to the group problem.

e. The *opinion giver* states his belief or opinion pertinently to a suggestion made or to alternative suggestions. The emphasis is on his proposal of what should become the group's view of pertinent values, not primarily upon relevant facts or information.

f. The *elaborator* spells out suggestions in terms of examples or developed meanings, offers a rationale for suggestions previously made and tries to deduce how an idea or suggestion would work out if adopted by the group.

g. The *coordinator* shows or clarifies the relationships among various ideas and suggestions, tries to pull ideas and suggestions together or tries to coordinate the activities of various members or subgroups.

h. The *orienter* defines the position of the group with respect to its goals by summarizing what has occurred, points to departures from agreed upon directions or goals, or raises questions about the direction which the group discussion is taking.

i. The *evaluator-critic* subjects the accomplishment of the group to some standard or set of standards of group functioning in the context of the group task. Thus he may evaluate or question the "practicality," the "logic," the "facts," or the "procedure" of a suggestion or of some unit of group discussion.

j. The *energizer* prods the group to action or decision, attempts to stimulate or arouse the group to "greater" or "higher quality" activity.

k. The *procedural technician* expedites group movement by doing things for the group—performing routine tasks, distributing materials, or manipulating objects for the group, e.g., rearranging the seating or running the recording machine, etc.

l. The *recorder* writes down suggestions, makes a record of the group decisions, or writes down the product of discussion. The recorder role is the "group memory."

GROUP BUILDING AND MAINTENANCE ROLES

Here the analysis of member functions is oriented to those participations which have for their purpose the building of group-centered attitudes and orientation among the members of a group or the maintenance and perpetuation of such group-centered behavior. A given contribution may involve several roles and a member or the "leader" may perform various roles in successive contributions.

a. The *encourager* praises, agrees with and accepts the contribution of others. He indicates warmth and solidarity in his attitude toward other group members, offers commendation and praise and in various ways indicates understanding and acceptance of other points of view, ideas, and suggestions.

b.   The *harmonizer* mediates the differences between other members, attempts to reconcile disagreements, relieves tension in conflict situations through jesting or pouring oil on the troubled waters, etc.

c.   The *compromiser* operates from within a conflict in which his idea or position is involved. He may offer compromise by yielding status, admitting his error, by disciplining himself to maintain group harmony, or by "coming half way" in moving along with the group.

d.   The *gate keeper* and expediter attempts to keep communication channels open by encouraging or facilitating the participating of others ("we haven't got the ideas of Mr. X yet," etc.) or by proposing regulation of the flow of communication ("why don't we limit the length of our contributions so that everyone will have a chance to contribute?" etc.).

e.   The *standard setter or ego ideal* expresses standards for the group to attempt to achieve in its functioning or applies standards in evaluating the quality of group processes.

f.   The *group-observer* and *commentator* keeps records of various aspects of group process and feeds such data with proposed interpretations into the group's evaluation of its own procedures.

g.   The *follower* goes along with the movement of the group, more or less passively accepting the ideas of others, serving as an audience in group discussion and decision.

"INDIVIDUAL ROLES"

Attempts by "members" of a group to satisfy individual needs which are irrelevant to the group task and which are nonoriented or negatively oriented to group building and maintenance set problems of group and member training. A high incidence of "individual-centered" as opposed to "group-centered" participation in a group always calls for self-diagnosis of the group. The diagnosis may reveal one or several of a number of conditions—low level of skill training among members, including the group leader; the prevalence of "authoritarian" and "laissez faire" points of view toward group functioning in the group; a low level of group maturity, discipline and morale; an inappropriately chosen and inadequately defined group task, etc. Whatever diagnosis, it is in this setting that the training needs of the group are to be discovered and group training efforts to meet these needs are to be defined. The outright "suppression" of "individual roles" will deprive the group of data needed for really adequate self-diagnosis and therapy.

a.   The *aggressor* may work in many ways—deflating the status of others, expressing disapproval of the values, acts or feelings of others, attacking the group or the problem it is working on, joking aggressively, showing envy toward another's contribution by trying to take credit for it, etc.

b.   The *blocker* tends to be negativistic and stubbornly resistant, disagreeing and opposing without or beyond "reason" and attempting to maintain or bring back an issue after the group has rejected or by-passed it.

c.   The *recognition-seeker* works in various ways to call attention to himself, whether through boasting, reporting on personal achievements, acting in unusual ways, struggling to prevent his being placed in an "inferior" position, etc.

d. The *self-confessor* uses the audience opportunity which the group setting provides to express personal, nongroup oriented, "feeling," "insight," "ideology," etc.

e. The *playboy* makes a display of his lack of involvement in the group's processes. This may take the form of cynicism, nonchalance, horseplay and other more or less studied forms of "out of field" behavior.

f. The *dominator* tries to assert authority or superiority in manipulating the group or certain members of the group. This domination may take the form of flattery, of asserting a superior status or right to attention, giving directions authoritatively, interrupting the contributions of others, etc.

g. The *help-seeker* attempts to call forth "sympathy" response from other group members or from the whole group, whether through expressions of insecurity, personal confusion or depreciation of himself beyond "reason."

h. The *special interest pleader* speaks for the "small business man," the "grass roots" community, the "housewife," "labor," etc., usually cloaking his own prejudices or biases in the stereotype which best fits his individual need.[26]

Groups need to work for balance among the three types of roles. Surely task roles depend upon maintenance roles, and maintenance roles are legitimized and become purposeful as a result of task roles. Our "hidden" agenda" discussion explains why individual roles are played in groups. A mature group permits its members to occasionally assume individual roles. Sustained behavior of this type by one or another group member suggests malfunctions in the group's climate. The more information members have about group roles and their own performance in groups, the more likely they are to improve this performance.

SOME FEEDBACK SUGGESTIONS

Group effectiveness—indeed, group supervision—depends upon commitment from group participants for success. Group members need to decide to improve group performance if they wish to bring about group effectiveness. Knowledge of present performance is often helpful in stimulating this improvement. Group members, for example, search for alternate methods of operation and try new group roles when they are dissatisfied with present group efforts. The Benne and Sheats material is easily converted into a feedback observation rating schema for recording the frequency and kind of roles group members presently assume. We present an observation sheet with sample items in Table 10-1. Responses to this inventory, of course, need to

[26]Kenneth D. Benne and Paul Sheats, "Functional Roles of Group Members," *The Journal of Social Issues*, vol. 4, no. 2, Spring, 1948, pp. 43–46.

TABLE 10-1. SAMPLE OBSERVATION SHEET

	Members				
	A	**B**	**C**	**D**	**E**
Task roles					
Initiator					
Information seeker					
Opinion seeker					
Information giver					
Coordinator					
Evaluator					
Total					
Maintenance roles					
Encourager					
Harmonizer					
Compromiser					
Total					
Individual roles					
Aggressor					
Blocker					
Total					

be analyzed in terms of what happened in the specific group. Is the group satisfied with its performance? Did the group achieve its purposes? Was the level of interpersonal tension within limits? Who assumed what role and when? Answers to those questions can be helpful in analyzing group performance. Further, group members become aware not only of roles they play, but also of those which need to be assumed to increase effectiveness.[27]

Role performance data can be supplemented by communications flow charts which record the direction and frequency of message flow in the group. These data can be collected and presented in the form of a communications sociogram. A series of such flow charts provides a short history of the group's communication pattern. Such charts can be fully understood only in relation to the live group—its purposes, actors, performance, and goals. Over time, however, certain consistent communication patterns may appear for a given group. This information, combined with role performance data, can add to the group's understanding of itself. As such, feedback needs to be presented by supervisors in a nonevaluative way. In the ideal, such information is gathered periodically by the group as it engages in self-evaluation.

[27]For a detailed discussion of group roles and more illustrative suggestions for collecting feedback data on group performance, see *Adult Leadership*, vol. 1, no. 8, January, 1953, the entire issue.

LEADERSHIP EFFECTIVENESS

In Chapter 4 considerable attention was given to the problems of leadership. While no carte blanche endorsement was given to a specific leadership or supervisory style, we did suggest the consequence of adopting one or another style. Indeed, we suggested that, over a period of time, schools predominately characterized by participatory styles would have positive effects on the human organization of the school. The synthesizing theory we present in Chapter 2 proposes that school success is dependent upon such positive effects. Yet at any given time alternate leadership-supervisory styles may be effective or not, depending upon the uniqueness of the situation. It seems obvious, for example, that evacuating a school during a fire requires leadership styles less than participatory. On the other hand, decisions of grade placement for students, psychological referrals, and certain curriculum development decisions are often best made as a result of group consultation. One style of leadership is not necessarily better than another, nor is one type appropriate in all situations. Appropriate leadership styles are particular to and dependent upon variables unique to a given situation.[28]

The "It Depends" Approach

A new theory of leadership effectiveness has emerged from fifteen years of research conducted at the University of Illinois through its Group Effectiveness Laboratory. This theory, developed by Fred Fiedler and his associates,[29] stems from a research tradition primarily associated with that of small-group psychology. The theory suggests that both task-oriented and relationship-oriented leaders are able to perform effectively in a group given conditions appropriate to and supportive of their leadership style. Further, the theory accepts the style of the leader as a given, and therefore recommends the arrangement of tasks and situations to accommodate leader styles rather than changing styles to fit situations.[30]

[28]While we endorse the particularistic approach as we discuss leadership as a general concept, we believe that most group situations found in schools favor some styles over others. This should be obvious from our discussions in Chapter 4 and from our treatment of formal leadership in groups, which is to follow.

[29]See Fred E. Fiedler, *A Theory of Leadership Effectiveness*, McGraw-Hill, New York, 1967, for a comprehensive treatment of this theory. More popular versions of the theory are found in Fiedler's "Engineering the Job to Fit the Manager," *Harvard Business Review*, vol. 43, no. 5, September, 1965, pp. 115–122, and most recently in his "Style or Circumstance: The Leadership Enigma," *Psychology Today*, vol. 2, no. 10, March, 1969, pp. 38–43. These references from the basis of our discussion which follows.

[30]Leadership styles are measured by an instrument which yields a Least Preferred Coworker (LPC) score for respondents. Using an Osgood Semantic Differential format, respondents are asked to describe their least preferred co-worker on each of sixteen dimensions. Those who describe this worker in a relatively positive sense are typed as relationship-oriented while those who describe him in a negative sense are typed as task-oriented. Fiedler presents impressive evidence supporting this method in chap. 3 of his book, *A Theory of Leadership Effectiveness*.

The Fiedler theory identifies three critical dimensions, variations of which largely determine the favorableness of the situation for one or another leadership style. The dimensions are: (1) position power of the leader, (2) task structure, and (3) leader-member personal relationships. Various combinations of the presence or absence of these variables represent the kind of power and influence which groups give to leaders. The *position power* of the leader refers to the status distance which exists between the leader and his group. It is often thought of as the amount and kind of authority associated with the leader's position. Fiedler considers position power to be the least important of the three dimensions. The second dimension, *task structure,* refers to the degree to which the group's work is programmed or routinized, as opposed to being vague and ambiguous. Curriculum and instructional problem solving, invention and creative decision making, are potentially less structured than administering the attendance procedure, safety program, or examination schedule of a school. The third dimension, *leader-member relation,* emerged from Fiedler's research as the most important factor in determining the leader's influence over his group. This dimension refers to the degree to which group members trust and like the leader. Whether leader-member personal relationships are good or not, whether the task is structured or not, and whether position power is strong or not are variables which determine the favorableness of a given leadership style. Our concern, of course, is: Which style is most effective in a particular situation? More specifically, what are the conditions which are supportive of relationship-oriented styles in groups, and what are the conditions which support task-oriented styles?

The Contingency Model

In Figure 10-6 we reprint a simplified version of Fiedler's contingency model[31] which shows the effectiveness of relationship-oriented leadership versus task-oriented leadership for groups characterized by different combinations of leader-member personal relationships, task structure, and leader position power.

Eight group situations are identified and categorized according to whether they are high or low on each of the three critical dimensions which determine favorableness of a given style. The group situations are arranged in declining order of influence for the leader, with cell 1 providing the leader with the most influence and cell 8 the least influence. The leader, for example, who is well liked by group members, who is working in structured

[31]The contingency model is constructed by plotting correlations of leadership style against the taxonomy of group situations. The approximate median correlations between leader LPC score and group performance plotted for each group situation (cells 1 to 8 in Fig. 10-5) are -.55, -.60, -.30, .43, .40, none available for cell 6, 0.3, and -.50. (Fiedler, *A Theory of Leadership Effectiveness* p. 146.)

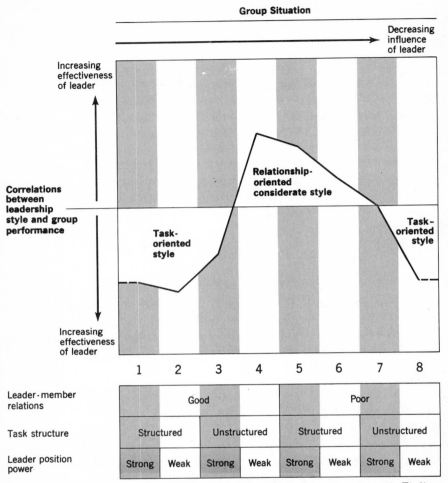

Figure 10-6. The contingency model for leadership effectiveness. From Fred D. Fiedler, "Style or Circumstance: The Leadership Enigma," *Psychology Today*, vol. 2, no. 10, March, 1969, p. 42.

tasks, and who has lots of authority can exert strong influence on the group, while his opposite, the leader who is not liked, who has an unstructured assignment, and who comes with little authority has difficulty in exerting influence.

The contingency model suggests that task-oriented leaders perform best in situations which provide them with substantial influence *and* in situations which provide them with very little influence. Relationship-oriented leaders, on the other hand, are most effective in mixed situations which afford them moderate influence over the group.

Educational Supervision

While each of the group situations described in the eight cells appears with some frequency in schools, the major share of the work of educational supervision occurs in situations described by cells 4 and 8. Unstructured situations are typical in educational policy development, in curriculum decision making, in instructional improvement, in in-service education, and the like. Group participants bring to group membership a variety of expertness which further defies structuring of tasks. In earlier chapters we have discussed the trend for schools to rely increasingly on authority and power derived from ability—from professional knowledge—rather than on authority derived from position. Position power is becoming less important in schools. Leader-member personal relationships are much too sensitive and particularistic to permit much generalizing. Ideally such relationships would be good. If this is indeed the case, then by and large the relationship-oriented style will bring educational supervisors closer to group effectiveness. The contingency model suggests that if such relationships are poor, the task-oriented leader will be more successful. We propose, however, that groups of professionals brought together in unstructured situations with weak position power for the leader and poor leader-member relations (cell 8), who are subject to task-oriented styles for *long periods of time,* will become increasingly less effective. This deterioration is likely to continue until (1) leader-member relations are improved, (2) members co-opt leadership functions, or (3) the leader is replaced.

How groups form, why people join groups, group motivation, norms, and dynamics, and the components of group effectiveness and leadership effectiveness in groups, are areas of interest and competence which are increasing in importance to schools as supervisory ways of behaving continue to replace administrative ways of behaving as the dominant means to school ends.

THE NATURE OF SUPERVISION: CONCLUSION

This chapter concludes the first part of the book. Our purposes in Part I have been: (1) to define and discuss the nature and breadth of supervision, (2) to map and relate components which make up the supervisory environment, and (3) to describe and evaluate supervisory assumptions and dimensions of supervisory behavior in terms of their effect on all inhabitants who compose the human organization of the school. Our discussions are based on two fundamental premises: (1) we believe that classroom doors do not have the capability to shut out hostile, frustrated, controlled, or closed school environments and, indeed, that learning environments reflect the climate of the school at large; and (2) self-actualization as a manifest goal for students cannot be achieved unless this goal is pursued, at the manifest level, for all school inhabitants.

SELECTED REFERENCES

Benne, Kenneth, and Paul Sheats: "Functional Roles of Group Members," *The Journal of Social Issues,* vol. 4, no. 2, Spring, 1948.

Cartwright, Dorwin, and Alvin Zander: *Group Dynamics: Research and Theory,* 3d ed., Harper & Row, New York, 1968.

Likert, Rensis: *New Patterns of Management,* McGraw-Hill, New York, 1961.

Part Two
SUPERVISING
THE HUMAN
CURRICULUM

Introduction: Human Learning and Personal Growth

Part I of this book has dealt with the process of supervision. It attempts to point out those supervisory behaviors which lead to self-actualization of all school inhabitants. Many of the behavioral dynamics described in Part I can be applied to actual instructional practices in the classroom. Granting, now, that a school were willing to adopt the supervisory processes described in Part I, we must consider the kind of educational program which will give substance to such practices as they focus on the primary client of the school, the student.

We are facing an explosive phenomenon in today's schools—student alienation. Granted that many elements in the larger societal environment contribute to this feeling of alienation, especially on college campuses, certainly we can say that some of the blame must be placed on the school's doorstep. A student does not have to wait until he goes to college to encounter impersonality and meaningless learning. Sometimes it begins in the first grade. One of the major problems facing primary and secondary school students is the climate of supervision which communicates a lack of trust and relies heavily on marks and promotion procedures to gain control and compliance. Another major factor, however, in a student's indoctrination into alienation is the curricular program itself. Because of both an overconcentration on memory as well as a hyperrational approach to knowledge and experience, students often perceive their academic learning experiences as belonging to a separate universe that has nothing to do with their real world.

In Part II, some attempt is made to face up to the task of building a human curriculum for students. This is not so much a task of developing a thoroughly detailed sequence of lesson plans which leaves the student in his customary passive role, but rather of providing a framework for learning in which the student will encounter reality on his own level. Neither, on the other hand, do we propose a human curriculum based on the assumption that students do not require any direction, any structure, or any challenge.

The human curriculum is one which attempts to correspond to developmental patterns of personal growth while introducing students into a human universe, a universe which they cannot manipulate at will, but one which calls out to them to humanize it further.

In order to clarify the focus of our attention and to indicate how the human curriculum offered in this book differs from others, Part II adopts the following sequence of chapters. Chapter 11 examines the salient features of the current curriculum reforms. The description of current curricular programs is brief because most readers will already be familiar with them. Critical comments are lengthy, however, because we hope to challenge some basic assumptions underlying these reforms as well as school environmental factors surrounding them.

Chapter 12 examines the issue of establishing educational objectives. Again, description of the theories for selecting and defining objectives is brief because the reader will already have seen these in previous educational study. More attention is given to developing a critical posture toward current practices.

Chapter 13 offers a theoretical model of the environment of learning. The reader is led to consider several varieties of learning contexts, only a few of which seem to be used in today's schools. This chapter helps to set the stage for the development of a human curriculum design in Chapter 14. This chapter presents a rather thorough elaboration of the assumptions behind such a program, leads the reader through the thinking process involved in selecting general and specific goals, and offers one kind of curriculum program which might flow from these goals. The reader should not accept this program as necessarily definitive or complete. It is offered both as one human curriculum design which we would choose and as a stimulus to thinking—which could very well lead to a human curriculum of a quite different form.

Chapter 15 considers the unpopular topic of evaluation. We say "unpopular" because it is so often neglected. Considerable effort in this chapter is expended in criticizing current methods of evaluation, the exclusive use of which contributes to the student alienation mentioned earlier. The responsibilities supervisory personnel have in changing the system of evaluation is underlined and a more comprehensive model is offered.

Chapter Eleven
THE PRESENT STATE
OF CURRICULUM PROGRAMS

In this chapter, we shall consider recent trends in curriculum reform, evaluate some of their strong and weak points, and discuss some of their implications for supervisory personnel. As we mentioned above, anyone exercising a supervisory function must be not only sensitive to the organizational dynamics of supervisory processes, but also, as Heffernan and Bishop indicate, familiar with issues and elements in curriculum development.[1] The last decade or so has seen extensive reform of curriculum content and organization. Anyone preparing for a supervisory position in education must become familiar, at some level of sophistication, with these curriculum reforms and the rationale behind them, for they have already received widespread acceptance in the schools. The present chapter offers a brief survey of the essential features of the curricular reforms and evaluates the climate of thinking that produced them. Since the treatment is brief, it should be supplemented by further detailed reading in the curriculum literature.[2]

FORMATIVE IDEAS OF THE NEW CURRICULA

Spurred by criticisms from inside and outside the educational establishment, and with a sense of national purpose shaken by the Russian threat to the balance of power, a variety of agencies—national, regional, and local—have engaged in a massive overhaul of school programs. Out of the ferment of seminars, consortia, and other gatherings of scholars, teachers, administrators, psychologists, and businessmen has emerged a mode of curriculum development which focuses on basic disciplines of knowledge. As a result of the knowledge explosion and rapid changes in society both technological and social, teachers and scholars have searched for the durable ideas, those having central and fundamental importance for organizing and comprehending a complex array of facts. Those who designed the new curricula have emphasized that key concepts, themes, generalizations, models, and theories

[1]Helen Heffernan and Leslie J. Bishop, "The Supervisor and Curriculum Director at Work," in Robert R. Leeper (ed.), *Role of Supervisor and Curriculum Director in a Climate of Change*, Association for Supervision and Curriculum Development, Washington, D.C., 1965, pp. 87–143.
[2]See the selected readings at the end of this chapter.

—in short, those cognitive components of the structure of the disciplines of knowledge—are the durable ideas.[3]

These recent curriculum designers have argued that the only way to manage the knowledge explosion and its confusing and variegated accumulaton of data is to focus on the structure of the discipline and on key concepts, concept clusters, and generalizations. This focus enhances economy of learning by enabling students to organize knowledge more readily around these key concepts and structures. In this way relationships and patterns emerge, and the student is enabled to transfer principles and attitudes for subsequent learning.

Alongside their emphasis on structure and central concepts, the new curriculum designers also stress processes of inquiry and discovery—methodologies employed by scholars in the disciplines for exploring new problems and phenomena. These processes include techniques of gathering, recording, and classifying data, of controlled experimentation, and of verifying evidence and validating conclusions. While each discipline has its own methodologies, general techniques which cut across several disciplines are accentuated, such as measuring, constructing hypotheses, and using abstract models or charts and graphs. Rather than simply presenting the student with the key concepts, the new curricula, by exposing the student to the raw material of the discipline and by using suggestive questions, attempt to lead the student to discover by his own inquiry what these key concepts or structural relationships are. Ability to think inductively then becomes a built-in goal of the curriculum. This discovery process puts the student squarely at the active center of the learning process and enables him to experience the exhilaration and enthusiasm of both search and discovery. In this way, he engages in the very processes of the scholar, although the problems and materials are adapted to his age and learning levels.

Another major emphasis of the new curricula involves sequence and continuity. This has led to a variety of programmed instructional units in which the unit is broken down into small, logically related elements which enable the student to progress at his own rate through a series of tightly connected steps. In other words, curriculum designers have experimented with learning material to discover what it was that, by its omission, caused a student to miss the point of the unit. Then they have included that particular link expressly in the learning materials. Thus, by a process of many trials, they have come up with learning units which any student, by progressing through each step, is supposed to be able to master. The concern for continuity and sequence has also led to the larger design of series of courses, for example, a K–8 arts program or a K–12 mathematics sequence. The emphasis

[3]John U. Michaelis et al., *New Designs for the Elementary School Curriculum*, McGraw-Hill, New York, 1967, p. 15.

is on the cumulative effect of learning simpler elements of the discipline and by building on these to move to more complex elements of the discipline.[4]

Organizational innovations which supposedly effect and strengthen the impact of the new curricula have also gained widespread acceptance. These include flexible scheduling, large- and small-group instruction, independent study, team teaching, and nongraded classrooms. As devices to increase curricula impact, these organizational arrangements do not logically flow from the emphasis on structure and key concepts. A group of teachers could team-teach a life adjustment program; classes could be flexibly scheduled and multi-grouped for typing and woodcraft. Indeed, a search through the new curriculum packages reveals very little awareness of these innovations in the use of space and time and the use of teaching personnel. This deficiency is probably due to the different origins of the discipline-oriented reforms and the organizational reforms.

DISCIPLINE VERSUS SUBJECT MATTER

When one places the curricular reforms of the past decade or so in historical perspective, it might be tempting to conclude that the pendulum has simply swung back to the earlier emphasis on subject matter. To conclude thus would be to miss, however, the unique and, indeed, most forceful aspect of the new curricula. For they are not new approaches to subject matter as educators have traditionally understood that term. Previously, "subject matter" was the content of the school courses or curriculum which was taken from the organized disciplines of knowledge and translated into subject matter to be learned. That is, the discoveries of science or literary criticism were taken out of their context and fitted to a theory of learning, broken down into manageable parts, and fitted into a scheme or organization which the curriculum designer, publisher, and teacher decided on. As school subject matter, it did not properly represent the syntax or the grammar of the discipline nor its substantive structure. Previously, educators assumed that this translation was legitimate and necessary. Scholars, however, have recently scored this mistranslation of discipline into subject matter.

> We have taught prosody in the name of poetry, thus killing an interest in poetry for ourselves and our descendants. . . . We have taught computation in the name of mathematics. . . . We have taught place geography in the name of geography, almost killing this subject in our schools. No geographer says that this is what geography is. . . . We have taught facts and principles in the name of

[4]See, for example, Jerome S. Bruner's notion of the "Spiral Curriculum," *The Process of Education*, Harvard, Cambridge, Mass., 1960, and John I. Goodlad's notion of "Organizing Centers" and "Organizing Elements," in *Planning and Organizing for Teaching*, Project on Instruction, National Education Association, Washington, D.C., 1963.

science; but science is a mode of inquiry, and the scientists now say what we are doing is not only out of date, but it is not science.[5]

Schwab, also, warns about the mistake of trying to fit material taken from a discipline—knowledge discovered according to the processes of inquiry and according to the criteria for validity which *are germane to that discipline*—to one simple theory of learning.

The structures of the modern disciplines are *complex* and *diverse. . . .* Diversity of modern structures means that we must look, not for a simple theory of learning leading to a one best learning-teaching structure for our schools, but for a complex theory leading to a *number of different structures,* each appropriate or "best" for a given discipline or group of disciplines.[6]

King and Brownell subscribe wholeheartedly to this distinction between a curriculum identified with the disciplines and a curriculum whose subject matter is borrowed from the disciplines, and claim the former as the *only* sound basis for a curriculum which emphasizes intellectual values.[7]

Not all among the new curriculum designers agree with this emphasis. Oliver and Shaver in the Harvard Curriculum Project in Social Studies distinguish between social science and social studies, the latter being based on the social sciences and history but adapted for use in a program of *general education.*[8] They maintain that a general education, social studies curriculum should prepare a student to make reflective, rational, critical decisions about public issues. To make these decisions, value judgments are involved, and no amount of pure social science, they maintain, can offer empirical procedures for deciding what is right or wrong. Their concern, then, is not *primarily* to introduce students into the methodology of sociology or to have students engage in sociological research, but is rather to expose them to value conflicts over public issues in order to prepare them for the appreciation of the complexities of public life in society and for the responsibilities of public choices.

This issue of a curriculum of general education versus a curriculum based on and incorporating the syntactical and substantive structures of the

[5]Arthur W. Foshay, "Education and the Nature of a Discipline," in Alexander Frazier (ed.), *New Dimensions of Learnings,* Association for Supervision and Curriculum Development, National Education Association, Washington, D.C., 1962, pp. 5–6.
[6]Joseph Schwab, "The Concept of the Structure of a Discipline," *Educational Record,* vol. 43, July, 1962, p. 197.
[7]Arthur R. King, Jr., and John A. Brownell, *The Curriculum and the Disciplines of Knowledge,* Wiley, New York, 1966, pp. 93, 117–125. See also Philip H. Phenix, "The Use of the Disciplines as Curriculum Content," *Educational Forum,* vol. 26, March, 1962, pp. 273–279, and Phenix, "Curriculum and the Analysis of Language," in James B. Macdonald and Robert Leeper (eds.), *Language and Meaning,* Association for Supervision and Curriculum Development, National Education Association, Washington, D.C., 1966, pp. 30–31.
[8]James Shaver, "Values and the Social Studies," in Irving Morrissett (ed.), *Concepts and Structure in the New Social Science Curricula,* Social Science Education Consortium, Inc., West Lafayette, Ind., 1966, p. 116.

disciplines is critical. Presently, the curriculum reforms have tended to stress the latter and will probably continue to do so. But the issue raises fundamental questions for educators about the basic purpose of public education. Previously educators assumed that the general purpose of public education was to prepare students for adult life in society, and hence the curriculum was a blend of three concerns: the psychological needs and growth processes of the student, the social adjustment to living with others from a plurality of ethnic and socioeconomic backgrounds in a political democracy, and, finally, the demands of a rational understanding of the student's cultural traditions and his present physical and social environment. When it was planned from this general education perspective, the curriculum contained knowledge derived from history, science, literature, and mathematics but organized it into learning units designed to contribute to the basic education necessary for the exercise of intelligent citizenship. Exposure to the rigorous and specialized methodology of specific disciplines, as well as the furtherance of scholarship, was considered the concern of colleges and graduate schools. Since large numbers of students did not go to college, the curriculum of the elementary and secondary schools focused on those general learnings requisite to functioning in our society. Even the college-preparatory programs were affected by this general education orientation.

Now, however, scholars from the disciplines claim that any learning of material borrowed from their discipline which is not learned *within the integrity* of their discipline, by their methods of inquiry, and related to the key concepts and substantive structures of the discipline is superficial, arbitrary, and not authentic learning at all. In order to acquire knowledge about the nature of the physical universe, it is necessary to think like a physicist, chemist, biologist, and astronomer and to use their methods of inquiry and to discover their structural principles—in short, to encounter and immerse oneself in the community of discourse of each discipline. To learn history one must become, at it were, a neophyte in the community of historians.[9] English programs have been developed in which language is the center and base of the program and is considered as a separate domain to be studied according to the structural principles of linguistics. Composition and literature are related to language, of course, but they are studied according to the key concepts and structural principles of the disciplines of rhetoric (for composition) and literary analysis (for literature).[10] In other words, learning something in school means learning it according to the distinct approaches of

[9]King and Brownell, *op. cit.*, p. 121.
[10]See, for example, Michaelis et al., *op. cit.*, pp. 52–130; Robert F. Hogan, "English," in Glenys G. Unruh (ed.), *New Curriculum Developments,* Association for Supervision and Curriculum Development, National Education Association, Washington, D.C., 1965, pp. 16–27; Francis A. J. Ianni and Lois S. Josephs, "The Curriculum Research and Development Programs of the U.S. Office of Education: Project English, Project Social Studies and Beyond," in Robert W. Heath (ed.), *New Curricula,* Harper & Row, New York, 1964, pp. 161–214.

the separate disciplines. Attempts to do otherwise, claim the reformers, distort what is learned and prevent the student from experiencing the integral and autonomous perspective of the world from the vantage point of that particular discipline.

CRITICAL REFLECTIONS ON THE NEW CURRICULA

The stress on the disciplines as forming the primary and, at times, exclusive content of the curriculum offers many, many benefits. It enables educators to refine, simplify, and purge from the curriculum much that is irrelevant and superficial and to strengthen their courses with material of lasting worth to the student. The new emphases, however, are not without their potential disadvantages, and educators with supervisory responsibilities should cast a critical eye not only on the rationale behind the new curricula but also and especially on the implementation of the new curricula in the school.

It may be helpful initially to take a long step away from the recent developments to study what has actually been happening. As one looks over the roster of committees which have spearheaded the drive to overhaul the curriculum, one quickly notices the abundance of professional scholars from university circles. The advent of scholars into the arena of curriculum planning and development should be cause for jubilation.

Our jubilation, however, should carry a few burrs of caution. Without for a moment questioning the altruism of these scholars, one must also realize that their enthusiasm for the disciplines is not entirely unbiased. Immersion in their scholarly discipline has obviously been fun, has consumed their energies for a better part of their lifetimes, and has convinced them of the contribution of their discipline to man's wisdom and welfare. To them, the growth of their scholarly community and the ensuing scholarly advances in discoveries appear as a benefit society cannot afford to refuse. In projecting downward the introduction of their disciplines *as such* into the high school and elementary school, they increase the probability of their particular profession benefiting from increased numbers of better-qualified youngsters moving into their field. Using the analogy of athletic recruiting, the professional football leagues stand to benefit considerably by college football programs, which in turn rely on high school football programs, which recently have benefited from Pop Warner football leagues for younger boys.

It would be ridiculous to claim a conspiracy on the part of the scholars to ensure some kind of future dictatorship of the intellectuals. Nevertheless, this appears to be the first time in the educational history of this country when a large-scale effort has been launched to equip almost everybody to be a minischolar, and a minischolar in several disciplines at the same time. It would be easy to parody the curriculum reform movement by suggesting that students attend classes wearing the long white coat of the laboratory technician muttering quizzically in a foreign accent, or that they don tweed vests and pipes and half-rimmed glasses when they go to the library. Such humor at the expense of men who have given so much to the advance of knowledge is crude and uncalled for. And it is true that schools have done a considerable disservice to the scholarly disciplines when they have used knowledge gained by scholarly research to inculcate a naïve or crude kind of patriotism or to serve crass utilitarian ends. It is also true that responsible rational living in a technological society demands intellectual rigor and clarity—a rigor and clarity which the scholarly disciplines provide.

The scholars' insistence, however, on the learning of modes of inquiry and structural principles of their discipline prompts several questions. How *much* familiarity with their disciplines is necessary for a person to carry on the daily affairs of living, especially for the large majority of persons who will not pursue careers in their disciplines? What kind of curriculum would we have if we invited business executives rather than academic scholars to assist in designing a curriculum? Or military men, or labor leaders, or theologians, or politicans? Obviously, there would be enormous differences in each case.

It could be argued that we lose something by acquiring knowledge in separate and distinct strands of inquiry. Reality is manysided, and it seems just as important to appreciate the natural symbolism of water in art and religious ritual, to understand the critical importance of water to hygiene and farming and industrial purposes, and to understand the geography of erosion and waterways as it is to know that the formula for water is H_2O. An interdisciplinary study of water and what it means to man's existence through the medium of music, poetry, architecture, history, geography, political science, archaeology, and anthropology as well as through biology, chemistry, and physics could open up a whole world of wonder and awe over such a seemingly simple phenomenon as a raindrop. Granted that one could not understand how water influences the formation of cities, how poetry can capture the many moods of water, or how it is that water rises when it freezes, without the painstaking efforts of scholars in their separate disciplines. Nevertheless, why must one structure a curriculum around a sequential parade through the disciplines rather than use organizing themes such as "The Many Moods of Raindrops," or "The Dance of Energy," or "The Texture of War"? Is an extensive, one-dimensional view of mass and energy, of biological life processes, or of the syntax of a language more profitable than a multidimensional view of energy, life, and language which does not adhere to the strict requirements of the disciplines?

This raises the question of how "objective" the knowledge gained through a particular discipline really is (if it is not readily seen as partial and limited). That is, with the emphasis on the disciplines as the only legitimate gateway to valid and true knowledge, it is conceivable, at least, that in the implementation of the new curricula (if not in the rationale behind them) the inference might easily be made that phenomena are exhaustively known through the abstractions of one particular discipline. In the interest of preserving the integrity of the discipline and of supporting its claim to valid knowledge, a few scholars and not so few enthusiastic teachers give the impression that their discipline gets to the really real truths of reality. Some behavioral psychologists who recently seem to have assumed the role formerly occupied by medieval metaphysicians sometimes give this impression when describing human behavior. This questioning of the adequacy of any one discipline to preempt all available truth is not meant to disparage the real merits of any particular discipline, but merely to stress the multidimensional characteristics of phenomena and to caution against a naïve acceptance of any one discipline or cluster of disciplines as exhausting what is potentially knowable in reality.

Again, what insurance does the public have that youngsters schooled in the disciplines will be more compassionate, just, responsible, and altruistic than they would otherwise be? How the schools are to go about teaching values has always been a subject for debate among American educators, but that the schools should somehow affect the values and attitudes of students has rarely been questioned. The methods of inquiry of the disciplines insist on objectivity, on impartial observance of the "facts," on categorizing phenomena under key concepts, and on classifying the relationships between and among phenomena according to structural principles. In accomplishing this task, a curriculum based on the disciplines serves a most important function in the education of youth. But man is not simply an intellect; he is a person with emotions and a person who must make many choices, for which the disciplines' methods of inquiry are inadequate. Wise men from Socrates to Severeid have admitted that knowledge is not virtue, that knowing the facts is no guarantee of making the just or prudent decision. Again, this criticism is not to encourage anti-intellectual perfidy, but rather to insist that training students in the skills of acquiring objective knowledge does not complete the job of a teacher.

Although the issue of efficiency will be treated in more detail in the next chapter, it is worth noting at this point the similarities between the highly rationalized, bureaucratic system discussed in earlier chapters and the tight logic of the streamlined curriculum packages. From a rationalized technical point of view, the reformers aim at maximum predictability of results from their curricula. In other words, they are seeking the financially most efficient and the technically most effective way to produce learning. But we must ask whether they have taken sufficient account of all the human factors.

TECHNOLOGICAL RATIONALITY IN TODAY'S SCHOOLS

Supervisory personnel need to reflect on the wider context of the curriculum reform movement—that is, as this movement grows out of our society's cult of efficiency and its underlying "technological rationality."[11] Such reflection is important because many school practices reflect this rationality, often to the detriment of both true learning and the human growth of students.

With a consumer-oriented economy aided by almost daily engineering breakthroughs in home appliances, automobiles, and communication systems, the American way of life has been saturated by a style of thought and values that places emphasis on organization, efficiency, and the regimentation of time, change, and motion almost for its own sake—in short, a concentration on the pragmatic and utilitarian. In stating this, it is important not to engage in nostalgic longings for some kind of golden age in the recent or distant past; rather, the point is simply to acknowledge that life styles in our society are being affected by the complexities of our national economy and the resonances of technological change.

Technological rationality has affected our thinking about purposes and processes of education. It is argued that our national interests demand highly trained personnel to continue our efforts in science, to man those managerial and technical positions in industry and government that are critical to our continued prosperity and our leadership among nations. Schools are expected to provide these highly trained persons. Therefore, educational programs of schools must emphasize the learning of those skills and competencies required by the positions to be filled in society.

Graduate schools, where formal training is completed (although training and intern programs in many professional, business, and governmental organizations put on the finishing touches), dictate to the colleges the requirements for entrance. The college, in turn, dictates to the high school the requirements for college entrance. And the high school college-preparatory curriculum is organized primarily to feed students into specific college programs, whether in commerce, education, engineering, or premedical. Even liberal arts programs in colleges are increasingly oriented toward preparing students for the pursuit of graduate education in specific majors. This orientation also places subtle demands on the high school and elementary school curricula (for example, the learning of a foreign language in order to be able to read scholarly journals in graduate school). This is to say nothing of those secondary school programs which prepare terminal students for immediate entrance into the labor market, or of those which equip students to pursue more particular training in junior college.

From the perspective of a social planner, such an orderly progression from elementary to secondary school to college and graduate levels makes

---

[11]James B. Macdonald has used this term in his criticism of current curricular theory in "An Example of Disciplined Curriculum Thinking," *Theory into Practice,* vol. 6, October, 1967, pp. 166–167. See Jacques Ellul, *The Technological Society,* trans. by J. Wilkinson, Knopf, New York, 1964, for a thoroughgoing analysis of the saturation of Western society by technological rationality. Herbert Marcuse, in *One-dimensional Man,* Beacon Paperback, Boston, 1966, presents a similar analysis.

sense. The system of government and industry is preserved through such a feeder system. From this view, the graduate schools should demand that colleges prepare prospective graduate students in those skills and competencies necessary to master the requirements of a graduate program. By the same logic, colleges rightfully demand that prospective students come with certain requirements fulfilled.

From the vantage point of the student, it becomes evident how this logic affects him. In order to be promoted from elementary to secondary school, he must have achieved a certain proficiency in basic language and computation skills. Ideally, this enables him to further develop these skills more specifically in dealing with expository writing and speaking, with foreign languages, with more complex works in social studies and language arts, with more abstract mathematics, and with biology, chemistry, and physics. As the adolescent increases his ability to deal with higher abstract reasoning processes, the secondary school refines his abilities to make generalizations, to discover relationships and the structural principles which undergird these relationships, and to organize and manipulate large bodies of factual information around central concepts by means of rational and logical processes. Theoretically, this growth in reasoning and discovery and in problem-solving skills enables the student to progress to the next level of his education. In college the student will further hone his mental abilities in more general studies for the first few years and then will begin to specialize in a major field. Then, of course, the undergraduate faces the last step in his preparation for a specific career—the graduate school. Here, courses are more specialized, going into microbiology, seventeenth-century history, market analysis research, or the teaching of elementary school mathematics.

As the student progresses from one level to the other, then, his education remains oriented toward the future: he must learn this in order to learn that in order to learn the other; he must pass through this stage in order to get to that stage in order to pass on to the next stage—and the more quickly he can get through these stages, the better. Accelerated programs and advance-placement programs—with all the prestige and status attached—all testify to an underlying hurry to get through each stage. In the process, everything becomes a means to an end, which in turn becomes a means to a further end. It becomes a question, as Grandstaff suggests, not so much of learning a subject for its own intrinsic merits, but rather of learning how to get promoted or how to get a grade leading to promotion.[12]

In a system dominated by technological rationality, everything takes its value according to the criterion of efficiency: what will accomplish the end intended with the least amount of wasted time and effort. Thus, in a school,

[12]Marvin Grandstaff, " 'Situations' as a Category of Curriculum Theory," paper presented at a summer curriculum seminar sponsored by the Center for the Study of Instruction, National Education Association, Summer, 1968.

a production-like process begins to take shape. Through elective systems, students have, to be sure, the choice of deciding on what kind of production line they want to place themselves. They can even jump from one program series to another—say, from an engineering program to a sociology program. The point is, however, that every program itself has a structure and moves along, according to its own logic, toward turning out a product. In this kind of system, it becomes difficult for the individual student to delay at one stage of the program simply to relish what he is learning for its own sake—simply to enjoy the present without thinking of how the present can be justified in terms of its use for the acquisition of something tomorrow. In other words, the production-line ethos of education continually holds out to the student the importance of change, of becoming, without encouraging the student to enjoy and appreciate being—being who he is where he is—and to appreciate other things and people for what they are in their own right and not as a means to something else.

At this point, someone might object that this orientation toward the future, the means-end use of things and people and the compartmentalization of time, reflects not so much any intrinsic logic of technology, but rather the more general, pragmatic attitudes of people who use technology. While there are some reciprocal effects of one on the other, the intrinsic logic of technology, if left to itself, if allowed to be the sole justification for itself, generates this kind of compartmentalization of time and such means-end relationships.

As the spread of technology, with its emphasis on efficiency and predictability, encompasses wider areas of life, a web of interdependent technological subsystems is built up. Transportation systems, computerized logistic systems, communication systems, training and retraining systems, marketing and purchasing systems, and many others spread interlocking tentacles so that a shift in one causes rapid shifts in other subsystems. In order to keep such a technological megasystem going, the lives of people involved in these systems become increasingly programmed to ensure maximum efficiency and predictability. There is nothing intrinsic to the logic of this kind of technology, which resembles a kind of megamachine, to allow for any other considerations extrinsic to its own demands. If the machine does not function smoothly, it is because the human beings involved occasionally refuse to operate as mechanical parts.

To say that the school has been infected with technological rationality is not to deny that students do occasionally learn to enjoy literature and history, science, and mathematics. It is to say, however, that the main orientation of the educational process is toward the future, toward getting into college or graduate school or landing this or that job. In other words, the schools are dominated more—though not entirely—by a pragmatic and utilitarian interest in knowledge. What the student learns—history, French, mathematics, and literature—has its own inner principles of rationality or order. But the social system of the school which provides the context of the student's education is guided by a technological rationality: the arrangement of his program, the fitting together of courses, is based on a technological rationality. In criticizing the limitations of the so-called new curricula, it is precisely the *acceptance* of this rationale, the packaging of material to fit tracks and promotion procedures—not so much the quality of any particular unit in the new package—that we want to call before the jury.

One-dimensional Learning

Technological rationality not only affects the progression of learning experiences and the student's approach to learning—in other words, affects the external environment of learning—it also affects *what* is learned. If the student feels that what schooling means is the acquisition of information and skills in order to pass exams, get promoted, and get a job, this level of interest and inquiry and effort will tend to be consonant with the quality of these goals—which are basically short-term and superficial. He "takes" from his encounter with the material to be studied what he needs to pass exams. Seldom will he study a problem or pursue an argument because of any intrinsic interest it might enjoy. Any brief reflection indicates that reality— entities, situations, problems, persons, and geographies—is multidimensional. A student who *uses* information and skills simply to achieve passing grades misses the rich meaning inherent in reality's vagaries. He gradually adopts a cognitive style of intellectual rape. And as in the crime from which that metaphor derives, the criminal misses the whole point of the human experience which the crime violates.

Current curriculum offerings appear far too simplistic in their appreciation of what actually goes on in a person when he "knows" something, when he thinks, when something means something to him. They seem almost to equate the structure of knowledge with the structure of the disciplines; at least, this is the distinct impression they give. Disciplines have structures, however, because man creates these structures: they are heuristic models enabling man to make generalizations and abstractions which can be empirically verified. But a man's experience of knowing, what goes on when he thinks, when he reasons, when he understands something, is far more complex than the simple deductive or inductive methodology of logic and science. These methodologies are abstractions from the extraordinary complex life of human consciousness. And when conscious experience involves not simply the grappling with a pragmatic problem but also the act of personal communication or the overt performance of some task or the making of something new, then the total behavior of the human individual is indeed complex. To reduce learning to the passive intake of information, to the processing of it by logical and heuristic skills, and to the solving of problems on exams is to ignore the perceptual, the emotional, and the functional elements of human consciousness.

The concept of human rationality as such is an abstraction; so is the concept of intelligence. The initial shock caused among educators by such a statement should indicate how easily many of them have accepted current curricular notions such as key concepts and processes of inquiry. But if they would take the time to reflect on their everyday behavior and look at all the "reasons" why they behaved as they did, they would find all sorts of ambiguous influences and fluctuations in their conscious experience. Reason and intelligence are human traits, but they never function in isolation from the fuller life of consciousness and perception. Only from a look over the shoulder, after the fact, can one construct the reasonableness or the logic behind one's actions. Even the scientist would admit that. Usually his discovery precedes the full-blown logical explanation of why such and such *had* to happen. Granted, his behavior is aided by the general rationality implicit in his methodology, and so he is not flailing around in the dark and coming upon his discoveries by mere chance. But, usually, the step-by-step logical explanation of his discovery of a relationship between properties of a given phenomenon comes *after* the discovery, not before it. Usually he proceeds in a far more tentative and hypothetical manner: "Let me see now, what will happen if I do this to that?"[13]

These critical remarks are not a call to haphazard and unorganized learning. We believe, however, that curricular-instructional programs need to be far more responsive to the growth processes of students and to the students' experience of the world. Chapters 12 and 13 suggest a more comprehensive framework for a curricular-instructional program which is not totally subverted to technological rationality. For now, it remains to suggest some implications of the foregoing discussion for supervisory practice.

[13]Not a few authors have gone to some lengths to document this complexity of conscious experience. Eugene T. Gendlin, in *Experiencing and the Creation of Meaning,* Free Press, Evanston, Ill., 1962, and in "The Discovery of Felt Meaning," in James B. Macdonald (ed.), *Language and Meaning,* Association for Supervision and Curriculum Development, National Education Association, Washington, D.C., 1966, pp. 45–62, has examined the function of felt meaning in cognition. His work bears similarities to that of several European phenomenologists, such as Husserl and Merleau-Ponty, to mention two. Polanyi's work on personal knowledge and tacit knowing also analyzes the implicit ground of explicit knowledge: Michael Polanyi, *Personal Knowledge,* Harper Torchbooks, New York, 1965; The *Tacit Dimension,* Doubleday, Garden City, N.Y., 1966. The work of these authors shares basic affinities with Kubie's work on preconscious processes involved in learning and thinking, and with MacMurray's essays on personal knowledge: John MacMurray, *The Form of the Personal:* Vol. I, *The Self as Agent,* Faber and Faber, London, 1956; Vol. II, *Persons in Relation,* Faber and Faber, London, 1961; *Reason and Emotion,* Appleton-Century, New York, 1937. All of these men are concerned with grounding rationality in the more total, organic life of conscious and preconscious experience, and with indicating the personal and social conflicts which result when man is split up into a thinking, rational human being and an instinctual, emotional animal.

IMPLICATIONS FOR SUPERVISORS

Whoever exercises supervisory responsibilities, then, needs to be aware of some of these issues implied in current and emerging curriculum patterns. With the stress on adequate knowledge of the structure of the disciplines, chairmen and others who occupy supervisory positions close to the instruction-learning system of the school may require some retooling in order to catch up with the revisions in their discipline. Certainly this has been true for mathematics and English supervisors with the recent change toward set and field theory and toward structural linguistics. If supervisors are to assist teachers in organizing curricular units around key concepts and structural principles and in assessing the usefulness of teaching materials currently available, they themselves ought to be familiar with these concepts and principles. Beyond this, supervisors need to be wary of the relationships and analogies between key concepts and methodological processes of inquiry in one discipline and those in other disciplines in order to help the teachers and students discover these relationships and analogies. Moreover, the supervisor ought to challenge the one-dimensional and highly compartmentalized vision of reality which prepackaged curricula might embody, and continually, in consort with teachers and students, seek the *human* import of what is being studied.

Because of the impact of the grading system and the tendency to focus on superficial uses of knowledge for passing exams and being promoted, supervisors must encourage sensitivity to other values as well as the purely academic. Many other things are happening to students in the classroom besides their acquisition of concepts and skills—things such as learning how to "sweet talk" the teacher, learning to understand another student's point of view, learning how to defend oneself from humiliation, and learning how to control impulses to anger or other emotional outbursts. Besides these more personal and subjective learnings, the context of curricular learning units— for example, a poem by Auden or a historical episode in the Civil War or the biochemical reactions in food digestion—has human implications which go far beyond the specific point being made in that unit. Supervisors should encourage teachers to dwell on some of these implications in order to enrich the student's encounter with that particular phenomenon.

Perhaps the most important implication for supervisors, and one which many will be slow to accept, concerns their responsibility for participating in both the evaluation of current curriculum packages and materials and the actual construction, if necessary, of revised curriculum programs. Supervisors, administrators, and teachers need to work together in this endeavor. Many administrators will avoid curriculum construction, claiming that that should be left to the teachers or to book publishers. While it is true that the teachers ought to possess sufficient knowledge of their discipline to make such evaluations themselves, nevertheless, the principal and the supervisor should be able to ask questions which will assist teachers in either specifying their goals, clarifying the point they are trying to communicate in a particular unit, or evaluating the results of their efforts. Supervisors, because their perspective takes in a broader range and quantity of students, can often judge more accurately the advisability of certain curriculum decisions. Because of their greater familiarity with the schoolwide effect of the curricular program, they ought to be able to provide a perspective which the individual teacher lacks. And their more extensive experience with a variety of teachers and students ought to give them the professional basis for helping the teacher and students develop a curriculum that suits their needs and preferences. While the hardware and software in new curriculum materials provide a rich source for organizing a course, the teacher, with the assistance of department chairmen and other supervisory personnel, must choose those materials which fit his particular approach to the course. In other words, curriculum packages and aids do not relieve the teacher and supervisor of the responsibility of building their own curriculum; they simply provide a wider and richer variety of materials to choose from.

SELECTED REFERENCES

Bruner, Jerome S.: *The Process of Education*, Harvard, Cambridge, Mass., 1960.

Elul, Jacques: *The Technological Society*, Knopf, New York, 1964.

Heath, Robert W. (ed.): *New Curricula*, Harper & Row, New York, 1964.

Michaelis, John U., et al.: *New Designs for the Elementary School Curriculum*, McGraw-Hill, New York, 1967.

Project on Instruction, National Education Association: *Schools for the Sixties*, McGraw-Hill, New York, 1963.

Chapter Twelve
DEFINING
GOALS OF THE
CURRICULUM PROGRAM

Supervisory personnel continually encounter the issue of goals or purposes in their work. A principal must try to specify the central goals of the total school effort and especially the goals of the instructional program. A department chairman worries about the guiding purposes of his department's effort on one grade level or over a three- or four-grade span. The central office supervisor tries to set general goals for the whole school district in terms of either grade levels or subject areas. Teachers, in an effort to clarify their courses to themselves and to their students, continually ask themselves, "What am *I* or what are *we* trying to accomplish?"

Teaching is supposed to be a purposeful activity. That is, teachers intend to make something happen to their pupils—to help them to learn, to grow, to become. One of the main reasons, however, why teaching is so often ineffectual is that teachers have not made actually operative the objectives which they quite easily recite for any inquiring observer. In this chapter we shall discuss the process of defining goals or objectives and indicate how the emphases in goal statements and assumptions behind them influence the selection of curricular-instructional content. Examples of two schools of thought regarding the general and specific purposes of schooling will be described and evaluated. In the process of pointing out certain shortcomings in the focus of these goal statements, we hope to develop the groundwork for a model of a human curriculum.

BEHAVIORAL OBJECTIVES

Ralph Tyler has been one of the moving forces in the effort to assist teachers and curriculum developers in the task of defining objectives. His basic model for curriculum development is dominated by this concern for objectives.[1] He and other curriculum theorists, such as Hilda Taba[2] and John

[1]Ralph Tyler, *Basic Principles of Curriculum and Instruction,* University of Chicago Press, Chicago, 1950.
[2]Hilda Taba, *Curriculum Development: Theory and Practice,* Harcourt, Brace & World, New York, 1962.

Goodlad,[3] have stressed the importance of specifying objectives in behavioral terms and have had a significant impact on the form of many new curriculum materials.

Tyler criticized the widespread practice of defining objectives in terms of content to be covered or devices to be used instead of changes in behavior of students. Many teachers still fail to specify their objectives for a particular class other than to state, "I intend to cover Robert Frost's poem 'The Path Not Taken,'" or "Today we're going to fool around with the slide rule (or the vacuum pump)." Or, when considering the objectives of their whole course, they simply state them as: "To appreciate poetry"; "To think critically." The difficulty with those statements of objectives is that they do not say what objective the *student* was supposed to achieve or what the student was supposed to learn. "Covering" a poem can mean anything from memorizing it to studying the internal rhyme scheme to comparing it to the Book of Job. Thinking critically can mean discussing an upcoming election, constructing a theory to explain some planetary deviation in our galaxy, or analyzing the faulty logic in a newspaper editorial. A well-defined objective should describe the kind of behavior which the student is supposed to acquire.

Objectives stated in behavioral terms must be seen in a behavioral continuum, that is, as behaviors which will lead to later, more complex behavioral patterns. Some kinds of behavior cannot be made exclusively an end in themselves—for example, learning how to compute on a slide rule. This must be seen as at one time an objective to be accomplished in three or four classes but at another time as a means to a larger end, such as the ability to solve problems in theoretical physics. In other words, a semester-long course has certain major objectives which will guide the selection and organization of learning experiences within the course. Any particular unit of that course will have its objectives, which in the larger perspective are means to the more general ends of the course, and any particular class will also have its particular objectives, which, again, become means to the larger ends. It is evident, therefore, that one can continue to specify objectives in behavioral terms until the behavior specified as an objective is so insignificant as to be ridiculous. Tyler himself argues for a moderate approach, stating that objectives should be stated at the level of generality of behavior that a teacher is seeking to help the student acquire—e.g., "to read a French newspaper intelligently," rather than "to identify a verb expressed in the subjunctive mood."

Objectives specified in behavioral terms allow for the assessment of the actual success of the teaching unit. That is, if the purpose of the unit is to help student X acquire the ability to translate fluently and at sight a passage of French literature of a given vocabulary range, then the teacher can

[3]John Goodlad, *School, Curriculum, and the Individual,* Blaisdell Publishing Co., Waltham, Mass., 1966; *School Curriculum Reform in the United States,* The Fund for the Advancement of Education, New York, 1964.

quickly find out whether student X can in fact perform the behavior stated in the goal of the unit. If student X cannot do so, the goal has not been achieved, and thus the teacher and student must continue the unit, perhaps with a new approach, until the goal is adequately achieved. By stating objectives in behavioral terms, therefore, teachers can easily evaluate the effectiveness of their course and of particular classes. The acquired behavior—for example, a formerly prejudiced student's ability to argue the case for the black laborer—indicates that the goal has been reached, that the learning experiences selected for achieving the goal were effective.

The clear statement of goals in behavioral terms also helps the teacher to select those learning experiences which will lead the student to the performance of the desired behavior. For example, the goal of a certain social studies unit might be stated, "That the student be able to perceive conventional terminology in diplomatic communiqués and discriminate between these linguistic and stylistic conventions and the actual political content of the message." Such an objective already implies the general type of material which the teacher and student will deal with as well as the kinds of class exercises they will employ. If the class is fortunate enough to be able to invite a person from the diplomatic corps to speak with them about his experiences, all the better. At least the teacher knows that he must select current as well as historical examples of critical diplomatic communiqués for analysis. How and in what order and with what precise emphasis he will introduce the material to the class will vary from teacher to teacher. But by and large, the clearly stated objective has already specified what the class will be doing for the next week or so. Notice, also, how relatively easy it will be to evaluate the success of the teaching unit. The class may disagree over the precise interpretation of a specific communiqué, but the teacher will be able to judge whether they are perceiving the conventional diplomatic terminology and whether they are going beyond it to the political issues.

We can begin to see, therefore, that objectives clearly stated, and specified as far as possible in behavioral terms, are critical to teaching and learning. Objectives impose a rationality or logic on the development of curricula and on instructional units. First we select the objectives, then we plan the learning experiences, then we organize the learning experiences into integrated and sequential units to provide for maximum cumulative effect, and then we evaluate the results to judge the effectiveness of the teaching and organization of the course.

Taba has refined this basic four-step framework for developing a curriculum into seven steps: (1) diagnosis of needs; (2) formulation of objectives; (3) selection of content; (4) organization of content; (5) selection of learning experiences; (6) organization of learning experiences; and (7) evaluation.[4] Actually, Tyler's work would not exclude the three steps added

[4]Hilda Taba, *op. cit.*, pp. 9–14.

by Taba, but her analysis makes them more explicit. Notice that *before* objectives are formulated, "needs" are examined. These needs include the needs of society, the needs of the individual student, and the demands of the disciplines of knowledge. Sometimes this first step is the most important since it affects all the other steps quite radically.

Goodlad's Model

Goodlad has further refined the Tyler model and offers perhaps the most sophisticated theoretical approach to defining objectives.[5] Basically this framework is concerned more with the decision-making process and the source for information regarding the decisions to be made than with the *content* of these decisions. (Figure 12-1.)

Goodlad distinguishes between three levels of decision making, moving from broad issues of purposes to specific decisions by teachers in the classroom on Thursday morning at 10:38 A.M. These three levels are: (1) the societal level, in which lay boards of education at the local, state, and federal levels decide on general purposes of schooling; (2) the institutional level, in which these purposes are made more specific by the professional technical staff of the school, involving teachers, curriculum specialists, and administrators; and (3) the instructional level, in which teachers decide on the specific behavioral objectives and specify what learning opportunities or organizing centers shall be used to achieve these specific objectives.

The data sources for information necessary to make these decisions are basically three: society and its awareness of its needs and aspirations; learners and learning theorists and developmental psychologists; subject matter specialists.[6] But before these sources are consulted, Goodlad proposes that this decision-making framework requires a consideration of basic values which underlie and enter into assumptions about which information from these sources will be selected.[7] (Figure 12-2.)

In his model, Goodlad presents us with a design of a rational system. Unfortunately, the model does not indicate the *political* contexts of educational decisions, in which more than pure reason determines the outcome. While Goodlad admits that this decision-making process is a political process as well as a rational process, he is content simply to state that truism as though what, in the political process, is chosen and put into practice is what society and the individual need and want, or at least as though nothing could be done about it anyway. Broudy adopts a far more critical and responsible stance when he scores the timidity of the professional educator in the face of politically mandated curriculum decisions.[8] That is, considera-

---

[5]John I. Goodlad et al., *Curriculum: Decisions and Data Sources,* Blaisdell Publishing Company, Waltham, Mass. (in press at this writing).
[6]*Ibid.*
[7]*Ibid.*
[8]Harry S. Broudy, *Paradox and Promise: Essays on American Life and Education,* Prentice-Hall, Englewood Cliffs, N.J., 1961, p. 169.

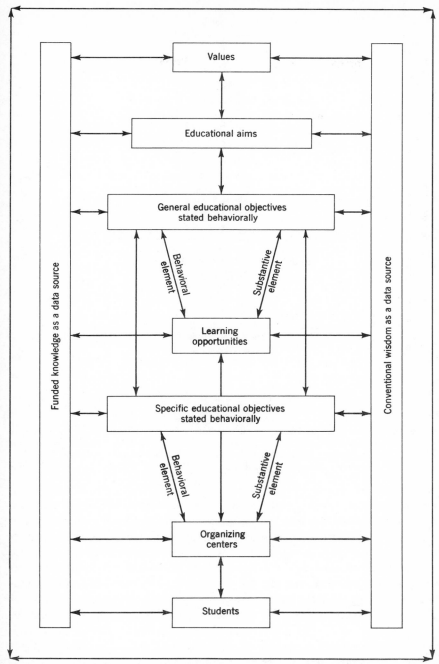

Figure 12-1. Goodlad's model of substantive decisions and derivations in a conceptual system for curriculums. From John I. Goodlad et al., *Curriculum: Decisions and Data Sources,* Blaisdell Publishing Co., Waltham, Mass. (in press at this writing).

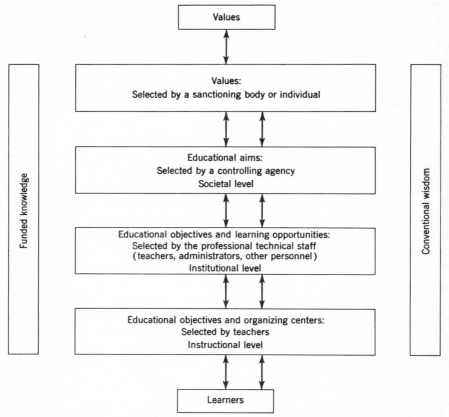

Figure 12-2. Curricular decisions, levels of authority and responsibility, derivations, evaluations, data sources, and transactions in a conceptual system for curriculum. From John I. Goodlad et al., *Curriculum: Decisions and Data Sources,* Blaisdell Publishing Co., Waltham, Mass. (In press at this writing).

tions of national defense, national pride, and international politics resulting from the shock of Sputnik led to a flurry of educational reforms. These reforms placed priority on learning certain subjects, such as science, mathematics, and foreign languages. There was to be no debate and no nonsense from professional educators, and by and large there was none. Whether this sense of emergency, generated by an escalation of competition from communist technology, will lead to continuation of these mandated curricula or whether the earlier concern for a broader curriculum, which would encourage the growth of a politically free and knowledgeable as well as technologically competent citizenry, will return remains to be seen. The point is that it matters considerably *who* makes the decisions.

Goodlad's model, with its insistence on rationality, on ends-means thinking, works in a world where rationality prevails but does not deal with the logic of political power—nor, indeed, with the logic inherent in technology itself. That is, a conceptual model must somehow stand *outside* of the systems it conceptualizes to describe how the various elements interact. Goodlad's model lies within the larger political and technological system. The dynamics of these larger systems can critically affect the elements described in his model and render them ineffectual, even though on the surface there is a semblance of rational decision making going on.

FURTHER QUESTIONS ABOUT OBJECTIVES

Any supervisor, therefore, must be familiar with the various strategies for identifying and describing objectives, for planning and organizing learning experiences, and for evaluating outcomes. The works of Goodlad, Taba, and Tyler previously mentioned provide a sound introduction to these strategies, as do the writings of Herrick,[9] Bellack,[10] Sand and Associates at the Center for the Study of Instruction, National Education Association,[11] Miel,[12] Phenix,[13] and King and Brownell.[14] The purpose of this chapter is not to summarize the works of these authors but to view their whole approach in its broad perspective.

Supervisors need to be clear when they are talking about curricular objectives. Discourse about objectives takes place on several levels of conceptualization. On one level the objectives may be very general, such as "The student should discover himself or realize his potential," or "The student should be able to think critically." These objectives are not invalid if taken on the level of general life objectives, to the achievement of which the school is supposed to contribute. On another level, objectives may have a social-political specificity: "The student should espouse the democratic form of government and express loyalty to his country." On still another level, now with more academic ring, an objective might be stated, "The student should be able to solve problems dealing with specific gravity." Some objectives, therefore, are long-range, some express social values, and some deal with measurable kinds of behavior.

The battle cry of "Down with nonbehavioral objectives!", which some curriculum theorists employ, is only partially helpful. It is helpful when it

[9] James B. Macdonald et al. (eds.), *Strategies of Curriculum Development*, Charles E. Merrill Books, Columbus, Ohio, 1965.
[10] Arno A. Bellack, "What Knowledge Is of Most Worth?", *The High School Journal*, vol. 48, February, 1965, pp. 318–332.
[11] See especially *Planning and Organizing for Teaching* (1963), written by John Goodlad, *The Scholars Look at the Schools: A Report of the Disciplines Seminar* (1962), and *Rational Planning in Curriculum and Instruction* (1967).
[12] Alice Miel, "Knowledge and the Curriculum," 1963 Yearbook, Association for Supervision and Curriculum Development, Washington, D.C., 1963, pp. 71–104.
[13] Philip H. Phenix, *Realms of Meaning*, McGraw-Hill, New York, 1964.
[14] Arthur R. King, Jr., and John A. Brownell, *The Curriculum and the Disciplines of Knowledge*, Wiley, New York, 1966.

stimulates teachers to specify objectives in behavioral terms when such specification is called for—usually in the design of short-term instructional units. There is little doubt that stating objectives in behavioral terms can improve inferior teaching, but by the same token it can stifle superior teaching. Certainly in the learning skills such specification provides an appropriate criterion for evaluating the degree of mastery of the skill. In the appreciation of value issues, however, or in ethical problems, such specification might imply a certainty about what is right or correct or better when there is little foundation for such certainty. The issue of patriotism, for example, raises many questions, the response to which will take any number of reasonable behavioral directions—from burning one's draft card to enlisting in the Marines.

This last consideration opens up this discussion of objectives to other questions. The four-step process of defining objectives, planning learning experiences, organizing learning experiences, and evaluating outcomes provides a neat and reasonable way of dealing with curriculum issues. It is a simple ends-means arrangement. We define the ends to be achieved, then plan the means to attain this end, and then evaluate whether the end has in fact been achieved.

Two very serious objections can be raised, however, to this arrangement. (1) Does the specification of behavioral objectives and the learning experiences leading to their acquisition imply that every student *can* and *must* behave in exactly the *same* way in order to validate the objectives? And further, does it imply that the *only* way to achieve the objectives is by progressing through such and such a series of preordained learning experiences? If the answer to both questions is affirmative, without any qualifications, then we have simply substituted one kind of dogmatism for another. Any talk about respecting individual differences becomes ridiculous, for even if students are allowed to progress at their own individual rate of learning, they must move toward the same fixed goal. (2) Do educators have the absolute, unchallengeable *right,* based on an assumption of competence, to require that their students will achieve certain objectives rather than other objectives? This latter criticism refers more to the broader objectives of a specific course or unit and not necessarily to the particular objectives of a single class period. If a student approached a French teacher with the request that the teacher help him to learn French, then the teacher, assuming that he was qualified to teach French, would have a clear mandate. But students simply come to school and *are told* what is good or not good for them to study, without being consulted. Educators think that they are relieved of any charges against them by pointing to the elective system. But even in these elective courses the student is seldom encouraged to set his own goals; they are usually set for him by the teacher or the textbook. James Macdonald criticizes this predetermination of curricular objectives:

It is idle to talk about humans who are self-directed, curious, creative, and self-fulfilling when they have been taught by the nature of curriculum tasks and conditions that they either should not be or are not able to be any of these things.[15]

The difficulty with unquestioningly adopting the ends-means rationale is that it can lead to many abuses. As was pointed out in the previous chapter in the discussion of technological rationality, this way of thinking often operates to the detriment of more valuable learning experiences. Curricular objectives derive, as we have seen, from three general sources: from social conditions and the needs of society; from the academic heritage of knowledge preserved and fostered in the disciplines of knowledge; and from the needs and potentialities of the individual. Within the ends-means rationale, it becomes altogether too easy, once either one of the first two sources of curricular objectives is chosen as most important, to subject the individual student to the demands of society or the demands of the disciplines. In this way, the school can very easily lose sight of its required commitment to the student and suppose its purpose is to program him according to the purported interests of society or the furtherance of the academic professions. In other words, educators may decide, when stating objectives, that the learning of a specific field of knowledge requires students to subject themselves to all the methodological rigor of that discipline, or that society's needs dictate the learning of specific skills by its future citizens.

Evaluation

An overemphasis on ends-means thinking in the setting of objectives leads to one other serious mistake in schooling, a mistake which supervisors must continually guard against. If curricular and instructional objectives are defined quite specifically in behavioral terms, then often there will be no allowance made for and no evaluation of spontaneous and concomitant learnings other than the learning specified by the objective. If, for example, a mathematics teacher has set up an instructional unit to get across the concept of inverse ratio and has defined his objective as the student's actual solving of a variety of problems dealing with inverse ratio—*but exclusively in mathematical terms*—he might miss the opportunity to encourage a student who suddenly perceives the general phenomenon of inverse ratio in human affairs, such as the inverse ratio between dictatorial powers and freedom of the press. Other operational concepts, such as *relativity, myth, system,* and *design,* have enormous range and can be used to interpret not only the particular phenomenon being treated in class, but a host of other analogous

[15]James B. Macdonald, "The High School in Human Terms: Curriculum Design," in Norman K. Hamilton and J. Galen Saylor (eds.), *Humanizing the Secondary Schools,* Association for Supervision and Curriculum Development, National Education Association, Washington, D.C., 1969, p. 41.

phenomena.[16] If the objectives are absolutized, however, such relational learning will be excluded, if not discouraged. And even if the learning which might spontaneously erupt in a class has *nothing* to do with the object of that particular lesson, the teacher should be free to pursue it if he perceives it as worthwhile.

FOCUS ON SOCIETAL NEEDS

In order to clarify how specific emphasis on either the needs of society or the requirements of the disciplines of knowledge can permeate the subsequent development of curriculum, we shall examine two schools of thought in curriculum theory. We will focus on the work of the most articulate spokesmen for these two schools—Broudy, Smith, and Burnett's *Democracy and Excellence in American Secondary Education*[17] and Phenix's *The Realms of Meaning*.[18] Although the former work deals primarily with secondary education, the rationale could be used to justify curricular-instructional programs at other levels. Phenix's work applies to both elementary and secondary levels of education.

Broudy, Smith, and Burnett set out to create a curriculum view which is responsive both to the school's obligation to a democratic mass society and to excellence of individual life in that society.[19] As their thesis develops, however, it is evident that the school's response to the goal of providing for "excellence of individual life" refers primarily to helping the individual come to terms with the realities of life in a mass democracy. Granting a nod here and there to the necessity of teaching students ways of effective political organization to achieve some control over or at least some check on the power groups in a mass society, the general thrust of their thesis is basically an acceptance of the fact that powerful groups in the larger society will dictate more and more what talents are necessary for work and citizenship in the technological world and an acceptance of the fact that the best the school can do is to look into the future, identify those general intellectual abilities which life in society will demand, and then equip the student through a program in general studies with the skills and cognitive maps requisite for life in that society. This seems like life adjustment education but now on a higher cognitive level. Broudy, Smith, and Burnett reveal this orientation when they identify one of the most important curriculum ques-

---

[16]See Arthur W. Foshay, "Shaping Curriculum: The Decade Ahead," in Glenys Unruh and Robert Leeper (eds.), *Influences in Curriculum Change*, Association for Supervision and Curriculum Development, National Education Association, Washington, D.C., 1968, pp. 5–6.
[17]Harry S. Broudy et al., *Democracy and Excellence in American Secondary Education*, Rand McNally, Chicago, 1964.
[18]Philip H. Phenix, *The Realms of Meaning*, McGraw-Hill, New York, 1964.
[19]*Ibid.*, p. 8.

tions. In the light of all the challenges to the nation—communist, economic, and military competition, an exploding technology, economic tensions, problems in the cities, revolts against the military establishment, and hunger among the poor—can society allow its youth to choose their occupations?[20] Many social planners say that American society cannot afford to waste its youth talent if the United States is to continue economic and political leadership among nations. Government, business, industry, and education tend increasingly to influence the individual to accept occupations which serve the national interest.[21] Certainly the post-Sputnik emphasis on science and engineering provides dramatic evidence of that. Thus the question is rephrased: "How far can we legitimately narrow the channels through which we send youth in order to develop vocational competencies which have an important and lasting place in the social order?"[22] The authors' response: "It clearly seems that there is a need for intensive grounding in general studies as a foundation for vocational preparation today, with specialization waiting for post-secondary training."[23] They add: "This seems to be the case if we wish to provide a maximum of choice to the student in his life. . . ."[24]

The argument we raise with members of the school which focuses on societal needs is twofold. First, they seem to accept as legitimate that the government and industry and education selectively influence youth, by means of their combined financial power and advertising control, to choose those educational programs leading to those careers which the technological society needs. The reversal of means-ends logic seems quite evident here. Secondly, even though technologically mandated specialization is postponed for four years by a secondary program of general studies, what have educators gained except time—time to further equip adolescents with more general cognitive maps which will help them to understand the complexities of life in an administered, technological, mass society? Granted that Broudy et al. make a far more generous plea for esthetic education in their general studies program than government and business would care to, nevertheless their concern to improve cognitive skills and conceptual acuity for adjustment to technological life in mass democracy seems too accepting of the dictates of the techno-structure. (Figure 12-3.)

There are times in their work when Broudy, Smith, and Burnett come close to providing a vision of the educated man not far from the one urged in this study:

The case for *common, general* education does not rest entirely, or perhaps

[20]*Ibid.*, p. 35.
[21]*Loc. cit.*
[22]*Loc. cit.*
[23]*Ibid.*, p. 36.
[24]*Loc. cit.*

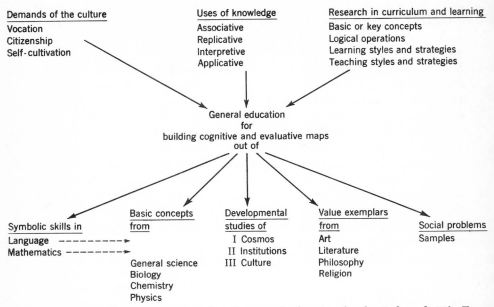

Figure 12-3. Design for common curriculum in general education (grades 7 through 12). From Harry S. Broudy et al., *Democracy and Excellence in American Secondary Education,* Rand McNally, Chicago, 1964, p. 160.

even primarily, on vocational considerations. If the analysis of the new, emerging mass society is correct, the needs of citizenship and self-development for general studies are even more urgent than the vocational needs. For, if the analysis is right, to exploit the possibilities of technological civilization for a society that can in any genuine sense be called democratic will call upon a very large proportion of our people, not an elite handful, to think and feel as educated men and women think and feel. The enlargement of vision this entails makes mandatory a common curriculum emphasizing the general studies.[25]

Such a statement could be interpreted to mean that this "enlargement of vision" refers to an ability to stand outside the pressures and confusing flow of American society and to critically evaluate from a broader *human perspective* what are the infringements on basic freedoms which technology and an administered society demand, not only of Americans, but of citizens of other countries affected by our foreign holdings and trade agreements—in short, an enlargement of vision beyond "national interest" and required social roles.

Broudy, Smith, and Burnett, however, seem inclined to view schooling far more pragmatically. They try to assess what will be the demands placed

[25]*Ibid.,* p. 45.

on students in their adult life as citizens, persons, and workers. They maintain that in modern society, every man's career will require specialization, while his role as citizen and as a person demands that he be a generalist.[26] Maintaining that specialization be postponed during the high school years, they seek cues for building a curriculum "not in the particular jobs that youth are likely to hold, nor in the diverse roles they will play in life, but rather in the ways that schooling or school learnings are used in modern life."[27]   Again, they seem to imply that a curriculum is to serve primarily an adaptive function, not to shortsighted vocational goals, but to long-range, general uses of knowledge in mass society. Such a position may be politically realistic, but it may not be entirely fair to the clients the school serves and ultimately to society itself. For one would expect educators themselves to have a vision of man's possibilities that goes beyond mass society's dictates. To be sure, Broudy and his associates do go beyond the present short-term specialization and fragmentation of current school offerings in strongly urging common general education for all at the secondary school level. But they do not go far enough.[28]

EMPHASIS ON THE DISCIPLINES

Philip Phenix's *The Realms of Meaning* represents another major attempt to provide a comprehensive rationale for a curriculum of general studies. His curriculum is intended for the period encompassing both elementary and secondary schooling. As the title indicates, its focus is primarily on the disciplines of knowledge. In this respect he differs from Broudy, Smith, and Burnett, although he and they agree on many points. Phenix is not unaware, however, of the needs of the individual and of society.

Because a person is essentially an organized totality and not just a collection of separate parts, the curriculum ought to have a corresponding organic quality.

[26]*Ibid.*, p. 61.
[27]*Ibid.*, p. 45.
[28]As with our subsequent discussion on Phenix, it is important to state here that the work of these men represents one of the few major attempts to offer a defensible rationale for a curriculum. They offer perhaps the most sophisticated approach to learning one can find in the literature. As they examine the logical and psychological demands on the secondary school curriculum, they insightfully distinguish between the uses of knowledge (associative, replicative, applicative, and interpretive) as they apply to facts, concepts, principles, and norms. They present a telling argument against the current misconception of the applicative use of scientific knowledge, a misconception which seems to underlie some current science curricula. Their distinction between categories of instruction offers an approach to various kinds of learning which is far more consistent with the material being learned. Their approach to molar problems provides for the kind of multidimensional learning advocated in our model. In short, our debt to their work will be obvious in our model of a humanistic curriculum even though we differ with them on some fundamental issues.

Since it is one and the same person who undergoes each of the successive experiences in his course of study, the plan of study can best contribute to the person's growth if it is governed by the goal of wholeness for the human being.[29]

Society, as well as individual persons, depends upon principles of community; corporate life, like the life of each individual, requires some overall plan. A curriculum planned as a comprehensive design for learning contributes a basis for the growth of community, while an atomized program of studies engenders disintegration in the life of society.[30]

The unique role of personal knowledge in all realms of meaning is of great importance both to the teacher and to the student. Every linguistic attainment, every empirical insight, every integrative perspective belongs to a developing person and is colored by the quality of his relations to himself and others.[31]

Since the object of general education is to lead to the fulfillment of human life through the enlargement and deepening of meaning, the modern curriculum should be designed with particular attention to these sources of meaninglessness in contemporary life. That is to say, the curriculum should be planned so as to counteract destructive skepticism, depersonalization and fragmentation, overabundance, and transience.[32]

The orientation of his philosophy of curriculum, however, is primarily toward the disciplines as *the* source of curriculum material. "If learning time is to be economized, *all* material should come from the disciplines, and *none* from other sources."[33]

Phenix's argument runs as follows.[34] Human beings are essentially creatures who have the power to experience meanings. A program of general education organizes and engenders essential meanings which it finds in six distinctive modes of human understanding. Phenix designates these six patterns or realms of meaning as *symbolics, empirics, esthetics, synnoetics, ethics,* and *synoptics.* He proposes that students be exposed to these realms of meaning and develop those skills of inquiry and judgment operative in each realm. Thus, these domains of understanding constitute sources from which curricular materials are to be drawn. He complements this emphasis somewhat by discussing principles for sequential ordering of experiences in each realm for different developmental stages of the student's growth.

Our proposal for a human curriculum differs from Phenix's on this point: While the realms of meaning or the disciplines may be a *source* for potential content in a curriculum, the individual person and his appropriation of meaning should be, nevertheless, the primary *referent* in developing a curriculum. The primary purpose of general education is not training and

---

[29]Phenix, *The Realms of Meaning,* p. 4.
[30]*Loc. cit.*
[31]*Ibid.,* p. 297.
[32]*Ibid.,* p. 5.
[33]*Ibid.,* p. 314.
[34]*Ibid.,* pp. 5–14.

expertise in the disciplines or realms of meaning for their own sake, just as it is not the preparing of students for adult vocational and civic roles. The purpose of general education is to lead the human person to a *discovery and appreciation*, for its own sake, of himself and others and the world about him. In other words, it is concerned with the growth of a human being who will act like a human being in his role as citizen and in his chosen occupation, one who will continually seek for the human significance of what he learns in the realms of knowledge. The primary questions raised when one focuses on the individual person as a source of curricular objectives are not questions such as, What knowledge is necessary for me to get by in a technological society? but such questions as, What does it mean to be a human being? What does it mean to know? How are human beings to live together in community? What does freedom mean, and how does a man exercise freedom in a human way? What is the meaning of evolution, of energy, of gravity, of harmony, of forgiveness, of loyalty, of time, of death, of war and peace, *for me*? Obviously, the domains of knowledge will be *sources* for finding partial answers to these questions. But the ultimate *referent* both in asking the questions and in interpreting the answers is the human person.

This leads us to our second major departure from Phenix's work. It concerns what he calls synnoetic meanings. He describes this realm of meaning in the following way.

> The fourth realm, synnoetics, embraces what Michael Polanyi calls "personal knowledge" and Martin Buber the "I-Thou" relationship. The novel term "synnoetics," which was devised because no existing concept appeared adequate to the type of understanding intended, derives from the Greek *synnoesis*, meaning "meditative thought," and this in turn is compounded of *syn*, meaning "with" or "together" and *noesis*, meaning "cognition." Thus synnoetics signifies "relational insight" or "direct awareness." It is analogous in the sphere of knowing to sympathy in the sphere of feeling. This personal or relational knowledge is concrete, direct, and existential. It may apply to other persons, to oneself, or even to things.[35]

As he analyzes this realm of meaning, Phenix focuses primarily on interpersonal relations and the direct subjective awareness of the totality of the other person. He also discusses self-awareness from a social-psychological and a psychoanalytic viewpoint. He dips into existential literature for further elaboration of the subjective experiences of anxiety, loneliness, absurdity, and freedom, and then moves on to poetry, fiction, and drama as carriers of personal meanings.

In general, he differentiates meanings in the synnoetic realm from meanings in the other realms: "Knowledge in symbolics, empirics, and esthetics is *objective,* or better, it depends on a *subject-object* relationship. Synnoetic meanings relate *subjects to subjects.*"[36] "Knowledge in symbolics, empirics, and esthetics requires *detachment,* while synnoetic meaning requires *engagement.*"[37] "Language, science, and art are concerned with *essences,* while personal knowledge is *existential.*"[38]

It would not be doing extraordinary violence to Phenix's delineation of realms of meaning to suggest that one could also consider these realms as realms of rationality. Thus, one might discuss the rationality of symbolic systems, of empirical disciplines, of esthetic disciplines, of synnoetic knowledge, of ethical systems, and of synoptic disciplines. We would argue that what would then be called synnoetic rationality is not a distinct type of rationality, but in fact lies at the heart and center of learning in all the realms of meaning. That is, what the person appropriates to himself, what has importance and value for him, is what he learns by appropriating its meaning sympathetically. As such, this learning set or stance toward reality which is called sympathetic rationality is operative in *all* realms of meaning when significant learning takes place—which is to say, whenever learning takes place. Phenix's distinctions between objective and intersubjective knowledge, between detachment and engagement, between essential and existential, are only superficially apparent. Superficial learning takes place with detachment, perhaps, but real learning requires a person to enter into, to dwell in, the meaning and significance of what he is learning. Thus, learning the function and structure of language, understanding the interrelationships of force, energy, and mass, and perceiving harmonic variations of a piece of music come about through sympathetic rationality. Perhaps the kind of learning intended by the use of this term is revealed by the difference between learning the definition of loyalty and learning the *meaning* of loyalty, between learning the definition of harmony and perceiving and feeling harmony, between learning the concept of evolution and letting its significance illuminate one's sense of time and resonate throughout one's feelings about oneself.

FOCUS ON THE INDIVIDUAL

What is good for assisting a particular student to become a healthy and mature human being ought, we repeat, to be the *primary* concern of the school and the curriculum. Knowledge of his world will come through his exposure to the disciplines of knowledge, and commitment to his society and its problems will be encouraged by analysis of his responsibilities as a citizen. But the human and personal growth of the student should remain pri-

---

[36]*Ibid.,* p. 194.
[37]*Ibid.,* pp. 193–194.
[38]*Ibid.,* p. 195.

mary in any general statement of objectives, and this concern must underlie any particular behavioral objective a teacher may choose for a specific class period or teaching unit. The reversal of this concern, that is, enshrining academic proficiency in physics or history *for its own sake* as the primary objective of a curricular and instructional program *can* in this ends-means rationality lead to the subjection of the individual student—regardless of his needs and wishes—to this goal. The same reversal can be found in those curriculum objectives which fasten on the needs of society either for trained specialists to fill positions critical to the "national interest," or on the needs of society to train citizens in a simplistic, uniform patriotism. For democracy is not an absolute—an end in itself—but rather a form of government freely chosen as a *means* to allow citizens to live in a cooperative venture. And the disciplines of knowledge are also means by which man comes to make sense of and comes to grips with his world. To make these ends in themselves in a curricular program can be self-defeating and has in fact led to some rather sorry examples of miseducation in our schools.

IMPLICATIONS FOR SUPERVISORS

1. *Supervisory personnel need to clarify their own assumptions about critical educational objectives.* Does the supervisor think about objectives of a curricular-instructional program from the perspective of the integrity of the discipline, or from the needs of the individual, or from the needs of society? In other words, when working with subordinates on objectives, does the supervisor stress one over the other, or does he maintain a balance between these three perspectives? How does he justify choosing one over the other? How does this emphasis influence his conception of the proper selection and organization of learning experiences? Can the supervisor and teacher explicate specific behavioral objectives as well as more general objectives?

2. *Supervisory personnel need to understand their subordinates' assumptions about objectives and to assist them in the clarification of these objectives.* The supervisor must discover quite early in his supervisory relationship what are the assumptions about objectives of his subordinates and clarify what basic differences they might have. If there are differences, can they afford a healthy opportunity for sharing ideas? Must the supervisor impose his assumptions on the subordinate? Do subordinates know how to specify goals in behavioral terms? Do they know when to?

3. *Supervisory personnel need to clarify the assumptions about objectives which students have.* Perhaps this clarification of what the students' objectives really are—and what they should be—might be one of the most helpful services the supervisor can render the students. Are the stu-

dents' objectives in conflict with the school's objectives? If so, how might they be reconciled, or at least understood? What sources of motivation that the teacher might utilize do the students' objectives reveal? Can the students' objectives be used as a source for developing curricular-instructional objectives?

4. *The supervisor needs to clarify the relationship between these objectives and the techniques of evaluating the achievement of these objectives.* Are objectives so stated that their achievement can be evaluated by some performance criteria? Are evaluational techniques of only one kind— tests—or are they varied? Are objectives determined by standardized tests? Are there some objectives the achievement of which cannot be realistically assessed? Ought they to remain as valid objectives?

SELECTED REFERENCES

Broudy, Harry S., B. Othanel Smith, and Joe R. Burnett: *Democracy and Excellence in American Secondary Education,* Rand McNally, Chicago, 1964.

Goodlad, John I.: *Planning and Organizing for Teaching,* Project on Instruction, National Education Association, Washington, D.C., 1963.

King, Arthur R., Jr., and John A. Brownell: *The Curriculum and the Disciplines of Knowledge,* Wiley, New York, 1966.

Phenix, Philip H.: *The Realms of Meaning,* McGraw-Hill, New York, 1964.

Tyler, Ralph W.: *Basic Principles of Curriculum and Instruction,* University of Chicago Press, Chicago, 1950.

Unruh, Glenys G., and Robert R. Leeper (eds.): *Influences in Curriculum Change,* Association for Supervision and Curriculum Development, National Education Association, Washington, D.C., 1968.

Chapter Thirteen
AN ENVIRONMENTAL DESIGN FOR THE HUMAN CURRICULUM

Our thesis throughout this book has been simple. The productivity of the organization increases as it encourages the human growth of its participants. Moreover, the job satisfaction of the participants increases as they channel their energy into the fulfillment of organizational or professional goals. When applied to supervisory practices in the school, this thesis means that essential to the supervisory role is a commitment to the human growth of teachers and students through satisfying and fulfilling experiences in the educational process. This implies that supervisory personnel not only employ those supervisory styles most conducive to human development, but also bring to their work an idea of a human curriculum—that is, a general model of a school program which offers those educational experiences which will lead students to human maturity.

As should be obvious, the proponents of the human organization are not in the health and recreation business. Whether talking about banking, advertising, or educational organizations, they envision effort and hard work leading to significant results, but in a human way, not in a machinelike or hyperrationalized system. An assumed premise throughout this book is that the one-dimensional view of schools based on the means-end model or the systems model is inadequate (though useful). That view is based on technological rationality: the objectification of the world and of persons through an abstractive process which categorizes and interprets schooling in a cause-and-effect, statistically quantified series of relationships. This results in an instrumental view of man himself which is somewhat spuriously justified by some advocates of the purely functional man, the goal-oriented, need-directed organism proposed by behavioristic psychology.[1]

Rather than cling to that arthritic view which denies any validity to technological rationality, we wish to assert not only its limitations when it is infelicitously proposed as the only form of rationality, but also its considerable power when employed in the service of human growth. Jails can be models of technological efficiency and yet waste enormous resources of human potential.

[1]Dwayne Huebner, "New Modes of Man's Relationship to Man," in Alexander Frazier (ed.), *New Insights and the Curriculum,* Association for Supervision and Curriculum Development, National Education Association, Washington, D.C., 1963, p. 145.

Curriculum theorists, as well as sociologists, psychologists, and philosophers, present telling criticisms of the ineffectiveness of present school programs, despite the attempts at curricular innovations. Goodlad, one of the foremost spokesmen for curricular changes, admits that there is a notoriously low correlation between academic success and personal stability, leadership, family happiness, and honest workmanship.[2] Despite conflicting reviews of his findings, James Coleman's massive study of educational achievement raises serious doubts about the effectiveness of even the most prestigious school programs. His study suggests that the individual's self-concept, and consequently his perception of his control over his future, is the single most important factor in achievement.[3] His earlier study of adolescent subculture underlines the tenacious attempts of adolescents to frustrate the designs of the system of schooling precisely because it communicates so little respect for them as persons, and because it fails to provide them with genuine opportunities for personal commitment. The works of Friedenberg,[4] Kozol,[5] and Holt[6]—even if one argues that they overstate their case—point to serious lack of human concern on the part of teachers and administrators.

This mounting disquiet over the inability of the curricular changes to make a bigger difference is not so much a proof of any *intrinsic* weakness of the new curricular approaches but represents, rather, a growing awareness that other human factors—besides the purely intellectual and academic—play as great a part, if not greater, in effecting mature and genuine human growth. The evidence from developmental psychology, as well as the more normative statements of anthropologists and philosophers, points to those *personal* human variables which lead to genuine human growth.

In this chapter we shall attempt to summarize some of the recent descriptions of these human variables and to construct a theoretical model of the human context of learning. As we shall see, such a model facilitates a critical analysis of the shortcomings of current curricular-instructional programs and provides a framework for developing curricular-instructional units which are more adapted to a variety of learning experiences. As the supervisor works with teachers or students, such a theoretical framework will provide a valuable source for discussing objectives and specific units of the instructional program.

[2] John I. Goodlad, "The Education Program to 1980 and Beyond," in Edgar Morphet and Charles Ryan (eds.), *Implications for Education of Prospective Changes in Society, Designing Education for the Future No. 2,* Citation Press, New York, 1967, p. 49.
[3] James Coleman, *Equality of Educational Opportunity,* U.S. Dept. of Health, Education, and Welfare, Washington, D.C., 1966; and James Coleman, *The Adolescent Society,* Free Press, Glencoe, Ill., 1961.
[4] Edgar Friedenberg, *The Dignity of Youth and Other Atavisms,* Beacon Press, Boston, 1965; *The Vanishing Adolescent,* Dell, New York, 1959.
[5] Jonathan Kozol, *Death at an Early Age,* Houghton Mifflin, Boston, 1967.
[6] John C. Holt, *How Children Fail,* Pitman, New York, 1964.

B COGNITION AND D COGNITION

Abraham Maslow outlines some of these other human factors.[7] In Maslow's description of human growth, an individual moves from the satisfaction of basic biological and security needs to the satisfaction of higher human needs such as self-esteem, autonomy, and self-actualization. As an individual approaches personal maturity, he becomes more capable of transcending those lower needs of self-gratification, security, and social acceptance. Instead of being *completely* absorbed in the process of becoming, of "becoming someone," of "making something out of life," of "striving for success," he is able to enjoy *being*, being who he is and where he is, and at the same time to enjoy and appreciate others for what they are and to appreciate the world and objects in it for their own sake (not in order to use persons and objects to solve problems or satisfy lower needs). We might recall here our remarks in Chapter 11 about appreciating and living in the present. A completely future-oriented, instrumental approach to learning deprives the present of its intrinsic value, in much the same way as the hero of Henry James's novel, *The Beast in the Jungle,* was blinded to the potentialities of the present by his fear and anticipation of the beast.

According to this distinction, then, between *being* and *becoming,* Maslow differentiates cognitions as B cognitions and D cognitions.

D cognition can be defined as the cognitions which are organized from the point of view of basic needs or deficiency needs and their gratification and frustration. That is, D cognition could be called selfish cognition, in which the world is organized into gratifiers and frustrators of our own needs with other characteristics being ignored or slurred. The cognition of the object, in its own right and its own being, without reference to its need-gratifying or need-frustrating qualities, that is, without primary reference to its value for the observer or its effects upon him, can be called B cognition (or self-transcending, or unselfish, or objective cognition). The parallel with maturity is by no means perfect (children can also cognize in a selfless way), but in general, it is mostly true that with increasing selfhood or firmness of personal identity (or acceptance of one's own inner nature) B cognition becomes easier and more frequent. (This is true even though D cognition remains for *all* human beings, including the mature ones, the main tool for living-in-the-world.)[8]

B cognition is less structured, more a grasp of the wholeness and immediacy of the object or person, more contemplative in posture, less instrumental or problem-oriented (with the subsequent splitting up of the object or

[7]Abraham H. Maslow, "Some Basic Propositions of a Growth and Self-actualization Psychology," in Arthur W. Combs (ed.), *Perceiving, Behaving, Becoming,* Association for Supervision and Curriculum Development, National Education Association, Washington, D.C., 1962, pp. 34–39. The reader might want to refer to Chap. 6 at this point and review what was said there about teachers. Most of the description of growth and personal meaning in teachers' lives can now be applied to students.
[8]*Ibid.,* p. 41.

person by abstraction). This is not to identify B cognition solely with a passive state of mind. B cognition can also involve action—not only intense intellectual concentration, but also the active exercise of manual and technical skills. It can also involve the mutual self-revelation and appreciation of friendship.[9] What differentiates B cognition from D cognition, or B activity from D activity, is the end intended. B cognition or B activity seeks no other end outside itself, outside the sheer satisfaction intrinsic to the knowledge or activity, whereas D cognition or D activity is instrumental—is used to solve problems or answer questions or gain a specified objective.

Maslow is quick to draw curricular implications from this distinction.

This development toward the concept of a healthy unconscious, and of a healthy irrationality, sharpens our awareness of the limitations of purely abstract thinking, of verbal thinking and of analytic thinking. If our hope is to describe the world fully, a place is necessary for preverbal, ineffable, metaphorical, primary process, concrete-experience, intuitive and esthetic types of cognition, for there are certain aspects of reality which can be cognized in no other way. Even in science this is true, now that we know (a) that creativity has its roots in the non-rational, (b) that language is and must always be inadequate to describe total reality, (c) that any abstract concept leaves out much of reality, and (d) that what we call "knowledge" (which is usually highly abstract and verbal and sharply defined) often serves to blind us to those portions of reality not covered by the abstraction. That is, it makes us more able to see some things, but less able to see other things. Abstract knowledge has its dangers as well as its uses.

Science and education, being too exclusively abstract, verbal and bookish, do not have enough place for raw, concrete, esthetic experience, especially of the subjective happenings inside onself. For instance, organismic psychologists would certainly agree on the desirability of more creative education in perceiving and creating art, in dancing, in (Greek style) athletics and in phenomenological observation.[10]

He continues:

This same tie between health and integration of rational and irrational forces (conscious and unconscious, primary and secondary process) also permits us to understand why psychologically healthy people are more able to enjoy, to love, to laugh, to have fun, to be humorous, to be silly, to be whimsical and fantastic, to be pleasantly "crazy," and in general to permit and value and enjoy emotional experiences . . . . And it leads us to the strong suspicion that learning ad hoc to be able to do all these things may help the child move toward health.[11]

If Maslow's description of the healthy person appears somewhat lyrical, he readily admits that the human condition also involves conflict, anxiety, frustration, sadness, and guilt. But as the person matures, he is able to dis-

[9]Cf. Huebner, op. cit.
[10]Maslow, op. cit., p. 44.
[11]Ibid.

tinguish between neurotic or petty pseudo problems and the "real, unavoidable, existential problems inherent in the nature of man."[12] Considerations of these aspects of human life, including the unavoidable reality of death, belong in the human curriculum. Jerome Bruner and Ralph Harper, for example, offer some enlightened approaches to the topic of death as it might be included in a curriculum design.[13]

The mature person, then, lives in two worlds: an inner world and an outer world. While the two worlds constantly interact with one another, nevertheless one can point to relatively distinctive experiences and different processes in each. A curriculum that is concerned with only the outer world —with D cognitions and D activities, with extrinsically motivated behavior, and with the world of impersonal, functional, and objective relationships— will produce, other things being equal, immature and stunted young adults.

For our purposes, then, we may employ Maslow's terms to describe one dimension of human growth. We may represent this dimension diagrammatically on a continuum.

| Appreciation and enjoyment | B cognition
B activity
B motivation
B inquiry
B creativity | | D cognition
D activity
D motivation
D inquiry
D creativity | Functional and instrumental |

PERSONAL MEANING AND CULTURALLY DEFINED MEANING

James Macdonald describes two other growth experiences found in the process of human development: the experience of personal meanings and culturally defined meanings.[14] When discussing the development of the self, he comments:

The self as a reflection of ego-processes strives toward meanings. These meanings are of two general varieties; they are perhaps best described by the prescriptions "know thyself" and "know thy world." The self is not "actualized" in a vacuum but in a world. The world is, however, primarily as it is perceived by the self. For the world to become only what one feels it is is to retreat into psychosis; but for the world to be accepted only as it is defined, in terms of rational, cultural knowledge, is certainly a form of neurosis. In neither case is the ego integrated into a functional, open, and reality-oriented structure.

[12]*Ibid.,* p. 45.
[13]Jerome S. Bruner, "Identity and the Modern Novel," *On Knowing, Essays for the Left Hand,* The Belknap Press, Cambridge, Mass., 1962; Ralph Harper, "Significance of Existence and Recognition for Education," in Nelson B. Henry (ed.), *Modern Philosophies and Education,* University of Chicago Press, Chicago, 1955, pp. 215–258.
[14]James Macdonald, "An Image of Man: The Learner Himself," in Ronald C. Doll (ed.), *Individualizing Instruction,* Association for Supervision and Curriculum Development, National Education Association, Washington, D.C., 1964.

It should be apparent to all that the growing self must have personal meanings and cultural meanings for adequate realization. Further, it follows from this that the two meaning systems are not separate compartments within the individual. They are (in a healthy state) functionally integrated into the purposive striving of the person.[15]

Combs also emphasizes the importance of personal meaning, although he agrees with Macdonald on the need to integrate the two kinds of meaning.

Any piece of information will have its effect upon behavior in the degree to which an individual discovers its personal meaning. To put this in more technical terms, we could say that the effect of any bit of information will depend upon its psychological distance from the self. Learning thus becomes the discovery of personal meaning. We might think of all the information a person needs in order to make an effective adjustment to life as existing on a continuum from that which is very close to self to that which is very far away from self. The problem of learning then becomes a problem of moving information from the not-self end of this continuum to the self end.[16]

He goes on to criticize the neglect of personal meaning in school.

In our zeal to be scientific and objective, we have sometimes taught children that personal meanings are things you leave at the schoolhouse door. Sometimes, I fear, in our desire to help people learn, we have said to the child, "Alice, I am not interested in what you think or what you believe. What are the facts?" As a consequence, we may have taught children that personal meanings have no place in the classroom, which is another way of saying that school is concerned only with things that do not matter! If learning, however, is a discovery of personal meaning, then the facts with which we must be concerned are the beliefs, feelings, understandings, convictions, doubts, fears, likes, and dislikes of the pupil—those personal ways of perceiving himself and the world he lives in.[17]

Personal meanings are meanings that are organized and integrated with the self-concept and carry not only cognitive but affective content. These meanings are unique to the person and derived from his life experiences. For a child who has spent every summer on Cape Cod, the meaning of Cape Cod would be illuminated or saturated with personal intonations which a geographer describing the New England Coast might not have. "Football" has a culturally defined meaning, but for a veteran professional quarterback that meaning would be colored and enriched by nuances from

---

[15]*Ibid.*, p. 39.
[16]Arthur W. Combs, "Personality Theory and Its Implications for Curriculum Development," in Alexander Frazier (ed.), *Learning More about Learning*, Association for Supervision and Curriculum Development, National Education Association, Washington, D.C., 1959, p. 10.
[17]*Ibid.*, p. 11.

his own personal experience of the game. The most personal meaning, of course, is the concept which the student has of himself. His relationships with others, especially with his immediate family, have molded over several years the student's self-image or concept. His sense of his own worth, of his capabilities, of his shortcomings and failures, and of what is worthwhile in life is a part of his self-image. All new experiences and learnings tend to be filtered by and through his self-concept. While the educational program, mediated by the teacher, is to introduce students into the broad and various realms of culturally defined meanings, the teacher must remain sensitive and responsive to the broad range of personal meanings of the student in order to assist the student in the task of integrating the two realms of meaning. This process of integration will result in a deeper grasp—both intellectual and valuational—of reality. The teacher, then stands between the two meaningful contexts and mediates and clarifies their integration. Macdonald asserts that the student's ego-integration is achieved "through the discovery and internalization of more and more productive meaning schemes in both spheres."[18]

Macdonald's categories differ somewhat from Maslow's B and D cognitions, for it is possible that personal meanings can be D cognitions and can be used for D activities. One obvious example of personal meaning used in D activities from daily classroom experience concerns the student's personal understanding of what he is trying to do. For all too many students involved in a particular classroom exercise, the point is not necessarily to learn something well, but simply to find out what the teacher wants him to say, and to say it. For that's how one gets good grades. Therefore the classroom exercise is, for the student, an exercise in grade getting.[19] The teacher who fails to understand this personal perspective of the student stands to suffer no small disillusionment. It is likewise possible that culturally defined meanings can ·be transformed into B cognitions and lead to B inquiry, for example, the student's insight into and appreciation of the tragic character of Othello, or his curious inquiry into the structure of the eye. Thus, we can represent these two dimensions in a conceptual model of curricular concerns.

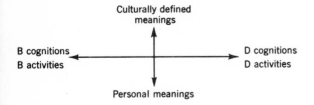

Culturally defined
meanings

B cognitions   D cognitions
B activities   D activities

Personal meanings

[18]Macdonald, *op. cit.*, p. 43.
[19]Cf. Marvin Grandstaff, "Situations as a Category of Curriculum Theory," a paper presented at the June, 1968, Curriculum Conference of the Center for the Study of Instruction, National Education Association, Washington, D.C., 1968.

ACTIVITIES OF THE INDIVIDUAL, OF FRIENDS, OF THE GROUP

Up to this point we have spoken of elements in the growth process of the individual as an individual. But the individual does not exist isolated and alone in the world. Although the fully mature and self-actualized person can retreat within himself from time to time to be alone to dream or savor the peace of his own reflections, or to contemplate a spring landscape or sunlight dancing on the water, most of the time we exist as persons in relation to other persons.[20] We are invested with significance by others who have need of us. We give life to others and participate in their lives. "We live and move and have our being not in ourselves but in one another."[21] Novelists, philosophers, and social psychologists have described the variety of influences of others upon the individual. The individual's attitudes, values, aspirations, and accomplishments are all affected by the ebb and flow of the matrix of relationships in which he exists. Huebner accents the importance of the encounter with others in the growth process of the individual.[22] Unlike the human relations school generally, and theorists such as Likert in particular, Huebner stresses not so much the formation of attitudes by the group or group belongingness—which are not to be denied as critial supports for individual growth—but the importance, rather, of conversation between man and man. Real conversation is the bridge over the aloneness that each man experiences, is the gesture across the chasms that separate the particular universes of individuals, by which they reveal themselves and transcend the limitations of their personal world. This is one of the reasons why childhood friendships are so important and, for the adolescent, why his initial romantic experiences are so expansive. Today's school experiences being what they are, the only experience most students have with the miracle of their own personal uniqueness is found on a date or in informal relationships outside of school. Research into why this experience of friendship and trusting intimacy has been excluded in any and all forms from the classroom might reveal the purely instrumental and hyperrational environment of the curriculum.

Relationships are established through conversation. The conversation between friends differs from the conversation of a group; but in whatever setting, it is through conversation that the individual makes contact with other individuals. To quote Huebner:

Conversation is thus an art. Not only an art of language, by which man finds new, esthetically satisfying language forms and symbolizes the experience of his world; but also an art which leads to the forming of oneself and the other.

[20]John MacMurray, *Persons in Relation,* Harper, New York, 1961, p. 211. Though difficult, this book offers a stimulating challenge to traditional views of knowledge.
[21]*Ibid.*
[22]Huebner, *op. cit.*

By speaking and by listening, man can become aware of what he is and what he may become, and may help his fellow man do the same.[23]

Notice that conversation can both enhance the level of interpersonal relationships and thereby create friendship, and also be a means of discovering new and satisfying ways of symbolizing the world. Hence, conversation has an objective as well as a personal referent; that is, through dialogue with a friend, with whom I feel secure enough to explore new meanings and expressions, I may discover new relationships between aspects of reality, new ways of understanding and appreciating a hitherto vaguely understood aspect of reality.

We may then speak of a general dimension of human growth which moves from individual thought and action to conversation with another, to action and discussion in a group. All three experiences are formative of the person and make up his environment of learning. Group activities and discussions contribute to the person's ability to relate to others, to share in group goals, and to surrender selfish attitudes and values for the benefit of the group. Sometimes, however, group participation in school activities can be made a fetish. Conversation with another person can usually be carried on at a deeper level than discussion in a group and can lead to the formation of the stronger ties of friendship. And there are times when it is good for the person to be alone, to work alone, to simply get away from all the talk and think things over on his own. This third dimension of human growth can be represented as a continuum moving from individual activity to conversation and activity with a friend to discussion and activity in a group.

Individual ◄─────────── Friend ──────────► Group

We may then add this dimension of human growth to the two previously described dimensions. The resulting model provides the context of the human curriculum.

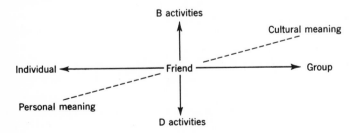

But what of the content of the curriculum? What about those structures inherent in and formative of the discipline that makes up the material of the curriculum? The model described above provides the context, the

---

[23]*Ibid.*, p. 152.

situation[24] in which the teaching and learning of core concepts and images, structural principles, and processes of inquiry and invention take place. The point is not to disparage curriculum content, but rather to place it in the context of *human* learning, and to insist that only by attention to the human context can curriculum content be integrated into the healthy personal growth of the student. One must reluctantly admit that knowledge is not virtue, but that nevertheless, knowledge integrated with a humanizing educational process will be far more likely to lead to humane behavior than an impersonal process in which the student is manipulated by fear of failure and the bogus reward of academic honors in order to get him to some preconceived academically or socially defined goals.

The model of the human curriculum, then, will be made up of four elements, one substantive (the curriculum content; though the content will be imbedded in the context, for purposes of analysis we shall treat it in abstraction) and the other three contextual. For purposes of clarification, the model is presented in its entirety and then broken down into its constituent parts in the following sets of diagrams (Figures 13-1, 13-2, and 13-3).

CLARIFICATION OF THE MODEL

In order to clarify the model, we shall locate learning activities in each quadrant. For example, in diagram alpha (α) an activity in the individual-culturally-defined-meaning quadrant would be the activity of a student studying by himself in the library the events surrounding the Declaration of Independence. In this activity the student might check two or three sources, but the learning consists mainly of the acquisition of historical information and, probably, a culturally conditioned interpretation of the significance of the events. If the student attempts to reflect on the political freedom he and his family enjoy as a result of American political democracy and in contrast, say, to the political repressions in certain Latin American dictatorships, the kind of learning would be enriched by including personal meanings and interpretations. This learning activity, then, would begin with the individual more or less accepting culturally defined meanings and then continue by relating these to his personal experience.

Let us suppose, however, that the student is white and on relatively good terms with a black classmate, whose individual study project was concerned with colonial slavery. Later that week in the cafeteria, student W and student B just happen to ask one another how their individual study projects are progressing. The resulting conversation might bring student W to a different understanding of his classmate's ambiguous feelings about the uncritical patriotic tone of the history textbook. This learning experience

[24]Grandstaff, *op. cit.*

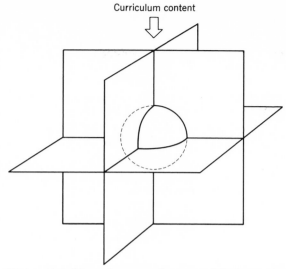

Figure 13-1. Three-dimensional context of the human curriculum. The three dimensions are represented by the three geometric planes. The curriculum content is represented by the sphere imbedded in this three-dimensional space.

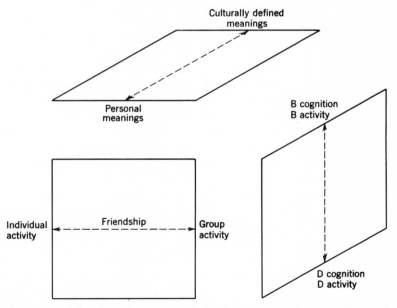

Figure 13-2. The three dimensions of the human curriculum are illustrated separately for visual clarification.

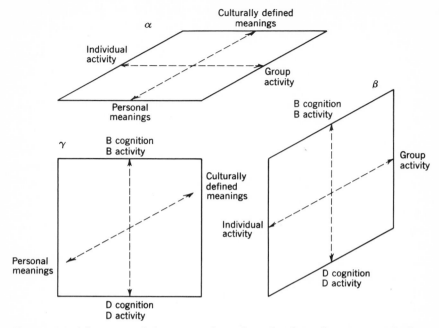

Figure 13-3. These sets of diagrams indicate how the three dimensions might be considered in pairs of two-dimensional constructs, again for conceptual clarification. Activities can be identified in each quadrant of each construct.

then involves culturally defined meanings and a critical analysis of them in the light of personal meanings in a dialogue with a friend. Had student B chosen the study project on the Declaration of Independence, the kind of learning which probably would have occurred would be quite different from student W's learning even though student W and student B might give the same factual responses on a true-false test.

Let us suppose, again, that student W and student B attend the same class that day for a group discussion on the American Revolution. Let us suppose that in the course of the discussion, besides considering the oppressive military, political, and economic pressures on the early colonists in New England, New York, and Pennsylvania, the discussion turned toward the right of any people to rebel against political, economic, and military oppression. Perhaps the treatment of the American Indian by our government might be injected into the discussion. Or let us suppose that the Castro-led revolution in Cuba came up and was debated hotly in terms of communist influence and ideology. Perhaps the political outcomes of both revolutions might be contrasted and evaluated. Now student W's understanding of the significance of the Declaration of Independence might change as the debate of democratic versus communist political and economic ideology provided a contrasting contemporary background for its interpretation. In this instance the context of the learning experience is composed of both personal and culturally defined meanings and group discussion and analysis.

Learning in all of these contexts frequently takes place in a school setting, but often by chance, especially as regards the injection of personal meanings. If teachers were more aware, however, of the personal meanings which each student brings to class, and of the enormous pedagogical effect of dialogue between two students, then they could plan the instructional unit to be more responsive to these contexts of learning.

Other examples of learning which might take place in different quadrants of diagram α would be a study of occupations, a study by rural farm students of price controls on crops, an analysis of a film like *Sixteen in Webster Groves* by students from an affluent suburb, a study of genetic laws of heredity, and a study of the automobile industry. Depending on the context the teacher wanted to plan for, different emphases and therefore different learnings would take place.

In the beta diagram (β) one could locate the activity of an individual student memorizing vocabulary lists in French in the individual, D activity quadrant. The individual student's efforts to master any skill, whether it be penmanship or reading faster or mixing colors in art class, can usually be classified in that same quadrant. In almost any kind of testing and grading situation the same individual, D cognition context would be operative. In any group competition, say in a grade-level spelling contest or science project contest, the learning would take place in the group activity, D cognition quadrant. A moment's reflection would reveal the enormous motivational potential in these latter learning contexts. Group problem-solving or project work, even without the overt competitive aspect, could also be considered as group D activities, for the group is still striving to use the knowledge to come up with an answer or a construct which will measure up to the teacher's expectations and earn a good grade.

In the same beta diagram, the examples of an individual student painting a picture in art class, listening to folk music, and studying the aerodynamics of the fruit fly out of curiosity or fascination would fall in the individual B activity quadrant. This is not to say that all activities related to art are necessarily B activities. A student who is attempting to replicate a landscape by Van Gogh in order to satisfactorily pass an exercise in oil-color mixing demanded by his art teacher may very well be engaged in purely D activity. In learning activities, however, where the student engages in more contemplative and appreciative behavior, the context can be more readily identified with the individual, B activities quadrant. At this point, the reader might try to recall and list learning activities from his or her own past school experience which would fall in this quadrant. The list would probably be quite small.

A final example in the beta figure to illustrate a learning context involving group activity and a B activity is a dramatic production by the group. Teachers by and large have not begun to use drama as a context for learning. Having students adapt a story from their literature or history books for a dramatic presentation often allows them a moving experience of conscious identification with character. By trying to get inside the personality of the character they are portraying, students come to understand the situation of the play sympathetically; they can look out on the world and on the other characters in the play from the eyes of another person. By internalizing and then externalizing the conflict, comedy, or tragedy of the dramatic situation, students can develop an understanding and sensitivity to the problems, joys, and miracles in their own lives. Because of the atmosphere of "make-believe" —which is often a more intense reflection of reality—students are relieved somewhat of the threat of exposing themselves and yet can get a feeling for real interpersonal communication. To use the dramatic context for learning does not require a full-scale production similar to that of the annual school play. It may consist of impromptu dramatizations with the simplest of stage props to suggest the "make-believe" atmosphere. Often, the excitement such imaginative experiences arouse leads students to drop many of their defenses and to work as a team to put on the show. Anyone familiar with group dynamics would point to this kind of experience as critical in developing group spirit and cohesion, as well as in allowing students to bring forth a part of themselves which they customarily hide. This is not to say that dramatic productions should be used for therapy. The emphasis should be on the objective dramatic situation. But teachers should be aware of the group dynamics involved in these experiences in order to prevent them from getting out of hand and to assist and clarify whatever learnings take place.

In the gamma diagram (γ), one can again conjecture about a variety of possible learning situations. A student who constructs a montage in order to express what war or patriotism or autumn means to him would be learning in a context of B cognitions and personal meanings. Interpretive readings of poetry might also be classified in his context. A context involving personal meanings and D cognitions or D activities might be one in which a student whose father works with computers and who has some knowledge of the versatility of computers takes a course in computer programming. As he learns the several languages of the computer, he will no doubt be spontaneously thinking of several applications of particular codings. Another example of this context would be a biology class exercise on the reasons for certain dietary foods where one of the students might have worked in a hospital kitchen. If the teacher knows as much as possible about the backgrounds of his students, he can utilize the experiences of students to help clarify some of the implications of the matter under study.

As was mentioned in Chapter 12, in the discussion of synnoetic or sympathetic meaning, lasting and significant learning occurs when the student is able to appreciate and "dwell in" what he has learned, to feel the human implications of some object or aspect of reality or simply to marvel at its intricacy or simplicity. This kind of sympathetic knowing can be experienced not only in a love relationship but also in knowing other aspects of reality. Scheler points to the importance of this kind of knowing in a world where technological rationality threatens to cut off man's roots in nature.

Hence the first task of our educational practice must be to revive the capacity for identification with the life of the universe, and awaken it anew from its condition of dormancy in the capitalistic social outlook of Western man (with its characteristic picture of the world as an aggregation of movable quantities). We must dissociate ourselves, firmly and unreservedly, from the gross error of regarding the sense of unity with the universe as merely an "empathic" projection of specifically human emotions into animals, plants, or inanimate objects—as sheer anthropomorphism, therefore, and a fundamental misapprehension of the real. On the contrary, it is man the microcosm, an actual embodiment of the reality of existence in *all* its forms, who is himself *cosmomorphic,* and as such the possessor of sources of *insight* into all that is comprised in the nature of the cosmos.[25]

Iredell Jenkins points to this kind of knowing in a person's esthetic experience of a deeper participation in his world.

Through aesthetic experience we become intimately involved with things, we participate actively in their interests and adventures, and so we see them as they see themselves. This point is most frequently put by saying that art deepens our sympathy for the things and situations—for the human persons and problems— it presents. It puts us more nearly in the place of the objects and personalities it depicts, and has us confront the world from their position rather than from our own. So it is held that through our appreciation of art we achieve a special sort of sympathetic understanding: we overcome the partiality of our prejudices and preconceptions, we live through situations from the inside instead of judging them from the outside, and so we are prepared to accept things on their own terms instead of rejecting them for not conforming with our demands.[26]

As the teacher prepares encounters with the central ideas or personages in a science or literature class, he should attempt to lead the students to these kinds of B cognitions. A student studying the dynamic gravitational relationships of the planetary system, for example, should be led to a sense of wonder at the mathematical precision of such a system. This would be an example of a learning context involving B cognition of culturally defined meanings. This experience could be coupled with D cognitions as the class studies the technical engineering problems of putting a space capsule into orbit around the moon.

[25]Max Scheler, *The Nature of Sympathy,* trans. by P. Heath, Routledge, London, 1959, p. 105.
[26]Iredell Jenkins, *Art and the Human Enterprise,* Harvard, Cambridge, Mass., 1958, p. 130.

These descriptive examples should indicate the rich variety of learning contexts which teachers can utilize to make their curricular-instructional program more human. It would be an interesting exercise for the readers to list their own series of activities appropriate to each quadrant of the three diagrams. Going beyond this exercise, readers might then attempt to construct from these lists a logically related sequence of learning experiences for a class unit focusing on one central idea. A complementary and equally fruitful exercise might be to select a topic from one of the discipline-oriented curriculum packages and construct classroom situations which would involve, either serially or simultaneously, all three dimensions of the learning context.

In Figure 13-4, nine subsets of the model have been encircled and

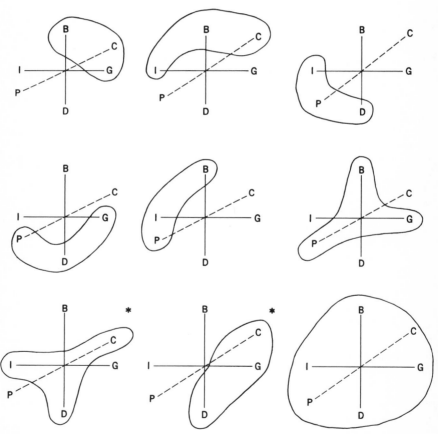

Figure 13-4. Nine possible contexts for learning. In the diagrams above, the letters stand for the poles of the dimensions described in the preceding pages. B stands for B cognitions; D stands for D cognitions; I stands for individual activity; G stands for group activity; C stands for culturally defined meanings; P stands for personal meanings.

*Today's schools focus primarily on IDC and GCD contexts.

labeled. Thus, the GBC subset refers to those activities involving Group activity, B cognitions or B activities, and Culturally defined meanings; the ICD subset refers to Individual activity, Culturally defined meanings, and D cognitions or D activities. And so on. The ninth subset includes all six poles of the three dimensions. This kind of activity or learning might be called a *peak* activity or learning, that is, that kind of extraordinary learning experience in which all elements in the human context become fused and integrated. A teacher is fortunate if she can stimulate such peak experiences once or twice a year.

As one searches for actual classroom experiences involving each one of these learning contexts, it becomes evident that the school in practice deals almost entirely with only two of these contexts: the ICD context and the GCD context. The other seven contexts of learning have by and large been neglected in both curriculum design and teaching strategies. Perhaps these contexts are seen to be more appropriately dealt with by the student counselor. It may be that much counseling involves these contexts, but that is no reason for excluding them as genuine learning contexts for the classroom.

In Figure 13-5, we attempted to show how much of the human context of learning is neglected in curriculum design and in classroom practice. The space within the solid lines represents the ICD and GCD contexts; the space within the dotted lines represents those other six neglected contexts of learning. In this diagram, the limitations of designing a discipline-dominated curriculum based almost entirely on technological rationality become more apparent.

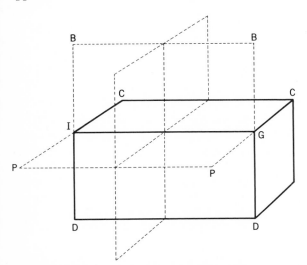

Figure 13-5. Today's schools use primarily ICD and GCD contexts and omit the following contexts: IBP, GCB, GPB, IPD, ICB, GPD.

Figure 13-6. Learning in today's schools.

If we consider student learnings—the outcomes of encounters with curriculum content—as the sphere embedded in the three-dimensional model, we can see in Figure 13-6 how much learning is neglected. This is not to say that learnings in the shaded area of the figure are *entirely* neglected. Such a judgment would be unfair to those many teachers who are struggling to bring students to these learnings. The primary focus, however, of much of the recent thinking about curriculum, as well as of the practice in today's schools, is on learnings in the one quadrant. In Chapter 14 we shall consider a curriculum which attempts to be more conducive to all varieties of learnings.

SUMMARY

In proposing the human context of learning as a model by which supervisors might assist and evaluate classroom procedures and curriculum design, we must once again insist on the genuine value of programming, processes of inquiry, structural principles, and organizing centers. The new curriculum movement rightly deserves the accolades of history for its significant clarification of these factors in the educational process. We hope to avoid, however, the blind acceptance of these insights as the panacea for human progress. That is, by what magic formula can we hope to "input" these insights into school programs and "output" an end to man's exploitation of man, an end to insane asylums, a reduction in alcohol and drug addiction, and a solution to the problems of poverty, racial conflicts, and international tensions? We need technological rationality, to be sure, if we are to confront these tragic human experiences, but we perhaps need even more a human community of trust and esteem and sympathy and forgiveness, and the foundation of this kind of community is to be discovered more in the realm of ethical and sympathetic rationality.

While an appeal to these basic human qualities of life is considered unscientific and sentimental by some, a curriculum which effectively programs these qualities of human life out of existence is self-defeating. To be fair, a curriculum focusing solely on interpersonal relations and esthetic contemplation can produce a flaccid and ineffective personality. It is not a question, however, of either-or. The schools can provide an atmosphere and a curriculum for both intellectual and personal growth. And, consonant with the theme developed earlier, one can enter upon personal growth most humanly through *knowledge* of the world and can grow intellectually precisely by an internalization and integration of knowledge in one's personal life.

The task of the supervisor is indeed complex. It is hoped that the preceding analyses have illuminated aspects of supervision which will enable the practicing or prospective supervisor to perform more professionally as well as more sensitively in the school setting. By clarifying one's assumptions and reflecting on various points of view concerning supervisory styles, teaching and learning styles, and comprehensive models to structure a meaningful context for learning, the supervisor should be better equipped to approach specific encounters with teachers and classroom situations. We would hopefully expect that supervisors will still trust their instincts in these situations, but let them be instincts grounded in some rational and comprehensive understandings of the requirements of the human organization and the human curriculum.

SELECTED REFERENCES

Huebner, Dwayne: "New Modes of Man's Relationship to Man," in Alexander Frazier (ed.), *New Insights and the Curriculum,* Association for Supervision and Curriculum Development, National Education Association, Washington, D.C., 1963, pp. 144–164.

Macdonald, James B.: "An Image of Man: The Learner Himself," in Ronald C. Doll (ed.), *Individualizing Instruction,* Association for Supervision and Curriculum Development, National Education Association, Washington, D.C., 1964, pp. 29–49.

Maslow, Abraham H.: "Some Basic Propositions of a Growth and Self-actualization Psychology," in 1962 Yearbook, *Perceiving, Behaving, Becoming,* Association for Supervision and Curriculum Development, National Education Association, Washington, D.C., 1962, pp. 34–49.

McLuhan, Marshall: "We Need a New Picture of Knowledge," in Alexander Frazier (ed.), *New Insights and the Curriculum,* Association for Supervision and Curriculum Development, National Education Association, Washington, D.C., 1964. pp. 57–70.

Chapter Fourteen
PLANNING
A HUMAN CURRICULUM

In the preceding chapter, the model of the environment of learning presented a point of departure for considering new possibilities in curriculum design. This chapter will outline one possible curricular design which attempts to incorporate those learnings neglected in many current curricular-instructional programs. Such a design does not pretend to be the only possible design for a general education program in elementary or secondary schools. Nor, indeed, will the design be developed in all particulars; rather, it is offered as an example of disciplined thinking in curriculum development, which *process* of thinking supervisory personnel might use in their work with teachers and students. Recalling the earlier model of Goodlad,[1] we shall first consider our assumptions and basic values, from which we shall derive general objectives. As we proceed to select learning content, we shall try to take account of those learning theories most consistent with our assumptions about individual growth and the nature of the disciplines of knowledge. The design will leave many questions unanswered, both because of the limitations of our own wisdom and because we believe that supervisors and teachers should attempt answers in terms of their particular school situation.

BASIC ASSUMPTIONS

1. The educator's primary function is to become obsolete. The job of the educator is to so influence the student that the student will gradually but eventually reach the point where he does not need the teacher, where he can pursue his own learning on the basis of his acquired knowledge and skills.
2. Indirectly related to the above assumption is the further assumption that *active* pursuit of knowledge and understanding, actual dialogue with reality, will produce the most significant and long-lasting types of learning. Whenever possible, therefore, the student must actively search, actively inquire, actively discover, actively organize and integrate. The teacher's job is to guide and direct this activity toward specified goals.

[1]See Chap. 12.

3. The school makes a difference in a child's growth, but not *that* much difference. If the school were nonexistent, other influences and experiences would "educate" the child. Besides, human beings are dynamic, constantly growing despite their best efforts to the contrary. The school simply speeds up the growth process and channels it in supposedly beneficial directions, rather than leaving the student to random, trial-and-error growth.

4. Unlike input factors in system designs of industrial or military organizations, the student is not like a piece of steel which arrives at the input station all neatly measured and qualified and stable. Steel and wood and stone do not grow and change during the very time when the production worker is trying to manipulate them. Students do.

5. Curricular-instructional programs should be designed in conformity to the growth patterns of students. The human growth needs of students should never be subordinated to objectives dictated by the needs of society and the demands of the disciplines. Theoretically, these three concerns—human growth, achievement of disciplined knowledge, and fulfillment of social responsibilities—should not be in conflict. In practice, however, they frequently are in conflict, and the concern for human growth usually is the one to be sacrificed. This practice should be reversed.

In order to clarify our assumptions of the growth patterns of the individual, the following conceptual diagrams attempt to sketch in broad strokes a picture of this growing human being. Despite their resemblances to cave drawings of prehistoric man, they might provide a helpful visual image of the student as he moves from infancy toward maturity.

Figure 14-1 attempts a rudimentary, three-dimensional model of growth which emphasizes the individual's gradual increase in freedom to explore his world. Initially, the infant's behavior is almost entirely dominated by his biological needs, such as needs for food, warmth, sleep, and basic sensory stimulation. As these needs are regularly taken care of, and as he becomes able to provide for them himself, he has more time and energy to seek more complex sensory stimulation and to move away from purely self-centered concerns toward whatever makes up his environment. His environment, he discovers quite early, is made up of people and things. Animals populate his early people-world, but gradually they, too, become part of the nonhuman world. This exploratory behavior is called *reality-oriented behavior* because through it the individual moves toward discovering things and people in their own right and not simply as gratifiers of his physical needs. As he moves toward things and people in their own right, he discovers that reality is quite complex—that he has to deal with each situation and each person in different ways at different times.

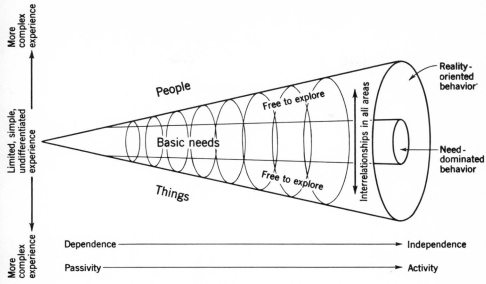

Figure 14-1. Relationship of free activity to behavior controlled by basic needs.

As the individual matures physically, he discovers that he can and is expected to manage many of the things which parents and siblings provided in his infancy, such as feeding, washing, dressing, returning his toys to the toy closet, and so forth. Moreover, he is allowed more freedom to explore his environment, first outside his crib and playpen, then outside of the house, and eventually outside of the neighborhood. This pattern of continued movement away from dependency toward independence to interdependence, and from passivity to increased self-activity, is basic to the process of maturing, of becoming a human person, and this process involves both emotional and cognitive development as well as physical development.

In Figure 14-2 the same three-dimensional model of growth forms the basis for sketching Maslow's descriptive categories of growth. It may be helpful at this point to review our earlier treatments of Maslow's motivational theory and Porter's adaptation of Maslow's categories into a hierarchy of needs.[2] What was stated in Chapter 8 as applying to the growth needs of teachers applies equally, in our curriculum concerns, to the individual student.

As was stated earlier in Chapter 8, Maslow's need dimensions, or levels, build on one another. That is, as a lower need is relatively well satisfied, the next higher need emerges and begins to occupy a person's conscious attention. Thus, as a student moves from satisfied security needs, he seeks more

[2]See Chaps. 8 and 13 on growth needs and deficiency needs.

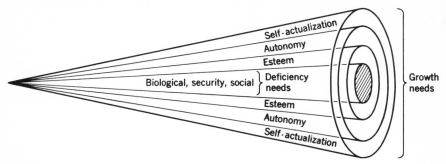

Figure 14-2. Human growth: deficiency needs and growth needs.

social satisfactions by belonging to a group, by making friends, and by striving for acceptance by a circle of acquaintances wider than his own family.

As the social needs become relatively satisfied, the student begins now to seek recognition for his own achievements. Here we notice the link between lower social needs and higher autonomy needs. His acceptance into a group as he sought to satisfy his need for affiliation was itself a recognition that he was not an absolute boor—that he had some likable or useful qualities. His later quest for more autonomy will have its roots in this earlier desire to stand out from the group by being respected for some skill or quality in which he excels.

Many students falter at the esteem level. Since they experience either failure in their schoolwork or little esteem—or sometimes indifference—from their teacher and an almost total lack of trust communicated by the disciplinary system of the school, they perceive that their need for esteem cannot be satisfied by participating in school activities. The only school activities that do grant them a measure of recognition are primarily athletics for the boys and cheerleading for the girls.[3] But this recognition comes not so much from teachers and administrators as from the students' peers at school. Except for the very bright and creative, therefore, and the athletes and cheerleaders, schooling usually does not provide sufficient esteem for most students. No wonder, then, that many students seek other sources of esteem—in becoming socially popular, in outside activities with gangs, in outside jobs, in private hobbies, and in other activities.

If the curricular-instructional program, on the other hand, could provide more experiences of achievement, of competence, of respect and status, then the student could feel more enthusiastic about learning. He would come to seek more esteem through his schoolwork and, as this was provided, would gradually accept more autonomous responsibility for his learning. In other

[3]James S. Coleman's *The Adolescent Society,* Free Press, Glencoe, Ill., 1961, documents this very thoroughly.

words, through the esteem and recognition granted him for his unique talents by *school* personnel (teachers and administrators, and not solely his peers), he might come to identify more closely with the objectives of schooling and to seek his fulfillment and self-actualization through learning activities.

Gradually, however, the student would grow restless over learning experiences which were exclusively under the control and direction of the teacher and the department. If he would develop his potential more freely, he must have more opportunities for self-expression and for creative explorations on his own. Once again even many "progressive" schools stop short of allowing these self-actualizing attempts on the part of students. Certainly the curricular-instructional program requires structure and organization for the less mature students, but it should not penalize those students who are eager to pursue more adventuresome goals.

Figure 14-3 is rather self-explanatory. It simply attempts to chart the different people and things an individual encounters as he moves from his passive and dependent condition into more active and independent participation with his environment. Reflection on the numerous skills and learnings required to deal with these people and things in his expanding environment leads to Figure 14-4.

Figure 14-4 attempts to indicate the development of habits, skills, and understandings which allow the individual the freedom to explore and participate in his environment. By mastering and internalizing any skill, the individual no longer has to consciously think about each minute part of the behavior involved in the performance of a skill. Rather, it becomes "natural," like breathing or walking, and thus the person's conscious energies are freed to explore new areas of his environment which he gradually assimilates into new skills, new understandings, and new interpretive maps of his environment. As he develops these skills and understandings, he is increasingly able not merely to explore the environment, but to interact with it—to develop deeper friendships, for example, or to take on a part-time job, or to solve problems in school assignments.

These basic learnings include social skills, such as learning appropriate manners for different occasions, learning something about sex, age, and authority role-relationships, learning to delay gratification in order to achieve a higher goal, and so forth. Other basic learnings involve physical skills, such as manual dexterity, visual and auditory perceptual differentiation, correct speech habits, athletic skills, and so forth. Besides developing symbolic skills, methodologies for inquiry, and attitudes and values, the individual accumulates a repertory of personal meanings. These are derived from experiences whose intensity left a lasting and frequently highly emotion-laden impression on him. Finally, the emerging self-concept lies at the heart of this developing core of the person and suffuses all of his accumulated learnings.

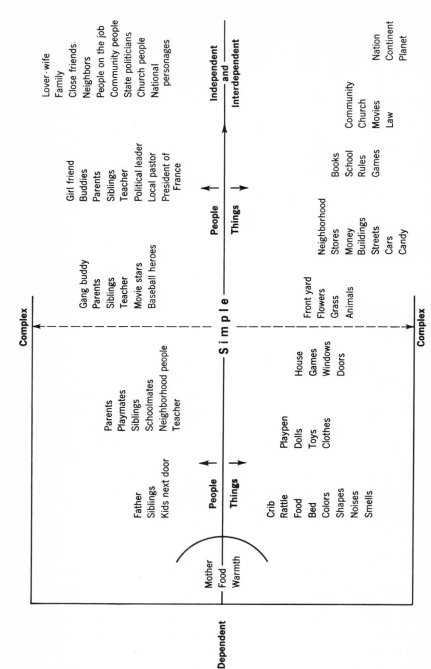

Figure 14-3. Environmental interaction chart.

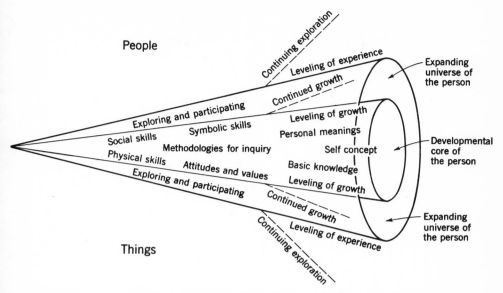

People

Things

Continuing exploration
Leveling of experience
Continued growth
Exploring and participating
Symbolic skills
Social skills
Methodologies for inquiry
Physical skills
Attitudes and values
Exploring and participating
Continued growth
Continuing exploration
Leveling of experience

Leveling of growth
Personal meanings
Self concept
Basic knowledge
Leveling of growth

Expanding universe of the person

Developmental core of the person

Expanding universe of the person

Figure 14-4. Developing freedom to explore and participate in the human environment.

All together, these elements of the developing core of the person determine the quality and degree of his freedom to participate in his human environment.

Notice that these growth processes can level off after a while, as the result of a variety of circumstances. Everyone is familiar with people who have stopped growing—who simply do not go beyond a certain point either in exploring their universe or in pursuing more intense human experiences. People sometimes caustically remark about this phenomenon: "Oh, you mean John X. Well, he died five years ago, but he's doing all right, I guess." When the core of the person stops growing, his experience of his environment levels off and he settles into a daily routine where things seldom change, except for the worse.

DEFINING GENERAL GOALS OF A HUMAN CURRICULUM

With this brief description and analysis of our initial assumptions and value premises, especially that the human growth of the individual student should be the primary focus of a curricular-instructional program, we may now proceed to define objectives which will respect the integrity of this growth pattern of the individual.

A human curricular-instructional program should lead the person out into the open and give him the best chance to be his best self.[4] As we have proposed in our assumptions about the growing person, the thrust and direction of his growth are toward increased freedom to explore and participate in the life of his environment. In order to achieve this freedom, the individual must become increasingly freed *from* both fear and ignorance. The fears from which the student must free himself are fear of himself, fear of the unknown, fear of authority, fear of insecurity, and fear of commitment and risk. The ignorance from which the student must free himself includes ignorance about himself, about the functioning of present society, about history, about natural phenomena, about the demands of interpersonal relationships, and about methods of inquiry and expression. Freedom from fears and ignorance enable the individual to respond to his environment with understanding, compassion, and decisiveness. It frees him from internal constraints and limitations, permitting him to make responsible choices. It enables him to be free *for* explorations into new areas of his world, free to accept new people into his life, free to commit himself to his work and to the service of his fellow man. And this freedom must be based on inner strength, confidence, conviction, style, and knowledge.

Gradually, this freedom from fear and ignorance enables the individual to give himself freely to others and to his world, to move toward that highest form of personal encounter, love. Doubtless, many educators will stir uneasily in their chairs at the mention of such a word. It carries connotations too romantic, or soft, or weak for the hardheaded business of education.[5] Because love is thought of as intensely personal and highly emotional educators assume that it is out of place to discuss it as a curricular objective. Besides, one's love experiences take place in a setting far removed from the classroom. All this may be true, but not exclusively true. Love has many faces and seasons; it is not simply candlelight and roses and glowing eyes. That is, if one broadens this very narrow meaning of the word *love* to include friendships, group solidarity, esthetic cherishing of works of art and science, love of country, and the brotherhood of man as well as romantic and marital love, then one can indeed speak of developing the freedom to love as a legitimate and central goal of the curricular-instructional program.

This goal of freedom to love, moreover, is not simply an individualistic affair (no pun intended); rather, it lies at the heart of man's societal quest as well. Looking at society and social institutions in a global fashion, one can ask whether all their particular goals add up to a generalizable goal.

---

[4]Frank Barron, "Creativity: What Research Says about It," *National Education Association Journal,* vol. 50, March, 1961, p. 17.

[5]See Dwayne Huebner, "New Modes of Man's Relationship to Man," in Alexander Frazier (ed.), *New Insights and the Curriculum,* Association for Supervision and Curriculum Development, National Education Association, Washington, D.C., 1963, p. 148.

Any number of philosophers will answer affirmatively, and that this goal is to *free* man for optimal growth as an individual and as a member of a community. Since man does not live isolated from his fellows, his freedom for growth is conditioned by a variety of communities of other men, all of whom are working for the optimal freedom to grow. One cannot deny the vicious use of power or the greedy accumulation of wealth on the part of many. But if one pushes back behind these behaviors, one usually finds frustrated, lonely, alienated people whose freedom to love even themselves has been severely inhibited.[6]

One can also view human history as man's struggle to free himself from his physical limitations, from geographically imposed hardships, from political oppression within his community or military and economic aggression from neighboring communities or nations, from ignorance about nature, and from ignorance about his own internal physical and mental illnesses. And once again, viewing this struggle from a global perspective, one can assert that the one way human history makes sense is to view it as man's search for freedom to be human enough to love—to enjoy the intimacies of family life, certainly, but also to love life itself in whatever form it offers itself to him. At this level of reasoning, therefore, the goals of man in society coincide with the goals of man as an individual. From this vantage point we can also see how a curriculum which focuses on the individual implies attention to his social milieu.

We affirm, therefore, that the overarching goal of the school is to further the student's growth toward these freedoms—to assist him in the processes of breaking out of the jail of his ignorance, fear, isolation, and alienation. Other social institutions contribute, to be sure, but the school is the one institution which focuses primarily on freeing persons from the limitations of ignorance and attempts to expand their horizons, to introduce them to the multifaceted wonders of life, and to focus, direct, and speed up their otherwise trial-and-error growth toward full humanity.

Goals, we must remember, are just that—ends to be achieved, not behaviors, necessarily, which will emerge quickly. When we state them, we should realize that their full achievement may take a long time, and we may not be there to see them realized through many cumulative experiences over several years. When teachers state general goals, therefore, they are describing what they expect the student to become by the *completion* of his educa-

---

[6]Without getting bogged down in arguing over psychological theories of the elementary driving force behind man's behavior, we may refer the reader to the developmental theories of Ernest Schactel, *Metamorphosis*, Basic Books, New York, 1959; Gordon W. Allport, *Pattern and Growth in Personality*, Holt, New York, 1963, *Becoming: Basic Considerations for a Psychology of Personality*, Yale, New Haven, Conn., 1955; and Abraham H. Maslow, *Toward a Psychology of Being*, Van Nostrand, New York, 1962. These men provide a sound theoretical basis for proposing the freedom to love as the central quest of man.

tion—which in one sense ends only with death. As educators, teachers' efforts should help the student as he is moving toward, but perhaps never fully realizing these goals. That teachers can never really say whether they have succeeded or failed in their efforts to realize these goals is therefore no reason to dismiss the goals as unrealistic. For unless teachers have these higher goals, the more immediate goals of day-to-day classwork will lack that vision necessary to elevate them from the level of pedantry and senseless routine.

We may summarize this discussion of general goals, then, by listing in order the kinds of freedom to which the curricular-instructional program should contribute. The statement of these goals should describe a high school graduate. Since freedom is a relative experience, we must understand these goal statements as relative, that is, as describing freedoms which are sufficiently enjoyed to lead to further growth. Elementary teachers, of course, will not see their students enjoying the freedoms of a high school graduate. But they will obtain some idea of the quality of freedom their students should enjoy by comparing their present state with the description of the final product.

General Goals

1. The student is free from fear:
   a. of himself
   b. of the unknown
   c. of authority
   d. of insecurity
   e. of commitment and risk
2. The student is free from ignorance:
   a. about himself
   b. about the functioning of present society
   c. about history
   d. about natural phenomena
   e. about the demands of interpersonal relationships
   f. about the methods of inquiry and communication
3. The student is therefore free to explore his world, to respond to it appropriately, and to participate in its struggles and joys.
4. The student is therefore free to communicate by means of language, ritual, and other art forms.
5. The student is free to organize his values and to commit himself to a hierarchy of values.
6. The student is free to accept the limitations of his freedom by both social and natural causes.

7. The student is free to serve:
    a. his family
    b. his friends
    c. his community
    d. his world
8. The student is free to love:
    a. himself
    b. significant others (beloved, family, parents, friends)
    c. others
    d. his country
    e. his world

Obviously, the achievement of such general goals will be difficult to assess. While teachers are not expected to be amateur psychologists, nevertheless they should have the mature sensitivity and common sense to make some general evaluative judgments about their students' movement toward these freedoms. It might provide a healthy exercise in self-reflection, moreover, to have students write their own assessment of how free they are at the beginning and end of each year—especially in junior and senior high school. Certainly, some objective tests are available to test some of the ignorance and fear items. Teachers and counselors, exercising great tact and sensitivity, can develop tests of their own. When using these tests, however, teachers and counselors should exercise great caution to protect the privacy of each student. By no means should a grade be assigned in those tests dealing with personal feelings. Teachers and counselors will have to go out of their way to build up the necessary trust to free such tests of any threatening overtones and to show the student that these tests are only to help him gain a better assessment of his own maturity. Such assessment may never be used for admission to college or to assist the efficient rating of students. For this reason, many educators will dismiss it as of no practical use. Simply because these concerns do not fit in neatly with the schools' rating, grading, and record-keeping procedures is no reason whatsoever for neglecting them. That they are neglected in many schools, and for that very reason, is a good example of the tail wagging the dog.

These overarching goals, however, require further specification if they are to provide clear and forceful direction to the curricular-instructional program. To propose freedom as a central objective of schooling does not mean doing whatever seems appealing at the moment. Any artist will testify that to be free to express oneself in an art medium requires mastery of the various techniques of the medium, a mastery which is gained by immersing oneself in the medium in order to gain control over it. This ability to *use* the medium to express subtle shades of meaning and to interpret the phenomena of experience demands hours of work. Frank Barron puts it well.

Education aims at freedom. But freedom is inextricably bound up with discipline, system, habit. To be free to write a novel requires mastery of grammar, style, psychology; to be free to think about theory of relativity requires much study of mathematics and physics. Education aims to increase such freedoms and a thousand more; in the meantime, however, behind and before each mastery, each accession to new freedom, lies routine, discipline, the developing of relevant habits.[7]

It is necessary, therefore, to describe those skills and understandings which the student must master to achieve the freedoms described in our general goals. Once again, these more specific objectives will be described as student learnings and competencies. These student learnings will be described as they should look at the *completion* of his secondary education, thus providing objectives which can be broken down into segmented patterns of growth for students at various age levels. This more specific description of the goals of the curricular-instructional program should lend itself more readily to measurement of goal achievement, but notice that they are still rather general and open-ended, allowing the student the elbow room necessary to personalize these learnings.

Specific Goals of the Curricular-Instruction Program [8]

1. The student is able to use the symbolic tools of thinking, communicating, and inquiring.
    a.   He has mastered the basic methods of logic, as can be shown by his ability to reason consistently in oral debate, to critically analyze newspaper editorials and political speeches, to draw inferences from general statements, and to construct valid generalizations from individual instances.
    b.   He has mastered the English language—a mastery which will be shown by his ability to use it orally and in writing according to accepted standards of usage and style and his ability to read and to interpret what he reads according to accepted performance criteria.
    c.   He has mastered the basic symbolic systems of mathematics, the natural sciences, and the social sciences. This mastery will be indicated by his knowledge of central concepts, of essential operations and functions, and of unifying theories, as well as by his ability to perform basic laboratory operations.

[7]Frank Barron, *op. cit.*, p. 17.
[8]The formulation of these objectives was heavily influenced by Philip H. Phenix, *Realms of Meaning,* McGraw-Hill, New York, 1964, and Broudy et al., *Democracy and Excellence in American Secondary Education,* Rand McNally, Chicago, 1964.

d. He has mastered the elementary forms of artistic expression. This mastery will be indicated by his ability to use the techniques of the art form (such as his use of color, symmetry, and perspective in painting, his use of verbal imagery and metaphors in poetry, his ability to interpret the personality of the character whose part he plays in drama, and so forth). Mastery in the arts would also involve knowledge of evaluative principles so that the student could both enjoy and make an informed appraisal of the work of art. It also involves familiarity with a variety of past and present works of art in literature, painting, music, drama, and sculpture.

2. He is able to systematize and interpret basic facts of the physical world and their interrelationships by means of conceptual structures. This ability would be indicated by his interpretation and analysis of health problems, conservation problems, new scientific accomplishments such as the space program, the use of thermonuclear energy, and so forth.

3. He is able to organize information into patterns of past cultural development. He would indicate such competence by his ability to explain central ideas and images which permeated all aspects of cultural eras such as classical Greek and Roman cultures, medieval culture, the Renaissance, and others, to locate the roots of many current social problems in past historical movements, to interpret the international scene against the backdrop of past international power struggles, and to identify at least some of the complex elements in such struggles, pointing out similarities and the unique character of different power confrontations.

4. He is able to understand and use the methods of regulating the social order. This goal refers to the student's understanding of the basic principles of our national, state, and local economy, of basic laws and why they were instituted, of political power and how it is used, and of democratic political action through voting, organizing lobbying groups, organizing grass-roots political action groups, and so forth. Such understanding and use of the methods of regulating the social order can be evaluated through simulated case studies or through molar problem solving which requires the student to draw upon a variety of understandings in order to interpret the demands of the situation and to make decisions which he can justify.

5. He is able to integrate and defend his values from a basic philosophic, ethical-religious, and esthetic stance. He will manifest competence in this area by his ability to make decisions in matters of conflict or in matters requiring evaluative judgment. The student does not necessarily have to be put in an actual conflict situation, but through exposure to hypothetical or simulated conflict situations he can indicate the consistency and reasonableness of his decisions and judgments.

Through competence in and mastery of these basic skills and understandings, the student will free himself from simple, undifferentiated knowledge and attitudes and develop more complex and interrelated understandings, skills, and attitudes. These competencies will enable him increasingly to transcend—to stand above—the limitations of particular experiences, needs, forces, and conventions, and thus to be free to understand and order his experience of his universe and to participate in the complex life of that world.

Evaluating Goal Statements

Before moving on to the next step in curriculum development, we should pause and evaluate whether our statement of more specific goals is consistent with the overarching goals of freeing the student for full human growth. Have we equated human freedom and personal development with intellectual competence in our two sets of goal statements? Some educators fall easily into making this equation. Wilhelms, for example, seems to come close to saying this: "Human becoming is not a thing apart from knowledge and skill; competence is its cornerstone."[9] Now, while knowledge and skill are essential elements of human becoming, they are not exclusively what becoming a human person is all about. Many learned and competent professional men reveal a distressing superficiality in their personal lives. Becoming human also involves developing compassion, loyalty, ethical sensitivity, and courage, establishing deep friendships, and being able to give of one's total self in a love relationship. These latter elements of human personal growth are not so much skills, for the concept of skill implies uniformly repetitive behavior, such as methodological research skills, or computational skills in accounting. Establishing deep friendships, Dale Carnegie to the contrary notwithstanding, takes much more than skill. Giving of one's total self in a love relationship flows more from a disposition, a readiness, to respond to a whole variety of interpersonal situations.

Can we *teach* courage, loyalty, compassion, and love in the classroom? Perhaps the question is purely academic, since it has been tried so rarely in classrooms that the evidence is insufficient to be able to say one way or another. Nevertheless, people *do* learn to love, to be courageous, to be compassionate. Where do they learn it, assuming that it does not flow from biological heredity? Exposure to models of courage, loyalty, compassion, and love, especially in the home, has something to do with it. The personal history of rewards and punishments throughout the student's life certainly has a shap-

[9]Fred T. Wilhelms, "Humanization via the Curriculum," in Robert R. Leeper (ed.), *Humanizing Education: The Person in the Process,* Association for Supervision and Curriculum Development, National Education Association, Washington, D.C., 1967, p. 22.

ing effect on specific behavioral responses in situations which call for courage, loyalty, and compassion. Discussion and analysis of examples of these virtues and their contraries help to sensitize the students to their own experience. And the quality of the student's own interpersonal relations also calls forth or stifles the disposition to behave courageously, compassionately, lovingly, or with loyalty. Without attempting to answer a question which has exercised philosophers from Socrates onward, however, we can say with some safety that present practice in the schools has been outrageously neglectful and irresponsible in its feeble attempts to deal with this important side of human growth.

But how has *our* statement of goals expressed this concern? The fifth goal, dealing with values, expressly attempts to underscore this concern; in dealing with the achievement of the other four goals, however, there will be ample opportunities to bring out the human and personal implications of these behaviors. Ultimately, no statement of objectives can ensure the achievement of growth toward personal freedom. Only by teachers' continuous efforts *throughout* the curricular-instructional program can the student gradually realize the personal implications of concepts and skills and attitudes and integrate them into his value system and his world view. In other words, learning these attitudes and dispositions in a school setting comes through a student's personal encounters with his teachers and peers as well as with models or examples of these human characteristics in school. [10]

SELECTING AREAS FOR LEARNING ENCOUNTERS

Moving now from a statement of goals to selecting areas for learning encounters, teachers and supervisors face another set of problems. If the total curriculum is being planned, then teachers and supervisors must decide what content from what fields of knowledge, such as biology, mathematics, literature, or history, to include. Then, within a specific course, there is the question of what topics to take up, what central concepts and principles will be emphasized, what authors or what historical episodes will receive major attention, and so forth.

Those planning a curriculum have to distinguish between the specific learnings they want to achieve and the content or subject matter by means of which they will accomplish these learnings.[11] That is, very often the purpose of a specific unit or class exercise may be to sharpen or develop a spe-

[10]See Broudy et al., *op. cit.,* pp. 221–230, for a sound treatment of the teaching of exemplars in value education.
[11]See Hilda Taba, *Curriculum Development: Theory and Practice,* Harcourt, Brace & World, New York, 1962, pp. 263–267, for a sound elaboration of this distinction, which is made by a number of authors in the field of curriculum development. This distinction is sometimes labeled as that between "content" and "process."

cific mental or perceptual operation, such as the analysis of relationships between facts or ideas (e.g., between suspicion and levels of communication, or between water resources and location of industry, or between the size of a peacetime army and the tenor of a nation's foreign policies). Any variety of content can be used to teach these mental operations, but the student must *also* be given an opportunity to practice the operation in his classroom experience. In other words, mere exposure to content does not ensure that certain mental skills will be learned. A student cannot learn how to paint simply by attending lectures on techniques of painting; he must undergo the actual experience of mixing paints, selecting a subject, studying and interpreting it, placing it in a certain perspective, emphasizing certain features, and so forth. A student learns linguistic elements of style by writing, not by defining the concepts in the grammar textbook.

Broudy, Smith, and Burnett's distinctions among the four uses of knowledge (replicative, associative, applicative, and interpretive) are also helpful here.[12] When planning a course or specific units of a course, the teacher and supervisor need to ask to what short- and long-range uses the student is expected to put the knowledge or skill he acquires. If it is primarily applicative—for example, the use of his learning how to compute on the slide rule—then it would involve much more drill than a learning which was viewed primarily as interpretive—for example, an experiment in biology which illustrates the process of photosynthesis.

Categories of cognitive and affective learnings also are helpful when trying to clarify the specific types of learnings intended by a specific unit of the curricular-instructional program.[13] By classifying what kinds of *knowledge* (knowledge of specific information, knowledge of terminology, knowledge of ways and means of organizing facts, knowledge of criteria for testing and judging information, knowledge of generalizations, and so forth), *intellectual skills* (interpreting statistics, analyzing relationships, judging logical consistencies in a debate, evaluating skillful techniques of style in a poem, and the like), and *affective responses* (accepting an ethical principle, appreciating the symmetry of an architectural structure, identifying with a character in history or drama, and the like) any particular learning experience should lead to, the teacher is more capable of deciding what particular pedagogical approach to employ in class—whether group discussion, a film, lecture, question-and-answer session, programmed materials, or independent study.

As we argued earlier, exclusive and rigid concentration on achieving

---

[12]Broudy et al., *op. cit.*, pp. 43–61.
[13]Consult Benjamin S. Bloom et al., *A Taxonomy of Educational Objectives: Handbook I, The Cognitive Domain,* Longmans, Green, New York, 1959, and David R. Krathwohl et al., *A Taxonomy of Educational Objectives: Handbook II, The Affective Domain,* McKay, New York, 1964.

very specific behavioral goals can stifle both teaching and learning. Sometimes certain curriculum units should be left relatively open-ended by allowing the student to encounter the material and make of it whatever he wants to. Many instructive experiences in our lives occur in precisely this way, when we approach another person or situation with no preconceptions or purposes in mind. Sometimes these free encounters lead to fascinating discoveries. Many such unstructured encounters should be built into a curricular-instructional program in order to develop independence, inquisitiveness, and spontaneity (and also to teach us something about spontaneous learning). This is not to say that such experiences would not sometimes be evaluated by students and teachers together. Too frequent and too detailed an evaluation of these encounters, however, can instill an artificial readiness to find something nice to report to teacher.

ORGANIZING THE CURRICULUM

Almost everyone who writes about education today remarks on the knowledge explosion. There is simply too much knowledge around to begin to fit it into a curriculum of general education. Bellack asks the logical question when faced with this problem: "What knowledge is of most worth?"[14] He responds:

> According to long and honorable tradition, knowledge is grouped for pedagogical purposes in four major categories—the natural sciences, the social sciences, mathematics, and the humanities (the latter an omnibus term that includes art, literature, philosophy, and music). These broad groupings of organized disciplines are generally recognized as basic culture interests of our society which constitute both the resources and the obligations of the schools. Each major field represents distinctive methods and conceptual schemes in which the world and man are viewed from quite different vantage points. Instruction in these areas has as its primary goal equipping students with key concepts and methods that inform and sustain intelligent choice in human affairs.[15]

In choosing these four general areas, Bellack hopes to counteract the practice of selecting discrete and individual disciplines which are then grouped side by side in curriculum strands. In such a fragmented curriculum the student ends up with a few separate ways of interpreting reality, but cannot integrate these views. The broad fields of knowledge furnish a framework for integrating these discrete perspectives.

Bellack also suggests that we follow the example of some British educators[16] and also stress the main modes of intellectual activity: the logical

[14]Arno A. Bellack, "What Knowledge Is of Most Worth?," *The High School Journal*, vol. 48, February, 1965, pp. 318–332.
[15]*Ibid.*, p. 322.
[16]See Oxford University Department of Education, *Arts and Science Sides the Sixth Form*, The Abbey Press, Abingdon-Berkshire, England, 1960.

(or analytic), the empirical, the moral, and the esthetic. Since any one discipline provides opportunity to employ more than one form of thought, students can be brought to appreciate other cognitive and evaluative dimensions in each discipline. Thus learnings in a curricular-instructional program can be viewed in two perspectives: (1) learnings of the conceptual schemes and methods of inquiry associated with the broad fields of knowledge, and (2) learnings which derive from the logical, empirical, moral, and esthetic modes of thought embodied in and also cutting across the four broad fields of knowledge.[17]

Bellack proposes, therefore, that a general education program include basic instruction in the four major fields (the natural sciences, the social sciences, mathematics, and the humanities). He also proposes that it contain studies of problems which arise in the world of human affairs which require not only concepts drawn from these four fields of studies, but also value decisions based on public policy, ethics, and philosophy. By dealing with these problems of human affairs—such as the nature of our welfare system, urban renewal, foreign policy, conservation, restructuring national voting procedures, taxation, and the like—students are led to view them in all their complexity by means of conceptual frameworks developed in the four broad fields of studies.

In suggesting this two-pronged approach to developing a curriculum, Bellack echoes a similar suggestion by Schwab:[18]

The plan would reconcile the demands of the discipline and the needs of our culture and society, where they are competitive, by considering the curriculum at each level of school as consisting of two parts. One part, to be called the nuclear curriculum, would contain materials from the disciplines, selected to fulfill those objectives of education which are determined primarily by the needs of the developing child and the aims imposed by our culture and society. Such materials would be taught, wherever possible, within the frame of the discipline from which they were taken. But where the exigencies of time, of learning competence, or other need required it, these materials would be freely removed from their theoretical or disciplinary context and put into the context of unquestioned principles designed for use.

The second, or cortical, component of the curriculum would be chosen by contrary and complementary principles. It would consist of materials chosen specifically because they are representative of the major disciplines. Such materials would display the more important conceptual frames of each discipline, its techniques of discovery and verification, and the variety of problems to which it addresses itself. Where alternatives existed, preferred materials would be those which also served present and recognized individual-social needs. But the criterion of representativeness of the discipline would be paramount.

[17]Bellack, *op. cit.*, p. 331.
[18]See the summary discussion in *The Scholars Look at the Schools*, Project on Instruction, National Education Association, Washington, D.C., 1962, pp. 51–52.

Five Categories of Instructions

This twofold approach is much more refined by the curriculum in general education (grades 7 through 12) proposed by Broudy, Smith, and Burnett. They propose a curriculum based around five categories of instruction: symbolic studies, basic sciences, developmental studies, esthetic studies of exemplars, and molar problems.[19]

They would use the courses in the basic sciences to introduce the student to the key ideas and methods of inquiry of the basic sciences of physics, chemistry, and biology. They also include the study of language and mathematics as a science. Their treatment of developmental studies, however, would seem to differ from Bellack's "basic instruction" in the social sciences. In these developmental studies dealing with the evolution of the cosmos and human life, the evolution of social institutions (family, church, economic system, laws, etc.), and the evolution of culture (the science, technology, art, literature, religions, and systems of ideas), the main purpose is to select cognitive maps, developed in many different disciplines so that they may be used interpretively. Because of lack of time to study the histories of art, science, religion, and philosophy, the interpretive concepts and theories learned in these developmental studies provide the student with frames of reference or perspectives for forming his view of his world. They enable him to understand something about the evolutionary origins of the human race, to see the general purpose served by social institutions, and to realize the interrelationships between important elements in his own culture, such as industrial development and the national levels of education.

Broudy, Smith, and Burnett introduce a relatively unique approach to value education in their esthetic studies of exemplars.

> The school . . . can present life styles as they appear in the arts, but not in the popular arts. Displayed in literature, drama, painting and music, life models acquire an attractiveness that engages the emotions as well as the intellect. They are invitations to feel and cherish as well as to understand.
>
> To follow this strategy, one can approach value education through what are called exemplars, as they are encountered in notable instances of literature and the fine arts. . . . To study all value exemplars via their artistic expressions is not a substitute for the study of ethics, aesthetics, and religion. However, given the limitations of time and the fact that attitudinal as well as cognitive components are essential to appreciative learning, the choice of the aesthetic vehicle for value education seems justified.[20]

Broudy, Smith, and Burnett seem close to Bellack's suggestion of the study of problems in the world of human affairs in their fifth category of

---

[19]Broudy et al., *op. cit.* The reader might want to refer to the diagram of their program of studies in Chap. 12, p. 234.
[20]*Ibid.*, pp. 224–225.

instruction, molar problem solving.[21] Molar problems are those large and complex problems in society the solution of which depends on a variety of disciplines, logical operations, and value judgments. A molar problem such as an adequate and fair tax system relies on knowledge of economics, population and income distribution, industrial production and financing, political structures and levels of government, and allocation of fiscal responsibility, as well as attitudes about welfare programs, the government's role in conservation, education, and national defense, free enterprise and the rights and responsibilities of government, and the like. The authors suggest that through encounters with these large, complex problems students learn (1) to clarify the statement, (2) to explore its ramifications, (3) to make guesses about relevant information and theory, (4) to explore the causes, logical and psychological, for disagreement, and (5) to formulate and then criticize alternative solutions to the problem.[22] These encounters develop the students' "habits of deliberation, the skills of using diverse interpretive frames, and the practice of attitudes needed for group thinking and decision."[23] The encounter with these problems "can be regarded as the integrative experience par excellence of the whole schooling process."[24]

As teachers and supervisors plan curricular-instructional programs, therefore, they should bear in mind these distinctive approaches to dealing with content. On the one hand, they may choose to stay within the discipline, concentrating on its unique perspective and methodology. At other times they may want to select ideas with greater potency which organize knowledge and information across the boundaries of the separate disciplines and to use these for specific kinds of both cognitive and evaluative learnings.

PRINCIPLES FOR DESIGNING A HUMAN CURRICULUM

Another perspective for a humanistic curriculum design in secondary schools is offered by James Macdonald.[25] Moving from the premise that a humanistic curriculum design should be focused directly upon "the creation of conditions for fostering the development of human beings,"[26] Macdonald presents a set of principles for developing such a curriculum design. Some of these principles have particular relevance to teachers and supervisors planning a human curriculum and are summarized below.[27]

[21]*Ibid.*, pp. 231–243.
[22]*Ibid.*, pp. 241242.
[23]*Ibid.*, p. 242.
[24]*Ibid.*, p. 243.
[25]James Macdonald, "The High School in Human Terms: Curriculum Design," in *Humanizing the Secondary School,* Norman K. Hamilton and J. Galen Saylor (eds.), Association for Supervision and Curriculum Development, National Education Association, Washington, D.C., 1969, pp. 34–54.
[26]*Ibid.*, p. 48.
[27]*Ibid.*, pp. 48–52.

1. Perhaps as much as one third of each day should be organized for "experiencing" activity in a completely nonjudgmental setting. This would include studying how knowledge is integrated in the real life of the community.[28]

2. The central coordinating theme for high school programs should be the study of man as scientist, as organism, as person, as role player, as dreamer. The central theme should not be the product of science, social relations, and the like, but the human process.

3. Programs should be so structured that those qualities of man that are characteristically human are continually emphasized in action. Man as a thinking, feeling, valuing, and symbol-creating being should be the heart of all activity in school. In order to develop this curriculum, arrangements must be so organized that teachers show these qualities as models and the students engage in these processes continually.

4. Curricular-instructional experiences should lead the student to an awareness of his potential to transcend the immediate personal and social situation. Students should be given every opportunity to clarify their values in relation to themselves, others, and the curricular content they are encountering.

5. All materials should be taught in the light of their historical and cross-cultural perspective in order to give students the opportunity to visualize a variety of cultural and historical patterns.

6. The curriculum should offer every possible opportunity for nonverbal education and expression, since freedom to learn and to realize potential may be more nearly achieved by perceptual training than by conceptual activity.

7. All instruction should make provisions for recognizing the symbolic process as a technique or means for conceptualization, not as an end in itself (the word is not the thing).

Macdonald's primary focus is on the human growth of the person. As was noted earlier in Chapter 12, this position places all other purposes of schooling, such as serving society's needs or furthering competence in the academic disciplines, in a subsidiary, though complementary, position. Many of the strategies of the Broudy, Smith, and Burnett curriculum design could be incorporated into Macdonald's vision of the curriculum; however, they would not leave the student as much elbow room for spontaneous, open-ended, and expressive activities or as free a choice of some of their learning experiences as Macdonald would. Macdonald appears, expressly at least, to take more account of the realm of personal meaning.[29]

[28]Some attempts at experiences along this line are already being attempted in Philadelphia's "school without walls." See *Life,* vol. 66, no. 19, May 16, 1969, pp. 40–42.
[29]See in Chap. 13 the discussion on personal meaning.

A HUMAN CURRICULUM DESIGN

The following curriculum design attempts to map out a program of general studies which seems consistent with the human goals expressed earlier in this chapter and which incorporates many of the strategies suggested by Bellack, Broudy, Smith, and Burnett, Phenix, and Macdonald. It also seems to be far more responsive to the human environment of learning described in the previous chapter. Since it is a design only for secondary education, it is offered more as an example of the process and content of a humanizing curriculum plan than as *the* one, definitive, human curriculum design. Teachers and supervisors planning their human curriculum will want to make their own adaptations. This design should be seen as a model to stimulate further thinking by teachers and supervisors.

The mere sketch of this program does not necessarily reveal the variety of approaches to learning that it offers. First, the courses on media and symbolic skills should provide more of an "activity" experience, with stress placed on the students' developing these skills of expression through experimentation with the media rather than starting out with a more passive study of the expressions of others, or textbook rules, or technical principles. Mathematics will probably be more structured than the other symbolic systems, simply because mathematics as a body of knowledge has rather well-established structural principles. In both the language and the art courses, however, equal attention will be given to the internal qualities of the media themselves and to the symbolic uses of the media. That is, students will experiment with such things as texture, symmetry, harmony, tone, perspective, rhythm, and pattern—in other words, they will study the intrinsic possibilities and limits of the media themselves. In this way they can learn what different shades, tones, hues, patterns, and forms in the media express *in and by themselves,* even before a human mind organizes them to express or communicate something. They will also learn how to communicate both verbal and nonverbal meaning. That is, they will try to say or express something, whether it be a feeling or a story or an image of human life in some kind of metaphorical fashion. These later learnings bear more on the symbolic *use* of the media for purposes of expression and communication.

Broudy, Smith, and Burnett presume that such studio courses or performance courses would be offered in the elementary grades, and they therefore concentrate more on the intensive study of great works of art.[30] First we find little evidence that elementary schools generally offer that intensive a program in art. Even were the elementary school to offer a rich and diversified art program—which we believe they should do—nevertheless, adolescents are far more capable of exercising a broad range of artistic skills, as a

[30]Broudy et al., *op. cit.,* pp. 176–177.

	I	II	III	IV
Media and symbolic systems	1. Verbal { Speaking, Interpretative reading, Writing }	1. Verbal { Rhetoric, Writing }	1. Verbal { Literary form, Poetic form }	1. Logic
	2. Art { Architecture, Photography, Design }	2. Art { Painting, Sculpture, Montage }	2. Art { Movie, Drama }	2. Art { Drama, Music, Opera, Ritual, Dance, Multimedia }
	3. Mathematics	3. Mathematics	3. Elective	3. Elective
Images of nature and universe	4. Physics	4. Chemistry	4. Biology	4. Evolution { Up to man, and society }
Images of society	5. Anthropology; Geography	5. Sociology; Politics	5. Economics; Law	5. Contemporary cultures
Images of man	6. Greek; Roman	6. Eastern; Hebraic; African	6. European; American { Early Christian, Renaissance, Enlightenment, Democratic }	6. Contemporary man

Figure 14-5. A human curriculum design.

result of their developing emotional sensitivity and desire for self-expression. Studio courses should not be relegated to preadolescence, for when that is done a judgment is pronounced on artistic creativity which no proponents of esthetic education would expressly propose. Adolescents do not suddenly change into intellects capable of unlimited abstractive abilities. They need to continue to develop their *perceptual* capacities, not only because conceptual learning follows and depends heavily on perceptual training, but also because the refinement of perceptual capacities leads to a far richer experience of one's world. As a student develops a greater sensitivity to perceptual qualities in his environment, he becomes more aware of his own feeling responses, and through being familiar with different media he is more capable of giving expression to these feelings.

Once again we see how expressive experiences with photography, painting, music, creative writing, and the like, allow far more room for the integration and expression of personal meanings. As the student attempts to put into communicable form what his world means to him, he is forced to reflect upon it, to put it into some perspective, and to evaluate relationships between meanings. Those who would argue that all this would be fine if we had the time for it, but school time must be used for more important matters, are missing the point. Unless a student grapples with meaning and integrates it into the very real and personal world he has built for himself, then all other attempts to bring about encounters with important matters will fail. And if a student is to make what he learns personal, he must have the *time* to make it personal, which often occurs only when he has to try to express meaning in his own terms. This stress on a variety of media also provides opportunities for expression and success in nonverbal media. Many students cannot open up to their own potentialities simply because of continued difficulty with verbal expression. Nonverbal expression cannot substitute for verbal expression, or vice versa, but success in one is often the key that leads to success in the other.

The art courses should also be viewed as synthetic learning experiences in which concepts and principles from the other courses can be brought together. For example, in the units dealing with architecture, principles from physics and geometry can be expressly introduced, such as vectors, center of gravity, stress, parallel lines, diagonals, and so forth. In painting, geometry and chemistry can be brought in quite easily when treating color mixtures and chemical consistency of paints, or when working with geometrical patterns, or shapes, or forms. Concepts and images from the images of man courses will also provide opportunities for students to express personal interpretations of, say, the character of Don Quixote, or Job, or Gully Jimson. While the stress in the language and art strands will primarily be on the students' activity and performance of the skills involved, some time would be devoted to studying a few select exemplars in each medium in order to point out artistic principles of expression. Study of these exemplars, however, should come late in the course.

The curricular strand dealing with language will concentrate on writing and speaking. Reading as a skill will be integrated with all the other curricular strands. This is not to deny that some students will require extra assistance in remedial reading programs, but whenever possible these extra programs should be integrated with the regular reading required for the other curricular strands. The writing activities should initially be related to the imaginative expression of perceptual experiences being developed in the art courses. Considerable attention should be given to both oral and written expression of personal meanings from the student's own experience and from what he has learned in the other courses. As the student progresses in his later years, he should attempt to express himself in a variety of literary forms, such as poetry, fiction, historical exposition, journalistic reporting, political editorializing, and the like, not so much to develop the professional's skill as to enable him to distinguish and interpret the different perspectives of each of these forms. The curricular strand dealing with language will be solidified by a more formal treatment of logic in the final year. The logic course, however, should expose the student to the qualitatively different types of logic imbedded in political debate, philosophical, theological, and ethical treatises, and the logic of poetry as well as the logic of mathematics.

IMAGES OF THE HUMAN UNIVERSE

As Bellack, among many others, suggests, the learned heritage of man has left him with relatively distinct perspectives or conceptual schemes with which to view and interpret his world. The "image" strands of the curriculum present three of these perspectives which are distinguished both by the phenomena under study and the general methodology of each broad perspective. We use the term *image* to describe these general perspectives in order to indicate that the central concepts employed are man-made constructs which enable us to interpret, measure, and find meaning in various aspects of the phenomena being studied. As Bruner notes, "The organizing ideas of any body of knowledge are inventions for rendering experience economical and connected."[31] As men attempt to make sense out of their world, they study it under a variety of conceptual perspectives or imaginary models, such as that of the atom, the state, economic systems, and "natural laws." Hence, using the term *image* conveys the limitations of these perspectives and yet the complementarity of images of one phenomenon.

The general orientation in each one of these image strands should be toward developing interpretive cognitive and evaluative maps which illumi-

[31]Jerome S. Bruner, *On Knowing*, Harvard, Cambridge, Mass., 1962, p. 120.

nate and sustain intelligent choices in human affairs, and not toward the applicative uses of the knowledge acquired in the pursuit of a professional career. In this we support Broudy, Smith, and Burnett's approach to the learnings in these curriculum strands.

Some science teachers may wonder why the traditional order of the natural science courses has been reversed. This particular approach is open to prolonged debate. Nevertheless, we chose this order because the evolutionary approach emphasizes that man is the highest organism to have evolved and that the elements of all sciences take on an added dimension when they are understood from the human dimension. This is not to anthropomorphize physics. Rather, it is to view man as cosmomorphic—that is, as embodying and bringing to a new completion all the lower forms of reality in his very person.[32]

Images of Nature

In the "images of nature" strand, then, the student is led to view nature from its most elementary forms and structures through the images of physics. He then moves on to study nature's increasing complexity in chemical structures and living organisms, and finally follows the long evolutionary journey of life up to man and to human society. Once again, the value premise behind structuring the sequence should be obvious: man represents the convergence of an immense cosmic will to live, and he is now called upon to assume conscious control over and give direction to the course of evolution.[33] And *that* particular evaluative interpretation of man's relationship to nature is worth a four-year effort.

Images of Society

The curricular strand dealing with images of society should provide opportunities for a variety of learnings. Once again, the stress will not be on developing a professional scholar or even a minischolar in any one of the fields. Rather, the student should be led to view his society from the different perspectives of the categories of these social sciences. Emphasis should be placed on those central categories and images which would enable him to understand the social processes and structures operative in his society and which will enable him to make informed decisions both as a citizen and as a mature human being.

---

[32]See the very instructive essay by Max Scheler, *The Nature of Sympathy*, trans. by P. Heath, Routledge, London, 1959, pp. 103–108. See also Pierre Tielhard de Chardin, *The Phenomenon of Man*, Harper, New York, 1959.

[33]See, besides Tielhard de Chardin, *op. cit.*, Hans Jonas, *The Phenomenon of Life*, Beacon Paperback, Boston, 1968, and Loren Eisley, *The Immense Journey*, Random House, New York, 1946.

In this curriculum strand the study of molar problems can be introduced and may be encountered with more frequency in the last two years. Broudy, Smith, and Burnett see molar problems as being large, complex social problems; but molar problems do not have to be so large that they consume a whole semester's work. Smaller molar problems can be introduced at different intervals in the course, to take up a week of class discussion, research, and proposals for solutions. These shorter molar problem-solving sessions, especially in the earlier years, would introduce students more gradually to small-group discussion and problem solving, as well as provide opportunities to *use* the knowledge they had mastered in that unit for at least a simulated look at a situation from the world of human affairs. Students should have the opportunity to use the skills and perspectives developed in their art, language, and science strands in some of their encounters with molar problems. For example, a particular group might want to make a movie, or to tell a visual story with photographs to illustrate the human problems involved in urban renewal—which might be the molar problem under study. Another group could perhaps construct an architectural model of building clusters in an urban renewal project. Another group might want to put on a play or operetta dramatizing the human comedy or tragedy inherent in urban renewal problems. Another group might want to study the problem of water supply, or to plan a better utilization of electric power resources, for a molar project in regional planning. As Broudy, Smith, and Burnett point out, these molar problem-solving units offer perhaps the most significant integrative learning experiences of the whole schooling process.[34]

In the "images of society" strand, instruction should also attempt to provide breadth and depth of learning by attending to the historical origins of certain traditions or theories in political organizations, laws, and economic systems, and also by exposing students to cross-cultural studies of how other cultures have dealt with problems of law, political organization, education of the young, marriage and family life, and economic life.

Since history majors will notice with some chagrin that history as a discipline has been omitted as a separate study, we should emphasize that, throughout the three image strands, there will be ample opportunity to deal with specific issues in a historical perspective. What is lost in terms of a comprehensive view of history should be amply supplied in terms of focus when students concentrate on historical developments of *specific* institutions and *specific* cultural traditions. They should notice that these strands will contain elements from the history of science and from economic, legal, and political history. Indeed, the planning and execution of this humanistic curriculum will elevate the history teacher to an even more important profes-

[34]Broudy et al., *op. cit.*, p. 243.

sional position than he presently enjoys, and should also constitute an exciting opportunity for him to work with specialists in discrete disciplines.[35]

Images of Man

The "images of man" curricular strand should provide opportunities to get at the evaluative learnings which have been stressed throughout this chapter. Following both Macdonald's and Broudy, Smith, and Burnett's suggestions, instruction will focus on those great exemplars of what man has been and can become, on man as dreamer, hero, and creator. This, of course, does not rule out dealing with man's tragic, alienated, and comical nature. Often, encounters with tragic and comic characters are the only way to discover—by dissonance or contrast—what are the truly beautiful possibilities in human life.

Study of the variety of images man has projected of himself will also provide for the development of a historical perspective of those key ideas that lie at the center of every great culture. Once again, the *variety* of images will also enable the student to develop a cross-cultural appreciation of man as he develops in different climates and under different geographical conditions. Since one cannot understand a great man in literature, drama, history, or art without understanding what ideals and ethical principles and visions sustained his life, the "images of man" sequence will bring the student to consider and evaluate these visions and ideals in terms of contemporary values, and his own vision of what he as a human being can become.

A moment's reflection will reveal many possible opportunities to relate this curricular strand with the other strands. Certainly, for example, students working with drama in the art strand would have the opportunity to put on several of the great plays from classical, renaissance, and modern times. The kind of learning which occurs when a person really identifies with a dramatic character in the process of acting out his part cannot be duplicated. Whether or not the student has the opportunity for this dramatic identification, he should be encouraged at every opportunity to feel his way inside the personality of the character he is studying—to try to see the world through his eyes and feel the things he feels.

The "images of man" curricular strand should present a balanced consideration of an individual exemplar (Socrates, Oedipus, Antigone, Ulysses, Aeneas, Julius Caesar, Job, David, Jesus, Buddha, Thomas More, Hamlet, Don Quixote, the Karamazovs, Kristin Lavransdatter, Stephen Dedalus, Willy Loman, and many others) and of generalized images of man (tribal man, industrial man, Renaissance man, secular man, urban man, organization

[35]Modern language teachers will like being dropped to teaching elective courses even less. Much of the literature previously taught in these courses can be taken up in the "images of man" courses. Students who want to learn to speak or read a foreign language can do so in elective and concentrated summer courses.

man, the common man, the playboy, the man of reason, man the romantic, Puritan man, and so forth). Encounters with individual exemplars should enable the student to identify with certain life styles he might try on for a while or permanently. Encounters with more generalized images of man would develop those critical evaluative maps and attitudes which would enable the student to interpret a variety of contemporary and historical life styles.

UNDERSTANDING THROUGH IMAGES

We know that many images in our imagination's repertory are comprehensive images which allow us to interpret large bodies of facts and experiences. The image of Willy Loman in *Death of a Salesman* gathers together in dramatic form the crosscurrents of economic, emotional, and social forces which can destroy contemporary man. This image enables us to interpret not simply the behavior of many contemporary salesmen, but also the widespread disintegration of family values and human integrity under the relentless twentieth-century compulsion for economic and social success. Macbeth provides another tragic image of the disintegration of men possessed by a craving for power. Ralph Ellison's image of the invisible man helps us to understand the struggles of black men to achieve identity and pride in a white society that does not "see" them. Picasso's "Guernica" and Goya's "Execution of the citizens of Madrid, May 3, 1808," coupled with Wilfred Owens's war poems, are graphic images of the horror and irrationality of war. T. S. Eliot's *The Waste Land,* Albert Camus's *The Stranger,* and Beckett's *Waiting for Godot* are other examples of images of contemporary man's experience of meaninglessness and absurdity which have filtered into the warehouse of our imagination.

Images are not merely interpretive lenses by which to contemplate and comprehend our experience of reality. In other words, they are not merely means to knowledge and understanding, but they bear within them emotional thrust, values, and value judgments, forming motives for our own choices. Going back to Willy Loman, we can illustrate some of the emotional import of this image. *Death of a Salesman* is not simply about the worldly failure of one human being; it holds up an image of our own spiritual failure.

Like all great worldly failures, Willy knows the violence of disenchantment. Lover of illusions, when he was disillusioned, he could not bear it. It is crushing to learn that success is relative and temporary. It is tragic to learn that worldly failure is absolute. To win is to win, really, very little as the world goes; but (as the world goes) to lose is always to lose everything. In the midst of ruin, one learns that each day of his life, nay, each hour, he has failed somewhere. Who is he who has the temerity to boast of success when every moment has yielded a harvest of errors and regrets and vanities. Like our faults, our most egregious failures are unknown to us, but they are there waiting like an infection for the moment of weakness, when the props of self-delusion are knocked away. Willy despairs when he learns that failure has always been imminent and has at last arrived.[36]

The violence of disenchantment is something we all fear, even though we suspect that our failures are more extensive than we consciously admit. Seeing at least a vague image of ourselves and our plight in Willy Loman cannot help but set up emotional shock waves and release hitherto forgotten longings for integrity. Images of the horror of war, as presented in "Guernica," as well as images of isolation as embodied in *The Stranger,* or images of tragic heroism as portrayed in *A Man for All Seasons,* express emotions and values as well as communicate understanding of the human situation.

This is not to propose a theory of art as a shaper of moral values. It is, however, to recognize that art does sometimes hold the mirror up to our own follies, does sometimes propose an ideal to which we are drawn, and always sharpens our sensibilities to the qualities of things and people. The point we are stressing primarily is that images convey and arouse feelings. In this sense, they appear to contribute to a fuller learning experience than mere conceptual learning.

One final reflection on the curricular image strands. As we move toward what McLuhan calls a total and simultaneous field (rather than discrete areas of subjects or disciplines),[37] we realize more clearly that images are partial, that they emphasize one aspect of experience, and that experience is reconstructed and appreciated by a host of images in the same and in different media. Hence, experience will be most fully enriched by a multidimensional, multimedia appreciation of it. This will involve exploring our experience of the human situation by means of images in music, film, literature, painting, sculpture, and dance, as well as through the images of the natural and social sciences.

SUMMARY

This chapter has attempted to point out a detailed approach to planning a human curriculum. In this attempt, care was taken to point out the *process* such planning involves, as well as to suggest *criteria* for selecting curriculum content, and finally a *proposed model* of a curriculum design with suggestions for implementing such a design. We have not taken up considerations of multileveled or multitracked implementation of this curriculum. Nor have

[36]Weller Embler, *Metaphor and Meaning,* Everett Edwards, Inc., DeLand, Fla., 1966, p. 11.
[37]Marshall McLuhan, "We Need a New Picture of Knowledge," in Alexander Frazier (ed.), *New Insights and the Curriculum,* Association for Supervision and Curriculum Development, National Education Association, Washington, D.C., 1963.

we talked about team teaching, programmed instruction, nongraded or mastery promotion systems, modular scheduling, and the like. These concerns must be included in planning and organizing a curriculum, to be sure. We felt, however, that we needed to focus on the basic content and student learnings in talking about a human curriculum and could leave these other concerns to be studied elsewhere.[38] The design presented here can be considered as a model (incomplete, as all models must be) of a human curriculum which teachers and supervisors can adapt and complete as they plan their own human curriculum.

SELECTED REFERENCES

Becker, Ernest: *Beyond Alienation,* George Braziller, New York, 1967.

Bellack, Arno A.: "What Knowledge Is of Most Worth?" *The High School Journal,* vol. 48, February, 1965, pp. 318–332.

Broudy, Harry S., B. Othanel Smith, and Joe R. Burnett: *Democracy and Excellence in American Education,* Rand McNally, Chicago, 1964.

Jenkins, Iredell: *Art and the Human Enterprise,* Harvard, Cambridge, Mass., 1958.

Kubie, Lawrence S.: *Neurotic Distortion of the Creative Process,* University of Kansas Press, Lawrence, Kans., 1958.

Maslow, Abraham H.: *Toward a Psychology of Being,* Van Nostrand, New York, 1962.

Polanyi, Michael: *Personal Knowledge,* Harper Torchbooks, Harper & Row, New York, 1964.

[38]See, for example, Broudy et al., *op. cit.,* pp. 244–274, for a sound discussion of ungradedness, unit and level organization, and patterns of progress.

Chapter Fifteen
EVALUATING THE CURRICULAR-INSTRUCTIONAL PROGRAM

Unlike other treatments of supervisory evaluation, this chapter will not deal with the supervisor's evaluation of teachers according to certain descriptive or prescriptive standards or processes. In other words, we are not here concerned with describing ways to rate the teacher against some comparative or descriptive scale. That approach to supervision is, we believe, relatively useless, except as a tool to improve the teacher's pedagogical techniques in the classroom, and then only if the teacher willingly enters into this relationship. The view of supervision proposed in this study describes the supervisor not so much as a rater of teachers' competencies, but rather as a consultant who works with the teacher to improve the curricular-instructional program and the day-to-day carrying out of this program. Hence, *evaluation* in this chapter will refer to evaluation of the program and the product of curriculum and instruction, and not to a supervisor's evaluation of a teacher.

This chapter brings to completion our analysis of the process of curriculum development. As we saw in Chapter 11 this process starts with clarifying general assumptions and values about formal education. The next step involves stating objectives, both general and specific. The description of objectives leads to decisions about appropriate learning experiences—which include both understandings and skills to be mastered. When these are organized into a curricular-instructional program and actually become the day-by-day classroom experiences, it is time for the final step of evaluation. As should be obvious, however, the process of evaluation should be operative throughout all the earlier steps.

EVALUATION AS TESTING

Unfortunately, this view of evaluation is seldom operative in practice. Evaluation is more frequently identified with the testing of students at the end of a course. At the conclusion of the semester or year, the teacher attempts to assess whether or not the students have reached the expressed objectives of the instructional program. One serious drawback to this practice is that, since it takes place primarily at the end of the course, the student does not benefit from feedback, which earlier in the course would have helped him to correct his mistakes and misunderstandings and have enabled him to recoup his losses in the later part of the course.

Even if the evaluation process includes testing throughout the course, the exclusive reliance on tests of student performance has serious drawbacks. First, let us be clear. Tests *are* valuable sources of feedback for both teacher and students. They *help* the teacher to discover whether the specific objectives of the unit are being achieved. But the teacher should be on the lookout for learnings other than those specified in his objectives. By trying to uncover, through written and oral student reports, interviews, and student checklists, these other learnings, the teacher can then analyze whether or not his choice of the learning experience was ambiguous or not really suited to achieve his stated objectives.

More importantly, the teacher might ask himself whether these spontaneous and unplanned learnings should be more expressly taught the next time around, whether these learnings provide valuable cognitive and affective ties with learnings in other courses, and whether they are the cumulative result of earlier learnings and can be reintroduced at a later time for a broader or more complex generalization. Let him also analyze the probable motivational factors which gave rise to the learning. Very often, for example, a student who has been required to absorb quite passively the prepackaged material of the textbook and simply repeat the specified operations on quizzes and exams will come to life when assigned a project which demands active ingenuity and inquiry on his part. This more active participation in the learning experience often touches off sparks of associational thought and imaginative applications for which the teacher had not planned. In these instances, the learnings and insights and accompanying enthusiasm which were *not* included in the teacher's set of objective may be far more intense and long-lasting than the intended objectives of the unit. Teachers and supervisors who are not willing to accept these fortunate accidents and to utilize them for further learning deprive the student and themselves of a wealth of experience, and have failed in one of their most important responsibilities as educators.

This approach to evaluation should lead to a further evaluational procedure. If student learnings are often spontaneous and variegated—if a student, that is, usually learns far more than the simple learnings specified in the objectives—then normally tests and other evaluative criteria constructed by the teacher will be inadequate to bring forth their expression. The teacher, therefore, should solicit the student's own evaluation of what *he* thinks he has learned. Such student evaluations should be on both an individual and a group basis. This will help to reveal the students' perception of the objectives of the unit or course as well as how well the learning experiences planned and organized by the teacher have helped them to reach the objective. This evaluative technique should also reveal those more spontaneous learnings and commitments of both the individual and the group touched off by the material under study, as well as assist students in the most valuable practice of self-evaluation. Because of the internal reflection required, such evaluation should also pay handsome dividends in solidifying and clarifying what it is they have learned; that is, this kind of self-evaluation is an irreplaceable *pedagogical* tool.

EXTREMES IN EVALUATION

Unfortunately, supervisors and teachers frequently go to extremes in evaluation. On the one hand, some hardly realize its importance and the very real difficulty of arriving at realistic evaluations. On the other hand, others allow one kind of evaluation, namely, tests, to dominate the entire curricular-instructional program. The first group may commit the lesser outrage, but they deprive themselves and their students of the necessary information by which they might change their courses and improve learning conditions. No teacher is so perfect that he can assume that his curriculum-instructional program is fostering optimum learning for all students. Neither can he assume that students are developing their capacities fully. The only way a teacher can discover how effective his work is and how much progress students are making is to evaluate by means of a variety of techniques: by both written and oral exams, by students' evaluation of their own progress and his teaching, by interviews, by bringing in outside evaluators, and so forth. No other professional person could long survive in his work if he did not seek feedback on results.

By far the worst offenders, however, are teachers who subvert the curricular-instructional program by emphasizing testing. Some allusion was made to the practice of grade-getting in the previous chapter, but this most prevalent practice must be more forcefully scored. There is much talk of alienation these days, especially the alienation of students from the school establishment. The system of testing and grading, in the opinion of many, as one of the more odious and dysfunctional practices in the school, is responsible for much of this alienation. And this practice causes alienation, not simply because students cannot stand being competitively ranked—although even this practice is hard to justify, once one denies the validity of the school's collusion with college and business recruiters—but much more because it alienates students from knowledge itself.

It is important for teachers and supervisors to see what happens when tests become the most important element in the curricular-instructional program. In such instances, everything the student and teacher do becomes oriented toward getting the right answer to test questions. This reduces knowledge—the protestation of teachers notwithstanding—to whatever one can use to pass an examination. Any teacher or supervisor who doubts this might try an experiment. Let him go into any ordinary classroom—the early primary grades might present some exceptions—and try to teach anything after previously informing the students that they will not be tested and graded on the material they will be covering in that class or series of classes. The response of the students will be almost totally uncooperative, not because students are pernicious by nature, but because the grading system has conditioned them this way. Work without getting graded for it! Their response will indicate how severely testing and grading procedures have perverted the conditions of genuine learning. Are these the self-directed, creative, mature young men and women our schools say they intend to produce? Can our democratic way of life endure when its future citizens will not read a book or discuss a political issue unless they receive some kind of spurious reward?

Even if we agree with or passively accept the school's being used as a highly efficient placement bureau for college and business recruiters, we must still ask the further question of whether the responses on tests adequately reflect the nature of knowledge that is supposed to have been learned.[1] Certainly in the case of culturally disadvantaged students, it has become evident that the tests show a cultural and class bias. The student may indeed possess the information or skill but not be able to understand the language in which the question is phrased. But this qualification can apply to a so-called advantaged student as well; a student who cannot produce the "right" answers may in fact still possess the knowledge in some meaningful form.[2] That is to say, a test question usually asks for the repetition of a skill or a piece of information in a very precise way, and the student's inability to hit upon that precise formulation of the response may be more an indication of his failure to subjugate totally his own intelligence to the teacher's way of expressing a given skill or fact or opinion than an indication of ignorance.

Moreover, testing as used in schools today is almost entirely an exercise of the student's memory, or, in Broudy's terminology, the replicative use of knowledge.[3] When this use of knowledge is elevated continually as the single most important element in school success as measured by tests, then the student will tend to concentrate exclusively on developing that kind of learning. Once again we can see how easily this can lead to alienation. The student does not have to become involved in what he learns—he simply plays the game of preparing and memorizing "right" answers; he does not have to think or interpret or analyze, except in a most superficial way. He can remain detached and feel no compunction whatsoever about washing his

---

[1] James Macdonald made this point in a speech on evaluation delivered at the 1967 Convention of the Association for Supervision and Development in Dallas.
[2] A point made by Macdonald in the same speech.
[3] Harry Broudy et al., *Democracy and Excellence in American Secondary Education,* Rand McNally Chicago, 1964, pp. 43–60.

mind clean with a walk in the park or a bull session at the drugstore, once the final exam is over. When testing continually asks for superficial learning, then that is the level students will be satisfied with. And then educators complain when students refuse to take schooling seriously!

Taking a backward step now, and looking at the whole process of setting goals, choosing learning experiences, and evaluating results, we can see that *in practice* the process has been reversed. That is, tests often *predetermine* the learning experiences and also reduce the goals to simplified behavioral objectives which the test can measure. This is an obvious case of the tail wagging the dog.[4] That is, curriculum developers, testing experts, and not a few teachers and administrators, despairing of being able to reduce more complex and general objectives to behavioral categories, settle for objectives which they think they can measure by standardized or departmental tests. And hence the deception is completed: learning is reduced to recall, and student progress and growth are measured by one-dimensional and superficial criteria. Teachers who succeed in getting their students to conform to such conditions pat themselves on the back for doing a superb job when their students achieve high grades. If the situation were not so tragic we could all enjoy the humor of this spectacle of a modern-day allegory of "The Emperor's New Clothes."

MISUSES OF TESTING

This complaint against present testing techniques must not be taken as simply dissatisfaction with the current lack of sophistication in testing techniques which may be improved in the future. It is much more a condemnation of three glaring misuses of testing: (1) allowing testing to dictate the objectives of the curricular-instructional program and the selection of learning experiences; (2) the dismissal not only of individual differences in the rate of speed in learning, but also of qualitative individual differences in learning itself, by testing only for common learnings, which can be assessed by simple behavioral performance criteria; (3) the creation of an unreal grading and promotional system by highly questionable competitive rankings according to test results, the validity and reliability of which are sometimes ridiculously superficial.

Supervisory personnel who allow these misuses of evaluation to continue as general practice in school are neglecting their professional responsibilities to their teachers and students. The whole thrust of our theory of supervisory practice and the considerable research behind it stand opposed to these misuses of evaluation. This is not to deny the usefulness of testing student learnings; it is rather a proposal to put testing in its proper place, so

[4] A point made, again, by Macdonald in his 1967 speech in Dallas.

that it will not result in the currently widespread absurdity of students being so busy studying for exams that they do not have time to learn anything. The primary purpose of the curricular-instructional program is to induce student learnings which will lead to human growth, not to collect intelligence-rating information for college placement offices and prospective employers.

EVALUATION OF THE PROCESS OF CURRICULUM PLANNING

To confine evaluation, however, to an assessment of student learning would be to touch on only one aspect of the supervisor's responsibility. In the case where the supervisor is a department chairman, a principal, or a central office supervisor working with teachers, the whole process of the teacher's development and implementation of a curricular-instructional program should be considered as subject to evaluation. In working with teachers on a joint evaluation of what it is they intend to accomplish and what in fact they do in the classroom, the supervisor should attempt to develop both a full description of the program and a set of evaluative judgments on each part of the process of implementing the program. In other words, evaluation must include not only the *product* or results of the curricular-instructional program, but the adequacy of the *program itself* and its implementation in the classroom.[5]

Supervisors and teachers need to describe the elements which contribute to three stages of the curricular-instructional program. The antecedent input variables, the transactional variables, and the outcome variables in the following diagram indicate these stages, the connections between them, and the methods of evaluation which might be employed.[6] Some assessment of the students' aptitude, their previous educational experiences, level of skill development, understandings of critical concepts, and so forth, as they enter into a school year or embark on a specific curricular unit, should be attempted. Because this critical first stage in any worthwhile evaluation process is so often overlooked, it is almost impossible to assess reliably what influences the specific class exercise had on learning outcomes. It may be impossible to assign an exact measure of the transactional variables' influence on the learning outcomes because of other environmental influences, such as

[5] Seè Robert E. Stake, "The Countenance of Educational Evaluation," *Teachers College Record*, vol. 68, April, 1967, pp. 523–540; Lee J. Cronbach, "Evaluation for Course Improvement," *Teachers College Record*, vol. 64, 1963, pp. 672–683; Ralph W. Tyler et al., *Perspectives of Curriculum Evaluation*, Rand McNally, Chicago, 1967; Fred T. Wilhelms, *Evaluation as Feedback and Guide*, Association for Supervision and Curriculum Development, National Education Association, Washington, D.C., 1967. These works provide comprehensive and creative approaches to evaluation to which the authors are indebted in this treatment of evaluation.
[6] See also the design offered by Stake, *op. cit.*

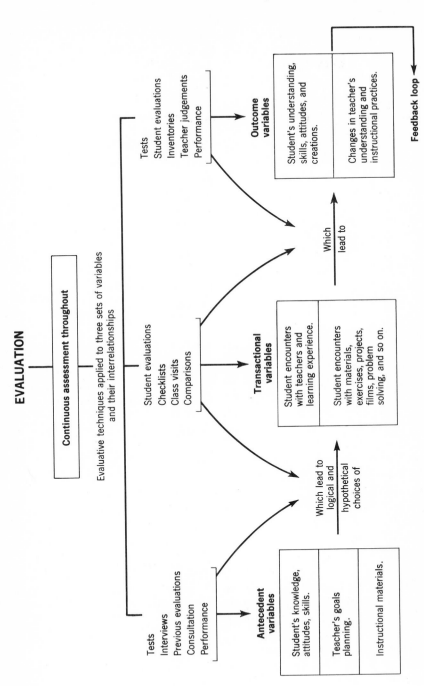

Figure 15-1. Continuous evaluation.

home life, peer-group associations, and the influence of other significant adults. Nevertheless, some valid general probabilities can be assigned to the influence of the transactional variables on learning outcomes if some assessment of the student's antecedent achievement is available. Certainly, if the student shows no advance at the end of the transactional stages in the skills, attitudes, and understandings which he possessed at the input stage, then the teacher and supervisor know that they need to revise their instructional program. Even this minimal effort of revision is often not made because the teacher has not sufficiently evaluated the student input variables.

Supervisors and teachers should then begin to assess the logic behind choices of the transactional variables. That is, when the teacher defines the objectives of the curricular-instructional program, he then proceeds to select learning experiences, or exercises, or learning encounters by means of which the student will acquire and develop those skills, understandings, and attitudes which have been set forth as objectives. In making this choice of transactional variables, the teacher either knows from past experiences that some learning experiences were very helpful in reaching the goals or else he conjectures that, logically or intuitionally, some particular learning experiences will lead to the desired student learnings.

Evaluating the Fit

The *fit* between objectives and transactional variables should be evaluated. Sometimes a pause for an imaginative speculation on alternative transactional variables will reveal that earlier choices of transactional variables were hasty, too unstructured, or unappealing to the interests of the students or were really not related to the objectives, or may even reveal unexpressed latent objectives of which the teacher previously had not been conscious. In other words, this step of the evaluative process involves asking, "Why did I choose *this* learning experience, *this* particular piece of material, to accomplish my objectives? Is this a logical choice? Is this the most appealing or dramatic experience for the student? What *exactly* will this learning experience accomplish? Does it relate to other objectives and learnings which the student has encountered in the past or will encounter later on in the course? Again, failure to spend sufficient time assessing the choices of these transactional variables has led to sloppy, disorganized, and wasteful classes. Certainly, there are no perfect choices for any one class; students vary in their interests and abilities. But teachers can continuously improve in selecting more powerful and engaging learning experiences by continuously evaluating their choices and trying to generate alternative choices.

Evaluating Transactional Variables

Evaluation of what happens in the students' encounters with the material which constitutes the transactional variables is critical. This means no more than being alert to how quickly and easily the students grasp what it is they are doing, to the kinds of questions they ask, to the difficulties the[y] ter, to their perception of relationships between this material and [ma]t treated earlier, to the level of enthusiasm they express toward this mate and so forth. Some first-rate teachers, alert to the responsiveness of the cla[ss] can sense that the class is going nowhere. They simply stop right in the middle of a lesson and change direction, discussing with the class why it was that the material was so flat. This kind of on-the-spot decision is difficult to make, especially if the teacher has invested considerable personal effort in preparing the lesson. But employing this kind of alertness and honesty is the only way to improve the quality of his teaching and to enhance the learning of the students. The students' appreciation of the teacher's honesty often pays handsome rewards in increased motivation.

Teachers and supervisors also need to evaluate the actual connection between encounters with certain materials and the improvement in student understandings and skills (the outcome variables). For example, certain learning experiences can be very superficial; the student may simply be tinkering with the algebraic formula or a literary concept and happen upon the "right" answer without really understanding the logic behind the skill he is developing or the general application of the concepts he is using. His learning may simply be repetitive rather than insightful. Here is where students' written or oral evaluations of what they think they have learned can be a most useful evaluative tool.

Comprehensive Evaluation

Finally a comprehensive evaluation of the whole curricular-instructional process at its completion—evaluation of the program and product—will enable the supervisor and teacher to plan those necessary program changes the next time around. This evaluation should obviously include two-way communication between the teacher and student. In such communication, the teacher indicates how much progress he thinks the student has made, what his strong and weak points are, what will need more work in the future, and what new directions he might take in the future. The student on his part indicates what he thinks he has learned, where the instruction was helpful or confusing, and what kinds of improvements the teacher might make in the future. Such an exchange is hardly possible by the simple use of report cards. Supervisors should work with administrators to see that school time is made available for teachers and students to have individual and group evaluation sessions. Obviously, this kind of two-way communication will be difficult with students in the primary grades, but some attempt should be made even at these levels.

This comprehensive evaluation should also include an assessment of the adequacy of the instructional materials, such as films, slides, teaching machines, supplementary textbooks, reference books, field trips, and so forth. Once again, failure to take this over-the-shoulder look at the usefulness of

:lusion of the course leads to the unreflective repe-
ass hours. The teacher should also ask himself
ıd space was helpful. Is there any way of revising
ʋ for longer or shorter periods, for small groups,
d attention to certain students? From this general
supervisor also need to reflect on the high points
ourse and to try to evaluate the probable reasons
sive final evaluation while the experiences of the
still fresh in the teacher's memory will enable him to make
those necessary decisions about changes in the program the next time
around. The teacher who rushes off to Christmas or summer vacation five
minutes after the last class is dismissed has lost an irreplaceable opportunity
to plan improvements for subsequent programs. Once again teachers and
supervisors need to lobby for time for such necessary assessments.

SUMMARY

It is apparent, then, that evaluation is a critical aspect of the supervisor's
professional responsibility. Evaluation must be continuous and not simply
end-of-year or end-of-semester assessment. It involves much more than rating
the teacher according to the test results of students, and much more than
the grading and promotion of students. Rather, the comprehensive evaluation process provides a continuous and responsible basis for decision making
throughout the curricular-instructional program. Only by means of an
ongoing evaluation process can the program be improved and adapted to the
human needs of students and hence result in more effective student learnings. The neglect of continuous and thoroughgoing evaluations on the part
of supervisors, teachers, and students can be cited as the single most perva-
sive cause of stale and irrelevant instructional programs. Continuous and
honest appraisal of the quality and effectiveness of the instructional program,
on the other hand, can be the necessary catalyst for imaginative curriculum
development itself, as well as for improved teaching strategies.

SELECTED REFERENCES

Cronbach, Lee J.: "Evaluation for Course Improvement," *Teachers College
Record,* vol. 64, 1963, pp. 672–683.

Stake, Robert E.: "The Countenance of Educational Evaluation," *Teachers
College Record,* vol. 68, April, 1967, pp. 523–540.

Tyler, Ralph W., et al., *Perspectives of Curriculum Evaluation,* Rand McNally,
Chicago, 1967.

Wilhelms, Fred T.: *Evaluation As Feedback and Guide,* Association for Supervision and Curriculum Development, National Education Association, Washington, D.C., 1967.

INDEX

INDEX